The Principle of Existence

Cause and Function of the Universe?

by

Harald Maurer

Translated into English by Marion Grob

Revised, extended, and up-dated edition 2004

Copyright 1987, 2004 by Edition MAHAG, Graz
ISBN 3-900800-10-8

Produced by:
Books on Demand, Norderstedt

Contents

	Introduction	7
1	T.A.O.	18
2	Disturbance	24
3	Encounters	30
4	Proton	36
5	Mass	42
6	Force	48
7	Electron	59
8	Games	66
9	Hydrogen	80
10	Light	87
11	Helium	96
12	Fusion	104
13	Crystals	112
14	Inertia	124
15	Gravity	135
16	Celestial bodies	149
17	Planets	174
18	Communication	185
19	Asymmetry	196
20	Galaxies	209
21	Entropy	219
22	Primordial molecules	226
23	Organelles	235
24	Information	249
25	Bacteria	263
26	Chromosome	272
27	Plan	281
28	Sex	291
29	Concept	297
30	Soma	303
31	Sensation	315
32	Consciousness	329
33	Relativity	344
34	Planetary Evolution	386
35	Purpose	413
36	Mind	418
37	Perfection	431
38	Eternity	439
39	Future	450
40	Footnotes	455

Nature is less complicated than it seems. Nothing makes me more optimistic that our generation actually holds the key to the universe in its hand already - that maybe we will be able in our lifetime to say why everything we see in this immense universe of stellar systems and particles is logically inevitable!

Stephen Weinberg

A single principle is sufficient to deduce everything from
everything!
Gottfried Wilhelm von Leibniz

Introduction

There are several methods to explain the world. The mechanistic, natural-scientific conception of the world along with Big Bang and evolution is struggling with the difficulty of discerning a beginning, a meaning, and an end in the never-ending series of causalities of the laws of nature. It describes nature with the effects that can be seen. The causes of these effects and phenomena remain hidden in the end; they are replaced by mathematical models and formulas. The reader, who wants to learn the truth after all, feels subjected to doctrines, premises, and axioms and is astounded to find that all physics and all chemistry - whose separation is in itself already disconcerting - is based on unexplained metaphysical concepts like gravitation, matter, time, mass, and energy. In that way, he learns how the world works but never why. But it is the why that makes the reader often resort to a work of non-fiction or consult some philosopher or other. Wherever he makes his researches, however, he will always gain the unsatisfactory impression that he learned only half the truth which does not make a coherent whole.

Without exception, philosophical ideas are substantiated esoterically or religiously and they mostly lack the scientific veneer of credibility. Moreover, philosophical answers are just too often inconsistent with the results of scientific research and have grown from one-sided reflections as a rule. Thus, Jaques Monod explains the world of life as an event between chance and necessity. But his opinion is on no account substantiated universally because it does not reveal why the world seems to be designed according to Einstein's general theory of relativity whereas on the other hand this theory cannot explain the phenomenon of life.

A flood of scientific non-fictional works has come over us in the last decades. They all have one thing in common: their almost inexhaustible obsession with quotes which gives the impression that all the authors copy from one another. And yet, the insights of science travel slowly. It takes a decade until new knowledge pervades the media and the quarter of a century until it enters the school books. At school, we are still taught that the world consists of a little world building machine, the atom, and that life is based on a little life building machine, the deoxyribonucleic acid (DNA). Both is wrong. It has long since become apparent that atom and DNA only represent informational events which are in fact subordinate to matter and life but which require their own cause. Unfortunately it is still inevitable to emphasise that the concept of the atom as a tiny miniature planetary system, in which electrons revolve around a nucleus, has to be regarded as outdated. However the atom might work, it does certainly not do so in the way that Rutherford, Thompson, and Bohr once thought it would... Particle and high-energy physics have long since cast a distinct doubt on this concept with the result that now we definitely do not know at all how the material events of this world come about.

In the attempt to reduce all laws of nature on this world to the effects of one single force one even discovered new forces which could not be subordinated to the old ones. Thus gravitation and the interaction of particles have remained practically unsolved up to today. With his general theory of relativity, Einstein gave a new image to gravitation; he revealed it as an apparent force and gave matter the property to bend the space surrounding it. When previously one had been faced with the question why matter should exert gravitation - which did not causally result from its pure existence - the question now is why it should bend space because this property also seems imputed somehow. Einstein himself knew about these weaknesses which did not keep his epigones from constructing black holes as if Einstein's formulas really were the ideal solution.

All those many theories, which are to substantiate origin and purpose of the world or to describe the development of life, have in common that they are on no account so smooth and free of contradictions as it may appear to the lay public. The evolution of life - although basically described in a logical way - has gaps which are immense. The doctrine of the inviolability of the genetic programme probably draws an arbitrary line in the same way as the doctrine, that the velocity of light cannot be exceeded, sets a limit whose existence has to appear mystical because as a postulate it remains unfounded and metaphysical. Because Einstein led us to believe in fact that this was the case - but we want to know why it is the case and suspect that one single final cause is behind all phenomena, behind the absolute velocity of light as well as behind gravitation or behind the DNA... Can this cause be found? Is there one single principle at the bottom of the world or rather in the world which makes it explainable by the facts of itself?

The scholars of this world would not conduct research if they did not have this expectation. They all have one goal: to find the common cause of all forms of phenomena - in fact in such a way that both the question about the nature of matter and about the mind can be answered satisfactorily.

Are such questions to be asked at all? Would not one final answer bring about the termination of these questions and could they not be just terminated immediately? They could if there weren't these prophets again and again who offered their manufactured answers for sale in order to make a profitable living on them. And if they didn't pretend that their polished, ready-made answers were the truth. Just as in former times - and even today - when the content of the religions was taken for real, at present one believes in the theory of relativity and the big bang in the same way - as if the first cause of this world had been mathematics or blasting technology. But it can't be neither! And the answer can only be found in a way that leads through all fields of knowledge of this world. Because the sciences have parted company: natural science and humanities have different objectives as if there were at least two causes for this universe...

Are the questions posed correctly at all? Is it necessary for the world to have a cause at all? Have we still not realised, maybe, that the logic of our thinking arose from a brain function which stems from the causalities of the visible and therefore throws us off the scent when we are considering the invisible? Or is human intelligence really sufficient to overcome this obstacle as well? Is it possible to break free from the subjectivity that forms our consciousness?

This book wants to show that it is not impossible. For each mystery there are at least two solutions: a complicated one and a simple one. Both versions have their supporters. One lot - for the most part insufficiently informed and unable to gain an overview - thinks that not everything is so simple; that the longing for simplicity is an obsession like any other; that in the end things always prove to be more complicated than in the formulations of the theorists. The others - for the most part scientists like Heisenberg - suspect on the other hand that the solution to the world's mystery has to be so simple that even the simplest theory one can think of will still describe the truth in too complicated a manner.

Strange as it is, the simplification of the world has consisted in the discovery of many forces and particles and particles of particles (quarks) up to today and there can be no question of a satisfactory answer. Because a lot of new questions have popped up. They are answered with a couple of theories, each of which dealing with the borderline cases of the previous one, and in the end each contradicts all the other ones... Can it go on like this? It can but it doesn't have to. Because there has to be a simple solution. Even those who don't want to deny God have to admit that this world has to be created in such an ingenious way that it works automatically so to speak. Ingenious solutions, however, have always been simple!

As simple as the solution proposed in this book might seem it will appear to be a paradox at first sight. But these are the characteristics and the fate of every new idea. Each opposes traditional views at first, and each is vehemently fought at first to be finally accepted only after the keepers and guardians of the old theories have died off.

On the way we will follow, we cannot deny the results of scientific research but their interpretations. The fact that bodies fall to earth is undeniable but it still has not been proven if the so-called gravitation forms the basis of this process nor where it comes from!

Man tends to divide the conceptions of the world and to make their halves clash. Where this method led him to is obvious. Should the right way not consist in uniting the halves again to create one science that comprises everything? In this unification the boundaries between physics and chemistry, biology and philosophy, etc. will fall - and therefore these boundaries will be of little concern to us in this book. No matter from which fields we will need data and knowledge, we will take it and merge it into a theory of our own without restraints.

The recurrent theme of this book begins in physics. Well, actually physics is not intended to give answers concerning the cause because it is a science of measuring, of mathematically handling phenomena which may remain fundamentally quite unexplained. It is described with metaphysical concepts like energy or work but these are measuring quantities which do not answer who or what is actually at work in order to evoke such enigmatic effects like gravitation or the strong nuclear force. But physicists are not without imagination. Again and again they are inventing substantial workers, as for example the "particles" whose exchange causes the effects. He who is satisfied with such answers may put this book aside. Because this book tries to explain why the physicists had to discover their theories and what is really behind the phenomena.

Will our theory be dynamite for arguments and discussions? Certainly not at once. In the eyes of the scientists, he who opposes the valid paradigms is a crackpot, a crank, or a troll and a zealot. As a rule, one tends to ignore madmen like that. Maybe one will condescend to look for errors in this book and one will certainly find them but basically these "errors" are irrelevant. One will confront us with other theories which will be defended by their supporters like the persuasions of a religion. And it will be held against us that we are trying to undermine the holy temple of physics, Einstein's Theories of Relativity, and that we are questioning the Special Theory of Relativity at all. This may make many a scientist suspicious of us. But when Einstein encroached upon the temples of Newton he met with little response in the beginning - and if Max Planck had not been interested in Einstein's hushed-up theory, probably the world would have been spared.

In this book, however, we will demonstrate why Einstein had to discover his theories and why the world behaves in fact as if it was designed according to the General Theory of Relativity although this theory represents a solution of the problem which is just as bold as it is unrealistic. The majority of the physicists will already raise the objection that the theories of relativity have been proven many times. Apart from the fact that theories cannot be proven as a rule, one can respond that these proofs are nothing but exactly the phenomena they dealt with and that all of them can be attributed to other causes. As it is, the pyramids of Egypt prove without a doubt that they were built in some way but the question remains in which way! Any theory in this respect can be proved with the existence of the pyramids, and in the same way, the perihelion rotation of the Mercurial orbit or the deflection of light in the field of the sun prove every theory which can substantiate them with good approximation.

The hypothesis in this book has without doubt a philosophical aspect that cannot be denied. One should probably invent a new definition for this way of looking at things. For the fun of it, what about: "philophysics". Because it brings about a fusion of several methods which has been rather taboo so far. It blends ontology and epistemology into a whole and does not stop at uniting mind and matter by explaining the mental subjects of the world causally with the physical ones. But one has to be aware of the fact that matter itself is no material product but arises from an event for which every word is legitimate - and that includes "mind". This fact also demonstrates the inadequacies of our language. That we are able to understand the world perfectly despite this flaw is to be demonstrated exhaustively. The book was written with great objectiveness. Nothing was categorised in advance, no thought was given if the message of this book was positivistic or nihilistic, materialistic or something else. Philosophers would label it "excessive reductionalism" but into which category it will be put in the end is for the reader to decide.

The book was written because there aren't any real answers rooted in the non-fiction and reference books of this world, and the fictitious worlds of philosophy, the spirits of the world, the various Providences or chance are of no use as the cause. Many readers, who were troubled by the questions of where from and where to, and who were searching for an answer in the wrong place, might have felt the same.

The book forms a community with the reader. That's why the word "we" is used so often, because it is hoped that the reader will take part in the discoveries that are to be made and that he will understand the train of thought. It is not a book that could be read for entertainment. It demands a high degree of imagination and fantasy from the reader. It would make no sense to continue reading if something was not understood. The thread would be lost, the connection destroyed. Because this connection dances among the once falsely dissipated fields of knowledge. As it is, it also embraces symbolically the dance of a world which we try to comprehend. Physics alternates with astrophysics which in turn merges with biology, astronomy, and psychology just as it arises. This is certainly a good way since it prevents monotony and will hopefully make this book, which is surely not easy to read, exciting enough to get through to the end.

Many readers will remember how they went to school and learned physics by heart in form of mnemonic sentences like: Like charges repel each other. No-one actually learned why that was so. It just was. It lacked any deeper comprehension. It will be a strange experience for the reader to suddenly understand all the things he once had to accept as given and to know why charges were invented and why their behaviour was postulated. Without doubt some things will meet with a lack of understanding, especially at the beginning of the book; the conventional school knowledge was drummed into our heads far too well, we all believe too much in the actual existence of charges or material particles to be immediately prepared to forget it all. But prepared we should be! For many of us, the TV-set at home may be proof for the existence of electrons - but these people should remember our allegory of the pyramids mentioned before...

The book should only give you food for thought. For lack of space, many ideas can only be sketched as an example, and the reader is invited to continue the process in order to find the principle, which we will discover, in his old school books and to subject what he already believed to know to critical examination - hopefully with the astonishing conclusion that he now understands completely why for instance all bodies fall to Earth at the same speed or why bodies cannot be accelerated beyond the velocity of light. Yes, all of a sudden he will comprehend such mysterious axioms like those of Galileo or Newton for it does not go without saying on any account that a body subjected to a linear uniform motion "will continue its momentum on its own" (in Galileo's own words). Even such an apparently trite process must have a definite cause which Galileo and Newton did not discover at all, though. Einstein could not demonstrate it. It is absolutely to be desired that an understanding for concealed causes of such a kind can be worked out completely without mathematics. Mathematics are an abstraction of our hypothetical reality. But we want to deal with that reality on which our subjective reality as well as that of mathematics are based.

Our brain is not an independent apparatus which produces an image of the world in our heads according to any accidental criteria, an image that would probably not have any real reference to the absolute reality (that's what some philosophers suspect). As we will see, our think tank is a real product of this reality, a reaction to the environment which has to be perceived - and for that reason, it is indeed able to comprehend the reality by which it is caused. Although our physical sensory world is only hypothetically real, no one will still deny today that our knowledge can expand far beyond the visible...

Of course, the book also contains some fantastic speculations. Often the question concerning the why is even easier to answer then that concerning the how. A completely new hypothesis about the origin of the planets will be developed to demonstrate that still not all possibilities have been discussed and that at least the current theories are not tenable. For the first time, a plausible reason for the distance which the planets keep to the sun arises from the discovered principle. These distances follow a law of nature that has been a mystery until this day and which counterfeit all elaborated theories due to the lack of explicability. Moreover the paradox of the angular impulse can finally be explained. That might sound a little sensational but it follows quite casually that both phenomena of astrophysics and of particle physics can be understood causally with the discovered principle.

Maybe there will be a time when some of the chapters of the current natural history will have to be rewritten; it has to be expected especially with regard to the theories about the development of the stars, the age of the stars, and the black holes. Because black holes cannot exist and the Big Bang didn't happen nor did the "missing links" ever exist in the evolution of life ... And one will be searching for them just as futilely as for the black holes, for the quarks as primordial matter of all matter, or for the Higg's boson as cause of the mass...

The fairy tales of alien astronauts who are said to have come to our Earth from far away stellar systems or who are probably still secretly visiting us in their flying saucers will have to be definitely put to an end. Daeniken's entertaining ideas will nevertheless be fuelled because we will discover that an evolution of life across several planets cannot be ruled out. Was there ever life on Mars? Was Mars once like present day's Earth? Did it have oceans like the Earth? Many things point in this direction and this book will give the answers to these and many other questions. It doesn't evade difficult topics like consciousness or death and comes to surprising results which may sometimes appear to be fateful without being really fateful. Maybe it is fateful to see our body as convenient instrument of a stubborn germ cell and just as fateful to have death revealed as the genuine end of our ego. But at the same time we will win the great freedom which we still have within the chains of causality: the freedom to give our life a meaning allowing it to be completely devoted to living. Because it would make no sense at all to fix all one's attention to the Hereafter which cannot exist.

Earth's history has consisted of a series of disasters of which the scars of our tormented planet give proof. One knows about ice ages and global earth movements, continental drifts and enormous impact craters but most of the causes are still shrouded in mystery. We will shed a light on the mystery, may the reader decide how much of the presented solutions he likes.

The why in this book is not a question for meaning. It is a question for cause. The question for meaning, the what for, will cease to apply because of the answers we will find. There certainly isn't any purpose that has to be fulfilled by the cosmos somehow. Nor is there any plan, any planner nor any destination. One single principle rules this universe; only one single force as a consequence of this principle forms and creates the world incessantly. How it does so only from the fact of its existence, how the cosmos becomes and always will remain cosmos out of itself, is what we want to demonstrate in the following chapters. As concisely as possible, we will achieve our goal without much esoteric embellishments and regardless of the prevalent opinions: to see the world as a matter of course in order to comprehend that it has to be as it is!

Many thoughts in this books have been expressed quite often - although in completely different contexts and interpretations. That nature did not consist of any primordial stuff but was a product of simple actions was already formulated by Schelling in 1799. We already find the spreading of the sphere of one atom across the spheres of other atoms and their mutual influence with Teilhard de Chardin. And in 1755 Immanuel Kant advocated the opinion that all matter, disintegrated into its basic materials, had filled the whole space of the world's structure... Kant also assumed - as the first one to do so? - that matter was also exerting repulsive forces. Alan W. Watts already demonstrated with amazing dialectics that an absolute nothingness could not exist at all and that the existence of a world had to be logically compulsive. The works of this philosopher, who died in 1973, are absolutely noteworthy in this connection. Even Newton and later the physicist Ernst Mach[1] suspected that gravitation and inertia could somehow have to do with the surrounding masses. A suspicion which has been often expressed by other physicists as well, even by Einstein.

We will find something of all the thoughts about this world in this book; although integrated into an order that probably has not been published in such a comprising complexity.

Our opinion regarding the DNA as a dynamic structure will appear a little daring because it violates a dogma of the geneticists. But mutation and selection are not sufficient for the progress of evolution at all. The possibility to write down environmental influences directly onto the DNA had and has to exist. Let's anticipate things a little: How should it have been possible, for example, that the coloured human race came into being by a mere accidental mutation? We surely have to assume that all primitive forms of the human being had originally been very hairy. To hide all the properties that made the climate more bearable (more pigmentation, higher quantity of sweat glands, different distribution of temperature receptors, etc.) under the fur from the beginning would have made little sense for nature which always only created the bare necessities. Thus coloured people surely turned coloured only after they had lost their fur through breeding, so to speak. Maybe the loss of hair was even due to erotic reasons but one cannot fail to notice the influence of the climate which began at the same time. Are we really to believe that one mutation among all primitive human beings, which specifically would have had to meet several dispositions and characteristics at the same time to make any sense, had suddenly produced a naked and dark-skinned human and that he of all people had been so attractive all of a sudden that only his tribe was considered for reproduction from that time on? Or was really chance at work several times in a most appropriate way at the beginning of this new phenotype?

When butterfly chrysalises are exposed to temperature stimuli, the hatched butterflies suddenly have wings of a different colour which are passed on to their descendants. In cold climate and without water yellow-spotted fire salamanders turn into the black Alpine salamander and their descendants remain so. These and many similar cases demonstrate that a regression to the old form will never happen. It looks as if an existing supply of information is gradually used up without being replenished. This fact finds expression in the law of the irreversibility of evolution. The cause of this principle, though, had been unknown for a long time...

Today there is little doubt that acquired characteristics - both phenotypic manifestations and behavioural patterns - are hereditary. But how are they passed on? The biologists don't have a good answer to this question. For them, the DNA has become a rigid machine. That it cannot be one is to be discovered in this book which will also try to convey something about the origins of the DNA. Since it is also one of the oldest questions of the world: what was first, hen or egg? There is an explicit answer to it: the egg! But nothing in it has the features of the future hen itself, it is not programmed with finished characteristics but only with cellular properties that carry the possibilities to react correctly to an environment.

Every bodybuilder knows how much living and eating habits can change the body. But where on the DNA is the programme for bigger muscles? Or for sun-tanned skin? Here the influence of the environment becomes particularly clear. They are made possible by open programmes of the DNA, i.e. variable adaptation mechanisms which exclude a rigid scouring of genetic information. Environment challenges and moulds. All organs and organisms develop according to this principle; without exception they all grow into the required functions and create a demanding, pressing, even compelling environment for one another.

We will discover that the common assumption that all living beings were descended from one type of primordial cell is extremely implausible. There must have been many different primordial cells and consequently a polyphyly, the development of forms from uncountable primeval forms. This thought isn't exactly new either, it was already formulated by the medical practitioner Max Westenhoefer. For us, it will also go without saying that brains didn't develop in order to discern the environment but that all brains were moulded by the environment - as a reaction to the actions in it...

It certainly is a great thing when matter can think about itself - but it is not a miracle. Nor is the whole universe a miracle. For the principle, there was no other possibility than to cause the world just like it is.A wise Indian guru was once asked what he thought of the theory of relativity. He answered: "Even you can invent a theory!"

Really, the ways are still open! Thus the reader is invited to draw his own conclusions about the hypothesis developed in this book. There is not enough space to discuss all the phenomena of this world - and a book with 1000 pages would deter readers too much....

Whatever the reader will consider and analyse after having finished this book he will find the principle of existence in it.

1 T.A.O.

Why does the universe exist? Why is there not just a nothingness in its stead?

In order to answer this question we have to examine the concept of "nothingness" a little closer. We created it by ourselves on the basis of our experience. This experience was born of the fact that objects exist in a given space and that they can be removed. But even when we remove, for example, all objects from a room, this does not mean that a nothingness is left because we have a definition for that what remains: air. When we remove the air, we oddly enough do not speak of a nothingness but characterise the new condition with one word that expresses especially the lack of air: vacuum. Well, we could also remove the whole room together with its vacuum; in addition, we could try to imagine the nothingness by removing the Earth, the sun, the galaxies, and the cosmos. Then we will maybe see an empty space but we are still bodily within this space and torment ourselves with the difficult mental image of the nothingness. Maybe we should remove ourselves as well - but who would then define the nothingness as such?

The nothingness is therefore not only unimaginable but absolutely impossible without a something that marks the boundaries - just like a hole which is inconceivable without its surroundings. We can only relate the term nothingness to the absence of defined objects. However, an absence of objects can only be possible if these objects exist in some way somewhere.

Obviously without giving it a thought, we know and use a word for a condition that cannot exist at all and pose an absolutely unnecessary question using this word. If there cannot be such a thing as an absolute nothingness, we are automatically forced to assume the opposite: existence: For that reason, it is quite comprehensible that "something" exists - but of course it does not go without saying that this something must have adopted the form of our universe of all things.

Anyhow, this first little discovery that there has to be at least something takes away the question where this something comes from. We cannot just remove the cosmos, because where should we put it? But if this is the case it was never brought into its place, because where would it have been before?

There has to be just something from a logical point of view... A simple matter remains to be answered: how does this something manage to become the universe as we know it?

Our simple train of thought forces us immediately to conclude that this something as an undefined, shapeless existence is actually timeless, i.e. it exists eternally. Neither "before" nor "after" is it possible that a nothingness exists.

The ancient Chinese had an equivalent for this shapeless, featureless existence which they called Tao. Tao is the unity, the cause behind the things we perceive. Buddhists often compared this Tao to a completely calm lake whose smooth surface reflected nothing. This is a good comparison which we will use as well. We will call our basic structure, the matrix, "The Absolute Organization", using the abbreviation T.A.O. to express the shapeless existence. This shapelessness is relative; even if T.A.O is not just an object it has to be of a certain condition. We have to imagine this condition vividly in order to detect the cause of all apparent laws of nature in it. Although an ambitious goal it is not too difficult to put into practise. We will only be credible if we are prepared to accept as facts the phenomena made irrefutable by the discoveries of science.

We will try to describe T.A.O., the Indefinable, and in doing so we will set up a fiction. But this, the only admissible fiction, only serves for better comprehending the function of T.A.O. as an energy relay and carrier of information. Any further fiction is forbidden to us.

All phenomena described in the following have already been treated and described by science - although without recognising their origin and their cause.

Well, T.A.O., the shapeless existence, does not look like anything because there is no eye to see it. Nevertheless, T.A.O. must have a recognisable structure in order to be distinguished from the nothingness. When researching this structure we have to look for the simplest thing that can be thought of. It has to be just a little bit more than nothing to be sufficient.

Just like the smooth surface of a lake has a structure, namely the spread of water molecules which do not reflect anything yet, T.A.O. must also have a structure, at least in form of a subdivision into separate units. It doesn't matter particularly if these units can be subdivided for certain or not. Let's just say this simple structure consists at least of points which lie next to or on top of each other as if the space was filled with an infinite amount of tiny spheres which keep in a regular order like the atoms of a crystal. Just think of the inside of the lake and its molecules and you will get a similar picture.

Naturally, even this structure has a cause which we will comprehend automatically later-on. For the time being, we want to be satisfied with this definition of T.A.O. as an arrangement of rather insubstantial and impassive points. Instead of T.A.O. we could also use some other word like "Matrix" or just "Space".

The physicist Mach already had the idea that the apparently empty space had to be actually granular somehow. The Pakistani physicist Abdus Salam expressed a similar thought more recently. We are thus in good company. Even if our matrix differs from the "obsolete" ether theories, the basic thought is absolutely comparative.

When we mentally enlarge this structure enormously, we will approximately get an image as shown in figure 1.

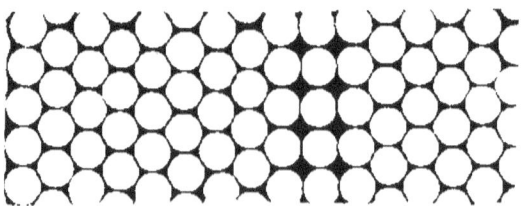

Fig. 1

A simple, motionless structure of points or little granules which are pressed together as close as possible. It continues three-dimensionally in all directions (fig. 3a). It doesn't have a size as long as there is not any scale in it. It has no beginning and no end because it exists eternally out of necessity. Neither is there time in the conventional sense because there aren't any events or any clocks to measure it. The nature of T.A.O. is therefore endless, timeless, eventless, without size, without scale - and yet of a granular structure which is supposedly at rest for the time being - leaving it open whether this condition is possible at all.

Anyhow, we want to draw one conclusion from what we just said: the space in which the universe takes place is not and never has been empty!

Well, the just described structure of T.A.O. is on no account pure fiction. Something exists and this something is at least an energetic condition; an accumulation of such conditions, to be exact. We could say: close to every something another something exists and so on... We can discover and understand the natural tendency towards structures of this simple kind by experimenting with, so to speak, flowing energies, for example with heat. A liquid heated from below produces convection cells. Figure 2 shows such a process, and we see immediately the principal similarity with figure 1:

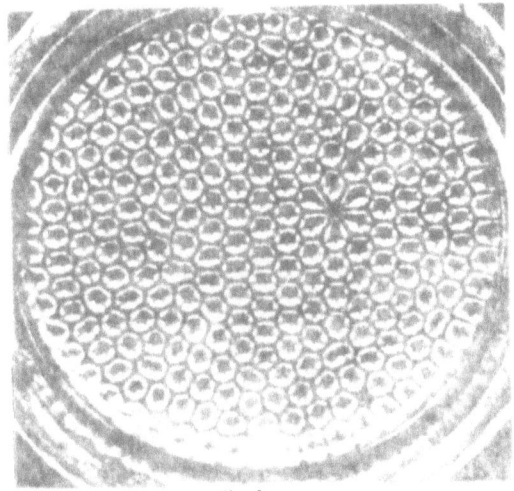

Fig. 2

The matter becomes even clearer when we make the thermal structures visible by means of the electric impulse photography developed by Dennis Milner und Edward Smart. Gleaming thermal spheres appear on a photographic plate which is subjected to an electric impulse between two metal electrodes. They demonstrate that energy does not just flow or disperse but structures itself into certain orders. These are called dissipative structures, and we will come back to them later. But now let's take a look at the thermal spheres on the photographic plate (figure 3):

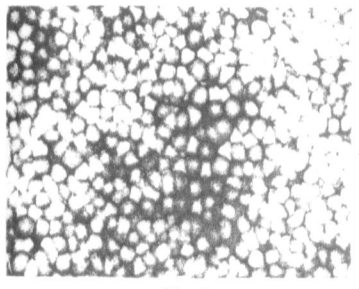

Fig. 3   Fig. 3a

At this point, we also see nothing but an enormous magnification of the structure of T.A.O.. Well, we cannot attach a certain size to T.A.O. itself but the events above give us an approximate impression of the dimensions in which we are roaming mentally. Atomic manifestations take place on a scale for which we invented the unit Angstrom. One Angstrom is inconceivably small, it is 1/10 000 000 mm. If we extended one millimetre until it covered the distance from one pole of the earth to the equator, which are ca. 10 000 km, one Angstrom would have become just one meter long. Well, one glucose molecule already measures about five Angstrom, and there is a distance of one Angstrom between its atoms. Molecules and atoms, however, are already gigantic objects compared to the structure of T.A.O. Therefore we can only enter these areas mentally; there wouldn't be any devices to measure these dimensions in any way.

Properly speaking we have to admit that this structured T.A.O. represents neither an existence nor a nothingness. It forms the basis for both terms. Something exists and yet it does not exist as long as it is not perceived. The nothingness and the existence, both mean absolutely the same. The image of this world is a process of looking at it. It does not exist without the eyes. T.A.O. is neither dark nor light, neither hot nor cold... Whatever we are looking for, we will only find structure and substructure. If all these structures were at rest in themselves there would be no universe. No universe... that doesn't mean on any account, however, the nothingness. Because the structure still exists.

Of all the numerous theories based on the ether, the lattice model by Walter Russell and John Worrell Keely ("The space is filled with a motionless flexible lattice!") is the one which is the most similar to our concept. Yet the lattice model is not logical and self-explaining but a forced design. Where should the lattice come from? The basic structure of the universe must be an inevitable, casual phenomenon, a basic order which is neutral in itself and yet must have the absolute property to carry the prerequisites and processes from which the phenomena and quantities we know, like charges, quanta, light, material mass, or inertia, can or rather must develop independently. We will see that if anything fulfils this expectation, it is the matrix of T.A.O..

Of course, we must certainly not mark this T.A.O. as primordial matter. It is not a material substance, it does not "consist" of something but it takes place, it has an effect... In our language, we have a word for something that has an effect: energy. Therefore, what we have found up to now is space - structured space - in which energy can have an effect. Nothing more. Whatever forms the basis of this effect can always be given any name one likes. We just call it T.A.O.. It is a simple, short word and contains a certain beauty. Already the Chinese choose it for this reason.

Fig.3b: Disturbance

2 Disturbance

When we disturb the smooth surface of a lake by supplying some energy to it in form of our dipped-in finger - and we can retract the finger immediately - it is to be expected that the surface generates waves which propagate. We did not really add something to the lake, we only lent it one finger so to speak, and yet the lake has a new appearance now. Let's compare our T.A.O. structure to a three-dimensional lake. In figure 1 we shifted one row of the structural points in order to see that in this case they will immediately need more space than before. All granules are standing in each other's way. Therefore every disturbance of this structure is gradually communicated to all other granules. Something is happening inside this lake, and it is only an informational event because the lake still consists of the same something. Just think about how multifarious the play of waves on a lake can be and how many patterns and new structures can come into existence.

When we disturb T.A.O. or when it is disturbed in some way, in fact something similar to the events on a surface of water will take place but in all directions of the space at the same time, i.e. three-dimensionally. So disturbance can change T.A.O. and enrich it with information. Though not any random form of disturbance is possible but certainly only that which casually results from the structure of T.A.O. The simplest kind of disturbance is an impulse moving through T.A.O. For this impulse we will also use the term shove or vibration. The form of this impulse is shown in some detail in figure 4:

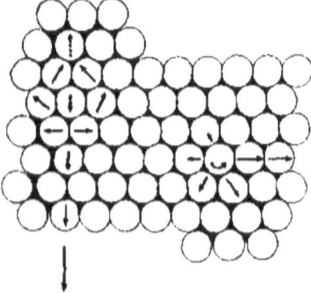

Fig. 4

On the left side of the figure we can see how a vibration - the impulse moves downwards - reacts back on itself, i.e. it is also transmitted in the opposite direction through the shifting of the granules. As a consequence, everything is at rest again after the shove. Therefore not an oscillation is moving through this matrix but a tremor. Later, we will substantiate in detail why there cannot be any oscillations within T.A.O.

Every granule transmits the disturbance to the next one but not immediately. It will take a short time until the next granule becomes aware of the impulse. There are no instantaneous causalities, a little time will always elapse between cause and effect. For that reason, time is already a product in this structure, the interval stands always between cause and effect first and foremost. In a simple way we thus discovered time within T.A.O.; and what we said about T.A.O. also applies to time: as long as no-one perceives and measures and above all interprets an interval between past and future, time in the conventional sense does not exist. Still it has an effect... Since we already talked about energy, in time we find a second important factor for the existence of the universe.

On the right side of the figure, we see an impulse coming towards us, from the front of the structure so to speak. Every disturbance of a granule is of course also transmitted to all granules which are arranged perpendicularly to the movement of the impulse. If the disturbance is a torsional vibration, the transmission cannot take place simultaneously but only in such a way that the impulse is surrounded by further disturbances in its direction of movement so to speak. We can define this form of impulse more exactly by simply saying: a disturbance spirals through the structure of T.A.O. Starting from an arbitrary point it seizes all other points of T.A.O. and therefore has a discernible direction of movement because the ancillary shoves caused by the main shove follow temporally behind. Since the individual granules always oscillate or vibrate only around their own area, there isn't any real movement^2 in T.A.O. The transmitted impulse is only information passed-on. The content of this information - that is to say form and extent of the disturbance - maybe means "energy" for a possible recipient which uses a language like we do - and actually he could already call it "light"... But one thing after the other!

Since every disturbance is equalised retroactively of its own accord - the granules are pressed back into their close-grained, dense texture - there will always be only one single disturbance or vibration running through the structure while everything becomes smooth and at rest again behind it. And we see a considerable difference to the allegory of the lake: an impulse does not cause a real wave! Just to emphasise it again: everything is at rest before and after the impulse.

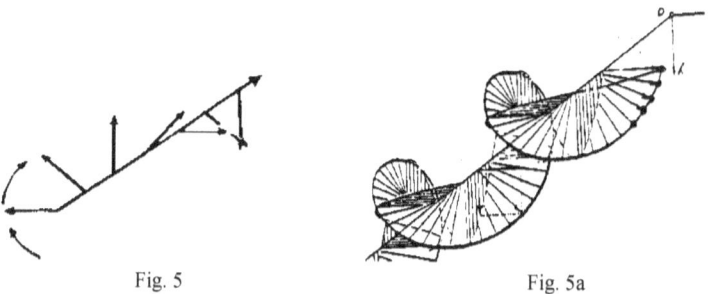

Fig. 5   Fig. 5a

When we dip our finger into a lake for a moment we generate a series of waves which spread in circles. Very metaphorically speaking, if we dipped our finger into T.A.O. for a moment, the result would be a single shove (and only one "circle") spiralling through T.A.O. It consists of two different movements: the forward movement and the perpendicular radiation of further shoves. Both components are shown in figure 5. This relay of impulses results automatically from the nature of the structure. The form of the applied impulse is significant. When we make a granule vibrate, the radiating shoves will be equally intensive in all directions; when we make the granule move only into a vertical or horizontal direction, the impulse passed on to the granules which do not lie in this direction will be weaker. In that way, we polarised the impulse so to speak.

Hopefully, it was not too difficult to understand the above. Despite its simplicity this function of T.A.O. is already something like the key to the universe!

We could also symbolise the form of the impulse by drawing a spiral (figure 6). After all, it includes both directions of movement!

Mankind has always recognised the symbolic meaning of the spiral[3] intuitively. Particularly in the Eastern religions it plays a significant role. As we saw, not completely without reason. But in T.A.O., there are only spiral paths - no stationary spirals.

When we disturb T.A.O. once - figure 6a, a) - and then a second time, a second shove will follow the first one without being in direct connection with it. Neither would a third one have anything to do with the previous ones – figure 6a, b). Frequency is the name we give to a succession of several impulses in the same direction within a certain time. The intervals between one shove and the next is called wavelength without signifying a real wave. For linguistic reasons, however, we will continue using the term wave because we are now aware of the little but significant difference.

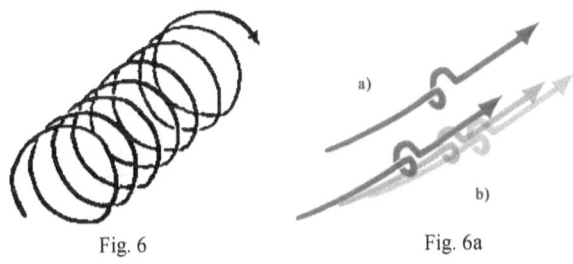

Fig. 6   Fig. 6a

When we designate one directional plane of the impulse as the "electric" one and the one perpendicular to it as the "magnetic" one, we will get a good expression for the sequence of several impulses: "electromagnetic wave". Well, this term is already in use, and of course, the process in T.A.O., as we just described it, is in principle nothing but an electromagnetic wave as symbolically shown in figure 5a. But the designations "electric" and "magnetic" don't have any special meaning for us yet.

If we wanted to build a model of T.A.O., we would have to put some fairly elastic spheres in layers one on top of each other and eliminate friction. There isn't any friction in T.A.O. The physicist would say that it was a matter of elastic shoving actions which didn't consume any energy. In such cases, he speaks therefore of the conservation of the impulse. But we must not imagine the granules of T.A.O. to be anything but vibrating about themselves as if they were connected by springs (fig. 6b).

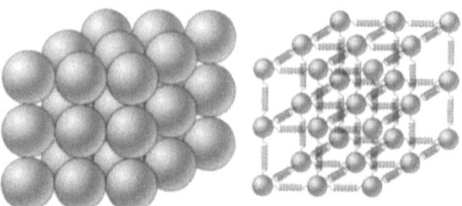

Fig. 6b

To put it in a nutshell: The structure of T.A.O. can be disturbed by an impulse which is continued on two directional planes. The sussession of several such shoves is not a wave as it may spread for example in material media (sound or gravity waves) because the impulses are not connected to each other in any way. Every serious analogy with oscillations or waves would be wrong. Later, we will see that many physicists drew a couple of wrong conclusions because of this incorrect analogy...

When the message transported by the quickly running individual shove is energy, we could also call it "energy quantum". This fact is done justice to by the quantum theory of physics which already acknowledges that all energies are transmitted in form of small portions, i.e. quanta. That this is not just a whim of nature but that it is not possible in any other way is what we just found out.

Fig. 7

In our hypothesis, we could of course also stimulate a granule in the centre of T.A.O to start oscillating or rotating or we could give it a shove (which would be the more correct way of looking at things). As a consequence, one impulse would run to the right and one to the left. And we would also discover that one impulse began spiralling to the right and the other to the left starting from the point of generation (figure 7).

Hence there are two spiral paths with different spatial orientation. With this trivial insight we are already in a position to describe the material events in this universe entirely, as strange as this may sound at this point. But all discoveries which are necessary to be made in the following are a direct result of this spatially different orientation of impulses. With the spatial condition we come across the third important factor of these few elementary basic concepts which are responsible for the existence of the world: space. The other two are: energy and time. All three concepts are the result of each other because if there were not any intervals between cause and effect, a spatially defined order would not be possible.

We should now think a little about what has been demonstrated so far in order to comprehend the connection between energy, space, and time intuitively. All concepts are based on T.A.O.– because T.A.O. is, as we will see, the carrier of energy, space, and time. All three concepts are effects, and as we will learn later, they only exist due to perception or "measurement" as the physicist would state it more precisely.

Actually, with these three elementary effects we already found everything that is to be found in this cosmos!

3 Encounters

The two effective planes of an impulse, which are perpendicular to each other, could also be symbolised by a cross. And again, it is not without a good reason that the cross has played a special role as a symbol in this world (figure 8).

This crossed interconnection of the effect finds expression only in the relationship between what is responsible and the observer. Every disturbance becomes only existent as such if something or somebody is actually disturbed. Although the shoves of the impulse are propagating in all directions, for an observer, only that shove exists which is coming towards him. In the language of the quantum physicists it means that every quantum only exists in the moment it is measured.

Let's just assume somewhere in the pitch-dark there was a fanatic boxer who did some shadow boxing in the truest sense of the word. While he is turning around, he is dealing out punches in all directions. We cannot see these punches but we feel them when we get close enough to the boxer. From time to time we will be delivered a punch. We won't know about any of the other punches - they are not hitting anything. For that reason, the perceiver always feels only those effects which are perpendicular to the body of the boxer and likewise to the body of the perceiver. The same applies to every energy effect of an impulse of T.A.O.. Every measuring instrument - as well as each of our sense organs - learns therefore only a fraction of the truth. Every energy which is perceived is only a small amount of the total energy of an impulse. When physicists talked about energy in this world, for a long time they always referred only to that small noticeable amount of energy - exactly that observable or measurable fraction. Starting from that fraction they drew their conclusions. Not until lately did they discover that many of these conclusions have to be wrong. We will talk about that later.

We already defined the spatial orientation of the shove spirals with "left-hand" and "right-hand". To make it perfectly clear we are now determining: a right-hand spiral is the propagation of a shove in clockwise direction, a left-hand spiral moves counter-clockwise. In general, we will call the sense of rotation of an impulse "spin"[4], a term which is used in quite a similar sense in particle physics. We also described already the creation of two spiral shoves at the same time and now assume that many disturbances of T.A.O. also cause many different spiral shoves which flow through the structure in all directions. In the same way, every other kind of vibration and straight shove is possible as well. But for the time being we are only interested in those propagations of energy which exhibit a spin.

Well, what happens when two such spirals meet? For this encounter there are two possibilities which are distinctly different in particular (figure 8a).

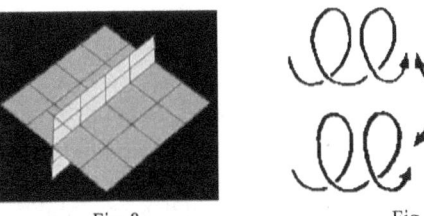

Fig. 8   Fig. 8a

Either two spirals with opposite spin meet. They will correspond in motion at the point of meeting. Or they have the same spin and will then collide diametrically at the point of meeting. Naturally the resulting effects will be different. But before we take a closer look at the consequences we have to find further differences and in doing so we have to proceed a little as if by textbook because it won't do any harm to understand the different forms of movement well.

For the time being we just assume that every disturbance, every impulse has the same quantity of energy, i.e. that the radii of the spiral paths have the same size. We know, although, that every shove in all directions is actually moving on endlessly spreading out over bigger and bigger areas of space. For that reason, its energy decreases by the square of its distance. But we can choose a defined section of this area in which the disturbance remains especially effective.

Well, there are following variants for the encounter of two impulses:

1) CORRESPONDENCE IN MOTION. That means both spirals are moving to the right or to the left at the moment of their collision. Therefore a spiral with a right-hand spin and a spiral with a left-hand spin have to meet in this case.

2) CONTRAST OF MOTION. At the moment of their collision the spirals are moving in opposite directions, i.e. two spirals with the same spin collide.

3) CORRESPONDENCE IN TIME. That means the shove of both impulses happens at the place of encounter.

4) CONTRAST OF TIME. Both shoves happen in different places at the time of their meeting, in the extreme case they are exactly opposite of each other.

The following illustrations show the possibilities which result from these four variants, symbolised by simple arrows and pictures of pipe-cleaners. Let's take a closer look at these possibilities.

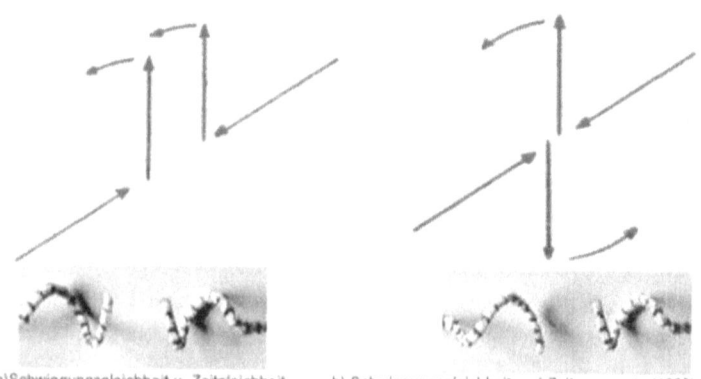

a) Schwingungsgleichheit u. Zeitgleichheit   b) Schwingungsgleichheit und Zeitgegensatz (180°)

a) Correspondence in vibration and correspondence in time
b) Correspondence in vibration and contrast of time (180°)

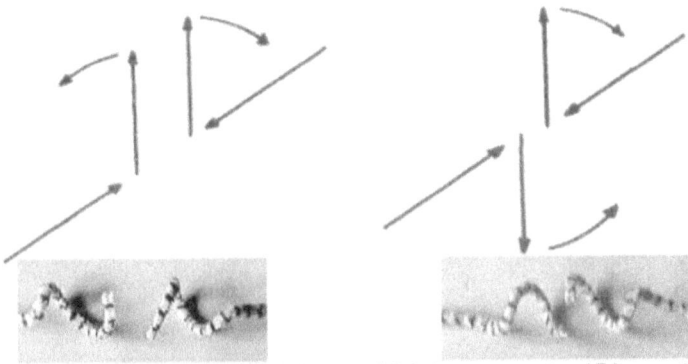

c) Schwingungsgegensatz und Zeitgleichheit
d) Schwingungsgegensatz und Zeitgegensatz

c) Contrast of vibration and correspondence in time
d) Contrast of vibration and contrast of time

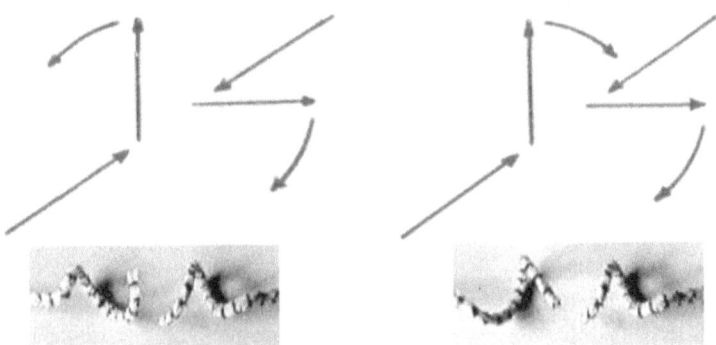

e) Schwingungsgegensatz u. Zeitgegensatz
f) Schwingungsgleichheit und Zeitgegensatz (90°)

e) Contrast of vibration and contrast of time
f) Correspondence in vibration and contrast of time (90°)

The contrast of time of 90° (e and f) is called temporal displacement in the following. Now let's study the pictures above, try to picture the encounters clearly in our mind's eye and think a little about them. We will obtain different results, and we will give these results pleasant names so that we will still know at a later time what we are talking about. Although it's not correct we will also call the movements vibrations.

re. a: PENETRATION

Each of the impulses meets with correspondence in vibration and in time and therefore has the chance to be continued. The impulses penetrate each other and continue their corresponding motion as if nothing happened.

re. b: INTERFERENCE

Two absolutely contrary shoves, which are rotating in the same direction, annihilate or enhance each other depending on phase position. Either both impulses will vanish apparently without a trace or they continue their motion intensified. These processes are called destructive or constructive interference.

re. c: MODIFICATION

Two shoves travelling in the same direction intensify each other but won't continue in their previous directions. A new shove is produced which travels on perpendicular to the original direction. The quantity of energy and the directions have changed.

re. d: RESISTANCE

In this collision, nothing matches at all. Both impulses will put up resistance against each other without cancelling one another out. They will rebound from each other. This process is also called reflection.

re. e: DISHARMONY

Temporal displacement by 90° and contrast of vibration. The impulses cannot continue but they don't annihilate each other either, nor do they intensify one another. Therefore they will remain on the spot of the meeting where they form a vibrating field which will exist only for a short time because of the contrasting vibrations and will dissipate into new impulses scattering into all directions. We call this event an unstable field. The physicist names an event based on the same process an unstable particle! We begin to suspect where our considerations will take us: process e) causes the first "material" phenomenon!

re. f: HARMONY

Temporal displacement by 90° and correspondence in vibration. This event resembles the preceding one. But the impulses do not meet directly, neither do they find a possibility to be continued in the original direction. They are toppling over one another so to speak and create a field there and then. This field remains stable due to the correspondence in vibration because the impulses will always run after one another. A harmoniously vibrating spherical body made of impulses develop as shown more clearly in figure 10.

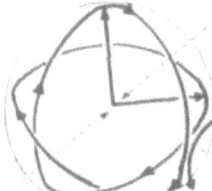

Fig. 10

With that we discovered nothing less than a stable particle. It is not a substantial particle but a field in which two impulses chase each other very quickly. We want to call this field proton because it is identical to the hypothetical proton of our atomic physicists.

Well, this resembled text book style but it could not be avoided. He who has problems in understanding these successions of motion in T.A.O. exactly, does not need to be sad. It is sufficient to understand that different forms of encounter between the impulses just have different results and that oscillating fields can form in some cases, impulses so to speak, which remain on the spot. Of course, all intermediate variations of these encounters are possible - T.A.O. is certainly filled with countless fluctuations and vibrations which - like the punches of the boxer - go into empty space. Physicists have already discovered this abundance of shoves into empty space which are virtual because they are ineffective. They called them "vacuum fluctuation" or "quantum foam".

For that bit of mental acrobatics we are now rewarded with the insight that there aren't any "particles" in the sense of the word at all but that matter is obviously put together of impulses dashing round and round in imaginary spheres because of their meeting each other. Therefore matter does obviously not consist of some kind of primordial matter but is a product of energy, space, and time! At the moment, however, it is still difficult to really believe this.

4 Proton

Well, let's draw an inference: the only basic presumption we assumed was that T.A.O. had to exist for logical reasons and that it exhibits the simplest structure possible. It cannot be defined more precisely. It does not have any further characteristics either. No matter what we call it, for the underlying T.A.O. it will be only just an arbitrary word. Maybe this reminds us of the first verse of the Gospel of John: In the beginning was the word...

We realised that the word, in our case the word T.A.O., had to be compulsorily existent - it is deductively inevitable. We could choose any other word for it: God, Spirit, or Force... Typically every story of the Creation on this earth begins with a word of this kind. We equated T.A.O. with space because space becomes space only through the existence of T.A.O. Its structure is a granularity representing just a little bit more than the Nothingness - but this structure is already able to transmit energetic information in form of impulses which have a slight similarity to waves. In the broadest sense these sequences of impulses can be called light.

Light of that kind of very hard gamma radiation (i.e. with a very high impulse frequency) had to exist prior to any form of matter. Surely there was also any other possible kind of impulse form, and it would seem to suggest itself to give each of these energy quanta a particle name of their own - if the physicists had not already done so (without exactly knowing what they were talking about).

The coincidence of spatial and temporal conditions produced building blocks of matter which, on their own, represent only energy without possessing any material substance or mass. They are energetic events and we called the first of these events which we discovered proton. About 99 percent of the universe consists of protons of this kind. When we speak about this proton as an element of this world, we call it hydrogen. It is the simplest element we know.

If there was only one single proton inside of T.A.O., this proton would be virtually as big as T.A.O. - i.e. in principle as infinite as the cosmos itself. Because all the vibrations of one field of impulses are running into infinity so to speak. A first and only proton would basically be the centre of T.A.O. around which the impulses would propagate radially. If there ever was such a first proton it would have defined that place in the middle of infinity where the universe developed. Moreover it lent a new spherical geometry to the space.

It does not matter if many protons came into existence spontaneously and at the same time or if they formed gradually at great temporal intervals. The question is why did T.A.O. not just simply remain at rest like a giant crystal - as big empty incomprehensible Nothingness? Obviously it is the same with the rest as with the Nothingness. It is not conceivable without its opposite and does never exist by itself. For that reason, there could have never been a T.A.O. at rest. What should the rest relate to as long as nothing happened in T.A.O.? And is it possible that "nothing" ever happened? That is a simple but significant consideration because it forces us to acknowledge that there could never have been a real beginning of the cosmos! To ask why there isn't a Nothingness instead of the universe would make just as little sense as racking one's brains over why T.A.O. - if its existence is unavoidable at all - just didn't remain at rest!

We also have to be aware of the fact that all concepts, even Nothingness or rest, could only come about with the events in T.A.O.! Sometime or other, today's image of the cosmos developed from that. Because up to the moment when impulses met in such a way that protons could come into being there was nothing else but a chaos of disordered impulses.

So to speak, two protons would divide up T.A.O.. Since they are distributing shoves in all directions, they are immediately in each others way. Because of the oscillations the granules of T.A.O. will without doubt require more space, a larger area than before - as we already demonstrated in figure 1. The more protons came into existence, the more space they took up. Vibrating and oscillating they fought for the space, displaced each other and drew the first boundaries. In this way, energy centres were created in T.A.O. as spherical fields which obstructed one another or penetrated each other as far as their energies (shoves) allowed. Only now did the protons obtain the atomic appearance which we imagine them to have. The mutual influencing and displacement made T.A.O. literally crystallise out into an enormous amount of protons which squeezed each other down to a structure of tiniest spheres so to speak ... not dissimilar to their underlying substructure, T.A.O.!

Now let's try to depict such a proton field (figure 11). The circle, however, is an imaginary boundary, though, which is never determined by one field alone but also by the adjoining fields. When we draw the spiral path which results form the movement of two impulses into all directions (see figure 10) into this circle we will promptly obtain the picture which the physicists De Broglie and Schrödinger once created of the atom.

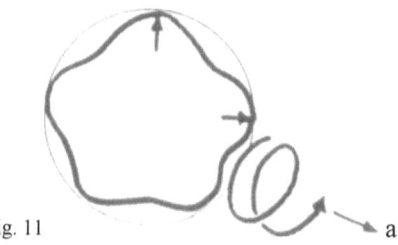

Fig. 11

The sketched in harmonious oscillation represents nothing else but an electron wave. The electron, often described as a building block of matter, is actually not a building block and not a flying particle. It is a wave in exactly the sense in which we understand the word wave. It is created by the two impulses running one after the other; the result is a wave-like oscillation circling the field spatially and which can adopt other forms as well. It differs from light above all in that its path is always curved and in its energy content since it was originally the result of two impulses. Therefore differences in spin and mass action are to be expected as well. If we called this energy whizzing around and around a particle, it would not be quite correct - but still the world predominantly believes that the electron is an object. But it is just as little an object as the proton itself.

When we imagine how the electron impulses oscillate across the indeed imaginary surface of the field it soon becomes clear that it will come to shoves again. Figure 10 revealed already that the result of two spatially displaced impulses has to make every granule they hit oscillate. We sketched the result in figure 11: a further creation of a spiral path (a). Every vibrating proton is therefore emitting new disturbances into all directions which are the same as light in principle but for their energy being much too low. Still, they are similar spiral shoves, and logically all these spirals streaming away have the same sense of rotation, i.e. the same spin. With that the space around the proton receives a new order. Let's just call it "polarised". And the force which flows outwards through the shoves and seems to envelop the proton like a shell, we will call electric field because the electron waves are to blame for its coming into existence after all.

When two protons meet they are not very nice to each other from the outset because they are simply in each other's way. A priori there is thus a repulsive effect which - not least of all - contributed to the development of the proton's boundaries. Now, the vibrations of the electric field are coming across each other as well. If the two protons are of like kind, like spirals will meet, too, as shown in figure 12 (A).

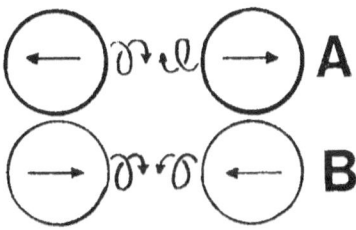

Fig. 12

This means the occurrence of meeting case d). This case is called resistance or reflection. That means in addition to their mutually existing aversion, the two protons put up resistance against one another; their aversion is intensified. With that an apparently new force is revealed. If we wanted to make the explanation of this force easy for ourselves as the physicists have done so far we could say the cause of this force was a "charge" and simply determine the proton was "positively charged". That would result in the postulate:

"Positive (i.e. like) charges repel each other."

But we know by now that the proton has not been charged with anything so that there shouldn't be any mention of charge. And apparently the term "positive" has to be just as ridiculous! But we are able to imagine that there could be a proton which is vibrating into the other direction. Then a spiral with a right-hand spin and one with a left-hand spin would meet (figure 12, B!) and then case a) would arise. We named it penetration - which means not more and not less than that the impulses don't take any notice of each other!

If we now postulated a force - to anticipate things a little - which had the tendency to squeeze the two protons from the beginning it would have an easy job in contrast to the case before. And ignorant of the true facts we would of course say: one of these two protons has to be "negatively" charged! That would be in accordance with the mnemonic sentence we learned at school:

"Unlike charges attract each other."

But with this we would be spinning a yarn (and the physicists have done so up to this day) which is quite unreasonably far off the truth because the second proton was charged with nothing either! Apart from the opposite spatial polarisation it is absolutely equivalent to the first. For that reason, we realise: positive and negative are actually spatial concepts. Just as well or even better we could say left and right instead!

Later we will discover that all atoms polarise the space around them either into "left" or into "right" in a characteristic manner and that almost the whole behaviour of matter is determined and controlled by that circumstance.

Obviously all protons of our universe oscillate in the same direction. If one appeared that was oscillating in the opposite direction, it would be a negative proton so to speak, i.e. an antiproton. If we shoved such an antiproton into a proton, the two opposing impulses would annihilate each other in the moment of their joint centre point: the two protons would dissipate into wild, disordered shoves. Thus, we discovered in a simple way that antimatter can actually exist and that there is nothing mysterious behind this concept.

Therefore, it goes without saying why obviously all protons are of like kind nowadays and why antiprotons can be created in a particle accelerator at best. If there ever were different protons, they would have immediately stood against each other in lively annihilation. Today's protons emerged victorious! Their remaining correspondence explains many a puzzle of nature like the violation of parity (that is the theoretically expected symmetry of the elementary particles) or the strange fact that living organisms only use left-handed molecular spirals. We will have to discuss these topics in more detail later.

At this point, we want to note down the following: we already expressed our assumption that protons - and with them in principle the known universe - arose from a kind of chaos of gamma or X-rays. But where is it written that the universe has been finished already? Could it not be possible just as well that there is still chaos surrounding the universe which began expanding from any place of T.A.O.? In this case, this X and gamma radiation should still be detectable somehow - for example as a radiation which would flow in on us from all around exhibiting a strong Doppler shift. Maybe we would identify it as heat at best. Well, this radiation really exists. It is the cosmic background radiation with wavelengths of $3*10^{-3}$ to 30 meters, and at least it does not prove the one thing: the Big Bang...

And could it not be possible that the war between protons and antiprotons is still raging in the universe, and that we would therefore have to detect mysteriously big expressions of energy coming from these areas which could only be explained with the mutual annihilation of matter and antimatter? These messages from the farthest areas of the cosmos really exist: gamma-ray bursts or quasi-stellar objects whose energy radiation is disproportionate to its (although rather unknown) size. Generally they are known as quasars. But we will present a different explanation for this mystery of astronomy. Prior to that we will think about why such an ethereal structure as the proton appears to be so solid that we call it matter.

5 Mass

Up to now we haven't found any primordial matter but only energy impulses within an insubstantial structure, quanta, which only became manifest because of the observer or because of the measuring instrument. Why does the world appear to be so compact, so substantial, nonetheless that the physicists had to invent the concept of mass? What does the visible and tangible of the cosmos consist of?

Fig. 13

Let's imagine a fan wheel. When we make its blades rotate and accelerate them, they soon look like a disc (figure 13). The faster the blades rotate, the more compact the image of the disc becomes. Soon we could not put our hand into it anymore. When the blades of the fan are so fast that they are almost everywhere at the same time, we have a wheel in front of us that offers considerable resistance, a wheel that does not exist in reality. But it would not go well with a wheel of the same kind.

If we wanted to throw an object through this compact disc, it would have to be very swift and very small. If we intended to shatter this wheel, we would have to choose a big and slow object. The acceleration of the blades reduces the duration of one revolution. The resistance they put up against us because of their rotation could be called "apparent mass" because logically it is only the kinetic energy of the blades which stops us from entering. Well, when we equate this energy with the observed effect, i.e. the mass, we realise that it is the rotational velocity of the fan which can change the fan's appearance. Thus the difference between energy and mass results obviously from a coefficient of velocity. This will remind many of us immediately of Einstein's famous formula:

$$E=mc^2$$

In this formula, a velocity, namely that of light, is also decisive whether an event appears as energy or as mass. But we will deal with this formula at a later point.

When we now remove all blades except for one and call this fragment, which is nearly invisible during rotation, "quantum of action" (a favourite trick of the physicists), we still don't find any "mass" in the whole model which would correspond to our observation. Therefore we don't want to use such an imaginary concept for mass as an argument at all. Up to now we have discovered only three concepts which are obviously responsible for the image of the cosmos: space, time, and energy.

The search for the world formula has been a goal that scientist have been striving for since time immemorial. Of course, the universe is not designed according to one formula – and therefore such a search is quite futile. After all, that would be as if a baker could make all his produce according to one single recipe! But if there was such a universal formula it could only be restricted to those three concepts which we discovered, and actually it would have to be immanent to or be the basis of all calculations of our so-called reality in some way. Shall we try to create a world formula with these three concepts? Would it be possible to express the relationship of these three abstract quantities mathematically?

When we pay close attention to how these three concepts are related to each other in our fan wheel, the following strange equation is the result:

$$energy = \frac{space}{time^2}$$

That should be all? Is this strange formula of any use? We are going to verify it immediately with a little mathematics:

Let's assume the fan blade of our thought experiment is approx. 32 cm long. The path of its revolution is thus ca. 2 meters. Now, we are making the blade rotate giving it a velocity of one revolution per second - i.e. 2m/sec. Since we do not believe in "real mass" we invent the term apparent mass[5] in order to paraphrase an action of mass of the accelerated blade (even if professional physicists are getting into a flap right now!). At the same time we postulate: the quantum of action of the non-moving blade equals 1 "blade" - and it doesn't matter in the least what we would like to understand by that because all dimensions and units of this world were chosen arbitrarily. Even the physicists use "Planck's quantum constant" in their calculations in a similar way. And 1 blade is just our empirically determined quantum of action.

Thus absolutely unconcerned we are calculating:

$$apparent\ mass = \frac{v}{t} = \frac{2}{1} = 2$$

2 what? 2 meters? But it looks as though the quantum of action of the blade has already doubled, i.e. 2 "blades". Well, it has to be more than the non-moving blade, hasn't it? But this does still not impress us considerably. In truth, we only just calculated the travel by means of the velocity. Newton did something very similar with the velocity of the planets (v^2) - and what he calculated by means of the orbital radius (r) was one fictitious cause of the planetary motion, a centre of "mass" in kg! For that purpose he needed additionally a coefficient of proportionality, the constant of gravitation, which he had to estimate by rule of thumb because Cavendish determined it only about 100 years later.

Well, therefore we won't be bothered by any objection and continue: we are stealing the time from the blade, and it is getting so fast that it only needs one sixteenth of a second for one revolution. Of course, that means that its speed becomes sixteen times higher (now the mathematics are getting into the same flap as the physicists).

$$apparent\ mass = \frac{v}{t} = \frac{32}{0{,}0625} = 512$$

The result is 512 "blades". Should this number now really express the present effect, possibly the action of mass (quantity of matter)[6]? Does the obtained disc now really act as if it had 512 times the effect of the blade? And is this effect nothing else but the effect of kinetic energy? If this was the case we should be able to calculate our originally assumed quantum of action of 1 "blade" from this apparent mass by means of the usual formula for kinetic energy (kin.E=1/2 m•v^2) which includes a mass after all. We rearrange the formula to get:

$$\frac{1}{2}m = \frac{kin.E}{v^2}$$

and unperturbed we substitute the kinetic energy with our apparent mass:

$$m = 2(\frac{512}{32^2}) = 2(\frac{512}{1024}) = 2 \cdot 0{,}5 = 1$$

Thus, we really get again the effect 1 which we assigned to the blade. This confirms our suspicion that our apparent mass means the same as kinetic energy and from that we have to conclude that every action of mass we become aware of is based on an energy that works through motion.

Velocity, however, is travel divided by time; when we include the concept of space in our formula we get:

$$apparent\ mass = \frac{v}{t} = \frac{travel(space)}{\frac{t}{t}} = \frac{travel(space)}{t^2}$$

By dividing space by the time squared we should logically get the value of that energy which leads us to believe in the action of mass. This can be easily verified, and for time we choose one sixteenth of a second which yielded the value 512:

$$apparent\ mass = \frac{travel(space)}{t^2} = \frac{2m}{0{,}00390625} = 512$$

Naturally we also get the number 512 this way. It reveals the magnitude of the "quantity of action" – the mass by motion. And indeed the fan disc would offer a corresponding resistance. Apart from one constant which we invented to define a unit of action we were calculating with absolutely abstract concepts. Hence the world seems to consist of literally nothing! He who raises the objection that in fact the fan wheel has not increased its mass but its density is on the right track. Because we will discover in the chapters "Gravity" and "Inertia" that in truth not the masses play any role for the gravitational effects of bodies but the density of the bodies.

Did we discover some kind of world formula with our little game? Of course not. But their relations are part of every calculation which is dealing with energy or mass. A universal formula for the existence of the world would have to be of similar design because it would have to do justice to this simple universe. The relation of space, time, and energy is at the bottom of all laws of nature, behind the free fall as well as behind the laws of conservation of energy and impulse which were postulated. All three concepts are inseparably linked with each other. Already this reminds us of the space-time of the general theory of relativity (but it does not refer to the systems of inertial of the special theory of relativity) and it applies to the whole cosmos which demonstrates this connection evidently by the expansion, the entropy, and the modification to interdepending "natural constants" (fine structure, gravitation, and velocity of light).

Exhaustively, the only genuine building blocks of the universe are: energy, space, and time. Although our formula used measuring units like seconds and metres – which don't have any absolute significance in the universe - we could at least demonstrate the connections. We are unable to actually calculate anything with them!

The constant 1 "blade", the effect, already depends on our perception. Therefore, the world is not a material event of substance, so to speak, but a kind of "mental occurrence" – just as many philosophers already suspected. Nevertheless the picture of a material universe in which masses have an effect on each other is created in our mind by the play of resistance and harmony and the multitude of encounters.

For that reason, we must not assume that those three concepts are genuine, established objects within an absolute reality – because we know after all that basically only T.A.O. exists. Space, time, and energy are effects of T.A.O., actually they are only informational events of the same kind as a holography which - consisting only of light - can reproduce an image of everything nevertheless! These effects or rather our perceptions of energy, space, and time are the only definable building blocks whereas T.A.O. remains indefinable for us in the end...

Every oscillating proton represents nothing else but our fan wheel. If one wants to do justice to the insubstantiality of this world and to develop an extensive theory about it nevertheless, only a general field theory will lead to the goal. Einstein knew that as well, and he was working on it until his death. But he was unable to accommodate gravitation and electric forces. Even the quantum theory to which he actually contributed, does not always agree with his theories of relativity without force. Therefore we will have to deal with this topic in more detail at a later point.

Physics already works with many field concepts. Fields are simply spaces filled by forces, impulses, or energies. The proton is such a space and the term "field" is more suitable for it than particle or even atom. All concepts connected with the word atom, both concerning its indivisibility and its independence as world-building, contestable object, have been regarded as outdated for a long time after all. In the following we will call the proton field "spherical field" as well in order to have our own name for our own child. And we will see the universe as a single infinite field in which everything is contained that can develop from energy, space, and time. And that also means the "masses" which - as we just saw - are only a special form of energy.

Fig.13a

6 Force

In the course of their research physicists discovered several fundamental forces. If they had hoped to gradually reduce the number of these different forces the contrary proved true in the end: modern particle physics discovered completely new effects which were apparently caused by completely new forces. But actually physics has always endeavoured basically to standardise all forces in one single force - as the sole cause of all effects. In their aspiration, physics was caught in a real frenzy of particles. One was not content with the building blocks of matter but also attributed the forces themselves to the exchange of further particles. In order to avoid that these particles came into conflict with the iron law of the conservation of energy many of them were simply called virtual, and one relied in the following on Heisenberg's indeterminacy relation which states that it is impossible to determine the position, the state, and the impulse of a particle at the same time anyway because the influence of the observer cannot be eliminated.[7] That is why it was even possible to operate with "borrowed" energies, and theories, which were more than over-subtle, were invented but in principle they do not explain anything though - because strictly speaking the exchange of "bosons" did in no way throw any light on the existence of the physical forces...

This exchange of particles of force was described by means of the FEYNMAN diagram (figure 14). It was based on a purely pre-arranged definition. Therefore it appeared to be unrealistic and did not explain why an exchanged particle should get other particles to attract or repel each other.

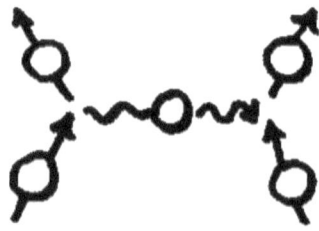

Fig. 14

The idea of the virtual energy, which goes back to Heisenberg who found out that there is obviously more energy available for the activities within the micro-universe than had to be expected from pure arithmetic, was not that bad at all. After all, we also realised that actually only a fraction of the energy can be noticed as an effect by any measuring instrument or any observer. If one only calculates with the effects perceived, one ignores - remember our allegory - all those punches of the boxer which went into thin air. But it is apparent that they do not go into thin air but are causing effects, too, which we just fail to notice.

Today one still knows the variety of at least six cosmic forces which are no fictitious forces like for instance the centrifugal force, the force of inertia, or the Coriolis force. Let's specify them one after the other:

1) The FORCE OF GRAVITY (gravitation) which, for instance, keeps the planets in their orbit or causes weight. Their particle equivalent is the graviton.

2) The ELECTRICITY (electromagnetic interaction) which acts upon charged matter, causes magnetism and holds atoms together in the molecules. Its transmitter is allegedly the photon.

3) The WEAK FORCE type I (weak interaction by means of charged electric current) which can change elementary particles, i.e. turn protons into neutrons. Its conveyor are the so-called W^+ and W^- particles.

4) The WEAK FORCE type II (weak interaction by means of neutral electric current) which has not been observed yet in nature but which materialised like an unexpected demon in high-energy physics. It is attributed to the W° particles.

5) The STRONG NUCLEAR FORCE (strong interaction) which binds the components of the atomic nucleus. The corresponding particle is designated meson.

6) The COLOUR FORCE (chromodynamic interaction), although a purely speculative force which is made responsible for protons not being able to decay any further because it does not release the quarks, those particles which are assumed to constitute the proton. The annoying glue that persistently prevents us from finding the quarks because of its interaction is made of gluons.

Naming the last force may elicit a smile because it appears indisputably funny. What on earth happened? What had the physicists suddenly gotten into and why? The blame lies with the circumstance that the accelerators of high-energy physics have produced more and more particles which had to be integrated into the atom one after the other. A whole zoo of particles soon romped about in the accelerators and one began to put them into categories. Every particle demanded by theory was found straight-away by sifting through thousands of bubble chamber photographs again and again. And obviously the physicists have not become aware up to now that they created these particles indeed and did not knock them out of the atom in any way.

Well, even we discovered a case of encounter between the impulses which provided an instable field (encounter event e!). Every possible kind of meeting is in principle possible. And so particles have been produced long since which appeared to be even heavier than some atoms but the confusion they created arose without a reason. They don't have anything to do with atoms at all.

It is a strange game that the physicists are playing and it shows how much stamina the human mind has in sticking to certain ideas. After all, clinging to the traditional belongs to the modes of behaviour which are characteristic of mankind; the history of science contains many examples how reasonable solutions to new problems were successfully prevented by that.

The crowning event of science's not getting anywhere is the theoretical invention of the quarks. But of course it will be possible to produce particles in the accelerators one day which are sporting all the demanded characteristics of the quarks ...

The whole thing reminds us of the difficulty that astronomers once had with the planetary motion. Since they were obsessed with certain ideas - for example Aristotle's philosophical demand for perfectly circular orbits - Ptolemy invented the epicycles; an idea which held the attention of several generations of astronomers. Even Copernicus himself - getting wise to the irregular movement of the planets - still had to resort to them. Of course the epicycles described the planetary orbits correctly and in a calculable way but they were nevertheless just downright wrong and it was not until Kepler had thought hard about it for several years that they were dismissed. But he who wants to can still discover them because the planets obviously describe these epicycles in their retrograde motion. And the proofs for the many, many particles of high-energy physics are just as obvious. They don't mean a thing and for that reason, we will not go deeper into the matter of the particles because in truth the world is not as complicated as it is constructed by the physicists.

Well, apart from the fact that all forces remained unexplained even under the assumption of particles, gravitation, of all things, could not be illustrated with this method, either – because nothing at all can be done with the gravitons. Though the cause of gravitation should be the easiest to find! Maybe it has remained such a big mystery only due to a fallacy...

For resolving this mystery we take a ride on the bus. In the beginning the bus is empty but more and more people get on board and soon there is a big crowd. We will notice in an unpleasant way that more and more people are pressing against us and that they are doing so with increasing force. If we did not know about the true facts we could over-subtly postulate a force which is inherent in us and has the mysterious property to attract people! And we would promptly labour under a fallacy. Because it is the pressure arising from the people in the bus which is pressing them against us...

Besides many others, the physicist Dr. Pages from Perpignan already had the idea that gravitation was in truth a pressure on the body. At that time he met with a gale of laughter on the grounds that one only had to reverse the preceding signs in Newton's equation and everything would remain as it had been before. But similar thoughts can already be found with Newton - maybe he thought this solution was a little too complicated. The oldest pressure-gravitation theory was issued by Georges Louis de Sage (1747/1756) who already made the mistake to argue with gravity particles which have not been found up to this day. The ether-vortex theories of René Descartes (1644) and Lord Kelvin (1867) were pressure theories – but so complicated that nobody comprehended them. Allegedly Quirino Majorana (1871 – 1957) even proved the pressure theory of gravitation in experiments but no-one took notice of his astounding experiments.

The physicist Mach also had some ideas which aimed at the influence or resistance of surrounding masses and were even discussed by Einstein. But for Einstein, all these solutions were unacceptable, he was the first to do away with gravitation at all revealing it as a fictitious force as defined by the forces of inertia. It didn't become more explainable by that but Einstein's equations have at least the merit that they can be used with any preceding sign. In fact, Einstein discovered the mirror image of the truth, so to speak, when he assumed that mass was curving space - although without coming across the original of the mirror image. Because like all the other physicists he started out from the assumption of a central mass (apart from the fact that in his theory the mass is actually represented by energy and impulse). But we will see in a minute that gravitation is created by the surrounding masses (fields) without exception:

We know that the propagation of the impulses of a proton is running into space until it meets with resistance in form of the oscillations of other protons. It is certainly not difficult to picture this more or less three-dimensionally. That these fields penetrate each other and, if considered in an over-subtle manner, that all fields of this universe are interwoven, is another useful concept. This principle applies to all spherical fields. Of course, celestial bodies are spherical fields as well because they consist of protons whose vibrations amount to big total fields. Since matter - as we already put it - stands in its own way, it is under pressure. It does not terminate at all where our senses perceive boundaries. Every field extends far beyond its visible sphere and is in contact with other fields. Just as on the bus, a force is created which we can best define with following sentence:

ALL MATTER REPELS MATTER!

Well, actually this is exactly the opposite of what has been assumed so far. And at first it appears to be completely insane which is a very good sign because it reminds of a remark that Bohr made when he rose to his feet after a lecture of Wolfgang Pauli and declared: "We all agree that your theory is crazy. We just can't reach an agreement in one question: is it crazy enough?"

We will see that this crazy idea is leading to astonishing solutions. Contrary to the gravitation which was an additional property of matter and seemed rather farfetched, the repelling force is produced automatically through the pure existence of matter. For that reason, it seems to be more logical, i.e. more satisfying in a philosophical way. Because we did not have to invent anything in addition; space, time, and energy are still sufficient for the functioning of the cosmos.

We call this self-substantiated principle the repulsion principle. It is the principle of Existence as such. Because there is only this one repulsive force! All other forces are validated by it. And behind this force, as behind everything we have previously discovered, is only T.A.O. and nothing else!

If we consider the cosmos to be filled with spherical fields and chose one as an object for observation, the question arises: who exerts more pressure on who - the individual field on the surrounding fields or the surrounding fields on the individual one? The question answers itself: of course the individual field is squeezed like hell from all directions! We call this pressure the universal pressure because it comes from the universe or universally from all other fields. Acting against it is the individual pressure of every field. This illuminates why the sphere is the preferred body in the cosmos. This individual pressure of the field contains also that part of the universal pressure which is having an effect right through the field because shadowing of the universal pressure is determined by the density of the field - and therefore this density determines the gravitational effect. At this point, we have to declare specifically in addition that we chose the term pressure for stylistic reasons only but physically speaking it is not correct - because actually we mean repulsion. So we are not developing a gravitation-pressure theory but a gravitation-repulsion theory! But universal pressure just sounds more tersely than universal repulsion. It is the same as with the word wave which we apply sloppily and inappropriately sometimes. Because the transmission of an impulse in T.A.O. is always done by means of vibrations and oscillations - not by means of waves. But after we have stated it clearly it won't be so terrible if we use that inaccurate but lovely word again and again. Therefore the resistance of "masses" against each other is never created by waves but by the tiny vibrational shoves which their fields exert on each other. But we will examine this more closely at a later time.

Actually, the universal pressure has the tendency to squeeze all protons as tightly together as possible. The spherical fields, however, create a force towards one another which is sometimes stronger than the universal pressure. We already know it: electricity. Because all protons vibrate in the same way after all: the space around each proton is polarised and this reinforces their repulsive effect which of course has existed from the beginning according to the repulsion principle. Therefore the universal pressure will not succeed so easily in squeezing the protons together. The electricity together with the ubiquitous repulsion prevents it effectively. It is the second force in our specification and clearly predominates between the fields. For that reason, the physicists have found long since that gravitation doesn't make almost any difference in particle physics whereas the game of the charges plays the leading role.

Many models for the origin of the world are based on the assumption that clouds of hydrogen formed into balls because of gravitation and that the celestial bodies were created in that way. This is rather incredulous! Gaseous hydrogen - hence protons - will always evaporate in all directions; its fields are too small in relation to the field of the cosmos. Think of the fan wheel where fields that were small and quick stood a better chance of going through the wheel. The same applies to fields in general because the resistance they offer to one another is always the product of the two coinciding quantities.

Although we will deal with gravitation and its further effects on the basis of the universal pressure in more detail later-on we can already claim that we resolved the great mystery of the origin of gravitation in a few sentences. Prior to that we had already discovered electricity. Now there is another force which is not to be underestimated and which is substantiated by itself nevertheless. Envision some kind of ruler before your mind's eye which is getting caught between universal pressure and individual pressure (figure 15).

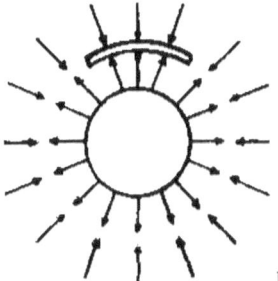

Fig. 15

We don't need a lot of imagination to picture the ruler being deformed. It is bent or curved around the field by space. If we didn't know anything about the geometrical conditions of the space, we would have to invent a new force as cause of this mysterious curvature. Maybe we should wittily call it curving force. When the ruler follows the curving force willingly, it simply bends around the spherical field according to its ductility. When the tormented ruler, however, is flexible and likes to remain straight, the universal pressure at the ends of the ruler outweighs the counteracting individual pressure of the spherical field in the centre of the ruler and the ruler is getting closer to the field. The ideal place for the pressured ruler would be the centre of the field where it would be left in peace, and this is exactly where it would go if it could. We will immediately understand that the curving force is the stronger the more we approach the spherical field. That means the extent of the curving force is proportional to the intensity of the field's curvature.

What are we actually discovering here? Due to the spherical arrangement of the vibrating fields the space is really "curved"! Fields curve around the space. What would Einstein say to that?

Now what happens when two protons meet? Normally their repulsion will prevail. But when we press them together with a little force, the curving force begins to take effect. That means each proton tries to bend the other around it, tries to deform it. We have to understand this choice of words correctly: of course, protons don't try anything, we should rather say: the universal pressure is bending the protons around one another... But as we know what is meant we can spare ourselves such stilted idiomatic expressions. For the protons, there is no way out, they will both literally bang into another and merge to form a new mutual field.

Again we should be more precise to prevent that the wrong images and the wrong questions arise: fields do not just move through T.A.O., they propagate! After all they basically exist only of electromagnetic impulses. Since these impulses are shoves of force they generate resistance or evade each other. For that reason, proton fields are not just oscillating states like the rings of waves on a lake which would override but never repel one another! With such a wrong image we could not substantiate that the force is generated between the impulse fields. But we can do so because we are talking about vibration fields whose impulses can also bounce off each other. This is the slight but important difference! Although they only propagate in T.A.O., oscillating, vibrating spherical fields can therefore influence each other in such a way that it looks as if a force was at work!

This merging force which, however, is only effective in the vicinity of proton fields and which we called curving force is nothing else but the strong interaction postulated by particle physics, hence the fifth force in our specification. It is a logical consequence of the repulsion principle and of the geometry of the space. It would not work without the universal pressure - which means that the strong interaction has indeed its cause in the surrounding "mass" but appears to be so strong that naturally it could never be explained with gravitation being immanent to the proton!

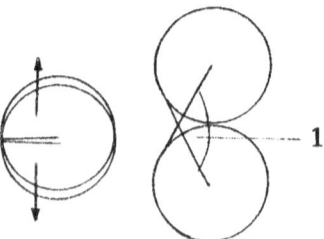

Fig. 16

According to popular theory, protons are positively charged and should be flying apart... the truth is they cannot be separated because due to the integration of their individual fields they combine to form new total fields. One would have to separate the fields again – but that is practically impossible. For that reason, the protons in an atomic nucleus do not lie side by side but inside each other (we will discuss this in detail later-on). Therefore the intensity ratio of the curving force (strong interaction) compared to the electric force (the effect of the universal pressure without the influence of curvature) can be depicted geometrically in a simple way without getting carried away by complicated mathematics (figure 16).

When two fields of the same size are drawn from a mutual centre up to the area where the curving effect is strongest, i.e. until their boundaries touch, the force changes in the same ratio in which the angle of the lines of projection (1) increases. In the centre of the fields, the curving force is practically identical with the normal universal pressure effect; when we equate it and thus the electrical force with 1 the angle of ca. 130 degrees indicates an increase of the dynamic effect by 130 because of the curvature. In fact, the strong interaction turns out to be about 130 times stronger than electricity. Compared to that, the gravitation depending on a central mass would have only an intensity of ca. 10^{-42}. The weak interaction changes the electricity only by a factor of about 10.

This interaction is also immediately comprehended: if a little less force is required for merging a proton and a neutron because the electric repulsion is weaker, we can make a new short-range force, which apparently helps us, responsible for this difference. This imaginary force is identical with the weak interaction type I. In this case, however, the neutron would not stay neutral, because it partially adopts the vibrations of the proton - as if a W^+ (or W^-) particle changed over. If we played the same game with two neutrons, the result would be again a difference in forces, and we would have to discover another helpful force: the weak interaction of type II which is obviously replacing completely neutral $W°$ particles because nothing has changed with the neutrons. We are realising that the different forces come about only because of the different natures of the fields!

Every time two fields unite, it plays a role if they are polarised fields or neutrons. Proton and neutron fields are actually perfectly similar to each other, only their spatial polarisation is different.[8] The different interactions seem to operate according to the prevailing case - but the whole game goes back to one single director: the repulsion principle!

The sixth force, the so-called colour force (chromo-dynamic interaction) is a hypothesis which does not find an equivalent in nature. Within the proton, there aren't any quarks or gluons. But there are all kinds of oscillation fields imaginable consisting of uncountable vibrations... a sea of particles because every kind of particle can be produced in principle. How "heavy" or how "big" it appears, how it is "charged" and which "spin" it has or how long it will exist depends on the conditions of the encounter in the surroundings and on the quantities of energy.

And so the physicists of this world will go on trying to shatter matter and to identify the thus newly created impulse fields. Quarks have not been found yet - that is prevented by the persistent colour force, after all! - but one day such a product from the accelerator will fit in with the ideas of the physicists and they will cry out: "Eureka, we found the quark!"

Although, in that case one will have to forget about the hypothesis of the colour force...[9]

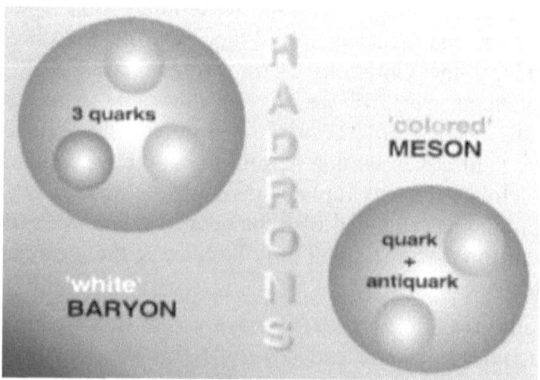

Fig.16a: The colour force

7 Electron

Universal pressure, individual pressure, and electricity always work in well-adjusted relations to each other. Usually a balance is created between them which determines the form of the event. A good balance, though, is only found in the so-called inorganic processes. Later we will discover that not achieving this balance is responsible for the creation of organic structures.

At close range, it is predominantly the curving force which decides what will happen in the end. The curving force itself depends on the size of the fields compared to each other (who is curving who?). The electric repulsion, i.e. the polarisation of the space, is the strongest adversary of the curving force. Therefore, it is not particularly surprising if two protons are rarely found closely bonded to form one atomic nucleus. A neutron is always involved because it willingly joins in and adopts the oscillations of the protons whereas two protons would have to be very exactly similar to each other in order to maintain harmony. For that reason, there exists a rather loose bonding of two protons as we can find it in the hydrogen molecule. Even a combination of three (H_3) is possible.

Proton and neutrons will always be squeezed only as tightly together as their resistance toward each other admits, that means until this resistance finds an equilibrium with the curving force. Before this happens, however, that repulsion, which exists out of range of the curving force, has to be overcome. The energy required for this comes for the most part from the motion of the fields or from the pressure of the environment. Barrier is the name we give to the point which has to be overcome before the curving force becomes effective. It is identical with the Coulomb Wall of the physicists and exists between all fields - there is even an equivalence between celestial bodies: the Roche limit. It goes without saying that this barrier does not have any particular significance for the individual impulses of the fields. Electron waves can easily jump across because the field of a proton does not develop spontaneously but is differentiated in time so to speak and evades an electron wave at convenient times. Physicists who regarded the electron as a particle were surprised by this effect and called it "tunnel effect". It has been interpreted by means of complicated quantum-mechanical formulas but the basis of its existence is very easy to understand. The tunnel effect is rated as the most significant evidence for the nature of the electrons being waves and for the electrons only simulating a particle character outside of the atom. Analogous to that there are, of course, similar effects to be found with light because the particles of light, the photons, are also constantly doing things which they ought not to do if one seriously considered them to be particles.

The barrier calls the tune in the dance of birth and death of matter. In all processes between spherical fields this barrier has to be overcome; therefore it always determines the occurring amounts of energy while the available magnitudes of the energy, for its part, determines the range and the strength of the barrier between the "particles".

Every particle or every element of our matter is in truth a Something without substance, a motional event as illustrated with the spherical field. The polarised space around a proton or any other "charged particle" - we already called this space "electric field" - is a mono-pole because it can adopt only one definite spatial spin orientation, i.e. either "right-hand" or "left-hand". Matter and anti-matter never complement one another but annihilate each other wherever they meet because there is practically no barrier between them. Neither does the barrier ever occur in any process either in which two opposite poles or polarisations come together.

Well, how should we describe an atom on the basis of our knowledge? Contrary to previous opinions it has neither a nucleus nor a shell. Actually there is only a vibrating spherical field - which will propagate in a real spherical manner only in the ideal case. Every kind of nucleus results from the method by which it is to be determined. It is always the result of the resistance between the measuring field and the measured one. An alpha particle (we will get to know it yet) will meet with resistance in a very definite range which is defined by the alpha particle itself and where it will be deflected. Rutherford detected the size of the atomic nucleus in this way - but what he really detected is only an area of higher energy density.[10] The atomic shell is also defined by the perception of resistance of a necessary measuring field. For that reason, atoms adopt different sizes depending on the energy level of the available matter; they determine these sizes for each other, however permeate one another only until states of equilibrium are achieved. The intensity of the impulses controls the distances of the fields to one another. Since the harmonious impulses remain self-contained only very definite distances are possible (wavelengths, frequencies). These impulses, one running after the other, (we already described in the beginning that it have to be at least two impulses) are nothing but what the physicists call "electrons" or "electron waves". And even if they are not really waves, after all every impulse dashes off as solitary as the "wave" of a whiplash, so that we continue using the word "electron wave" or "electron".

It is thus the electron wave which creates the spherical fields first and foremost but it propagates on every other suitable structure as well. Since it is a very strong energy quantum, the assumption that it is a - although very light - particle was surely very tempting. But one soon discovered that this particle had almost no dimensions, and there were clear indications in many experiments that it could be a wave. As in case of the light, that is why one brought oneself to the dualistic interpretation that the electron just had to be both simultaneously. But both is just plain wrong! It is neither a real wave nor a particle. And of course it is not the carrier of any charges either.[11] But because of its spatial polarisation it causes those effects which tempted the physicists into assuming the existence of charges!

Although it was postulated that the electron was a solid building block of matter and bound to the atomic nucleus, it had to be disconcerting that electrons can be separated from their atomic bonds extremely easily. They evaporate from hot metals, they can be enticed by the light to emerge, they tunnel through energy barriers ... and for the most part every impacting electron releases several others (secondary electrons). Surely this can only be explained by the dance of the impulses as we outlined it. Since polarisation and electron wave always belong together, the electron waves willingly follow preset polarisations (magnetic fields). We will comprehend it when we are taking a closer look on magnetism.

Even every electron wave can theoretically have a left-hand or a right-hand spin as well. But since all protons of this world are obviously "standardized" in a similar fashion, all electron impulses oscillate in the same direction. An electron oscillating in the opposite direction would be an anti-electron, i.e. a positron. A variety of impulse events which are producing electron waves without being bound to a spherical field - this is in principle possible, too – are producing a positron at the same time as well without exception - as we already discovered – and left-hand and right-hand spirals can come into existence at the same time. Such events rarely take place in nature - mainly in cosmic radiation - but can often be found in charged particle accelerators. For electron waves, the same, already known conditions of encounter apply. When an electron meets a positron, variant e) or c) will occur depending on the temporal displacement of the impulses. Thus in the first case, an unstable particle is created which can adopt the qualities of almost any kind of particle - conditional on the applied magnitude of energy. Such kinds of particles, quasi-atoms, are called positroniums. These artificially created disharmonious spherical fields often appear to be considerably more solid than protons but they only exist for the fractions of a second.

More often there is an encounter according to case c); it is called modification. In this case, the two impulses annihilate each other in fact but their energy is not lost without a trace but radiates in more or less straight shoves (without spin) from the place of meeting. Energy shoves of this kind already have a name on their own: neutrino.[12] Every time when energy gets lost on the back way, it is setting off through such shoves. Theoretically they can in fact disturb other impulses or indirectly impart vibration to the fields - i.e. interact with them - but their own spatial expansion is small (ca. 10^{-44} cm in diameter) and therefore there is not much that offers resistance. For that reason, neutrino shoves are travelling through the globe as if it wasn't there. Only one in about 10^9 neutrinos bumps into a particle field, reacts with it and changes or destroys it in the process.

Since almost every impulse event inevitably causes linear shoves, the cosmos is literally filled with neutrinos. They pulse through our body without damaging it in the least. In the same way, they also travel through every kind of measuring device and therefore can be proven only indirectly. But for the most part, shoves of this or a similar kind are the basis for that field surrounding matter which causes the displacement of the field and consequently the effect of gravitation.

Like any other form of impulse, neutrinos, for their part, can cause electron waves because the encounter modification can of course also take place in the opposite direction. Such electron waves can turn out to have significantly more energy than normal electrons – in that case we talk of heavy electrons (muons) - and from such electrons, on the other hand, an atom can develop which is a real energy giant compared to other atoms. A field of this kind is then called a muonic atom.

It would be a thankless task to describe all the events which are possibly by means of the electrons. Practically all particles are able to transform into one another - a fact which causes quite a headache to the physicists. Yet this fact is very easy to comprehend if both the particle character and the wave property are negated - and if the impulse field is taken as basis just as in our concept.

Neutrino shoves are not always impulses which are as straight as a die, sometimes they even have a spin. In this case the neutrino acts like a little electron, so to speak, and with that even an anti-neutrino becomes possible. For that reason, there are at least three kinds of neutrinos, of which only one can be really completely neutral (when I wrote down the book for the first time this fact was still unknown. In 1995, the physicist Frederick Reins was awarded the Nobel prize for the discovery of special differing types of neutrinos). To look for a symmetry in all these particles would be a homage to the angel of the bizarre...

Neutrinos come into existence spontaneously during decay or fusion processes. Like so many other particle formations they are not found as "building blocks" in the atom itself. Actually only the bigger sister electron exists without exception in the atom, and to be exact, practically every hydrogen nucleus consists of electrons because in principle there isn't any difference between nucleus and shell after all as we would like to emphasise again. Proton and electron are a homogenous structure. Whether this structure is "bare" or whether it "contains" an electron, it is only the result of the various possible spatial polarisations which can occur and create an "ion" with it.

De Broglie (as the first one?) defined the particles as waves of matter and the atom as a kind of diffraction halo. He had to cope with the difficulty to apply the parameters of the particle to the wave as well. As it is with a real wave, the phase velocity stands in a definite relation to the wave velocity. The result was that the phase velocities in electron waves seemed to be faster than the velocity of light. Only when looking at things in a relativistic way was the result a velocity that corresponded to a particle. This problem is not automatically applicable in our concept because there is no phase velocity in a series of purely chronological impulses. It is, however, clear that even in our considerations only such frequencies are allowed which don't disturb each other since otherwise they would cancel each other out; they would interfere until they were annihilated. Consequently, a harmonious sequence has to be maintained; therefore, electron waves only occur in definite, self-contained paths - which correspond to Bohr's quantum conditions. These points are absolutely not in favour of a particle theory either but probably it will take some more time until the misleading designation can be deleted from the blueprint of matter (even if modern physicists already emphasise that they had never meant "particles" in the literal sense).

Well, let's say a few words about the neutron. So to speak, neutrons are islands of rest in the middle of a pulsating universe. They are manifestations of not being and this is meant in the deadliest sense of the word! In fact, on the one hand they act as an agent for the protons which can maintain their vibrations without disturbance because of them. On the other hand they will bring disharmony into the best proton structure if they hit it slowly enough. Since the neutron does not vibrate much on its own, it has an enormous power of intrusion or penetration but is less stable because it maintains a lighter structure. The neutron remains rigorously restricted only within atoms because it is practically held together by protons. When a neutron is isolated it will soon adopt oscillations; the physicist says it decays into a proton and an electron. On the other hand there are of course no anti-neutrons; this will probably shatter the nice symmetry which the physicists hoped to find in matter...

Figure 17 tries to illustrate the microcosm. Atoms appear as oscillating spaces through which electron waves are pulsating. One should almost say: there aren't any electrons - but blossoms, funnels, and trumpets... The various shapes are created by the different states of energisation. In the next chapters we will discover how these forms of oscillation determine and control the behaviour of matter.

Fig. 17

8 Games

Now we already know enough to better understand many phenomena of this universe in which the games of the impulses lead us to believe. The most evident phenomena, which finally led to the current state of development of our technology, are electricity and magnetism. Even if these are apparently two phenomena, it is actually only one and the same game that has to be discovered. Even matter is an "electromagnetic" product.

A "charged" sphere is a place around which the electron waves on the surface oscillate as harmoniously and rectified as around a proton. The result is, as we know, polarised space, i.e. a field which we have to call electrostatic field, properly speaking, because it remains on the spot after all. Now, let's take a closer look at such a field (figure 18).

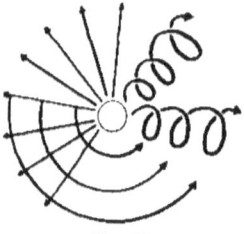

Fig. 18

We recognise our "spirals" which lend a special polarised order to the space. These spirals consist of two motional components. Firstly, we see the outward bound (radial) direction which we symbolised with straight arrows, secondly there is the lateral (tangential) component which can be represented by circles. Both directions are perpendicular to each other. We already named these two planes of action when we introduced the concept of the "electromagnetic wave". For that reason, we want to call the outward bound arrows the electric field and the circles the magnetic field.

Both fields lie practically inside one another but will never become effective at the same time. Nevertheless we can say: we are dealing with an electromagnetic field. With this field we want to carry out some experiments. First we make it rotate. In doing so, we blur the outward bound arrows of the electric field, the circles, however - which are also moving away from the sphere - present a completely new picture as can be seen in figure 19.

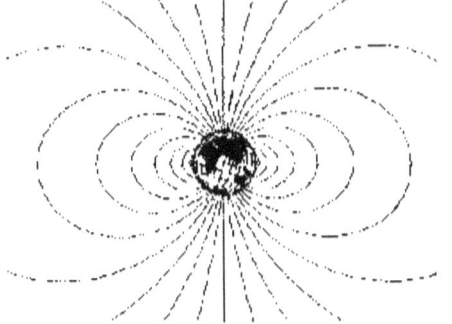

Fig. 19

This picture shows the familiar lines of force of a magnetic field. We observed its effects often and attributed its existence to little "molecular magnets". At a higher school, we learned maybe that this field stems from the spin of the electrons; but we did not really comprehend it just because of that. This is to change now. We are extending our experiment a little by making the charged sphere revolve, i.e. we move it in a circle. When we visualise what is going to happen now, it will soon become apparent to us that a picture very similar to the one before has to come about (figure 20).

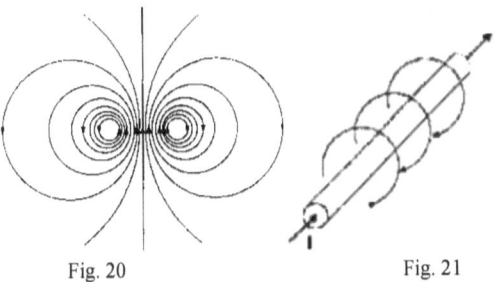

Fig. 20   Fig. 21

Again the arrows have blurred and we notice that they cancel each other out completely. The circles, however, only annihilated each other within the circle which we were drawing with the sphere. Outside of it they maintained their structure. Thus, we produced a magnetic field again - exactly the same that we know from every permanent magnet. Instead of moving a sphere we could also take a wire loop and let the electron waves (and with them the spatial polarisations they are causing!) flow down this loop. The physicist Oersted was the first to have this idea in 1820 already. He formed a wire loop and fed direct current to it. With the needle of a compass he detected a magnetic field and concluded that a magnetic field developed around every current-carrying conductor (figure 21).

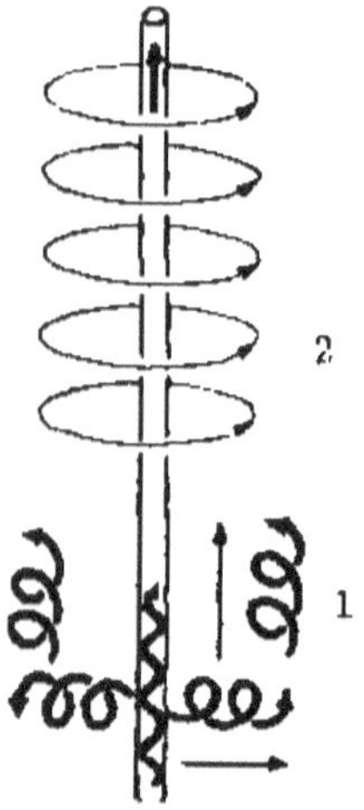

<<< Fig. 21a

We already know that electric charge is nothing but polarised space which can be defined as left-hand or right-hand. This polarisation is moving along with the charge - when the impulses of the electrons are following an ordered direction along the conductor. In that way a new polarisation is created running along the conductor. It goes without saying that this polarisation has a spin, too. Thus, there are two kinds of polarisation: the purely electrical one which moves perpendicularly away from the conductor and the magnetic one which follows the conductor. Between two identical conductors the perpendicular polarisation would cause resistance, i.e. repulsion (according to our model of encounters) when the charge is at rest. With a moving charge, however, this structure is dissipated into a new structure as shown at point 1 in figure 21a. It has the same spin all around which results in an overall motion around the conductor as is illustrated by the circles at point (2).

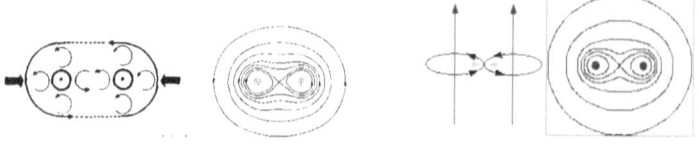

Fig. 22

Therefore two conductors through which the current is flowing in the same direction are oscillating in the same sense between each other (figure 22). This time we are looking at the spins practically from the front. Then we see how the oscillations evade each other, thus an identical oscillation prevails but that also means: no resistance! The conductors are squeezed together by the universal pressure, i.e. they are apparently attracting each other! Since the oscillation which runs in the same direction can oscillate around both conductors, a mutual magnetic field develops surrounding both conductors.

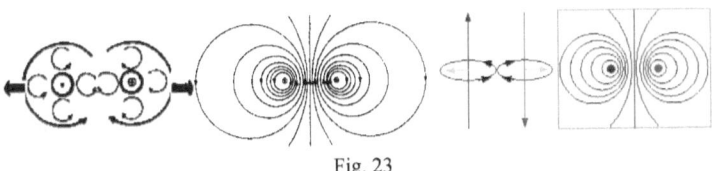

Fig. 23

The opposite is true for conductors through which the current flows in opposite directions (figure 23). Here the spins in-between won't evade each other but they crash against one another and create resistance. Result: the conductors repel each other because their repulsion existing a priori is intensified and overcomes the universal pressure. Figure 23a shows the two different phenomena again from another perspective.

Therefore the conductors of a coil lying next to another attract each other. They form a mutual magnetic field which surrounds them - for that reason, it enters the coil at one end and exits at the other end (figure 24).

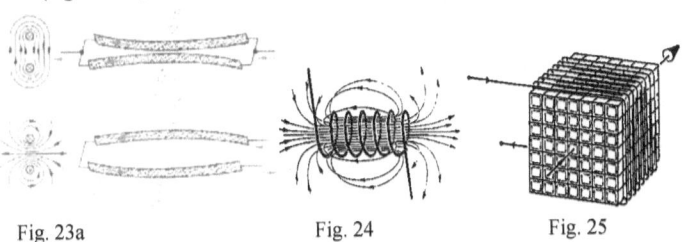

Fig. 23a   Fig. 24   Fig. 25

Again the result is a magnetic field like that of a bar magnet, and therefore we know that the magnetic effect of a bar magnet has to be attributed to moving "charges". It is a matter of purely superficial electron impulses which flow around the bar sorted in rank and file and polarise the space (figure 25).

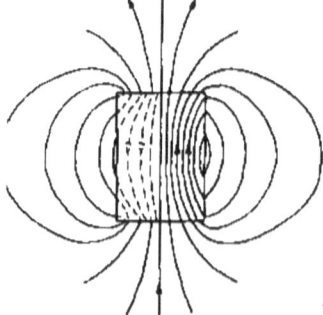

Fig. 26

Figure 26 shows that the lines of force of the bar magnet also enter at one end and exit at the other end. When we look vertically onto the pole, i.e. as depicted in figure 27, we should clearly see the polarisation (remember figure 21a) flowing from pole to pole[13] in our mind's eye.

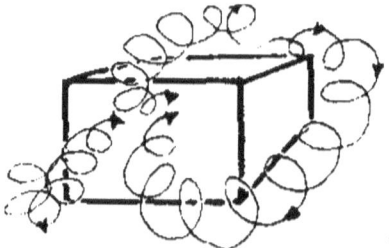

Fig. 27

The polarisation creates a closed circuit. Now we comprehend the behaviour of the two poles towards each other immediately; they aren't north or south poles but spaces with left-hand or right-hand oscillation - and again our familiar conditions of encounter apply: identical oscillation accomplished by left-hand and right-hand spin leads to attraction (case of encounter: penetration), we say: unlike poles attract each other! Opposite oscillations (identical polarisations meet) lead to resistance, i.e. to repulsion according to the guiding principle: like poles repel each other! When we were learning these mnemonic sentence by heart at school we certainly didn't know their causal background at all!

Fig. 28

Figure 28 shows how the circuit of two unlike poles can close. The apparent attraction, which now occurs, comes directly from the universe! When we turn one of the magnets around, opposite oscillations come across each other immediately and the repulsion of the poles overcomes this force from the universe! We can imagine this process quite vividly and he who feels like it can get himself two magnets to make some experiments on his own. He will suddenly understand their behaviour as never before. And we begin to suspect where these games will lead us: because with these magnetic fields we are actually increasing and decreasing nothing else but gravitation! But we will only fully comprehend this in the chapters "Inertia" and "Gravity".

Well, what will happen if we put a conductor, which does not carry any current, into a magnetically polarised room? In the conductor, the electron waves usually move all over the place in total disorder. Well after all, electric spin and magnetic spin are closely coupled with each other (just like, for instance, the toothed wheel and the worm in the picture). When the conductor has been neutral before because its electron waves did not prefer any direction, we are now subjecting it to the order of the magnetic spins. The electron waves are forced to submit to this polarisation and are aligned. This condition, however, is already called charge! It does not require much fantasy now to imagine the result when we are moving the conductor within the magnetic field (figure 29).

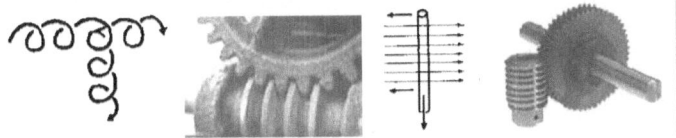

Fig. 29: Coupling of the spins

In doing so, we are moving the conductor through the spirals of the magnetic field to the effect that the spirals of the electron waves are also provided with a movement along the conductor. The charge is moving, and the moving charge is nothing else but electric current! It now flows through the conductor and this process is called induction.

When we are not moving the conductor, the spirals of the magnetic field for their part flow through the conductor aligning the electron waves. Again the interlacing of the polarisations takes effect and pushes the electrons to move on. They take "their" atoms along and in this way the conductor is moving in its longitudinal direction. This dynamic effect is called Lorentz force – after the physicist who discovered it. We can intensify this conductor movement by letting a current flow through the conductor. The current will of course get into a resistance situation with the spins of the magnetic field. This is nothing else but the reversal of the induction process, i.e.: movement causes current, current causes movement...

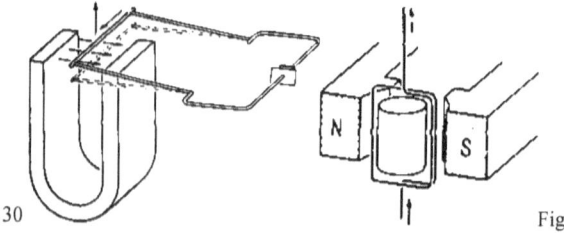

Fig. 30　　　　　　　　　　　　　　　　　　Fig. 31

This means we have done nothing less than invented the electric motor - if it did not exist already. The direction of the current determines the direction of the movement which gives expression to the strict coupling of the spins of space and electron. Figure 30 shows these connections.

When we put a conductor loop, in which the currents are flowing in opposite directions, into a magnetic field, the loop receives a rotational momentum (figure 31) because opposite motional forces are created. After all, the conductor loop itself creates a magnetic field as well which either repels or attracts the poles of the magnet.

With the polarisation of space by means of the spins and their coupling we hope to have gained a deeper understanding of the behaviour of matter which is predominantly determined by electric and magnetic effects. Electron waves are always the backdrop; all repulsive or attractive effects follow directly from the repulsion principle. Therefore two magnets which attract one another demonstrate directly the power of the cosmos surrounding us! In an intensified manner, two magnets which repel one another represent the general maxim of: all matter repels matter!

Already at this point, it proves itself clearly that the assumption of a pressure - or more correctly of a repulsion - instead of a "gravitation" does not leave everything as it has been at all but that it can make processes explicable which could only be explained by inventing further forces before. We don't have to continue to use invented forces and concepts like positive or negative and north or south pole as arguments. All polarisation effects described up to now arise casually and logically and always in accordance with one and the same principle!

Every kind of matter can be magnetised more or less. Some elements, in fact basically all of them, will start immediately to build up their own magnetic field under the influence of a magnet if their electron waves find sufficiently low resistance in the atomic range. The spin of this individual magnetic field is always opposite to the spin of the inducing magnetic field. For that reason, there will always be a repulsion which will be superimposed by the corresponding main effect. A typical example of this behaviour, which we call diamagnetism, is for instance bismuth. The predominant effect - attraction or repulsion as explained - on the other hand is called paramagnetism. It is marked by the exact coupling of electric and magnetic spins.

Some elements, like iron, nickel, cobalt as well as the rare earths gadolinium, dysprosium, and erbium, or certain types of alloy, obey the magnetic field particularly thoroughly and tenaciously; they are ferromagnetic. How weak or how strong the alignment of electron waves can be understandably depends on the atomic structure of the elements. Every alignment can be destroyed again by the effects of disordered vibrations, like heat or mechanical shock. All ferromagnetic substances are of a crystalline structure, i.e. they are dominated by great order from the outset. The little molecular magnets of our scholastic wisdom are pure fiction, though, they just don't exist.

When the alignment of electron waves is maintained in an element (or at least partially) we call it remanence or remanent or residual magnetism.

There are many other varieties of magnetism. They are all based on the same cause: the polarised space – or rather the polarised T.A.O.. For the same reason, there are the phenomena of electrostatics which are particularly easy to comprehend. For that reason, we want to examine them in more detail.

Let's recapitulate: charge is polarised space; like charges lead to repulsion, opposite polarisations to attraction. Every kind of energy flow, like for example a closed circuit, is only possible when matching vibrations come together. From time to time, this encounter can be enforced or enabled by setting a vibration in advance. But first let's take a look at figures 32 and 33:

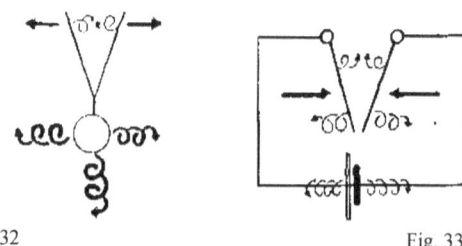

Fig. 32   Fig. 33

When we mount two thin silver plates to a polarising (i.e. "charged") sphere, the plates will adopt the same polarisation, too. Result: the plates repel each other! As can be seen immediately in figure 32 for a sufficiently well-known reason.

A battery supplies oscillations of opposite effect: plus = right-hand and minus = left-hand. Therefore opposite polarisations are fed to the plates of the interrupted circuit (figure 33). Result: they are apparently attracting each other because now they are pushed together by their environment (universal pressure and/or other fields)! As we will see in the following, right-hand and left-hand oscillations encounter each other even in the battery itself creating a continuous circuit which immediately makes the current flow when the plates are touching.

Now there are elements - i.e. very particular atomic structures - which only allow certain polarisations, either only "right-handed" ones or only "left-handed" ones. When we put two of these elements together, the result is a predetermined direction of oscillation which will only admit a current conduction if the spin of the flowing oscillation matches the predetermined one, because otherwise resistance will arise (figure 34).

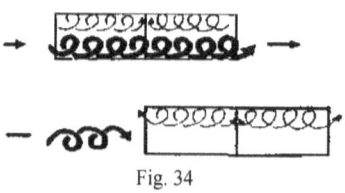

Fig. 34

This goes certainly without saying but nevertheless we just described the principle of the diode.

When we arrange three layers according to the motto right-left-right (or left-right-left) and switch on two electric circuits as shown in figure 35, circuit 2 cannot flow via the L-sector before circuit 1 has not partially disturbed or rather superimposed the left-hand oscillation in the separating element with its stronger R-oscillation.

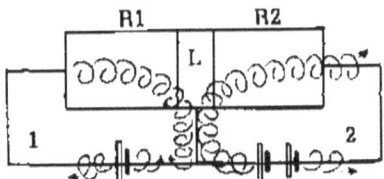

Fig. 35

This disturbance can be modulated, i.e. vary in its magnitude. That which is flowing over the bridge established in the L-element - which should be very thin to enable the oscillation to cross over from R1 - via R2, maintains this modulation (the current is controlled without inertia) and, if it is desired, it can be even stronger than in the electric circuit 1 when a higher current conduction is transferred. With that we discovered an amplifier but it exists already and is called transistor. The elements used, which so persistently admit the current to pass in one particular direction only, are called semiconductors. Contrary to metals whose electron waves can oscillate at random, semiconductors have a structure which admits oscillations only in particular spots (the physicist calls them "holes"). From that, only one particular direction each is defined.

But we wanted to talk about static electricity. When we look at the space polarisation of a charged sphere (figure 36) we come to the conclusion that the spins of the polarisation hinder each other a little. This hindrance is the lower the more space there is available for oscillating - as is the case on the smaller sphere on the right.

Fig. 36   Fig. 37

When the two spheres of figure 36 carry the same charge, the electrostatic effect of the smaller one is significantly higher, i.e. its field is stronger. A pear-shaped body (figure 37) exhibits the highest field intensity at its largest curvature. Small peaks can carry very high potentials for that reason. When we will figure out later that electrostatic effects are also important in the action of tiny molecules and atoms, we understand already that they can be stronger on these minute "spheres" than one would expect.

The other way round, if one wanted to draw off electrostatic charges from the atmosphere, one would do well to chose a lighting rod that is as pointed as possible for the same reasons.

When we put an uncharged sphere into an electrostatic field, the sphere will adopt the polarisation in such a way that it will fit into the polarisation of the field (figure 38). That means the side close to the field becomes a left-hand oscillator if the field oscillates to the right. This results automatically from the fact that the right-hand spiral of the field is of course a left-hand one when seen from the sphere whereas further right-hand spirals continue on the other side of the sphere.

Fig. 38

As it is, the sphere is divided into a "positive" and a "negative" charge. On it, a suitable potential prevails - and we call this process influence. It is easy to fathom because nothing else could happen in this case. When we take two spheres we can separate them after the influence took place and remove them from the field. Then they will actually carry opposite charges.

This process becomes significant for us when we discover that the molecules of life adopt spin programmes, too...

An electric, spatial oscillation can even be preserved. Two plates oscillating in opposite directions maintain the oscillation that is between them even after the electric source has been removed because the oscillation cannot flow off (figure 39).

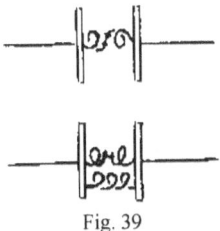

Fig. 39

The preserved potential comes free again when we close the circuit. A capacitor works in such a simple way. So to speak, we can hold on to the oscillations between the plates of the capacitor by placing an insulator of a certain kind between the plates. In fact, this insulator does not allow the oscillations to flow off but it integrates the polarisation into its own structure in such a way that we can no longer draw it from the capacitor. When we remove the insulator it leaves the vibration behind and the capacitor is still charged. Insulators which are good at this game are called dielectrics. They readily adopt the oscillations on their surface but won't keep up the oscillation without the capacitor plates. It is unnecessary to emphasise that the identical spins create the case of encounter "resistance" on the capacitor plates (figure 39, top) and that charging is not possible for that reason.

All electron waves can be aligned magnetically to an extent differing from element to element. As we already emphasised, all forms of matter are of an electromagnetic nature. But when this designation was introduced or rather when it was derived from other words probably nobody suspected its significance. Light and heat also influence the order of electron waves. For example that's why selenium becomes conductive under the influence of light or why heat can be transformed into electric current in a thermoelectric couple.

A thermoelectric couple is a particularly simple object: two metals (one oscillating to the left and one to the right) are soldered together. Then it is only necessary to make one of them loose its vibrational equilibrium (which it found with the other metal) by heating it - and a current starts flowing via an electric circuit. With that the lost equilibrium is restored or at least sought. Here we also find the game of spatial polarisations within the spheres of influence of the fields (atoms) and of the situations of encounter.

Many crystals are composed of atoms (ions) which are oscillating to the right and to the left. Thus they already oscillate with themselves in a polarised form. In order to release these internal charges one only has to subject the crystal to pressure or to deform it; the internal polarisations are then coming to the surface and can be used as current conduction. The phenomenon is called piezoelectric effect. When the crystal is deformed by heat (in doing so it will expand irregularly) the process is called pyro-electricity.

Are we really to believe that electrons are a rigidly bonded building block of matter? After all we see that one can practically do with them whatever one feels like. It is even possible to centrifuge them, that means they can be very easily separated from a metal by moving the piece of metal very quickly. In that way the electron waves are left behind, so to speak (figure 40).

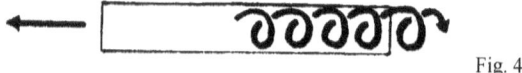

Fig. 40

Light waves have similar properties, too, but we will discuss this in our chapter about the Theory of Relativity.

Well, we have learned a lot about electricity by now. We realised that all causes of the electromagnetic forces are to be found in the polarised space and that the causes of this space lie in turn in the electron waves of which the atoms are composed. We comprehend the significance of electrostatic dynamic effects in material actions as well as the materialisation of magnetic fields.

Every rotating or moving charge produces magnetic moments. As it is, every rotating proton has its magnetic field as well. For the most part, neutrons are expelled from proton bonds and will always take a little of the oscillation with them. Therefore a completely neutral neutron exists only in theory. Experimental neutrons exhibit almost always a magnetic dipole moment when they are rotating. The sense of rotation of a spherical field ("particle") is also designated spin, by the way.

But before we go on to learn more about the games of matter in the next chapter "Hydrogen" maybe we should think about what we have discussed up to now and take a look at figure 41: it shows atomic fields in 1 200 000-fold magnification - the play of waves on the lake of matter... The individual light spots correspond to various atoms stemming from the evaporisation of a submicroscopically small, pin-point sharp crystal wedge of platinum.

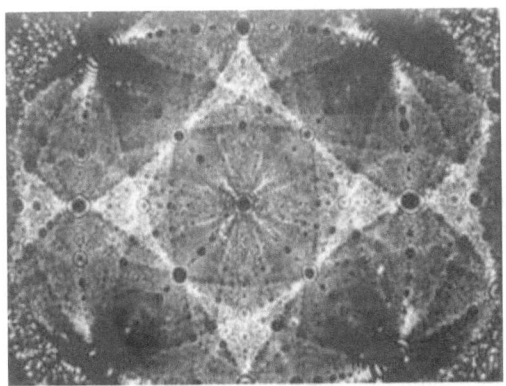

Fig. 41: Atomic fields

9 Hydrogen

We already got acquainted with the first and simplest kind of an atom: with the proton, a spherical field which structures or polarises the space around it and for that reason always carries a charge in the language of physics. Depending on the form of polarisation, "negative" (left-hand) or "positive" (right-hand) charge is possible, we then speak of negative or positive ions. The polarisation of the atom can also be mixed (unordered) and thus give the impression that the atom is "neutral". With hydrogen, however, this condition is more likely a special case – for this atom chiefly appears as an ion in the interaction of the elements.

Since hydrogen atoms repel each other strongly they mainly exist as gas. This gas can only become liquid or solid (crystalline) under high pressure and simultaneous extraction of energy (cooling). This is possible because the electromagnetic state of oscillation of the atom can be influenced by radiation or absorption of "heat".

One will get sufficient information about the universal significance of this atom in every book about chemistry or physics, therefore we will keep to the most essential properties. Like all the other atoms hydrogen manipulates the electromagnetic information or the energetic states in form of emitted or absorbed "light". Due to its simplicity the hydrogen atom acquired particular significance in the exploration of the atomic structure and origination of light. When its light arc emissions were examined a strange regularity in its spectrum was found. Based on this regularity, Niels Bohr developed an atomic model which was very successful although one soon had to realise that the atom could by no means correspond to this theory of quantum shells or orbitals.

Bohr substantiated his quantum jump theory of the origination of light by means of the observation of one single hydrogen atom. But we ask ourselves if it is really admissible to assign this phenomenon of the creation of light to the electron waves of one single, isolated atom. Because nowhere in this world do such lonely hydrogen atoms exist. One single hydrogen atom (proton) would not be possible at all; its existence is always determined and maintained by other atoms - predominantly by other hydrogen atoms...

Well, let's examine the hydrogen atom a little closer (figure 10). Precisely defined, it is not such an ideal spherical field as in our generalisation of it. When we take a snapshot of the field we see that the two shoves orbit the field asymmetrically. When they are on one side, there is nothing on the other side at the same time - except for the matrix, T.A.O. Remember our fan wheel again: when we want to move a second wheel into the first one we just have to make sure that the blades don't get into each others way. The wheels would have to run in synchronicity, and both could exist without disturbing one another (figure 42).

Fig. 42

The area which the two wheels share is called the overlap integral. Because of this circumstance, two hydrogen atoms could lie side by side and maintain a mutual image of oscillation. The harmony of their electron waves will not be disturbed by that. Extreme cooling increases the overlap integral so much in certain situations that several fields can merge to form one single field ("giant atom") (Bose-Einstein condensation).

The mutual area of oscillation is already a simple kind of linkage between two atoms; we call it the covalent bond. It leads to an extension of the electron waves around the new formation. But this bond is not very strong, it is predominantly maintained by the universal pressure (environmental pressure). This is on no account a complete fusion of two protons because the two atoms feel just enough of the curving force that they form a loose friendship. For that reason, hydrogen is usually found in pairs. We call such a pair a hydrogen molecule (H_2). The magnitude of its bond - stronger than any gravitational effect of central masses and weaker than the curving force - received the name Van der Waals force. Due to the previously applicable theories it could not be substantiated with gravitation (although it appears to be very similar to it) but in truth it is of course also a consequence of the universal pressure. The correct way of looking at it is that not a "bond" of two fields came into being but that a new mutual field has formed - i.e. there should be no talk about bonding forces at all.

The mutual impulse field is depicted in figure 43. This is more or less what a hydrogen molecule looks like (projected two-dimensionally). The depth of the penetration into each other is determined by the motional condition (energy) of the oscillation image. The more energy is supplied to the system, the farther away the atoms will move from each other.

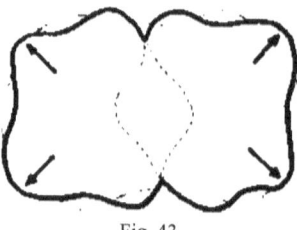

Fig. 43

It would be conceivable that there were further attachments of hydrogen atoms; that hydrogen would form chains (clusters) similar to water. That this does not happen is due to the utilization of space, as we will soon see when we are making some adjustments to the form of the hydrogen molecule. Two fields facing each other always exert the repulsion principle on one another. Apart from the place where they overlap, they shove the rest of the other field away. For that reason, the fields are getting a little deformed. We could say that the two fields shadow the universal pressure a little for one another and each is squeezing itself into this shadow. The final appearance of a hydrogen molecule would therefore have to be approximately as we tried to make clear in figure 44.

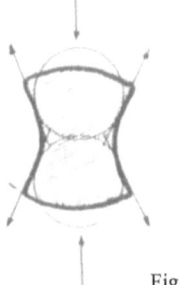

Fig. 44

The mutual pressure deforms the molecule to a doorknob- or dumbbell-shaped formation (for very similar reasons, a single hydrogen atom could also adopt such a doorknob- and dumbbell-state of course). The immediate environment also plays a role in that because the hydrogen molecules are most often among their own kind and fill the space as tightly as possible. The interaction of individual pressure and universal pressure (environmental pressure) therefore creates a picture as shown in figure 45.

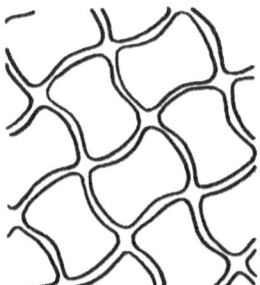

Fig. 45

We will also find analogous events in the fields of the sky, for example with Earth and moon. As it is, the moon is clearly deformed into a kind of pear-shape and literally held in its shadow while the same process squeezes the Earth into an egg shape and causes tides on both sides. Thus it is not some "force of attraction" exerted by the moon which makes the waters rise but the universal pressure diminished by the moon which allows it (figure 46).

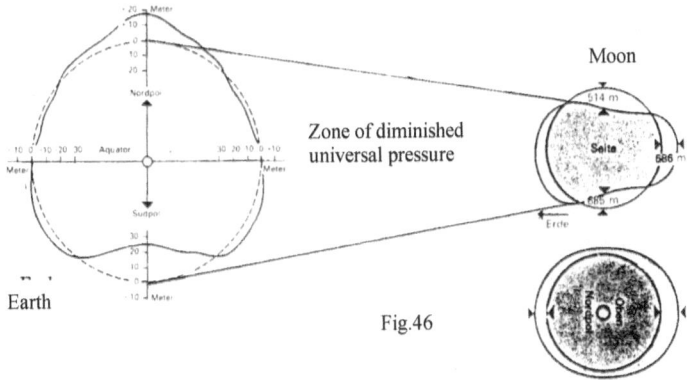

Earth

Zone of diminished universal pressure

Moon

Fig.46

One single hydrogen atom would have to be very big after all to be considered as the cause of light waves.[14] This has purely dimensional reasons because the wavelength of light could be scarcely fit into an atom. Hydrogen molecules, however, rather supply such wavelengths which we know from the hydrogen. If we assume that every energy supply can also only lead to quantised modifications to the distance of the two fields because of the quantisation of the electron impulses, we will discover that the proportions of the molecule change with corresponding regularity due to the described shadowing effect. Thus the surface proportions of the dumbbell-shaped double field are discontinuously shifted towards each other to a very particularly determined extent.

We projected this proportion in figure 47 by simply making the shadow of the pressure act upon the respective other field - starting out from quantised increases in distance. And here is the most astonishing thing: the proportions of the lines created in that way indicate exactly the lines of the hydrogen spectrum according to Balmer! We enlarged the proportions and compared them with the Balmer series: they have the same spacing! This means that the wavelengths of the hydrogen have something to do with the front surfaces of the hydrogen molecule. Even if one suspects that the molecule in the light arc is breaking up due to the high energy applied the mutual shadowing of the atoms still remains thus maintaining such an operative mechanism. Through that it is revealed that the electron impulse around the atoms triggers new impulses, which follow each other chronologically, and that these frequencies correspond to the spatial modification to the front faces (1 and 2 in the illustration). We can demonstrate it in a simple geometric way. We should not forget in our considerations that light is not a real wave but a chronological succession of individual impulses.

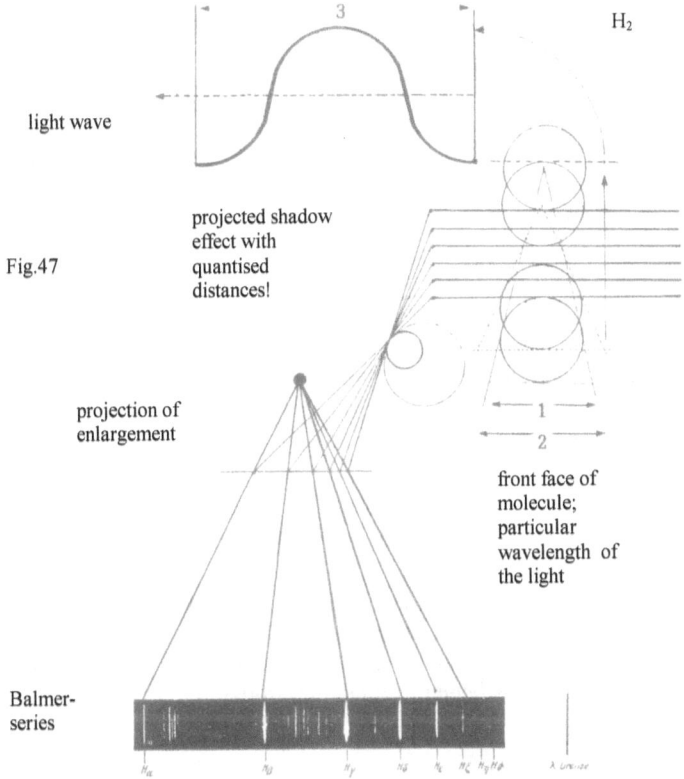

Fig.47

A wavelength (3) is produced which apparently exceeds the magnitude dimension of the molecule by far but this explanation is more satisfactory in many respects than the electron jumping from orbit to orbit according to Bohr which has the flaw to be in stark contrast to electrodynamics and burdened by the knowledge that an electron orbiting around the nucleus like a planet cannot exist from the outset because it would have to fall into the nucleus after a few nanoseconds. That is to say, if seen as a particle, it would continuously loose radiation energy.

Since the atoms always change their distances to each other discontinuously – because of the inevitable levelling out of new overlap integrals - they act only in unobtrusively emitted or adopted magnitudes of energy. We see, quantum physics is on no account only an illusion!

It is predictable that elements which make us suppose an outside structure that is very similar to that of the hydrogen atom on the basis of their chemical properties alone will supply very similar spectra as well. As it is, we find the Balmer series again with lithium, sodium, potassium, rubidium, lanthanum, and francium. From an electron-theoretical point of view all these elements are assigned one electron on the outer shell.

So this is what we discovered: due to the repulsion principle the uniform modifications to the distance of two (or even several) fields towards each other lead to quantised dimensional changes in the fields which exercise a direct influence on the radiated impulses, i.e. their frequencies and wavelengths. The connection is obvious and easy to comprehend. This effect results for the reason that atomic fields partially "shadow" (shield off) the universal pressure (environmental pressure, pressure, or shove coming from other fields) in accordance with their energetic density replacing it with their own pressure (repulsion).

Later this shadowing effect of the universal pressure discovered with the hydrogen will lead us to a surprising discovery on the subject of the macrocosm and will lift the veil from a law of astronomy which has been unsolved until today.

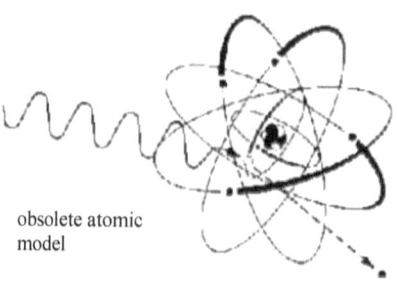

obsolete atomic model

Fig.47a

10 Light

A golden yellow field of grain surging in the wind should now appear before our mind's eye... But what is a field of grain doing in a chapter about light? Does this not stretch the term "General Field Theory" a little too much? On no account, because the pensive consideration of a field of grain will help us find and comprehend some extremely important definitions about the spreading of fields and impulse propagation in the field of T.A.O.. By now the domino principle will certainly be clear to us, after all the transmission of impulses in T.A.O. follows this concept - and we already know that the "dominoes", i.e. the "granules" of T.A.O. are not bodily moving from A to B but that only a transmission of energy (properly speaking a transmission of energetic information) is taking place so that a domino velocity is out of the question while there is a velocity in the spreading of the apparent wave. Hence, it is not an "object" that is moving - and we realised that there is no such thing as a "real" movement[2] of material bodies in the universe at all. This is justifiable in a philosophical point of view as well because logical reasons for the existence of real movements could not be given easily!

Fig. 47a

The domino principle can be applied to the stalks of a field of grain. They, too, can shove each other and transmit information without leaving their place. The structure of the field of grain resembles the matrix of T.A.O. and we can well imagine that we could pull away the field when the wind is blowing a lane or an eddy into the stalks - the lane or the eddy would remain in the same place. On the other hand, the eddy could move or the lane could go wandering - and the field would not follow!. This is also the more important picture for us because the universal field, T.A.O., does certainly not move - and within its matrix there are also only movements of the information or energy transfers - no matter what we like to call them. Impulses fields – just like the eddy in the field of grain - can propagate completely within T.A.O. - and within these impulse fields other fields can be vibrating as well - and all these fields are only connected by their own plane of action (as symbolised with toothed wheel and worm). They can move within T.A.O., penetrate or "fight" each other, interfere with, intensify, and annihilate one another... T.A.O. remains unmoved during all this like a field of grain in a storm.

A proton which - as we already know - is a field of impulses does not move through T.A.O. like an object but it propagates like an eddy in a field of grain! This is an unexpected, absolutely unbelievable conclusion. It means that a thrown stone does not simply fly along solidly but that it pulsates through the matrix! Its field vibrates through the "granules" of the space; actually the stone consists only of a vibrational image of an arrangement of atoms, and this vibrational image moves on by means of continuous induction and sequencing of further vibrational images, in the same way as an EM (electromagnetic) wave induces its fields one after the other... One could almost say the stone "beams" itself through the fields of the universe - and this applies to every field![15] Even a playboy behind the wheel of his Ferrari is "beaming" through the world in this way. And despite the 220 kilometres per hour on the motorway nothing really moves - but a field of information in form of a Ferrari plus driver is propagating! All objects in this universe move in the same way - from atoms to giant galaxies. And that what is moving is not only the visible and perceptible range of the field but everything that makes the field and is part of it; everything it sets into torsional vibration or fluctuation all around it – all of that follows the movement! We will realise that this knowledge is tremendously important and that we will be confronted with it again in the chapters "Inertia", "Gravity", and "Relativity".

At this point we want to deal with the light only. In fact, the usual depiction of an EM-wave shows us the rectangular connection of the planes of action (E-field and M-field) quite well. But it also leads us astray because it gives the impression that we are dealing with a wave in the form of an oscillation. But we know the difference and we know that the individual fields are created by the succession of independent impulses which leads to the fact that they may appear as if they had the properties of both a wave and a particle.

Light is message and messenger in one. It is practically caused and absorbed again by all the fields provided that matching frequencies coincide. Therefore every atom can only gather very particular light waves and absorb their energy. As a rule, the wavelengths concerned are always the same and can also be created by the correspondent atom itself. The most frequent reaction partner of light is the electron, and obviously the particle theory of the electron leads to the particle theory of the light. But the photon is pure fiction. From our point of view we will comprehend the photoelectric effect (Einstein was awarded the Nobel price for its discovery) in a completely different way. The concepts wavelength and frequency, however, will be used with light in the general sense because the difference to the genuine wave is rather irrelevant with most phenomena and becomes only significant in those cases where connections of the phases with each other would have to lead to absurd results. For example, long waves would have to run faster than short ones. As a result, the velocity of light would therefore depend on the colour which is certainly not the case

We can easily symbolise a series of light impulses with a couple of beer mats threaded onto a string (instead of with a spiral) (figure 48).

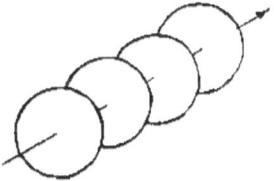

Fig. 48

The density of the beer mats marks the characteristic of the light, the colour - or whether it is a matter of X-rays, gamma rays, or radio waves. By means of this simple beer mat model we can conduct very nice experiments in our minds. After all, we are talking about a helical, circular shove which creates a series of - let's say - discoid fields ("wave fronts"). The circular shove dashes tremendously quick around the travelling direction of the impulse. Since the progressive movement itself takes place at the velocity of light, the helical movement - though it is of course also a fictitious movement like the first - even has to exceed the velocity of light significantly.

As we already discovered in the beginning, our various conditions of encounter apply to the impulses of light unrestrictedly. It is therefore possible that "particles" are created from strong light impulses (gamma rays) as we already discussed in the chapter "T.A.O.". What we want to examine now with our beer mat model are the phenomena of diffraction and refraction.

Well, the velocity of light is on no account universally standardised but it depends on the medium in which the impulse spreads.[16] In a vacuum, in which T.A.O. remains nearly at rest, this velocity is only determined by the properties of the matrix. In material media, the impulse meets with resistance at the vibrations of the atoms and is slowing down. If the impulse encounters an obstacle only on one side, it is retarded only on this side whereas the part of the impulse outside of the medium will maintain its speed. The result is a change in the direction of the impulse as demonstrated in figure 49.

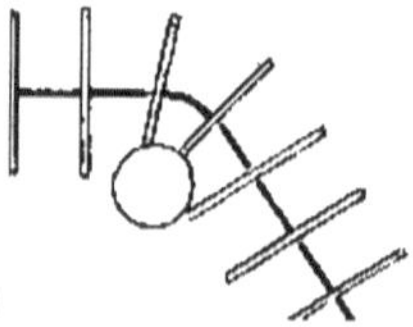

Fig. 49

Light is therefore diffracted at edges or by small bodies. This diffraction is the stronger the closer the beer mats follow each other, that means the shorter the wavelength of the succession of impulses. At the same time, differences in the path length occur, the impulses override each other, and they interfere. For that reason, we receive an interference pattern on a screen which we use to catch the diffracted light. The diffraction fringe rings in figure 50 demonstrate very nicely how the individual colours are diffracted to a different extent.

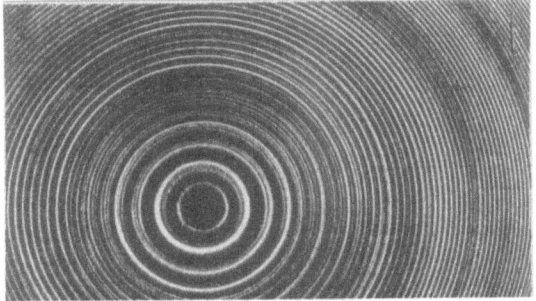
Fig. 50

The refraction of light is just as easy to comprehend. When a sequence of impulses enters obliquely into a retarding medium, again only a part of the beer mat is slowed down whereas the unaffected part overtakes the retarded one a little bit. Understandably the light is therefore again subject to a change in direction (figure 51). Again this change depends on how many mats are retarded within a certain time. The more mats, the stronger the refraction. The impulses of red light are farther apart than those of violet light, therefore the first is refracted less than the latter. The degree of refraction is characteristic for every medium, too. In the same way as upon entering a medium, light is also refracted upon leaving it - but in the opposite direction.

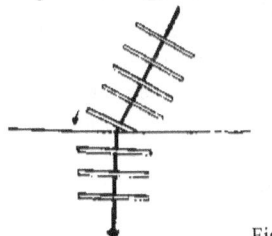
Fig. 51

Why light slows down in a medium is easy to explain: the fields of the atoms often oscillate inverse to the direction of the impulses of the light. Although it is still travelling at the velocity of light it is delayed a little. Since light of a short wavelength is of course delayed more often, a prism makes the individual wavelengths exit in different directions. The picture we receive through it is known as spectrum (figure 52).

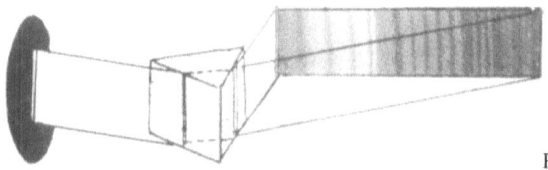

Fig. 52

Of course, the reversed process is also possible: a field of atoms oscillating in the same direction as the movement of light, takes the light impulse with it and advances it a little. This process is called anomalous dispersion. This means that the index of refraction for light of short wavelength is getting smaller than that for light of long wavelength. This is characteristic of only a few substances; their sympathetic oscillation leads most often to an increased absorption of the light which conveys part of its energy to the fields. A typical example of this behaviour is for instance exhibited by solid fuchsine. It is a popular exam question for students of physics if this acceleration of the light within a medium contradicts Einstein's Special Theory of Relativity. The mental dilemma, however, only occurs when one regards light as a genuine wave in which the phase velocity depends on the frequency. In our opinion, however, there is not always a compelling connection. With that, the mysteries have not been solved completely, though, because the individual light pulse apparently adopts superluminal velocity as well after all. In this case, however, it is a deception - the inability to exceed the velocity of light remains secured since the transmitted impulse is a secondary impulse emitted by the absorbing field.

When an impulse collides with a field it can be "taken along" by an impulse which happens to be running in the same direction. This has more or less the effect of a "short-cut", that means the normally helical light pulse is drawn forward a little at that moment. The effect per atom is in fact infinitesimal but sums up to measurable ranges by the multitude of atoms. In essence the physicist designates phenomena of this and of similar kind as phase shift. Since the emerging impulses are actually no longer identical with the ones that entered due to the distortion, at best a piece of information that was modulated is partially destroyed – but the original form is still discernible.

What is passed on in the fuchsine is therefore not exactly the entered impulse; that what emerges from the field of the fuchsine, however, carries a part of the message (colour!) of the original impulse. Obviously there has to be something which could possibly be faster than light: information (if we disregard the circumpolar movement of impulse shoves in T.A.O.). That means if light means energy transport without the transport of matter, transport of information could also be possible without the transport of energy. This would not affect the Special Theory of Relativity in any way.

It is also possible to speed up light to superluminal velocity by means of the tunnel effect, as Professor Günter Nimtz from Cologne or Raymond Chiao from Berkeley demonstrated. However, the researchers have been violently attacked, as if to say: "Such statements cannot be reconciled with the current physical conception of the world and actually such nonsense should not be discussed at all." The speed limit for light is therefore subject of particular discussion at the moment. But the expression superluminal velocity does not make any sense, anyway. Because as already explained, this velocity depends on the medium, and theoretically it has a postulated peak value only in vacuum - but an absolute vacuum does not exist anywhere! What is more, relative superluminal velocities are also possible, as we will soon learn...

When the refraction of the light upon exiting is so strong that it is refracted back into the medium, we are talking about total internal reflection (figure 53).

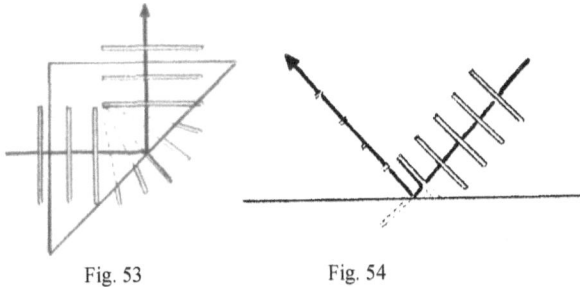

Fig. 53   Fig. 54

In this case, the impulse oscillates only partially out of the medium, it gets faster on one side and changes into the direction in which there is again a retarding medium. This transition of the totally reflecting surface resembles the tunnel effect of the electron. Prisms of this kind are employed in our binoculars. They are practically "bumping" the light off. Optical fibres work in a very similar way according to the same principle.

The nice round beer mats of our model can also be broken, as shown in figure 54. The light striking a reflecting surface first fractures one side of the mat, is tilted in a certain angle by the impact and promptly looses the second half of the round shove. Result: the impulse is only travelling to and fro on the same plane. We already defined such an impulse as polarised. The impulse can also loose its halves when penetrating narrow crystal structures.

The effect of polarised light on matter is a little different from that of unpolarised light. The conditions of absorption and reflection change. Metal absorb it much better than normal light. Therefore it affects thin metal structures by disturbing their order. For that reason, a farmer will never leave his scythe lying in the moonlight (moonlight is reflected and thus polarised light). Moonlight also blunts razor blades and changes chemical reactions. So when the alchemists of the Middle Ages carried out many an experiment only by moonlight they didn't do it for mystical reasons alone.

Neither is it a fairytale that blunt razorblades become sharp-edged again in pyramids. We certainly know after all that every matter continues into space - even in a polarised one - and that it is thus influenced by other fields. The pyramidal incidence of the space changes sharp metal structures and makes them sharper yet. In that way, every interior space of a particular geometrical hollow body has its characteristic function (beer, for examples, turns bad in cornered barrels).

By means of our repulsion principle we could throw light on many phenomena of parapsychology which are negated by the sciences. But this would already be enough material for a book on its own. Here we only want to show that light does not have any mysterious properties and that its game can be comprehended quite easily.

Even gamma and X-rays or radio waves are subject to the same rules. Diffraction and refraction exist for them, either, although under other conditions each. And of course electron waves can be treated in the same way as light waves. In this case diffraction, reflection, and refraction take place in electric or magnetic fields for the most part because as a rule electron waves are slower than light waves. After all, they are practically "compressed light" because they are composed of impulses (just remember figures 10 and 11). We will again deal with electron waves when we examine the photoelectric effect ,and the question of the velocity of light will occupy us once again in the chapter about the Theory of Relativity. Figure 55 shows diffraction rings which come into existence when a bunch of electrons is passing through a crystal. Did you notice the similarity to figure 50?

But now it is time to learn how the variety of matter comes about without requiring a Creator who intervenes from the irrational...

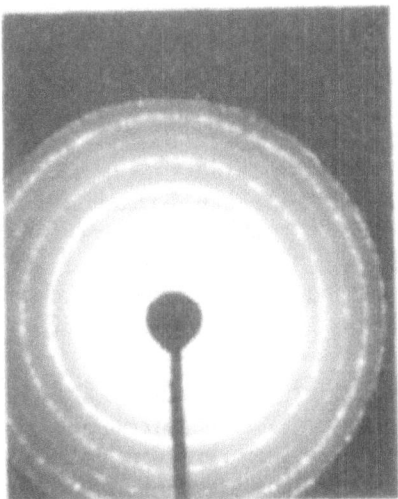

Fig. 55

11 Helium

Since universal pressure and curving force are caused by the surrounding fields they contain a strange aspect: if the cosmos around us was obliterated, all apparent forces of attraction would vanish and we would fall back into chaos or dissolve into a vacuum - in which a new universe could begin again, though. Since the universe around us will never be obliterated but expands as a result of the shoving pressure, naturally enough exactly this pressure is abating continuously. For that reason, matter will fall victim to decay on the whole – and it is to be hoped that a compensating creation of new matter will take place (as Fred Hoyle postulated it in his Steady State Theory of the universe) in order to sustain the presence of the universe.

While trying to create matter from gamma rays in the particle accelerators, the scientists already made it up to mesons - or at least that's what they believe. Since they do not want to wait for hundred of thousands of years until a proton comes into existence by pure chance through any constellation of radiation they try to produce matter by applying the highest energies. It is very likely that one day this will be successful if they don't lose interest in financing the awfully expensive and actually futile particle accelerators any longer. Some have already been closed down and some will never be finished at all.

Since we do not require the hypothesis of the Big Bang for the origination of the world, we don't have the theoretically demanded high temperatures at our disposal which are said to make the development of protons possible – but they are not necessary in general. We can assume that protons are not only merged in the nuclear reactors of the suns but that protons are even produced there – presumably as an extremely rare event. But one single proton every few thousand years is by the way sufficient to replace the loss of matter in the universe due to expansion. Yes, one single proton! For that reason, it must have taken quite a long time until the entire matter of the universe had been there all together.... But the universe is not the ash of a divine New Year's firework after all but a product of eternity! And the fusion of protons to higher elements ought to be even rarer an event. But these processes will only set in when a great amount of protons is available under certain conditions. That way, even rare fusions can manage to produce the higher elements in the course of time which are relatively scarce anyway.

We already described the energy barrier which the universal pressure has to overcome in order to bring two spherical fields so close together that the curving force forges them together. After surmounting the repulsion two fields shoot into each other like fired by spring force. They create a new mutual field which strives for spherical shape in fact but can only achieve it within the framework of possible energy distribution. Therefore atoms or "atomic nuclei" are only completely round in an ideal case. For the most part they are pear-shaped, oval, or dumbbell-shaped, even fields looking like peanuts are possible.[17] The ratio between resistance (repulsion) and curving force (apparent attraction) determines the size of an atom; in every newly created field a new ratio of these forces is developing. The criterion for judging this important reaction is the surface of a field, so to speak a kind of resistance shell.

Under their surfaces two individual protons hold a certain energy density which grows into a new field with double the volume upon merging - but under a surface which is suddenly smaller than the sum of surfaces would have been before. On this surface, which became smaller in comparison, the universal pressure all of a sudden finds less points of application for its force than before with the individual fields. On the other hand twice the energy is pounding against the new, diminished interior surface. That means: the equilibrium ratios which existed before are destroyed, first the surrounding fields advance, then the new spherical field swells up impulsively until a new ratio of the equilibriums has been established. This impulse is so violent that it causes an intense spreading of all sorts of electromagnetic radiation. This enormous energy impulse does not remain a secret to the environment; we call it fusion energy! With that both a part of the energy inherent in protons was released and the power of the universal pressure was brought into effect immediately.

So the new resistance shell of the newly accumulated field is comparatively smaller – as the geometry of the sphere entails. This also explains the so-called mass defect. The mass of the new field now appears to be smaller than the sum of the individual masses in total - but actually that should nearly go without saying.

In this connection we should know how to detect the masses of such small fields. The instrument developed for this purpose is called mass spectrometer. The atoms to be analysed are first passed through an electric field and then through a magnetic one. The difference in the velocity of the atoms (canal-ray beams) is compensated by means of sophisticated methods of deflection. The degree of their deflection in the electromagnetic field allows several possibilities to conclude to their mass which is defined by the inertia of their behaviour after all. Because of that it becomes immediately apparent that every surface variation of a merged field finds expression in changed charging. Therefore it is deflected a little bit more in the magnetic field thus indicating a lower mass. We should not forget after all that mass is an abstraction which does not stand for any substance! Therefore neutrons with low charge appear to be a little bit heavier than protons because they hardly show any reaction to the magnetic fields. But in truth neutrons are exactly as "heavy" as protons!

About a quarter of the field's energy is released when two fields are merging because the surface of the new field is diminished by about this amount. The "loss of mass" corresponds to the energy released. The technical utilization of this phenomenon is hindered by the fact that usually more energy has to be expended on pushing the fields across the barrier of repulsion than is gained in the end. But there is a trick to dodge this difficulty which surely finds its application in the sun. We know of course that the field of the proton is a product of time and space. This means there is a moment at every point of the field when the field does not exist at all so to speak. It is now within the realms of probability that a second field is making an attempt to approach in just that moment - and is possibly "absent" itself from exactly the same point. Then a kind of tunnel effect takes place. That means if we shove a hydrogen molecule completely into another one in just this way, we will actually obtain such a fusion field. It can be found in nature and is called deuteron. Just like hydrogen, it forms pairs and it received the name deuterium (D_2) in that form. Thus deuteron consists of two protons which do not lie next to each other, though, but inside one another forming a one hundred percent overlap integral that way. Our fan wheel suddenly has two blades!

When we bang another field into the deuteron or rather smuggle it in through the tunnel effect we obtain again a gain of energy and a loss of mass - but also a new field with a new name: tritium. We can also imagine, however, that this new field oscillates asymmetrically, has difficulties in maintaining the harmony, and therefore will decay again very soon. The third fan blade causes disturbance, it is cast out and promptly looses its oscillation. What comes out of the field is therefore a neutron. For that reason, tritium (a helium isotope) is radioactive. It decays again to deuterium. But deuterium does not live forever, either, and can decay back to hydrogen again. In all these processes new situations of equilibrium between universal pressure and individual pressure are established. The separated fields are expanding again but will be compressed immediately by the universal pressure (before it finds a bigger surface of application!), and again energy is released impulsively!

The fusion processes we just described can be continued further. When we bang two deuterons into each other or four hydrogen atoms or two tritium fields, it is possible that a new field is created in which four protons are involved, so to speak. This is possible because the impulses do not occupy the same spaces - two are, let's say, at the front and two at the back. They are able to fill the field by evading each other without disturbing one another. This fan wheel with four blades is called helium. It is nothing less than the principal building block of the world!

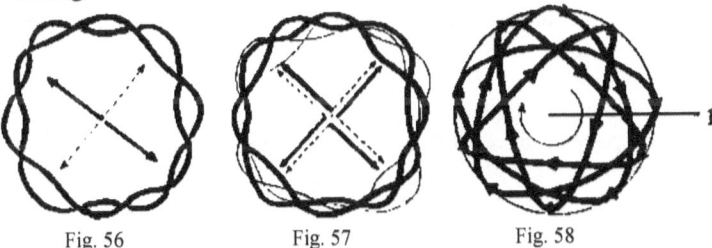

Fig. 56   Fig. 57   Fig. 58

Figure 56 symbolises the fusion of two protons to form one deuteron. The duplication of this oscillation field is shown in figure 57: helium. The figures reduce the events to the plane of the paper - we will get a better picture when we try to draw the paths of the impulses according to the three dimensions of the field. The obtained picture is approximately similar to the one depicted in figure 58. It makes us realise immediately that the directions of all impulses are the same.

The field is tightly packed with impulses, thus achieving a maximum of energy density. A further tunnelling in of an impulse is not conceivable anymore. In addition, we see clearly that the impulses create a circular oscillation in one (or several) place(s) of the field (1). This characteristic place of a field can be found at least once in all fields but it can also occur several times. The ability of the atom to bond results from this oscillation which we call valence. Since this oscillation is again a product of time and space it can turn out - independent of the total polarisation of the atom - to be polarised left-handed or right-handed. We will come back to that later.

The energy density of a field is always inversely proportional to its surface. The dimensions - i.e. the distances to one another - change accordingly. If one gram of hydrogen atoms still has a volume of 10 cm^3, one gram of helium will not require four times this space but only ca. 27 cm^3. The following principle results from that: the higher the energy of an atom the smaller it gets. This makes immediately sense if we take into consideration that two atoms restrict one another where forces of the same magnitude come together. This applies also with regard to the universal pressure which sends every field to its appropriate space. But this means also that one helium atom adopts a different size among helium atoms than among iron atoms...

As one can imagine the helium atom has a tremendously compact nature. Physicists also call this dense field alpha particles. From the view of particle theory it consists of two protons, two neutrons, and two electrons. But understandably it is impossible to actually extract such components from a helium atom just because they do not really exist within it. For this reason alone, it is completely impossible to fission a helium atom. When it is bombarded with other particles, a series of shoving processes takes place but an alpha particle remains an alpha particle. Even highly energetic gamma rays rebound literally... For this reason, helium is the first in a series of particularly proud atoms: the noble gases. Like the other representatives of this category it enters into molecular marriages very reluctantly and only in exceptional cases and does not even form lose pairs like hydrogen. Well, it is not imperative at all that helium can only come into existence indirectly through deuteron and tritium. Meeting processes with four protons involved are possible just as well. It is certainly a very rare event that four "disturbances" coincide and establish a harmonious oscillation field – however, it is not impossible.

Thus, there are many different possibilities for the development of this principal building block of the world and it is therefore not surprising that helium is the second most frequent element of the cosmos and, strictly speaking, it is found even more frequently because all other atoms of this world are combinations of helium, hydrogen, deuterium, and neutrons. And they are sentenced to decay back into these basic elements again one day. We will also call these basic elements primary fields. Their further combination into new elements is a simple jigsaw puzzle...

When two helium fields cross their barrier until the curving force takes effect, they can penetrate each other only a little to create a mutual field. Certainly they would fall apart again after a few fractions of a second; the ratio of the forces towards one another is bad. The situation is immediately different when three helium fields come together. This trinity already offers the universal pressure more possibilities to link them together; each of these fields practically lies on one Lagrangian point of the others, and therefore this intimate bond is found very often. It is about the most important atom of life: carbon.

We can well imagine what this carbon atom looks like: three helium fields, consequently three alpha particles, pressing against each other like the slices in a lemon (figure 59). The shells indicate only an arbitrary range of energy, the atomic field itself is of course invisible. So a carbon atom is structured quite simply. It is also the most asymmetrical atom among all the elements but this is exactly the basis for its enormous versatility.

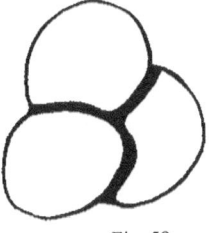
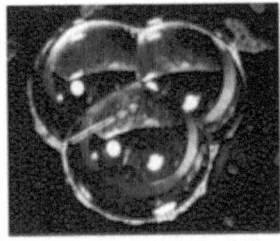

Fig. 59   Fig. 59a

Of course, several other elements can be combined from helium fields just as easily. The combination of four alpha particles is called oxygen, ^{16}O. Five alpha particles produce again a particularly symmetrical field: neon, ^{20}Ne. As to be expected, it is thus a noble gas. Six alpha particles result in magnesium, ^{24}Mg. Seven - silicon, ^{28}Si. Eight - phosphor, ^{32}S, Ten – calcium, ^{40}Ca. Thirteen – chromium, ^{52}Cr. And fourteen – iron, ^{56}Fe!

Should we be particularly surprised that the elements just listed are the most frequent manifestations of matter within our universe? Obviously their production is quite unproblematic... Eleven combined helium fields could be one scandium isotope. Twelve make titanium, an element that is also frequently found.

Well, we could proceed with the deuterons in the same way as with the helium fields. But deuterons are not so stable; it is very unlikely that they play a great role in the constitution of matter. Therefore all atoms are built predominantly of the primary fields proton and helium while neutrons make living together a little more bearable. According to the pattern indicated above, we could work out a complete crystallography of the elements but it would get a bit too far away from the issue to run through all the combinations here.

About 1500 of such combinations exist. Approximately 75 per cent of them are unstable; they will change into stable nuclides sooner or later.

According to our point of view, atoms with even mass numbers (^{20}Ne or ^{32}S) should be particularly frequent and have a particular stability. This is indeed correct: all the atoms of such a kind are particularly permanent and more frequent by at least a power of ten than nuclides with an odd mass number. This proves their composition from primary fields; all these elements consist of helium and hydrogen, so to speak. The even mass number is mainly determined by the alpha particles (= 4 protons or 2 protons and 2 neutrons). Moreover, there are additionally attached protons and neutrons which already reduce the stability. All elements with an odd mass number are therefore predominantly unstable. Exceptions make only light elements like (2 x 3=) ^{6}Li, (2 x 5=) ^{10}B and (2 x 7=) ^{14}N. Even the hydrogen molecule ^{2}H has an odd mass number (2 x 1) and can be separated for that reason.

162 sorts of atoms are composed of helium and hydrogen pairs (and not deuterium!) for certain. Too many primary fields and neutrons already disturb the cohesion significantly; therefore, particularly heavy atoms have a tendency to radioactivity which we will discuss in more detail at a later point. A formation of molecules

as in the case of hydrogen occurs especially with asymmetric atoms; their possibilities for attachment are particularly distinctive – for that reason, they are able to combine with each other quite well. Their asymmetries are easy to comprehend because the more primary fields are coming together, the more symmetrical the structure has to be. Therefore, asymmetries and the formation of molecules are found especially with lighter elements with odd mass number up to nitrogen, ^{14}N. But carbon is also seized by great infatuation for its own kind because of its remarkable asymmetry, just like oxygen which prefers to form a molecule of three, O_3, that bears the name ozone. In principle, exotic manifestations are also possible with every element because nature is not universally "standardised".[18]

In all cases the preference of the atoms to enter into a bond (i.e. not to prevent it) depends on the spatial structure and their oscillational properties (= electricity). Each time these qualities have their origin in the arrangement of the primary fields which form the "atom".

12 Fusion

By now, we have gained a basic understanding of how matter came into existence. Let's recapitulate: the first impulse fields originated from a chaos of gamma and X-radiation ("Disturbing impulses within T.A.O."). These impulse fields remained on the spot, so to speak, and created a variety of spherical or primary fields. They displaced one another and demanded space between them. They destroyed each other and carried on fighting until they formed standardised primary fields in a way. Even without particular expenditure of energy, that is to say by means of tunnel effects, it was possible to create elements up to helium. Both kinetic energies and pure chance could already combine these helium fields to higher elements as well but another process must have been even more important:

In the pressure developing through mutual displacement, vast zones of higher density were created, energy centres in space which are generally known as stars. This is all the more possible when elements developed previously, which were a little heavier and felt the universal pressure more strongly than hydrogen. For that reason, stars existed long before there were any galaxies because the latter only developed when the stars began to displace one another.[106]

The process of creating higher elements continued in the stars, and for the time being simple combinations of helium and hydrogen developed. This cosmic jigsaw puzzle products are knows as the first 26 elements of the periodic system of chemical elements: hydrogen, helium, lithium, beryllium, boron, carbon, nitrogen, oxygen, fluorine, neon, sodium, magnesium, aluminium, silicon, phosphor, sulphur, chlorine, argon, potassium, calcium, scandium, titanium, vanadium, chromium, manganese, and iron - and maybe even cobalt und nickel...

About half of these elements constitute practically the complete matter of the universe. At a later time - in processes which are comprehended nowadays - the heaviest elements were created in the stars. They actually only spice the cosmos because their occurrence is very rare.

Scientists classified all these elements into the periodic system of chemical elements according to their similarities. The periodic system comprises about 109 elements. We should not misunderstand this system of classification, it does not express any harmony among the elements. They were produced in a lively mess but since their building blocks had already been typified, so to speak, the result had to be that in each case four of these building blocks always made one oxygen atom, no matter where and when they came into existence.

The order of the periodic system is man-made - this order has been broken by isotopes, isomers, and isobars (not to be confused with the lines of equal barometric pressure on a weather map) long since. For all atoms there are hybrid forms which cannot be assigned to this or that element because of their chemical activities.

In order to explain the chemical properties of the atoms mankind invented a couple of theories. The electron for instance was declared to be the smallest "bonding machine" and it was assigned to stipulated regions where it has to stay. If we take into consideration that a proton really exhibits an electron wave (originally composed of two T.A.O. impulses) and that the helium atom has two of these waves for that reason (see figure 58), we have to admit that these ideas were applicable and that especially quantum mechanics shows the connections with good mathematical approximation. But quantum mechanics only treats the effects and leaves the causes in the dark. It describes reality more or less as if we described a football game only by the movements of the ball without seeing the players. The movements of the ball would be exact but their causes would be hard to find... Moreover, quantum physics is struggling with the problem that it is measuring quantum systems with quantum systems what successfully prevents objective distinctions between illusion and reality.

All models of atoms, waves, or particles applicable today have been derived only empirically from the effects and therefore do not correspond to the causal truth. Neither does the combination of primary fields according to our depiction create a functional, tangible object but only a total field which – traversed by impulses – does not reveal any real boundaries and dissipates in a universal total field in principle...

The attempt to shed light on the interior of atoms by means of X-rays has failed. All atoms supply a continuous X-ray spectrum which (contrary to the volumes or the melting temperature, the ionisation potential and the optical spectrums) does not reveal any periodicity. Therefore the plan of the inner electrons is purest fiction. But we know that the basic impulse which causes the electron waves, propagates really or potentially infinitely from the centre of the field outwards. The nucleus of higher elements is also actually only a piece of space structured by oscillation and spherical in the best of cases with a higher content of energy or motion.

Since electron waves as such already include the concept of the proton as well, the connection between the number of imaginary protons and theoretical electrons is really given in the figurative sense. But the positive charge of the proton and the negative charge of the electron are chimeras. Therefore the matter appears to be neutral - we already mentioned that - because the atoms always establish an equilibrium with each other. They can penetrate each other up to those energy densities which defy each other with the same magnitude. No matter how we disturb this equilibrium, it is the end of neutrality. Within an atomic system we have to disturb only a few atoms. We can remove them or shake them by filing, chafing, beating, or by using acids or by letting light, heat, and pressure act upon them; every manipulation we can think of and which is suitable to prevent the equilibrium will provide us with energy in form of radiation and electric current. The electrically neutral atom is a theoretical construct; the material events around us are predominantly directed by ions.

The various elements differ from each other in their energy content, in their spatial structures, in their electrical and magnetic moments. Thus every kind of atom already carries a programme which determines its behaviour towards other atoms. The chemists developed theories for these programmes which we should examine in more detail.

We already got to know one form of bond between atoms: the covalent bond of the hydrogen. Well, the term bond is fateful in so far that it tempts to assume the bond took place due to forces inherent to the atom. Most of the bonding theories proceed from this assumption and therefore most inconsistencies can be found in these theories. Even quantum mechanics did not get any further in this case. According to that, hybrid bonds would arise, for example, which could never remain stationary or double bonds which rule each other out. Therefore, one still has no idea of the true atomic states of complicated molecules, let alone what binds them together...

For that is reason I suppose it is necessary to emphasise it again: the strength of all bonds results from the universal pressure. Thus it really comes directly from the cosmos. For that reason, bonds are never caused by the atoms themselves but are on the contrary always prevented more or less successfully! In other words: bonding as such results actually from the environmental pressure created by the lack of space (caused by other atoms or fields - even the cosmos is a field), and in the end it depends on the states of the bonding partners if they create a long lasting mutual field or not. Hydrogen bonds because of its impulses - the overlap integrals - which are evading each other temporally. This form of fusion is frequently found.

The interaction of universal pressure and curving force manifests itself, as already indicated, in the Van der Waals force which could previously only be explained by means of many supplementary hypotheses. With that every covalent (or electrostatic) bond had to represent a great secret. Because the assumption that two electrons could oscillate together - not a bad image in itself - did explain on no account why the associated atoms stayed together. The heteropolar bond (electrovalence) has always been easier to understand; in this case the electrical attraction could be made responsible - even if this attraction as such remained a mystery.

In an atom, oscillations which are travelling in the same direction can be superimposed to create new oscillations. The physicist Jean Baptiste Fourier was the first to detect this principle. For this purpose let's take a look at figure 60:

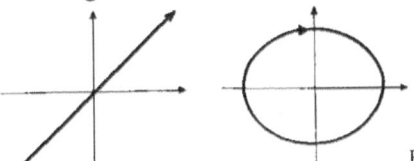

Fig. 60

When a body simultaneously makes two harmonious oscillations of the same frequency and of the same oscillational direction, the result is again a harmonious oscillation of the same frequency whose amplitude and phase depends on the amplitudes and phases of the two oscillations and their difference in phase. Two oscillations of the same frequency but with different directions of oscillation will provide elliptical orbits when they are superimposed. These orbits can degenerate into circles on the one hand and into linear oscillations on the other hand.

The figure on the right shows the process important for us. Fourier oscillations also play a significant role in quantum mechanics. On the whole we can say: completely new oscillations are created on the surface of an atom; spirals circle either clockwise or anti-clockwise depending on the direction and the difference in phase of the generating impulses. These new oscillations are - just like the space polarisation in which they are integrated - flowing away from the atom. With some licence, oscillations of that kind can be compared to Chladni's sound patterns which are produced on a metal plate stimulated into oscillation.

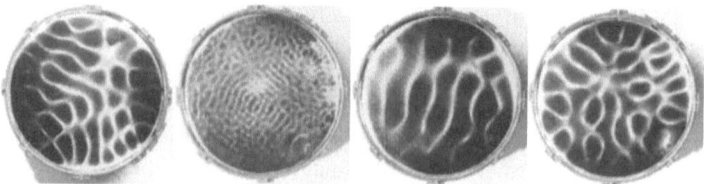

Fig. 60a: Chladni's sound patterns

Thus it becomes clearer that on the basis of these circling oscillations new structures are created around the atom which can be quite varied - but which are characteristic for every particular type of atom. Therefore left-hand polarisation on atoms oscillating to the right is also possible without them belonging to anti-matter for that matter. Again, we have to emphasise that we are not dealing with "real" oscillations but that these new structures are products of interference of the electron impulses. Oscillations occur only in the scope of atomic systems, i.e. in (ionised) gases for example or in solid bodies. For better comprehension, however, we will continue to call them Fourier oscillations.

It is always only in certain defined parts of the atom that Fourier oscillations occur, and exactly these parts and the quantity of their occurrence determine the valence (bonding power) of the atom. Experience showed that there are at least two such places located on an oxygen atom. One of them is clearly depicted in figure 61. The oscillograph, fig. 61a shows also the further circular polarisation on the "atomic shell".

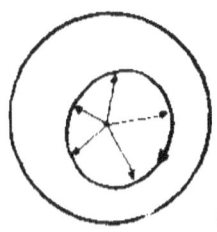 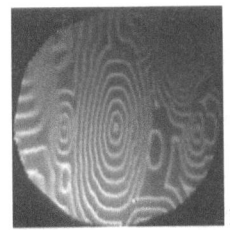

Fig. 61   Fig. 61a

Our conditions of encounter also apply unrestrictedly to the oscillational polarisations of the bonding areas. We could now simply determine that hydrogen oscillates to the left and oxygen to the right. Thus, there would be no repulsion between them, at least not in the places of the Fourier oscillation. Result: the two atoms seem to attract each other like two magnetic poles of opposite signs wherever and however they meet. We say: both atoms have an affinity for each other!

Two atoms bonded in that way make a new field as a molecule, deform one another and strive for spherical shape in the game between individual pressure and universal pressure, though. Again the new overall surface is reduced in comparison to the individual surfaces – having the already known effect. Only the occurrence of energies is significantly lower in this case than when two fields are tunnelled through, in which case we are already speaking of nuclear energy. But still this bonding energy is not to be underestimated. Again its strength comes from the universal pressure and thus from the cosmos itself!

In fact hydrogen and oxygen are oscillating in opposite directions. When they meet they do it with a bang ... and from the intimate affinity of one hydrogen molecule and one oxygen atom for one another the most important molecule of the universe originates: water!

Water is a primordial substance of the universe. Water must have come into existence already before there were any galaxies. Frozen to ice it has been wandering through the universe for ages and whole celestial bodies (comets) consist mainly of it.

The love of hydrogen and oxygen for each other does not stop completely after they have bonded. Therefore many water molecules create chains, so-called clusters, with each other. This is the cause of the liquid consistency, the flowing property.

Oxygen, however loves many other atoms as well and is very adhesive everywhere - not least of all that is the reason why water is wet and moistens all surfaces which are well disposed towards it. Because there are also molecules which don't like water in the least. It is always a game of the Fourier oscillations and of electricity; an extremely important game, though, because without water and without its aversions and preferences there wouldn't be any form of life at all...

Even the fusion of oxygen and deuterium molecules is possible; in this case we are talking about heavy water. Although both wet and liquid it puts up great resistance against its neutrons and thus it is often used as moderating substance for neutrons in nuclear reactors.

As we already know, light fields which are poor in energy, like hydrogen, are relatively big. In addition, a water molecule (H_2O) is a dipole. One side is polarised "positively", the other side "negatively" (figure 62).

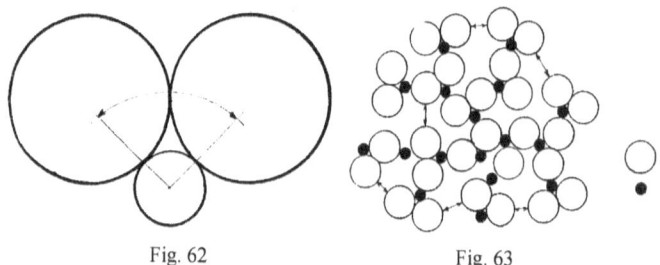

Fig. 62 Fig. 63

When we withdraw energy from the water (we take away motion by heat abstraction), on the one hand the formation of clusters increases and on the other hand the repulsion of the big hydrogen molecules acts stronger towards each other. Water is paying meticulous attention to combine only right-handedly and left-handedly. The result is shown in figure 63. In the final analysis a strict order develops due to the repulsion of the hydrogen atoms; water is deformed into a kind of crystal and we call it ice.

Understandably ice expands although the molecule itself does not change in any way. When we make the molecules move by means of heat waves, the hydrogen atoms start oscillating towards each other again; they share the existing place like the workers of a day and a night shift share one bed, and therefore they can move up closer together again. The hydrogen bridges are getting weaker, the water is getting liquid again and reduces its volume. At 4 degrees Celsius it occupies the least space.

A freely falling drop of water which is dominated by the same universal pressure all around significantly demonstrates the cosmic trend of matter towards the sphere (figure 64).[19]

The surface tension[20] of this sphere results from the opposition between the individual pressure (of water) and the universal pressure (of the environment). The repulsion principle makes it easy to comprehend so that we don't have to struggle with abstract concepts like work (which would have to be spent to lift a water molecule above the surface and which doesn't explain the spherical shape either).

This stress ratio of forces, which liquids exhibit in a particularly impressive way, exists basically between all matter. It is the cosmic pressure - and this results inevitably from the existence of exactly this universe...

The ice mentioned before provides us with our cue for another important structure of matter which we have to tackle with now.

Fig. 64

13 Crystals

The simplest and best answer to the question for bonds is found in crystals. A definite order transpires in them on the basis of the three-dimensional, geometrical arrangement of the atoms. We already saw a crystal in the ice which exhibits a typical dipolar bond. In addition to oxygen, hydrogen also forms very similar constellations with fluorine (HF).

Matters stand even simpler in pure electrostatic relationships where atoms form a lattice structure as ions of opposite kinds. The best example is common table salt, NaCl. Sodium is, just like hydrogen, a left-hand vibrator; chlorine oscillates to the right-hand. Therefore both atoms have an affinity for each other like oxygen and hydrogen. For that reason, they love to bond (figure 65).

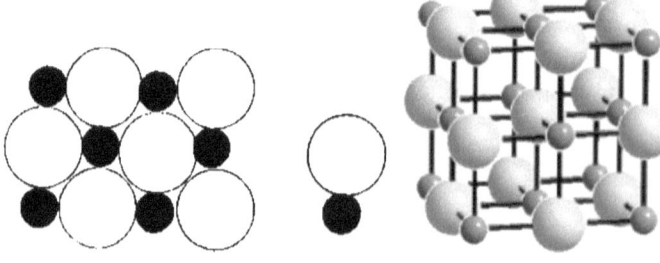

Fig. 65

As is to be expected, sodium as the atom with lower energy (OR 11) is bigger than the chlorine atom (OR 17). Several NaCl molecules turn towards each other automatically in such a way that every Na-atom is surrounded by the attracting Cl atoms and every Cl atom by the approaching Na atoms. Of course the bonding power as such comes again from the pressure of the environment and from the polarisation. All NaCl molecules are forced into their behaviour, they don't have any other possibility. We could say: sodium und chlorine are programmed to become common table salt!

Since sodium loves chlorine in the same way as chlorine loves sodium and since there are bonds between all atoms, common table salt is a so-called giant molecule. Similar conditions can be found with all salts, as for example lithium with fluorine and so on...

Covalent bonds also develop crystals which are not to be sneezed at. Every time when atoms of the same kind create a lattice of bonds we will find a beautiful crystal, mostly a gemstone. Above all, germanium and silicon are highly imaginative master-builders in this connection. But probably the most interesting structure is that which comes into existence when carbon decides to marry several times. Carbon has various facilities for attachments but only one takes up the least space (figure 66).

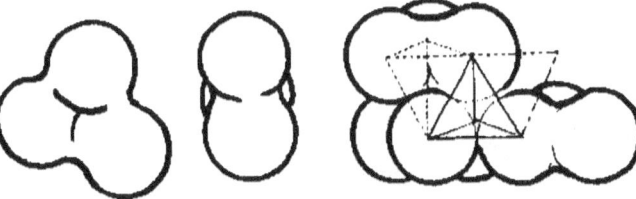

Fig. 66

This results in a structure in which the geometry of the triangular pyramid (tetrahedron) is concealed (figure on the right) and which therefore becomes extremely stable and hard; we know this structure as the diamond. Despite the know hardness of this jewel the bonding energy of its carbon atoms is lower than that in common table salt, because it is only a covalent bond just like hydrogen. But the compact bedding of the atoms - they lie in each others "dents" – is the basis for their low potential of mobility and displacement and thus for the stability of the crystal. Carbon atoms can of course combine in a completely different way; the atoms, for example, are displaceable on one plane, and this product is therefore soft and called graphite. The tetrahedron principle in carbon encouraged a concept of the model of this atom which is both simple and incorrect (figure 67).

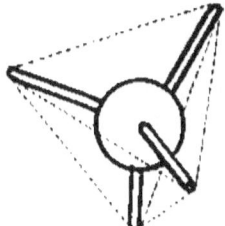

Fig. 67

This model was successful on the one hand but also created considerable difficulties on the other hand. According to the periodic system of elements as well as to quantum mechanical points of view, the carbon atom should only have two possibilities for bonding. But one knows that it can make up to four bonds. But if it was quadrivalent, it wouldn't be possible for the benzene ring to exist because the benzene ring represents a linkage of six carbon atoms in ring form. At least three bonds could not remain stable according to the model of figure 67 because they would exclude each other. With our model, however, the benzene ring can be portrayed without inconsistency (figure 68).

<<< Fig. 68

Such a benzene ring offers further good possibilities of attachment for other atoms or hydrogen molecules. We will encounter these possibilities later when we are discussing organic molecules.

How well our model represents reality is revealed by the X-ray diffraction pattern of a benzene ring (figure 69), which can already be produced today with modern methods...

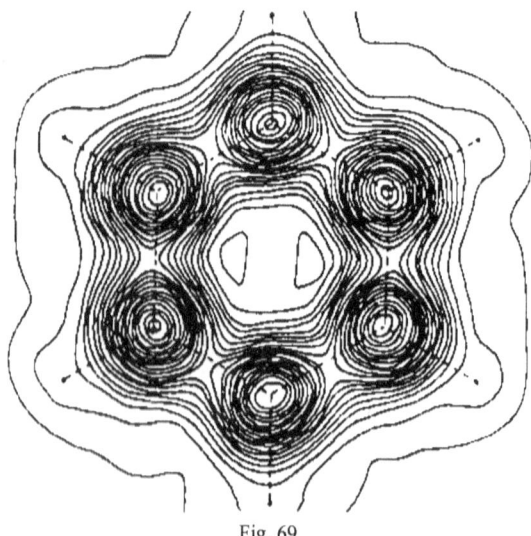

Fig. 69

The concentric lines show the distribution of the electron waves. We also make out how the individual fields bend into a total field. This structure was already identified by Kekulé more than one hundred years ago; it has remained unclear, however, how it comes about. The solution of the riddle, though, is - as we will see - much simpler than allowed for by the usual bonding theories.

But let's return to the crystals. All forms of crystals can be divided in 7 systems and 32 crystal classes. That means that nature also makes use of all (mathematical) possibilities. Every form of crystal which we can think of exists somewhere on this world. Since crystals are such robust structures they do not easily oscillate with irradiated impulses. For that reason, they absorb little light and are therefore more or less transparent. With some of them the transparency lies within the infrared or ultraviolet range of the electromagnetic waves. For similar reasons, crystals don't transmit almost any electron waves when temperatures are low and the crystals are pure. When there are any impurity atoms in the crystal the result will be effects which are known from semiconductors.

Let's examine another type of crystal which is not so stable as the structures discussed above. It, too, arranges atoms in a lattice but this arrangement is quite casual. The atoms are just piled on top of each other, bound by the universal pressure and the curving force and relatively easy to separate. This kind of crystal is called metal.

Practically all elements are able to create a metallic bond. Even gases will become metallic under a correspondingly high pressure. Since the electron waves don't dictate each other's oscillational spaces in this lose relationship but remain unbound, metals are good current conductors. The physicist says, metals are filled by a kind of electron gas, so to speak, and notices with displeasure that this actually contradicts the conventional atomic models. Because it had to remain completely incomprehensible why electrons - otherwise rigidly bound to the atomic nucleus - should now suddenly gain their freedom ... this was the more mysterious since electrons were known to be responsible for the chemical constitution of the atom.... Our viewpoint can lead us out of this dilemma in which the electron does not even exist as bound particle and the continued transport of all energy is done by the atoms (fields) themselves (and their communicating oscillations can also be called electron waves).

With that we are already acquainted with all forms of bonding. The simplest form is the pure Van der Waals cohesion, it holds matter together on the whole and is created by the pressure of the surrounding masses (fields) of the universe. At close range, the curving force plays also a decisive role. Organic molecules combine in this flexible form but other bonds also occur like the discussed heteropolar (ion) bond (common table salt) or the covalent bond (diamond) and the dipolar bond (ice)...

When physicists attribute the metal bond to the free electrons (what they really do in some theories), they get a little grotesque and demonstrate how much a theory is often more proper than right to them provided it supplies just any explanation - no matter how bizarre this explanation may be. It might have been somewhat plausible that electrons oscillating in the same direction and taking up the same orbit should evoke bonds, and the truth is not that far away from it. But that the exact opposite is to have the same effect will only be believed by somebody who did not follow the explanation. Yet it is absolutely understandable that the Van der Waals force has to be stronger in metals than in the light elements. The magnitude of the attack of the universal pressure depends on the energy density it will find. For that reason, it affects high-energy metal atoms stronger than light elements (not least for that reason that these atoms are heavier than one low in energy; we will discuss the exact connections later). The found equality (or difference) of forces determines consistency, tenacity, and stability of the corresponding metal. When we shift the equilibrium in favour of the universal pressure the pressure will squeeze the atoms even closer together (we can achieve this for example by abstracting heat.)

As we will see in the chapter "Inertia" the T.A.O. matrix also fastens the atoms which refuse to comply with any modification because of that – which, as a surprise, causes the inertia in connection with the velocity of light. The interaction of individual pressure and universal pressure in atomic bonds is not a clearly obvious matter anymore. When we provide the atoms with energy, they will win over the environmental pressure, the metal gets softer - but the universal pressure (and this means the one from the universe) will triumph nevertheless: it finds a greater surface of application because of the expansion of the red-hot metal and makes it heavier. The triumph is short-lived because when the metal is completely liquid it gets a little lighter again. And when it takes on gaseous form the universal pressure has not much say anymore; as individual fields, small and lithe, even metal atoms fly through the big "fan wheel" cosmos without any effort. This freedom stems from their motion as we will completely understand when we treat inertia as an aspect of T.A.O. But usually the atoms of a metal, although vibrating or oscillating, lie next to or on top of each other in precise order (figures 70 and 70a).

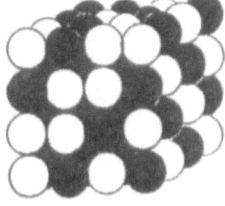
Fig. 70

Fig. 70a: Silicon atoms

In the same way as metals, crystals, and molecules are held together by the universal pressure at long last, accumulations of matter are kept together, which form whole celestial bodies. Matter is therefore in fact of atomic nature since it is composed of subordinate units but it is still an inseparable ensemble. Every atom would have to decay into radiation immediately if it was not kept within its boundaries by other atoms.

Causalities arise as a result of the game of the polarisations from which we derive the "laws of nature". We should not misunderstand these regularities. There aren't any laws of nature. Mankind created this kind of laws by combining observational quantities in the attempt to manifest a reality as independent of conceptions of the world and clichés of thinking as possible. Even the principle of T.A.O. tries to introduce a reality according to the laws of nature. Just like potentials, electrons, particles, and quarks, it cannot be observed directly but should be suitable on a deeper scale to find the most fundamental of realities which we can get hold of. The apparent regularities of material processes in T.A.O. are conditional on space and time and run off casually and inevitably because all sorts of atoms contain the programmes of their behaviour– exactly in the simple meaning that a ball contains the programme for rolling in contrast to a cube – and the cube contains one for stability…

We already know some results of these programmes very well: the common table salt and the water. Where these programmes can lead to on the atomic shells is what we want to show simply by experimenting a little with the molecules. Let's throw a little salt into water! What happens? Sodium is a left-hand oscillator - as we already determined - chlorine oscillates to the right. For these processes, the physicist knows the names cation and anion. In accordance with their programmes (valences) the atoms now begin to react to each other: the sodium atoms come immediately under siege from the oxygen atoms of the water, the chlorine atoms from the hydrogen atoms. As a result the water molecules come into conflict with each other since the hydrogen atoms don't want to have anything to do with one another. They repel each other and tear chlorine and sodium apart (figure 71).

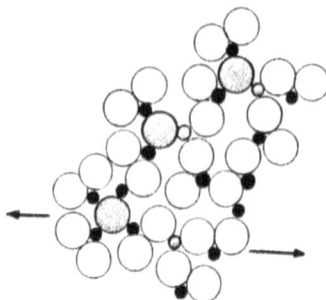

Fig. 71

We say: the salt dissolves. All chlorine atoms are now surrounded by hydrogen, all sodium atoms are enclosed by oxygen...

Analogous to our example with the common table salt, all salts consist of cations and anions and in each case their solution proceeds in the same way. It takes place completely automatically through the programmes of the shells, due to their aversions and affinities which prevent or permit bonds.

Water molecules alone have already enough to do with maintaining their joint fields and clusters, they are neutral to the outside and therefore don't conduct any current. With the dissolved ions the matter is totally different. Deprived of their original togetherness their longing for left-hand or right-hand polarisation remains.

When we are passing a current through the solution by immerging one metal bar which is oscillating to the left-hand and one which is oscillating to the right-hand into the water, the game of attraction and repulsion begins immediately according to our system of encounters. The chlorine atoms are heading to the one bar, the sodium atoms to the other. And now they take their revenge on the water molecules, so to speak, by tearing them apart. Chlorine carries away hydrogen, sodium does the same in the opposite direction with oxygen. We can establish that the water disintegrates into its components. Sodium delivers the hydrogen atoms to one bar, chlorine supplies the other one with oxygen atoms, at the same time they take along their polarisations - which means for both bars the same as if their own polarisations had moved through the water and closed an energy circuit.

Consequently, the liquid has become conductive and such a conductive liquid is called electrolyte. When we use copper salts (or any other metallic salts) for transportation, the copper atoms are deposited on the cathode which we can copperplate in this way. When we take caustic potash solution (KOH) as an electrolyte, the transporting potassium moves lively to and for, settles down for only a short time and does not enter into a bond - but is reprogrammed again and again into left-handed by the cathode and into right-handed by the anode.

These processes of the electrolyse are to illustrate how atoms or molecules are forced into very particular behaviours and specific directions of motion. Even the processes in living organisms often resemble these electrolytic processes. There, the molecules also apparently decide in favour of the places where they have to go - but in truth they don't have any free choice at all.

Every time when electrical processes are responsible for motion and destination of the molecules we speak of electrophoresis.[21] This process is in fact used especially in laboratories for separating compounds but we will also discover it in living cells. It is a big director in the drama of matter and life in which it doesn't matter if we are talking about organic or inorganic molecules. They all follow their programmes, which they carry in their interference patterns in the same way, and they are irreversibly forced to respond to the oscillations of the environment, the polarisations of the space, and to act accordingly ...

Now we can already create a current conduction in a very simple way by immersing a left-hand oscillator and a right-hand oscillator into a solvent. After all we can divide all elements, especially the metals, into left-hand and right-hand oscillators from the start because that's what they really are.

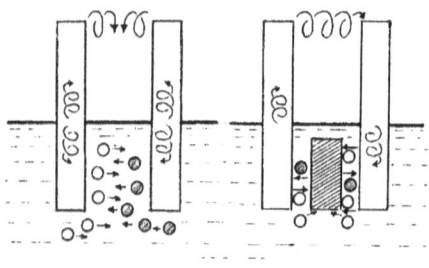

Fig. 72

Let's take a look at figure 72, on the left-hand side: in an aggressive solvent (an acid) metal atoms which carry the same information as the metal bar are detached. However, this also changes the equilibrium within the metal bar (it certainly did not lose any atoms at its dry end), and immediately a potential is building up between its ends. The ability of the solvent to do this, together with the properties of the metal is called solution pressure. It is characteristic for every metal in so far as it always evokes the same left-hand or right-hand oscillations. We can therefore determine the polarisation tendency of the corresponding metal by means of the solution pressure.

The physicist records all these unequivocal properties in an electromotive series in which the terms left-hand and right-hand are of course replaced by the illogical designations positive and negative.

The dissolved metal atoms of our experiment immediately set off to the metal bar which oscillates in the opposite direction. With that they transmit the oscillations of the metal bar through the solution and a utilizable potential is produced at the metal ends of the bar as we know it from the flashlight battery. Elements which can be used in such a way are called galvanic cells. In this process, every galvanic cell supplies currents of specific power, some of them more, some of them less. Therefore there are great differences of potential between these galvanic elements from the beginning which lead to an energy flux if we find ways and means to make compensations for them. And these ways and means are legion.

On this occasion, however, it can be possible that both elements are right-hand or left-hand oscillators and therefore wouldn't normally be suitable for each other. This obstacle can be avoided by inserting a third element which oscillates in the opposite direction. An oscillation bridge is created and it causes immediately a current conduction between the metals which again only results from the attempt to find an equilibrium with each other. This trick is for instance used in our nickel cadmium batteries. Of course, the linking element can also be the acid itself which contains opposing ions. But this trick has still another application: the enzymes of our body make use of it by employing co-enzymes as pole converters. In that way, they come together with molecules which would otherwise be averse to any linkage. Usually the body cannot produce these co-enzymes - swimming mediators in the solution of cell protoplasm – on its own. We take them in with our food, and they are nothing else but vitamins. Not all vitamins without exception have a function as co-enzyme but most of them do.

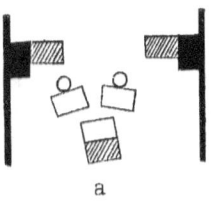

H_2 ▢
SO_4 ▰
Pb ▮
O ◯

a

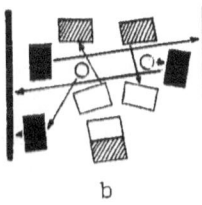

b

Therefore all atoms already know - as we tried to demonstrate - regulation and compulsion. A determining energy flux governs them; they release energy or conserve it. Of course, this makes the creative activity of matter a bit hard to grasp and confusing at first glance. Everything is in motion - although not indiscriminately but according to programmes which proceed with the actions in like manner just as they are created.

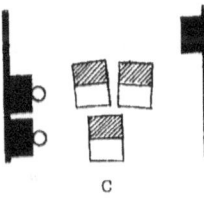

c

In order to understand this game - how matter handles energy, stores it, and releases it again - even better we will take a look at the accumulator of our car (figure 73; a to d):

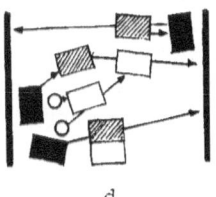

d

In order to store electric energy we choose an inert metal which will not be corroded too quickly by the sulphuric acid.

Lead is quite suitable but in principle we could use other metals as well. We just put two lead plates into a container. Then we add diluted sulphuric acid and the accumulator is ready. The acid is gnawing at the lead so to speak and lead sulphate ($PbSO_4$) is deposited on the plates.

Now we make current flow through the plates, i.e. we make them oscillate in opposite directions. The detached lead atoms adopt this programme (figure 73, b) and head for the plate oscillating in the corresponding opposite direction. The left-hand oscillators snatch the oxygen atoms oscillating to the right-hand and transport them to the plate oscillating to the right where plumbic oxide (PbO_2) is depositing. The isolated hydrogen molecules seize the SO_4 groups which have been left from the lead sulphate when the lead went on its journey. And what is brewing here, is pure sulphuric acid, H_2SO_4.

Suddenly we have more sulphuric acid than before whereas the water has vanished for the most part. One plate carries oxygen atoms, the other doesn't. The oxygen atoms programme the lead to "right-hand", the naked lead plate still polarises to the "left-hand" (figure c). The higher concentration of the sulphuric acid indicates the stored energy. The accumulator is charged...

There is a voltage between the plates because the plates continue to oscillate in opposite directions (oxygen - right-handedly, lead - left-handedly). When we bridge the plates with a conductor we create a current conduction by means of vibrational harmony which does not remain without consequences: the sulphuric acid is torn apart and immediately forms an alliance with the lead again whereas their abandoned hydrogen molecules are seized by the oxygen which detaches from the right-hand electrode again because the voltage is equalised (figure d).

While the accumulator throws up current, water and lead sulphate are produced in it again. When all the lead dioxide has been used up the accumulator is discharged and presents the same sight as in the beginning (figure a). In our example of the accumulator it is essential that all reactions which went off were determined by the oscillational behaviour of the atoms involved. The polarising conditions of encounter are responsible for determining the directions and destinations of atoms and molecules.

In a simple way the events in the accumulator reveal how atoms apparently seem to know what they have to do, and with that they are demonstrating how they transport energy and even store it for later by means of their completely forced action.

We were dealing with the accumulator in order to make it easier to understand later-on how and why molecules react with each other in the living cell and how and why they manipulate with energy. Although these processes take place far more multifariously and more complicated than illustrated, the causes are basically the same as those in the accumulator: atomic programmes and impulse sequences of the electric current...

Well, if we are very bright guys we will prepare our accumulator in such a way that it is in a charged condition from the outset. We will cover half of the plates with lead dioxide from the outset. When we pour highly concentrated sulphuric acid into this accumulator we promptly get an already charged battery which supplies us with current although it has never been charged. From the ratio of sulphuric acid to water we can see at any time how much energy is still contained in the arrangement.

Oxygen serves for producing a surplus abundance of oscillations and an opposite polarisation in the nickel cadmium battery as well. The electrolyte used is caustic potash solution which - as we already mentioned - does not change. In charged condition the electrodes consist of nickel(III) oxide and cadmium. When current is supplied, cadmium is converted into cadmium oxide and nickel(III) oxide into nickel(II) oxide. During the charging process these chemical reactions go off in the opposite directions. The oscillations in the electrolyte are transmitted by the OH molecules of the caustic potash solution which develop at the anode and return from the cathode to the anode as H_2O. Here, too, all oscillations match each other exactly in their spatial orientation causing attraction and repulsion, combination and separation. We find this simple principle in chemical processes again and again and, as we will see, it culminates finally in the probably most interesting manifestation of matter: life...

But before we give our attention to matter in more detail we should fathom out which modes of behaviour are going on between such big fields as celestial bodies and which explanations science has found for them.

14 Inertia

What we know so far is fundamental for understanding this chapter: the matrix of T.A.O. is absolute and immobile. It transmits impulses through vibration or fluctuation of its units ("granules"). It can be concluded only from the absoluteness of the matrix that these impulses stay together (!) and transmit information (energy, light, force, etc.); one of many manifestations of these impulses is the EM wave, another manifestation (coming into existence secondarily) is the "polarised space" as electric and magnetic field. In principle, these polarisations accompany all electromagnetic phenomena. The material manifestation of the impulses is the atomic field, an area of rotating impulses, point of origin of a field in which electric and magnetic field are latently contained, a field which is essentially unlimited and adopts its material dimension only through resistance towards other fields and whose unpolarised ("straight, neutral") shoves, however, form the field of repulsion ("neutrinos, gravitons") which is in penetration and in touch with other (in principle with all) fields of repulsion of the universe.

An atom moving within T.A.O. makes use of the matrix, i.e. its impulses propagate within the matrix in the same way as an EM wave. In other words: the atom transmits itself, it induces itself and thus pulsates through the matrix - it does not move like a compact object (because this would not work at all: how should freely oscillating impulses stay together and how should the atom move without the impulse-maintaining and field-stabilising structure of the matrix?). For that reason, there isn't any "real" or direct material movement[2] of atoms or atomic conglomerates within the matrix - and thus within the universe.

This way of looking at things is absolutely astonishing, and we will see what a far-reaching effect it will have. In view of such a multitude of movements within our world our imagination refuses to accept the image that bodies are oscillating through space in a somehow shadowy way - but we already know enough about this "nothingness" of energy, space, and time which we call "mass" to admit such an image – because even according to conventional theories matter consists almost only of gaps! But atoms cannot just simply "shift" their oscillational image autonomously - but they have to direct these vibrations through the matrix. This is absolutely plausible and logical. We are as little aware of it as of the oscillating atomic fields themselves - because our perception takes place on a scale high above it - but we will be talking about that later-on.

Now let's imagine a three-dimensional picture of such a field of repulsion: the field around a body consists of the same impulses which also form the magnetic field - but they are not polarised. The particle physicist would fantasise about neutrinos which were spherically flowing away from the body - and that wouldn't be so far off the truth at all. And one could even postulate gravitons, with the difference that they don't convey an attractive force but a repulsive one. After all, the oscillations which have a repulsive effect within T.A.O. constitute the field. Just think of the streams of particles and the solar winds flowing away from our central star. Now let's picture this in a more refined, more delicate, more "transparent" way and we will have a much clearer impression of the situation.

The field develops from the continuation of the atomic impulse fields; the energies and dimensions are extremely small and cannot be measured - but exactly this is the reason why they penetrate other fields without any effort- we know after all that gravitational fields, just like magnetic fields, can scarcely be shielded - and therefore we also know that magnetic fields have to be a manifestation of the gravitational field. Inside the universe a total field consists therefore of the sum of all the repulsion from the surrounding "masses" - this results in a certain state of tension (pressure is not the correct word) which disperses the bodies (expansion of space!). In order to surround a body which is getting into this field of tension, with a gravitational field nothing has to happen in particular because the repulsive pressure of the universe streaming in from all around partially penetrates the body and re-emerges weakened on the other side - there it sums up with the individual pressure of the body and is directed against itself. But let's take a look at it on the graph.

As simple as the whole matter is, it is no very easy to depict it graphically... Concerning the two attempts at a graph (fig. 73 a and b): The vectors streaming in from the cosmos are weakened when they re-emerge from the body, they also symbolise the individual pressure of the body which is, however, very low. The body brought into the field of the universal pressure "shadows" the field so to speak and is partially penetrated - therefore it seems obvious to attribute the effect of gravitation not to the mass but to the density of the body. Actually these are the facts which really apply. Here is a corresponding thought experiment:

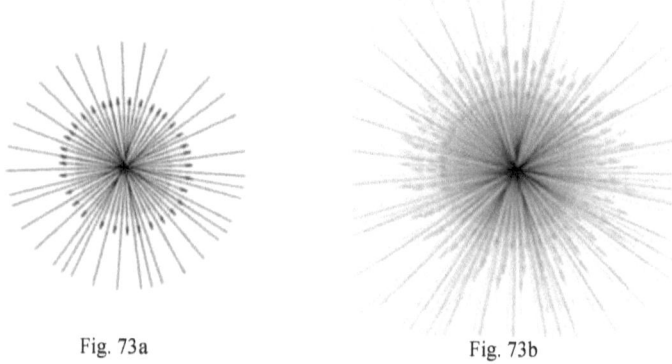

Fig. 73a   Fig. 73b

If we drilled a hole straight through the globe and threw a stone through it, it would take the stone 42 minutes to cross the globe and then it would return in pendulum fashion. It would take the stone the same time to cover the distance there and back as for orbiting the earth in a narrow circle once - about 84 minutes. If we did the same in the asteroid belt with a fist-sized asteroid and a grain of sand, we would obtain the same result provided that the asteroid would have the same density (!) as the Earth's globe (5.5 g/cm^3)! This proves that it is the density of the body and not its mass as such which plays a role in gravitation and in the acceleration of free fall.

And with these preparatory considerations we will take a closer look at the whole matter: Galileo discovered that a uniform motion in a straight line does not require a cause but "continues out of itself". He postulated: a body left to its own devices moves in a straight-lined and uniform manner. This theorem is called Galilean Principle of Inertia. We read in many books on physics that this profound insight was the beginning of modern exact natural science. This is a strange claim because Galileo's observation does not explain anything but describes only an effect which everybody can observe.

If we ignore that straight-lined is a very relative concept because we know that already the structure of space can curve, Galileo's consideration is without any doubt true. But which cause is behind this principle of inertia?

Every body shows a certain ability of offering resistance to an acceleration. Newton expressed the extent of this ability by means of the inert mass. This fiction was just as magnificent as it was teleological[22] because in principle it does not explain anything, either!

The physicists Mach and Hoyle and even Einstein had the vague idea that the cause of inertia had to be found outside of the corresponding body somehow. In fact, it looked as though something was offering resistance to the motion of a body - as though the body was moving within a medium. This is partially true for that reason that the matrix of T.A.O. is formed by and pulsed through by the surrounding mass fields. But the inertia doesn't have its cause only outside of the body!

Our figure 15 shows already very clearly how the field of a body exerts an individual pressure directed against the environmental pressure of other fields (universal pressure). All protons or atoms as individual fields sum up this one body to a total field which resembles the individual fields in its effect and represents just a bigger, practically infinitely expanding field (figure 74a).

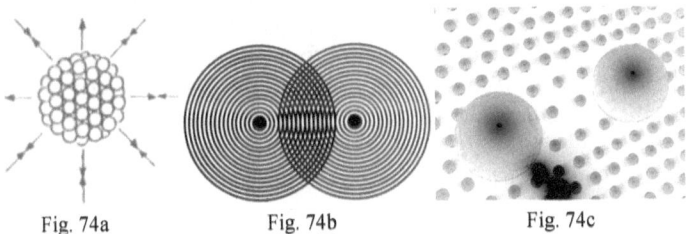

Fig. 74a   Fig. 74b   Fig. 74c

Figure 74b is to make clear how the fields penetrate each other as far as their motional state allows. Repulsion develops as if one squeezes rubber balls into one another. This repulsion has directions, it is directed against the antagonising fields – and this is the difference between the repulsion principle and the previously known pressure-gravitation theories. This difference is important because all the previous theories proceeded from the assumption of a pressure stemming from some invented particles (gravitons) (fig. 74c) which hover between the bodies. This entails the problem that this pressure is constant and that the particles between the bodies have to disappear somehow in order to offer those outside the possibility to press the bodies towards each other. There are some bizarre explanations for it, like streams of particles and absorption theories, which we don't have to deal with because they are illogical and couldn't even explain why there is something like a "centre of gravity".

Instead we will deal with a "flawless" field theory. The boundaries of matter are not where we perceive or see them. Every object that we touch has been in contact with us - with our field - long since. All matter - even celestial bodies - practically penetrates each other with its expansive fields. The difference between the object and the empty space is defined by very specific energy values. Our finger becomes a finger and the object it touches becomes an object in the very place where the two fields offer each other sufficient resistance. Our senses prepared themselves to put a boundary in this place so to say. Yet, the fields reach far beyond these boundaries and indirectly they can even be made visible by some kind of high-frequency photography. We know this phenomenon from books about parapsychology - but it is an absolutely normal process. In the same way as we can render the ultrasonic screams of a bat audible by creating differential tones in our frequency range of hearing by superimposing other ultrasonic frequencies (this also works excellently with dolphins), we can, at least partially, relativise the visibility boundaries of a field by bringing them into the range of visibility by means of superimposing a high-frequency electric field. This method is called electrography or Kirlian photography[23]. Bodies particularly rich in energy, like organisms or the poles of a battery, show a very distinctive, clearly visible field which certainly also reveals every energetic change in the body. A leaf portrayed with this method shows how its field is streaming off boundlessly into the environment (figure 75).

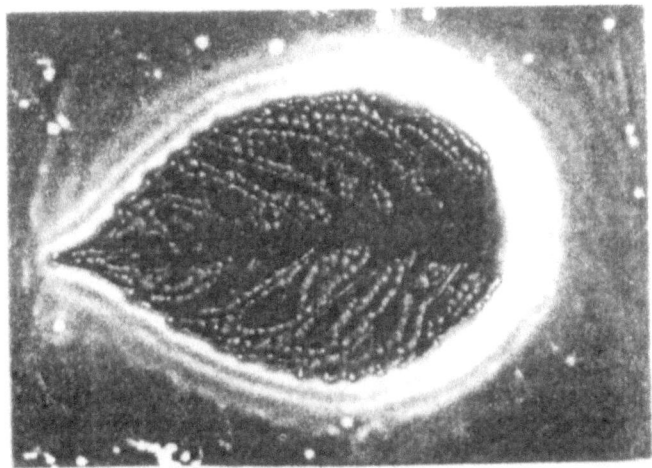

Fig. 75

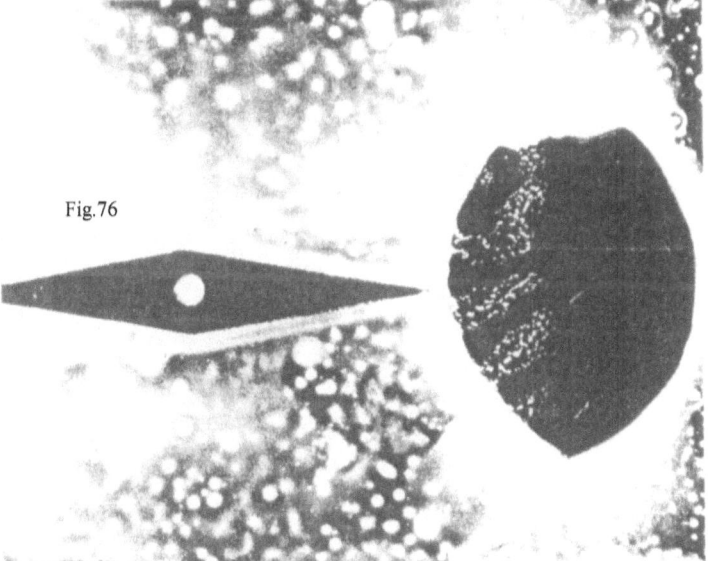

Fig.76

The field of a compass needle touches the field of a leaf before the visible boundaries come in contact with each other (figure 76). Individual fields sum up to a total field like the three leaves in figure 77 demonstrate.

Fig. 77

A horseshoe magnet shows the polarised space by which it is surrounded in a particularly impressively manner (figure 78).

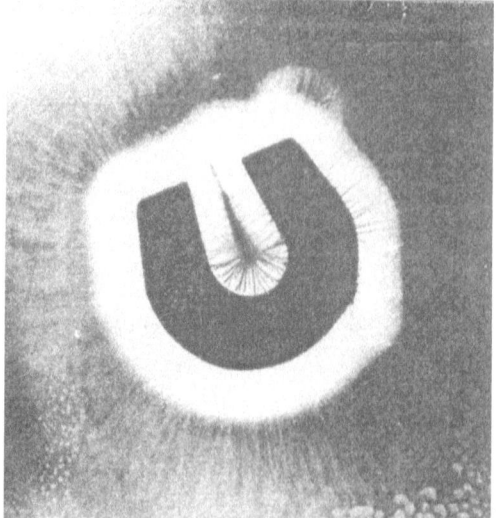

Fig. 78

The field differs succinctly from the fields of organic structures - we literally see that it has to be stronger and more orderly.

In principle every atom, every object, every body, and every star has this field around it. It is just the continuation of its Self beyond the range of the physiologically visible and has nothing to do with such mysterious concepts as Aura or Od. These names – which have been used for the detected fields of force of matter by parapsychologists for a long time - have dubious overtones because the scientists have persistently refused to examine and interpret these phenomena. Little wonder because their theories did neither predict them nor did they allow for an explanation.

If we remember our fan wheel we understand immediately that mass is equivalent to the energy content (the motional state) of a field. According to Newton, mass is defined by the inertia of a body. The following tempting thought would appear to be the right thing: this inertia is nothing else but the resistance which the adversaries universal pressure and individual pressure (or rather the reduced universal pressure passing through) find with each other.

In a motionless state, every body is in equilibrium with the universal pressure. Well, let's just push it out of this equilibrium (figure 79).

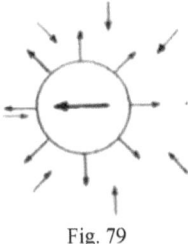

Fig. 79

We could simply say that the resistance increases in the direction of the motion. We would have to exert a force to move the body out of its resting position against this resistance. Opposite to the motional direction, however - i.e. "behind" the body – the resistance is reduced because a "hole", a reduction of the pressure, arises in the universal pressure so to speak. Metaphorically speaking: in front of the body something could "accumulate", behind it something could thin. What could that be? The matrix of T.A.O.? But it does not move. It cannot be squeezed together or thinned! Therefore our explanation is obviously wrong. And now we know why Mach, Hoyle, and Einstein did not pursue the thought of a surrounding gravitational cause any further (which was an omission but the medium, "ether", which was up for discussion at that time did not support this idea).

When we apply a force upon a body, for example by pushing it with one hand, it means that the fields of our hand meets with resistance at the fields of the body - and that the impulses of the atoms at the boundary of the body are influenced by it first. They retreat. And we know of course that the body does not move compactly but that its individual atoms propagate through the matrix... The atoms pass on the modifications to the impulses - thus the body moves at "intervals", i.e. it propagates... And this explains some very essential things: firstly: the exerted force propagates through the body - it does not act instantaneously onto the body. One atom shoves the other... and that means also that the body does not move at all on both ends at the same time - because the force is passed on with a finite velocity: we know this velocity already: it is the velocity of light! Secondly: all atoms of this body are (roughly speaking) gyroscopes after all - with rotation or spin. Therefore they cannot be shoved into new impulse sequences and impulse spaces just like that but they put up resistance. They will do it as long as we apply the force - i.e. accelerate. And that is already the solution to the mystery of inertia! Thirdly: when the body does not move compactly at all and a force marches from one end to the other (in direction of the movement) and presses against one impulse field after the other, the body gets a little bit shorter in the direction of the movement. The physicist Lorentz would be glad now because that is exactly what he had suspected after all (and Einstein would also smile a little but we are going to cure him of it)! But that's for later to be seen. When we don't exert any more force the atoms don't change any further, either. They go on drawing their circles... and nothing else happens ... Once levelled out, the body just continues to propagate... It is not only about the atoms being something like gyroscopes (which they are really not) but also about every change of direction costing the impulse some energy... and about the direction of the impulse paths within the matrix being changed when we set a body in motion. He who thinks of the Lorentz force already mentioned in the chapter "Games" is not so wrong!

With the knowledge of the internal relationships we can describe the events a bit more superficially again. The resistance created by inertia retroacts like a resilient medium. We had to exert a force in a certain direction and with that we enriched the field of the body by the contributed amount of energy. This energy is now contained in the body - and we call it kinetic energy. Exerting a force on a body is in addition a symmetrical process (as we will see more clearly with gravitation). It is not one field touching the other but it's always two fields touching one another! That means the exerted force is always perceptible for both sides. This is nothing else but Newton's third law of motion which says: principle of action and reaction - every body on which a force is exerted experiences a force of the same magnitude in the opposite direction... The sum of these forces is always zero. This demonstrates immediately that there is just no difference between motion and rest. So to speak, rest is motion compensated by a counter motion of the same magnitude.

Fig. 80

When Galileo made his discoveries he did not know, though, why things were as they were. Due to our way of looking at things we can comprehend Newton's principles without any contradiction. The principle of inertia (a body free of force is moving in a straight-lined uniform way), principle of action (when a force acts upon a body it will accelerate it), and principle of reaction - all of them logical and simple processes within the matrix of T.A.O.

Concerning the principle of action it has to be emphasised again that, just like the EM wave, the propagation of the atomic fields within T.A.O. has a finite velocity because of the stipulated structure, the velocity of light. Even the acting force is spreading at the velocity of light within the moved field. Therefore we could never accelerate a body beyond this velocity! Moreover, we will come across the velocity of light again in a surprising way when dealing with gravitation in the chapter "Gravity".

One of Einstein's postulates seems to come true. But he approached this circumstance from another point of view, and we are yet to see how this leads to absurd results in the final consequence: when a body cannot be accelerated anymore it behaves as if it had an insurmountable and thus infinitely high inertia. However, mass is defined by this inertia, and "gravitation" by mass. Since the mass appears to be infinitely great now as well, the gravitation would have to be infinitely strong and it would make the whole universe contract into itself immediately... But as we just realised there is no reason at all to draw such a conclusion. The body cannot be accelerated beyond the velocity of light, and otherwise nothing exciting happens.

But with that the velocity of light is in no way an absolute limiting velocity because we only have to accelerate two fields almost up to the velocity of light in opposite directions. Compared to the other one, every body will then have superluminal velocity. According to Einstein, this should never be possible, either. We will demonstrate later why this postulate occurred to him and why it has to be wrong.

The principle of action and reaction can also be reversed by saying: every body which exerts a certain force in a certain direction, is subjected to a force of the same magnitude in opposite direction.

In short, this is the recoil principle and it surely goes without saying. When we throw a stone by hand, everything we described is going to happen, not only to the stone but also to our hand. Yes, even our hand will become a little bit shorter. But luckily we do not feel it...

What happens to a field that is between (at least) two other fields (figure 81) will be explored in the next chapter...

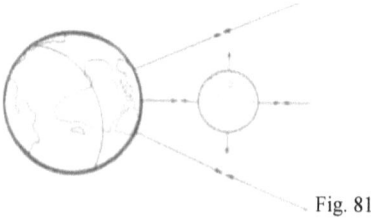

Fig. 81

15 Gravity

The gravitational force which two bodies seem to exert upon each other manifests in an accelerated motion towards one another. Galileo was the first to discover that in the gravitational field of the Earth all bodies fall at the same speed. This had to be a mystery considering the different weights of the bodies. Galileo's laws of falling bodies and Kepler's laws made Newton establish that the cause of the equal acceleration of all bodies was to be found in an attraction between the masses which makes both the apple fall from its tree and keeps the moon in its orbit around the Earth. He realised that the force between the falling mass m_1 and the mass of the Earth m_2 had to be proportional to m_1 (because of $F=ma$ it follows $F/m=a=const$) and that an equally strong opposite force was acting on mass m_2 and that therefore F had to be proportional to m_2 as well. Consequently this means for the dependence of the gravitational force on the two masses involved: F is proportional to m_1m_2. In other words: $F=ma$ expresses the inertia of the falling body, the mass results from inertia and exerts a force upon the mass of the Earth which is identical with the one that the mass of the Earth exerts on the falling body.

If ever a conclusion has been purposeful in science it was this one. For surely the Earth can never know what mass is just falling down on it and adjust its force to the inertia that is coming down. This automatic adjustment of forces is strange because gravitation is a symmetrical phenomenon which always only occurs between at least 2 masses in which case the masses are the cause of gravitation ("gravitational mass"), whereas one mass alone represents the inertia ("inertial mass") and these masses are obviously equivalent, i.e. have exactly the same properties. This means: one cannot find out if a force acting on a mass has been caused by the gravitational force or if it occurs as inertia in an accelerated frame of reference. This insight was therefore the starting point for a relativistic theory of gravitation: Einstein's General Theory of Relativity.

Einstein put an end to gravitation by - tersely said - "curving" the space, equating the gravitational mass with the inertial mass (i.e. adopting the principle of equivalence from Newton) and just letting it fall down the curved space – and in doing so, the concept of "mass" was somehow lost along the way. We already underlined that

Einstein discovered the "mirror image of reality" with that (because masses and attraction forces do not really exist after all). But before we deal with this mirror image (in the chapter about "Relativity") we will deal with reality.

When we take a look at figure 81 we should ask ourselves what applies more pressure (or maybe we should rather say thrust) on the moon (which is not true to position and scale here) – the Earth or the universe? Since the whole (!) universe is all around the Earth and the moon there is only one answer: without any doubt the pressure from the universe is considerably stronger. Since the weaker pressure from the Earth is acting against it the moon is not in equilibrium with its environment. But it is possible to immediately detect when the moon makes a movement in direction of the Earth, which the moon is certainly forced to do by the force of the universal pressure. Well, the universal pressure does not stop being an applied force, and therefore the moon receives an acceleration as defined by us in the chapter about "Inertia". In this example, it is the Earth's acceleration of free fall; as everybody knows, it is 9.81 m/s^2. (In the next chapter we will learn why the moon doesn't just fall down.)

The field of the falling body is only in equilibrium with the forces acting all around it and therefore weightless when it has this acceleration. When we (or the Earth's surface) disturb this equilibrium by preventing the compensation of movement, the force of the universal pressure results in a noticeable pressure between the surface of the Earth (or a pair of scales!) and the field. This pressure can be measured, its quantity is called weight. At the bottom of this casual mode of expression lies that complicated dynamic effect which we discovered in the inertia: the transmission of the thrust force of the Earth's field through the "falling" body at the velocity of light and the transmission of the thrust force of the universal pressure through the same body at the velocity of light from the other side! One can assume that the nature of the body does not play a significant role for this transmission of power and that it only determines the density, the impression of the mass, and the gravitational magnitude. We therefore require a factor for the ratio between the density (which can of course be just the same for a little stone as for a giant star!) and the gravitational magnitude which expresses this proportional ratio, i.e. a gravitational constant because without this constant the law of gravitation would be completely worthless!

And here is the next strange fact: that one was really looking for such a constant in view of the variety of masses in the universe and the variety of gravitational effects allegedly caused by them and - even stranger - really found one! Because according to Newton's law it is not possible at all to discover a constant in the range of the Earth which is to apply throughout the universe! Because his law only describes the relation of two masses with a god-given force (because it is not logically comprehensible). For that reason, the constant would have to be given by God as well and to be inherent to matter in the same mysterious way as gravitation itself. Can one measure such a thing?

One could. And one could do it only because the universe is really filled with a measurable force. It is the universal pressure! Cavendish measured the force of the universal pressure when he established the constant of gravitation. It was not the force of attraction between the masses of his gravitational or torsion balance. Let's go deeper into the matter (fig. 81a. Fig. 81b shows the original apparatus):

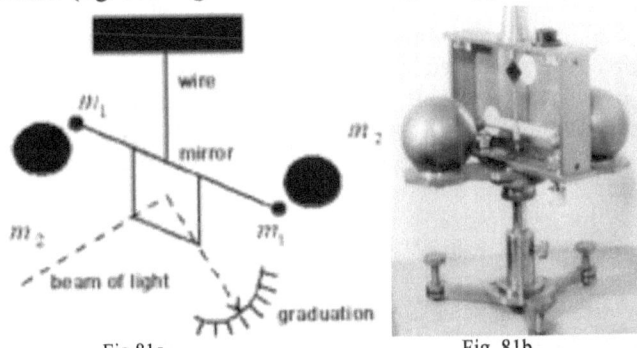

Fig.81a Fig. 81b

When the two bigger spheres are approached by the smaller spheres the latter are compressed by the universal pressure. The force applied to shove the smaller spheres leads to a twisting of the torsion wire until its resilience equals the thrust force. The torsion is shown on the graduation. Now the two bigger spheres are moved to the other side of the smaller spheres. In doing so the smaller spheres are shoved in the opposite direction. The constant of gravitation can now be calculated by means of the law of gravitation:

$$F = G \cdot \frac{m_1 \cdot m_2}{r^2}$$

There have been various modifications and improvements of the measuring methods. In principle, it is always the acceleration of two test masses which is measured in comparison to each other. This acceleration is nothing but the inertia being surmounted by the universal pressure, i.e. by means of the universal field which is composed of the tiniest shoves pulsating along at the velocity of light. And this field acts upon a body which allows being affected, invaded, or penetrated at the velocity of light at the most. If one tries to measure a proportional action factor in this event between two "inert masses", one will measure nothing else but the relation of these velocities to each other! When we take the reciprocal value of c, i.e. $1/c$, as quantity for the resistance against the force penetrating at c (= velocity of light), we obtain the factor for the inertia for one mass. As a result, the factor for the gravitational proportionality of two masses is therefore $2 \times 1/c = 2/c$. ($1/G$ would be the quantity for "rigidity" of space and time in the General Theory of Relativity). The gravitational force at the surface of a mass of 1 kg (density 1) is about $6.6713*10^{-9}$ N, i.e. twice the reciprocal value of velocity of light $6.6713*10^{-9}$ m/s. This numerically astonishing correspondence has already been noticed by some astronomers but they will probably take if for coincidence. It doesn't seem to be coincidence, though. But one should not take the figures too seriously either because the constant G is not precisely known (and presumably it is not even a constant at all), and although the constant c is known quite exactly – nobody has ever proved whether it is a constant (there aren't any "natural constants" after all).[24] The connection of c with gravitation, however, does not only become even clearer in the General Theory of Relativity but it actually takes on a fundamental significance. And before we jump right into the theory with our train of thought we will consider the background of Newtonian dynamics in a more superficial manner.

Every falling body regulates the power of application from the Earth's pressure and the universal pressure by means of its size (the size of the field of resistance). That means the universal pressure affects a small body with less force, and the Earth exerts a lower counter-pressure, too. A big body is affect with more force by the universal pressure - and the counterforce of the Earth is also stronger! Because of this automatic compensation all bodies fall certainly at the same speed! And we have to accept that heavy mass action seems to be indeed the same as accelerated inert mass action –

which is not surprising because the heavy mass action does not exist as the cause of gravitation at all. Thus there only exists some kind of "mass" - and it is only an effect and not a "primordial matter" of which matter could possibly consist. For that reason, Newton's "quantity of matter" strikes us as being so applicable because it could also be translated as "quantity of the event(s)"! And that is how it really is: we are not dealing with objects but with events.

The weight of a body reveals to what extent it looses the equilibrium with its environment. When the compensation of the counteracting Earth pressure is gone, the bodies previously falling at the same speed are suddenly of different weight, of course. Thus this gravity is defined immediately by the quantity of energy representing the field through its (lack of) motion. We call this quantity potential energy. It is absolutely identical with the kinetic energy and to be equated with it as we already discovered in our example of the fan wheel.

In fact, a moving body carries the exerted force that is moving it but it appears to be free from a force when the motion is uniform because the universal pressure acting against it compensates this force. When the motion and with it the compensation stops the force is released again and performs further work. Since the internal content of energy - as we noticed when we discussed the inertia - was really increased by modifications to the impulse which also increased the inertia by the amount of this force - which in turn increased the action of mass - the physicist can simply calculate the energy carried along by means of the mass of a field and its velocity. However, we have to keep to half the mass (1/G!), i.e. $kinE = 1/2 m*v^2$.

A body that hits the ground and burrows a big hole receives its energy for doing so directly from the cosmos. Once exerted, a force can be transmitted from body to body without loosing energy. This is known as the conservation of the impulse. And for that reason, we have called any disturbance of T.A.O. impulse from the beginning... And now the question is: Do really all bodies fall down to earth at the same speed without exception? The astonishing answer to this question is no! Because we must not fail to notice an important factor in the game of universal pressure and Earth pressure: the geometrical arrangement of the forces in relation to each other and the curving force resulting thereof! As we already know this force originates from the tendency of a body to resist deformation.

Something very similar applies to the inertia, too, if we remember our discovery that every body is fundamentally deformed by the exerted forces!

In a space with a given curvature, like the space around the Earth, the magnitude of the curving force results from the relation of two fields to one another. Well, we realised that the acceleration of free fall stems from the relation between Earth pressure and universal pressure. Actually a constant acceleration should only arise if these two opponents were of the same size in every place and all the time. But they are not.

Our figure 15 already illustrated the geometry of the distribution of pressure. The farther we get away from Earth, the weaker the universal pressure becomes oddly enough. Its field lines are getting thinner as it were (the reason for this is that the pressure streams in spherically). The closer we get to the Earth, the stronger the Earth's pressure becomes. The field is getting denser. Since the field of the falling body is situated between these forces, there are always a few more lines of force of the Earth pressure acting on the field than lines of force of the universal pressure. This would result in a constant slight surplus for the Earth pressure if the curving force did not intervene and compensate this difference. The curving force of a body falling to Earth, however, is conditional on its expansion. Generally speaking that is the reason why dense materials are actually always a little lighter than those which are loosely bonded (a fact which physicists have been unable to explain). And therefore bodies which are expanding are getting a little bit heavier! In a very big falling field the curving force becomes so strong that it will break the body before it falls down to Earth. The rings around the planets, of which we will speak later-on, are created in this manner. And a difference between vertical and horizontal masses is the result which has been unknown so far.

On the other hand, however, a very small field does not feel much of the curving force of the Earth. And now the Earth's pressure wins the game: the very small field will not fall down to Earth - and if it came into existence on the Earth's surface, the Earth would send it into the universe immediately!

Thus a field of this kind would have to be very small, and in addition it would not allow to be bound to other fields. There is only one such small, independent field on Earth: helium! And for the described reason helium is continuously disappearing from Earth without leaving a trace although it is produced in vast amounts by the radioactivity of the Earth's rocks. For the same causes, helium flows upwards on the wall of every containing vessel without bothering about gravitation. This "mysterious" state is called superfluid - and we see that this property is not so mysterious at all. Hydrogen is catapulted into space as well when it occurs separately in the upper layers of the atmosphere. But luckily hydrogen loves to bond and so quite a bit is preserved. Well, we should think of the pressure and the composition of the solar wind and of all those vast amounts of particles which are sent on a journey into infinity by the stars of this universe because they are small enough to escape from the lurking curving forces of the cosmos...

We are not yet finished with the subject of gravitation by a long shot. Many phenomena which have been regarded as mysteries of physics up to now can be unravelled by turning gravitation upside down. For example, it is absolutely impossible to explain by means of gravitation why celestial bodies or actually all masses are gravitating leisurely for infinitely long and why they are exerting attraction forces onto each other without receiving any energy from anywhere! Even Einstein's masses are quite occupied with the curvature of space - and nobody knows where they get the energy from in order to do so! These gravitational theories have a mystical component: no matter if they generate gravitation without supply and regeneration of energies or if they show other masses in Einstein's space-time which curved paths they have to fly on in order to age as strongly as possible (yes, we will not be spared to examine this one, too) by means of using energies of mysterious origin as well, basically they are just not logically comprehensible.

The repulsion principle does not allow for this dilemma in explanation. The displacement, the repulsion, or the pressure, they are achieved after all by the energy flux from one body to the other. We will come to see that this energy flux is the motor which actually keeps the whole universe going.

For today's physicists the phenomena of the inert and the gravitational mass remain an unsolved mystery. They fabricate a structure of the matter by means of "particles" which they created in the accelerator, and they explain the occurrence of forces by means of the interactions of these particles. The so-called standard model of this particle theory is an incomplete collection of hypotheses consisting of the quantum electrodynamics, the theory concerning electroweak processes, and the quantum chromodynamics. This model will never be completed for certain. Although it is possible by means of the standard model to reduce the far more than one hundred particles discovered to elementary ones with spin 1/2 (fermions) and to ones with spin 1 (bosons), which convey the forces between the fermions, but the successes of this standard model are rare and many fundamental questions remain unanswered.

Examinations of the particles with regard to their action of mass have produced confusing results. The various subatomic particles vary considerably with regard to their masses. While the photons, basis for the electromagnetic force, and the gluons, basis for the strong force, don't exhibit any mass, the Z and W particles weigh as much as 80 protons or one "atomic nucleus". The top quark is said to be even 350 000 times heavier than an electron. Why the mass of the particles differs so much cannot be explained according to the standard theory. And the existence of the mass naturally remains absolutely mysterious. According to the proven patterns, to blame every phenomenon on some particle or other, the Scotch physicist Peter Higgs invented a boson as a kind of saviour particle which is to grant the mass to other particles through interaction. The stronger the interaction the bigger the mass. The particle practically forms a field through which all other subatomic particles like electrons, gluons, or quarks have to pass. One has hoped to prove the Higgs boson at least indirectly if so much energy comes into effect by the collision of particles accelerated to extreme velocities that a new particle was created and its existence became "provable" on the basis of the combination of particles into which it decays. The search for this important particle, however, has been futile up to today.

Since one has not found any other convincing concept so far as to how mass is achieved, the idea of this Higgs field has remained attractive at least in theory up to today. The Higgs boson has therefore not only advanced to a kind of holy grail of the experimental particle physicists but it is also the last missing brick in the vault construction of the standard model. Without this upper last brick the whole edifice will collapse![25]

Already in the early eighties one believed to have sighted the Higgs boson in the spallation generator DESY in Hamburg. In 1990, it became evident that it had been clearly an error but researchers at one of the spallation generators in CERN "sighted" the "saviour particle" again ten years later. From thousands of "events" (traces of particle paths) they choose three which possibly maybe perhaps could be leniently interpreted as indications of the volatile particle if need be. Typically this "discovery" took place immediately prior to the planned closure of the accelerator - and this closure was cancelled off after the "discovery". But after several years of analysing the data it was final: there isn't any Higgs particle. The search for it was in vain, the masses of the particles have to be explained in another way. When the result of the analyses were published, the researchers who participated in the Higgs experiment admitted to having "corrected" the data of that time a little in order to prevent the closure of the accelerator.

Now it is claimed that the Higgs particle exists only at considerably higher energies which would make significantly more efficient accelerators necessary. This is based on a suspicious theory called "supersymmetry", which pleasantly enough predicts even several Higgs particles at the same time and this at fantastically high energies (which are no longer verifiable).

The theory of the Higgs field is - just like "quantum foam" and "vacuum fluctuation" - only one of the attempts of the physicists to re-introduce the concept of the ether by the backdoor because without the help of the ether the origin of the mass will remain unexplainable (and even with its help because there is no mass after all but only an effect of this kind). If the physicists continue their thoughts consistently they will inevitably end up where we already are, in the absolute matrix of T.A.O. and with the principle of displacement and repulsion - which will finally culminate in the fact that the cause of all natural events, which determine our reality, is to be found in that single force which would have been thought the least capable of it, "gravitation"!

How this force in the background directs the physical phenomena is to be illustrated in several examples. The pressure from the universe seems to shove everything mercilessly in front of it or together... That would have come to a bad end long since if there weren't little "tricks" to outwit the universal pressure and to partially overcome the repulsion. Plants were presumably the first one to use one of these tricks...

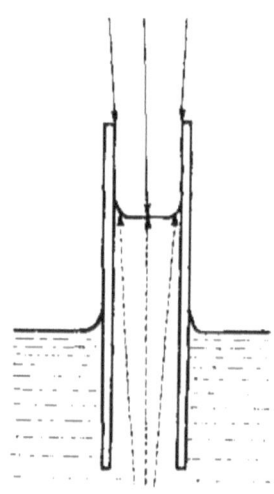

Fig.82

Fig.83

Physics as a pure science of descriptions has only the possibility to explain one mystery with another mystery. The whole physics practically consists of such philosophically worthless descriptions. For example, we were explained the capillary effect with other forces like cohesion and adhesion most of the time which are as mysterious as the capillary effect itself. One thing is for certain anyway - in a narrow tube with parallel walls liquids rise against the gravitation!

But we comprehend this effect immediately and quite casually when we take a closer look at the geometric proportions. Figure 82 depicts these proportions in a considerably exaggerated manner. We see that the parallel walls of the tube shield off the lines of force coming from the universal pressure which don't enter in parallel on any account. As a result the universal pressure opposing the Earth pressure is suddenly lower inside the tube than outside the tube; therefore the Earth pressure elevates the water until the equilibrium between Earth pressure and universal pressure has been restored again. The practically non-existing curving force favours this process further because the cross-section of the water column is small.

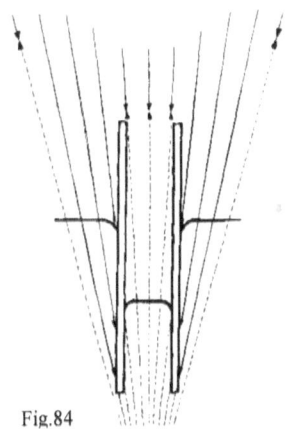
Fig.84

We already know that objects do not necessarily terminate where we perceive their boundaries. The fields around material bodies depend on the proton fields. It therefore suggests itself that mercury sets up a stronger, bigger field around itself than water. Of course, mercury is considerably richer in energy than water and we can easily prove the strong field of mercury by generating electromagnetic waves with it. For this purpose we only need to toss some mercury in a bowl. Because of this property we can say that the material limits (the limits of perception) of mercury are "lower" than those of water - as it is attempted to make clear in figure 83 (mercury on the left, water on the right). Because the field which is denser and richer in energy experiences the resistance from the universal pressure sooner! And now we are going to carry out the same capillary experiment with mercury whose liquid property we certainly don't doubt (figure 84). Again we exaggerated considerably but at least we will see that this time the field of mercury or rather the Earth pressure is shadowed by the walls of the tube because the field of mercury reaches far beyond the visible surface. This leads to a victory of the universal pressure and a capillary depression is the result.

Of course, we simplified these two examples considerably, yes, even illustrated them in a rather primitive way[26]. But it is to give us at least a little impression of how the complicated game of individual pressure and universal pressure can lend different tensions to the surfaces of liquids. The processes in the atomic impulse fields are exactly the same as those which we discussed for inertia - and we realise that surprisingly the universal pressure is also behind the capillary effect because the atomic impulses are specifically influenced by the game of shadowing and impacting the repulsion. The classical explanation of the capillary effect postulates that liquids "make every effort" to form a surface which is as small as possible - the effect is thus explained with an inner cause. Why should a liquid "make any effort"? This apparent endeavour comes from outside, from the dynamic effects of the universal pressure which shapes everything into spheres. One has to think a little about why the capillary effect is able to work in every situation, even in a vacuum or in the universe. Yet the repulsion principle does not only take place between celestial bodies but has its effects in the microcosm as well. Although it is simple in principle, the connections in this area are quantitatively an enigma. The material of which the tube is made plays also a role. If it is composed of water-repellent molecules (or if we use a non-wetting liquid), the repulsion of these molecules is already so strong that there will be no capillary ascent.

We could certainly go deeper into the topic but now we know at least where the force which makes water rise into the highest crowns of the trees really comes from – although the processes of electrophoresis and osmosis also play a role in it...

The mathematically interesting difference between our "Newton reversed theory" and Newton's own is (apart from the reversion of the basic principle) the inclusion of the curving force which implies a difference between horizontal and vertical masses, a difference which can even be calculated - with a little difficulty - from Einstein's General Theory of Relativity. Understandably, this difference was not yet spotted by Newton. Since one already starts calculating with a modified theory of Newton (M.O.N.D.) anyway, the inclusion of the curving force will considerably improve the mathematical handling of astronomic gravitation phenomena.

Again we have to invite our readers to go on a voyage of discovery through their old school books in order to realise how easily they will now understand many of the mnemonic sentences they once learned by heart. And just those phenomena of physics which have remained mysterious so far can be substantiated and explained in a particularly easy way with our viewpoint.

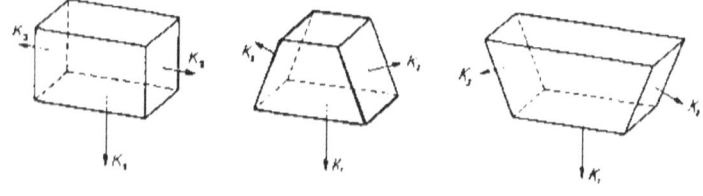

Fig. 85

Another example (figure 85). The picture illustrates the so-called hydrostatic paradox (also known as Pascal's experiment). A liquid filled into a vessel with a basis F weighs heavily on the bottom of this vessel. It generates a pressure K1 onto the bottom. Oddly enough this gravitational pressure is independent of the shape of the vessel. Provided that the size of the bottom and the height of the liquid correspond, the same pressure acts on all parts on the bottoms - the lateral forces K2 and K3, on the other hand, are different.

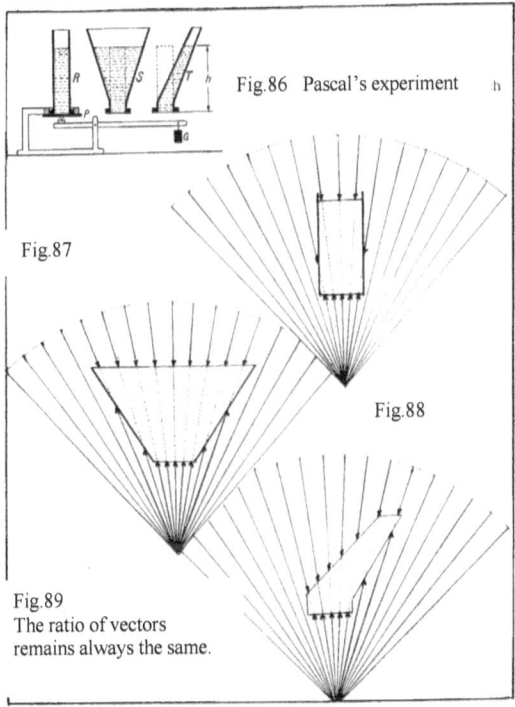

Fig.86 Pascal's experiment

Fig.87

Fig.88

Fig.89
The ratio of vectors remains always the same.

So this must strike us as a paradox because the amounts of the liquid and thus their weight must be different from vessel to vessel. The mystery cannot be solved easily by means of the usual gravitational theory alone. Again the physicist reaches for new forces, in this case it is the upward pressure within liquids, without being able to explain exactly where this upward pressure is coming from. We, on the other hand, know immediately that a compensatory effect has to take place, very similar to the one for the free fall. When we draw the lines of force of universal pressure and Earth pressure in their spherical connection to each other and hold the vessel between these lines we can see that there will always be a certain relation between Earth pressure and universal pressure and that this relation will never change regardless of the shape of the vessel (figures 86 to 89). It is just a small step from this fact to the principle of Archimedes but maybe the reader wants to puzzle over that a little by himself...

What we wanted to demonstrate was this fundamental simplicity which the repulsion principle lends to all material processes of this world. Magnetic poles, electrostatics and electrodynamics, electrolysis, gravitation, and capillary effect, there is nothing mysterious about them. All these observable facts and all the many phenomena which we are unable to treat here due to lack of space simply exist because the universe exists and "is under pressure".

Material events or laws of nature do not constitute the cosmos autonomously and they don't cause it. Exactly the opposite is the case: the natural phenomena are the eternal game within a universal field of force whose fundamental simplicity (T.A.O.) just admits certain possibilities and rules others out. The only force which can be derived from the universe itself shapes and moulds the structures, impulses, proportions, and masses of our reality.

Time, space, and energy are already perceptions of our consciousness, the first, the only, and the last fundamental concepts within our attempt to understand this world by virtue of our mental activity. We cannot find more because there is not any more to find!

16 Celestial Bodies

In the previous chapters we already understood inertia as a resistance, which the impulses of a body composed of spherical fields put up against the applied force and against the alteration of their paths within the T.A.O. matrix. Of course, the body does not "move" like a compact object but the exerted force propagates from atom to atom and the impulses just shift their vibrations correspondingly in that direction into which the force is pointing. This relocation of the impulses stores the new situation away so to speak - and that is a movement in the sense of Newton's first law of motion. We could say in short: the motional state of a body results from the internal relative movements of its impulses to the T.A.O. matrix - through which one is able to (or has to!) "climb" or "swing through" in just any desired direction. Since every force acting on the body hurries through it at the velocity of light at the most, its rigidity corresponds to the reciprocal value of c (1/c) - and since this also concerns the second body exerting a force, the proportion of the inertia of two bodies compared to one another results from the reciprocal value 2/c because the resulting gravitational constant is not the magnitude of "attraction " of the two bodies but the magnitude of the inertia which the bodies put up against each other when the universal pressure is squeezing them together.

Fig. 89a   Fig. 89b

This inertia is of course proportional to the content of the impulses of the bodies, i.e. its "amount of atoms" and the "kind of atoms" determine its resistance - from the force which overcomes this we calculate the "mass" - and from the mass the force. And we know that basically neither of the two exists. After all there are only the impulses... And what is happening through them is just the sum of all impulses involved - we are thus not dealing with forces at all but only with impulses. For that reason, the physicist does not speak of conserving the force but of conserving the impulse. This is demonstrated in the best fashion by the spheres transmitting an impulse (fig. 89a).

We all know these impulse spheres; the most astonishing with them is the fact that the number of spheres swaying away always corresponds exactly to the number of spheres that were shoved. The process, however, is easy to comprehend if one realises that a quantity of impulses ("mass") which is supplied at one end of the device has to get out again at the other end after it has "pulsed" through the spheres. Two spheres correspond to a certain field size which is transmitted through the atoms - and this certain field size just corresponds to two spheres again at the other end. Amazing that such a dynamic process requires the absolute matrix of T.A.O. as prerequisite - but without this matrix the spheres would not exist - and their motions least of all.

Well, a billiard ball does not just roll along either but its internal vibrational image only corresponds to this motion[2]. It is transmitted through the matrix and it transfers its impulses to the "next" billiard ball. And when we make it only rotate, again we see nothing but the process which we found with the straight-lined movement - its internal impulse image corresponds to the initiated rotational moment (or is "storing" it) and it continues rotating infinitely... And then that is just the "conservation of the angular impulse"! As we will see in a minute the occupation with this angular impulse is not only lots of fun but it is also particularly important for understanding the motion of celestial bodies. And since we want to concern ourselves with celestial bodies and planets we take this little digression upon ourselves now.

Rotation is also a motion which could only be changed by applying force. In the ideal case, the axes of a gyroscope stay where they are for that reason - they are fixed in space. That is no particular wonder anymore after all we know. And now let's watch a ballet dancer for a moment and how he is doing pirouettes...

Fig. 89c

What we can observe is something very strange: when the dancer extends his arms during the rotation he turns more slowly ... but when he draws his arms in, his rotation becomes suddenly faster. When disturbing forces (friction etc.) would be eliminated, he could play his little game endlessly and regulate his rotational frequency simply by extending his arms or legs. Yes, this extending would even have a fixed connection with his velocity! If we ask a physicist why this is exactly so, he will say: "Due to the conservation of the angular impulse!" "And why is this angular impulse so keen on conservation?" we could ask and would be told: "I don't know, this is a law of nature!"

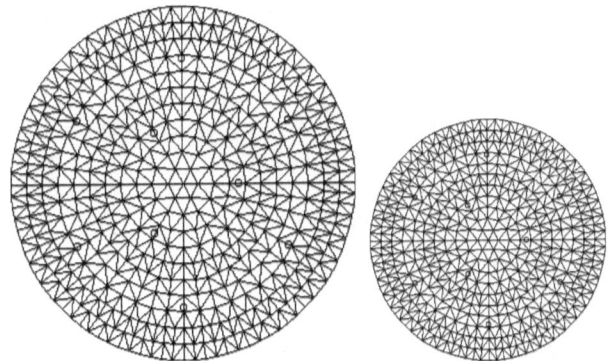

Fig. 89d

Let's assume we made a field, i.e. a body, rotate. We inflicted a modification upon its internal impulse oscillations which corresponds to this acceleration. So to speak we introduced another "image" - precisely the image of a rotation. For the body, this is a new "normal state" - it retains the internal image and what we perceive is a rotating "object". What we actually perceive is a field which is composed of impulses on certain specific paths. These impulses have an ultimate propagation velocity (c !). The result or the sum of all these impulses and their inner directions result in a definite rotation and speed of rotation.

When this field is getting bigger (ballet dancer extending his arms), the impulses take a different direction. They can only do that at maximum at the velocity of light because the structure of the T.A.O. matrix determines it this way ("distance between the dominos"). For that reason, the velocity of rotation is loosing this amount since - as long as the enlargement of the field takes place - the impulses of the field are moving outwards just a little. The new velocity of rotation (angular velocity) is the result of the radial and tangential components of motion. This is of course (only apparently!) slower than before. The whole process, however, will not work in this way unless there is some restriction to the speed of (light) propagation by the T.A.O. matrix! We thus see with amazement that the velocity of light (again!) plays a role in the conservation of the angular impulse.

When the ballet dancer retracts his arms the process takes place the other way round. The impulses of the field twist their direction round during the alteration, the resulting angular velocity of the total field is getting higher. The impulse or energy content of the total field remains always the same regardless of any change in size – and still the velocity of rotation changes! Again the velocity of light is to "blame" for this phenomenon. If the atomic impulses could go beyond or drop below this velocity of propagation, they would adapt to the modification - and the body would not change on the outside and maintain its angular velocity!

Figure 89 d tries to support our imagination a little. The various directions of the impulses are symbolised by the lattice. Enlargements or reductions of the field will change the direction of the lattice components to the outside or to the inside - as shown by the small diagonals. The paths of the impulse change correspondingly and can always only be passed through at c.

Who does not think of Einstein when he hears the word velocity of light? Who of the "insiders" does not already suspect that this causal existence of "c" in the phenomena impulse, conservation of impulse, conservation of angular impulse, inertia, and gravitation could have something to do with the General Theory of Relativity?

He suspects correctly - but we are not yet at that stage by far! Because the next thing we will examine is what the whole business of angular impulses has to do with Kepler's laws.

Well, some facts have to be noted down in particular. The rotational velocity is proportional to changes of the radius. The ballet dancer extends his hands and his rotation slows down. But within one unit of time his arms are passing over the same area as before ... and when he retracts his hands he rotates faster, though, but the area covered per unit of time is again the same. When we follow one point of a rotating body and measure the area which the radius covers within a second this area will always remain the same even if we vary the size of the body – only the velocity will change accordingly. A stone tied to a string and spun in a circle is getting faster when we reduce the length of the string while doing so – but the area which the string passes over within one unit of time always remains the same! That has to be expected for we did not change anything in the energy-impulse content ("mass") of the stone, of course. This connection of the velocity with the radius and with the area covered is called the "law of areas". And we will learn on the following pages that we already described Kepler's second law with that...

When we tie two spheres together and make them rotate, we see how they appear to revolve around a mutual centre of gravity in reverse motion. In fact, the movements of the two spheres "depend on" each other in the sense of the word - but in truth there is no centre of gravity. And now we will examine why the sun plays a very similar game with its planets.

As simple and ingenious as Newton's law of gravitation may appear it did not uncover the cause of gravitation. A particular weakness of Newton's dynamics (ND) consisted in the action at a distance across the empty space between the bodies attracting each other because this opinion did not explain for example why the attraction of the sun to the Earth is preserved even during a solar eclipse when the moon moves between Earth and sun. Against every logic is also the phenomenon that a force which acts linearly between the centres of gravity of the bodies - and is doing so from both sides! - decreases with the square of its distance. Moreover Newton's second law of motion says after all that the mass of a body is the mass of its inertia. The bigger the mass of a body, the bigger therefore its inertia. So when two bodies with different masses are set in motion by the same force, the body with more mass will react slower than the one with less mass. This observation, however, does not apply in case of the acceleration due to gravity because we know of course that all bodies fall down at the same velocity. Newton himself tried to disguise the weakness of his theory by explaining that the gravitational force acting on a body increases with the mass of the body. It is doubtful if Newton could believe this strange explanation himself.

Figures 46 and 81 already tried to illustrate the relationship of two celestial bodies - for example Earth and moon. Let's take another close look at it - this time with the sun and a planet (figure 89 e):

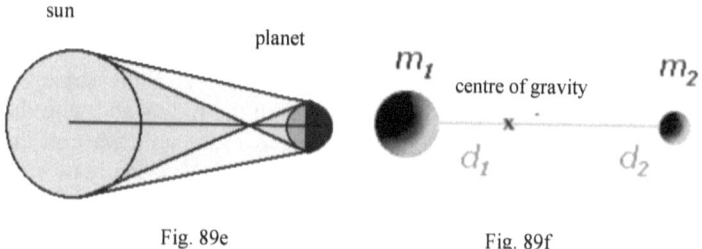

Fig. 89e   Fig. 89f

Beforehand some inevitable clarifications: when we want to describe the properties of the field which displaces the field of a second body, the best thing to do is using the properties of light for this purpose. The universe is not just vaguely filled with light but we can distinguish the stars from each other by the directional relation between source and observer - this relationship is well described in the physics of geometrical optics. Just like the light of the stars pours down on us, the subtle shoves of the universal pressure field pour toward the sun from all sides. These shoves (we already compared them to neutrinos or gravitons, though they are surely smaller by an order of magnitude) don't have a spin. When they have, we are dealing with a magnetic field (!). Even the phenomena of geometrical optics are very useful as an analogy for these universal pressure shoves, like for instance reflection (resistance), penetration, and absorption. Due to the lack of spin, however, the phenomena of wave optics (diffraction, refraction, interference etc.) do not take place! The game of the universal pressure with the celestial bodies is thus a game with "light" and "shadow"; i.e. their bodies shadow these subtle shoves. Shadows, incomplete shadows, complete shadows (umbras) - all these phenomena which we know from the light, especially from solar or lunar eclipses, also occur in the universal pressure field. Moreover we have to assume that these universal pressure radiation is partially let through by the bodies and that another part causes the acceleration of the body while a further part feeds energy to the body since it is absorbed. Because we won't have the astrophysicists talk us into believing that stars and suns keep on shining and gravitating for millions of years without receiving any energy from anywhere. In truth there is a continuous give and take of energy (energy flux) through the universal pressure fields.

The ingenious simplicity of Newton's laws of gravitation is now getting lost in the repulsion principle for the reason that we are no longer dealing with the effect of a force which is located in the centre of a "mass" but have to consider completely different factors. Thus not only the density of the bodies involved plays a role but also the material composition. The beautiful linear integration of the action of mass therefore has to give way to an exponential one. In addition there are the geometrical effects of the forces ("curving force")... The matter is really not getting any simpler with this - but we can nevertheless use a simplified description because we want to explain relatively simple phenomena - like for example the movement of the planets - with it.

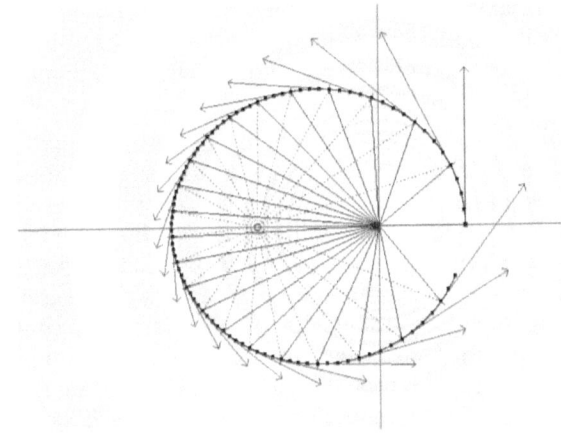

Fig. 89g

Figure 89 e shows the pressure shadow between the sun and a planet. The two bodies are pressed towards (!) each other in this shadow. This will always create the impression as if the smaller body is falling on the bigger body because it is subject to higher acceleration from the universal pressure due to its lower inertia. Since the planet is also subject to a corresponding counter pressure from the sun because of its size the rate of approach of the two bodies is always the same regardless of their mass ratio! That is to say the magnitude of this acceleration of free fall results always only from the ratio between the pressure of the central body and the universal pressure! It does absolutely not matter what is trapped in-between and "falls" towards the central body. But that had already been noticed by Galileo...

Even if nothing "falls" onto the sun, it has a field around it as a result of its shadowing effect and of its individual pressure in relation to the universal pressure. "Falling" bodies move from the area of the incomplete shadow into the area of the complete shadow... i.e. the closer the body comes to the surface of the sun the lower the lateral influence of the universal pressure gets - and the higher the acceleration of free fall. In figure 89g we illustrated the field around the sun with grey circles. When we assume that the sun would eject matter into space, like launching a satellite, we would have to realise that there is really something like a "curved" space around the sun which determines the movements of this satellite. The missile is moving against the universal pressure and the universal pressure is pressing it back into the "shadow" - depending on the speed of the missile a path results which either leads back into the sun or ends in the endless expanses of the universe. The "borderline case" between these extremes is a (nearly) endless fall around the sun...

Well, Kepler claimed in his first law that all planets were moving in ellipses whose focal point was the sun. If this was really the case, the orbits of the planets could actually be perfect circles. But when the sun launches a satellite - as we already know - the same force is acting upon the sun as the sun is exerting on the satellite: the sun is also repelled by the satellite. And the sun does exactly the same as the satellite: it goes into an orbit within its field, too. And even if this is quite an imperceptible movement because of the sun's great inertia it has far-reaching consequences - reaching as far as the range of the invisible field because the field is certainly also moving. This minute modification propagates within the field (at the velocity of light) - and apart from the fact that this would be nothing else but a gravitational wave as demanded by Einstein - it has certainly an influence on the path of the satellite. After all, the modification in the sun's field happens much faster compared to the velocity of the satellite, and since the sun is shifting in space together with its field, the satellite does not find the ideal orbiting condition anymore but is pushed back to the sun a little "earlier" (in the aphelion). The result is an elliptical orbit! The same consequences apply to the sun. Its orbit becomes an ellipse, too (but a very small one). The two ellipses revolve around a point which is named centre of gravity (fig. 89 f) because this is where the two bodies - if they fell towards each other - would meet because of their different velocities, not attracted by gravitation but shoved together by the universal pressure! It is therefore not a "centre of gravity" ... and in truth there is no such thing as a centripetal force or a centrifugal force or a gravitational attraction or anything like that. If we had to replace the alleged gravitation in the relationship of sun and Earth by a steel cable, the cable would be about 3,700 kilometres thick, in case of Jupiter it would even be 17,000 kilometres ... this makes the theory of gravitation rather implausible. But even if things are actually much simpler, they are not at all simpler to describe and least of all simpler to calculate. Newton's equations on the other hand do not refer to the cause but to the effect - and for that reason, they are working quite precisely. But they fail, for example, when it comes to the rotational movement of very big masses, like galaxies, where even Kepler's laws are rather ignored. We will have to deal with that, too.

In our universe, it is not masses which act upon each other by means of attraction but the fields of energy and impulse "tell" the space how it has to "curve" - and the "curved" space tells the fields how they have to move... Yes, again we have a moment of sudden insight! Because that is nothing else but the main statement of the General Theory of Relativity! Newton noticed that the subject of the focal point was wrong ... and Einstein noticed that the subject of gravitation was wrong... And in the same way as Newton's theory was both right and wrong by describing the effects on the basis of fictions (mass and gravitation), Einstein's theory describes field events in an almost excessive way - only more on the basis of geometry and mathematics - the cause of which can very easily be explained with the existence of fields of matter and the repulsion principle.

When the moon is between sun and Earth during a solar eclipse it cannot affect the attractive force of the sun because this force does not exist at all. But it can shadow the pressure from the sun a little and replace it with its own. While a gravitational modification in contradiction to Newton will be scarcely detectable in the complete shadow of the moon the weakening in the incomplete shadow is unequivocally measurable because in fact the boundary areas of the moon shadow the pressure from the sun but the pressure of the moon radiates spherically and therefore does not hit the area of the incomplete shadow on the surface of the Earth at the same time. For that reason, one can notice gravitational modifications at the beginning and at the end of a total solar eclipse - but during the occultation everything will stay within the framework of previous theories[27] or the Earth's gravitation will increase a little! [109]

We have to record as substantial facts: due to the mutual influencing of the fields (this also takes place when bodies "capture" one another) circular orbits are impossible in the universe. They will always be elliptical. Due to the circumstance that two fields are playing ping-pong with each other so to speak and are shoving each other to and fro between individual pressure and universal pressure, one has to conclude that the process is consuming energy. This is finally the end of the god-given gravitation! And before we rack our brains over these complicated connections we will examine Kepler's other two laws in order to learn at last why the moon does not fall down and why it knows that it belongs to the Earth although it is also moving in the field of the sun...

In the first online version of this book it said succinctly that a planet had to change its velocity to the same extent as its orbit was changing - and that this was exactly Kepler's second law. The response was a considerable number of criticisms ... that it was not just so easy to explain... And the critics are of course right, even if the criticised sentence is correct in principle it does not explain anything basically. When Kepler formulated his second law at first nobody knew what to make of it, not until the physicists discovered that nothing but the conservation of the angular impulse was at its bottom.

We already found out with the aid of the ballet dancer why there is this law of conservation. And we tied a stone to a string and were spinning it around while we were shortening the length of the string, and we discovered that the angular impulse is maintained in this case as well by a corresponding change in the velocity of the stone - and for that reason, the areas covered by the string within the same periods of time remained of the same size...

Well, it does not matter at all whether we tie a planet on a string ("gravitation") or if its path is determined by the fields of space curved by the pressure from the sun and the universal pressure. The planet is not to be robbed of its angular impulse and no moment of rotation is added either – of course it cannot be added because the planet is in a fall free of forces. But since it is shoved into an elliptical orbit by the solar field and its own field, its speed - as with the stone on the string - changes accordingly. A planet changes its speed of revolution in such a way that its radius vector covers the same areas in the same periods of time. This is Kepler's second law, the so-called "law of areas".

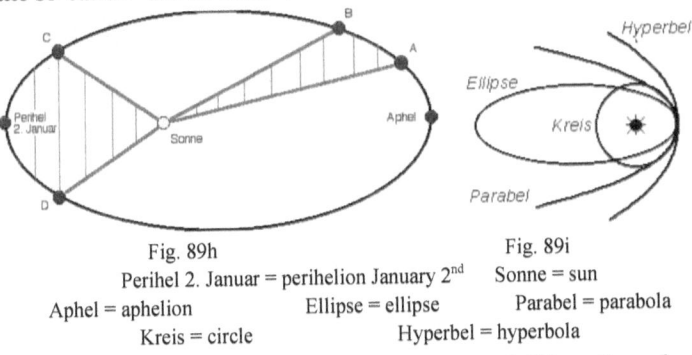

Fig. 89h
Fig. 89i
Perihel 2. Januar = perihelion January 2nd Sonne = sun
Aphel = aphelion   Ellipse = ellipse   Parabel = parabola
Kreis = circle   Hyperbel = hyperbola

The principle also works the other way round. When the velocity of the planet is influenced, its distance to the sun changes. Retardation by means of "tidal friction" as with the moon leads to an increase in the distance to the central body. In addition to that, though, the bodies are in contact with each other through their extended fields and transmit rotational moments to one another. We will see later-on that this has once played an important role in the relationship of the sun to its planets.

As already pointed out the planetary orbits are always ellipses. Strictly speaking all movements within our universe are ellipses or elliptical sections (conical sections). So even hyperbola and parabola are included in the ellipse (fig. 89 i). The reason for that is that always at least two fields influence each other and only if the mass ratios are very different can the path come very close to an ideal circle.

Maybe our attempt to undermine Newton's theory with the question why the attractive force of the sun does not suffer from the moon standing between sun and Earth was not convincing enough. After all, the moon only casts a small shadow on the Earth... But why does the moon know that it belongs to the Earth? Why is it not just getting lost? Why does the enormous "attractive force" of the sun not just pluck it off pulling it toward the sun? The moon, whose orbit is approximately on the same plane as the orbit of the Earth, travels with the movement of the Earth at one time and against it at another. Related to the sun, this velocity is smaller at one time and greater at another... the same as with the more massive Earth which allegedly fights the attraction of the sun by means of the centrifugal force. The much smaller moon has obviously no need to do so and the sun does not care for it, evidently it respects the intimate relationship of Earth and moon and leaves the satellite alone. Because actually it would just have to snatch the moon in the very moment when it is even standing still in relation to the sun...

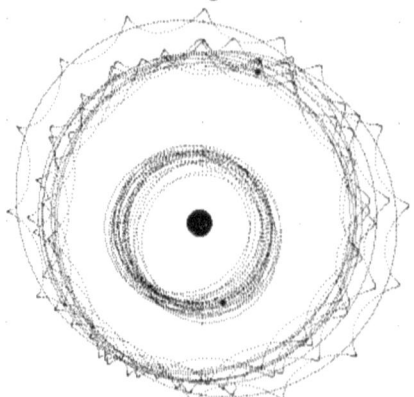

Fig. 89j

What, the moon stands still from time to time? When we take a look at figure 89j which shows us the orbits of Venus, Earth, and our moon we will not only see what a wobbly affair it actually is but also that the Earth is always running away from the moon and that the moon is chasing after it... The path of the moon turns into a kind of garland and the erect points of the garland show the moments in which the satellite is standing still with regard to the sun - in addition to which the attractive forces of Earth and sun would have to add up in this point...

Since the "attractive force" of the sun is actually rather unscrupulous and snatches every body whose acceleration of free fall is not compensated by the "centrifugal force", the moon should have long since fallen into the sun. We are confronted with the three-body problem sun-Earth-moon - and for that reason, we can definitely forget Sir Isaac Newton. Because with him, this question is extremely hard to answer or not solvable at all. If we take the General Theory of Relativity into consideration as well, we will already be unable to handle a two-body problem! But the GTR ignores the problem anyway because it doesn't know such a thing as "gravitation".

The truth is that we have of course a many-body problem with all the planets and moons and especially with the asteroids. We only chose the Earth's moon as an example because the problematic nature becomes particularly obvious here because of the vicinity to the sun. The greatest mathematicians of this Earth have wasted their efforts in vain to solve the orbital relation of the three bodies analytically. According to Newton's dynamics, the whole matter should not work at all which is strange somehow because Newton derived his theory from Kepler's laws. We see that a lot is rotten in the State of Denmark. Though one could yet concede that the sun revolves around the Earth-moon system (because it does not matter who is rotating around whom) in 365 days and that therefore a constant distortion of the moon's path towards the sun would have to result as a maximum. But even a distortion of this kind is not detectable!

Of course, the quantitative comprehensibility does not necessarily become any easier with the repulsion principle. But the loyalty of the moon to its Earth can be explained absolutely logically with our theory. Because the sun does never attract the moon but it repels it actually. The sun is shoving the moon against the universal pressure and the universal pressure is shoving it back. The moon is turned into a ping-pong ball - which, clinging in the pressure shadow between the moon and the Earth, jumps to and fro. Do we have to waste any more words on a problem which is so easy to solve when the attractive force is eliminated? He who keeps struggling with gravitation, centripetal force, centrifugal force, mass, and angular impulse will soon end up in the deep water of unsolvable differential equations. And if someone was ever so daring as to tackle the problem by means of the GTR?

Soon we will see that all celestial bodies are playing ping-pong with each other (even the sun is racing along at 20 km/h and the planets are following it).

But now we will take a closer look at Kepler's third law. The astronomer discovered a mathematical relation between the distance of a planet and its orbit. This relation says:

"The squares of the sidereal periods of revolution of the planets are directly proportional to the cubes of their mean distance from the Sun."

With this law, the relative distances of the planets can be determined solely by means of their sidereal periods of revolution. However, there are slight deviations with the aphelial planets, i.e. the law only works absolutely exactly with the perihelial planets.

A simpler and exacter method of calculation, which makes it possible to derive the distance of a planet from the sidereal periods of revolution in Earth days (when the distance is chosen in millions of kilometres), can be found by simply multiplying this distance with the square root of this distance and dividing it by 5: the result will always be the sidereal period of revolution in Earth days! Conversely, it is possible to determine the exact distance of the planet to the sun from the sidereal period of revolution in Earth days - and amazingly this method works even more precisely than Kepler's third law!

Thus there is obviously a regularity in the distances of the planets to the sun. This regularity can also be gathered from the law of planetary distances by Titius and Bode by means of which at least the asteroid Ceres was found. Since this law - a simple mathematic progression which corresponds to the orbit radii of the planets - was thought to be a coincidence because of the lack of scientific basic factors it never had any serious significance in astronomy.

Like the other two, Kepler's third law was also just a conclusion or a mathematical formulation of observed facts. It does not contain any indications to the cause of the planetary movement, the orbital radii, or to the nature of the effective forces. Kepler contented himself with a description of how and where the planets are moving. The application of Kepler's laws is thus not an explanation of a physical event but simply the account of an observational quantity which was only grasped mathematically by Newton about one hundred years later. But neither Newton nor Einstein could causally unravel the mystery which is contained in the many regularities of our planetary system. The Titius-Bode law was soon considered as a whim of nature and laid to rest by the astronomers. But we will demonstrate that this law and the peculiarities concerning the planetary movements can be explained in a very good manner by means of the repulsion principle. In doing so we will come across two more characteristic planetary movements (the rotations of their ellipses and the variations in their plane of motion), which Kepler had not yet discovered und which Newton could not explicitly include in his law...

Certainly we can already get a good idea about how the fields in T.A.O. structured themselves by mutual displacement into energy centres, agglomerations of atoms and molecules which - pressurized from all sides - formed central masses and bodies. Neither did it remain a secret to us that impulses cannot just flow indiscriminately but are forced into very particular paths by fields and "curved spaces". The concept of how stars could develop should not give us any trouble now.

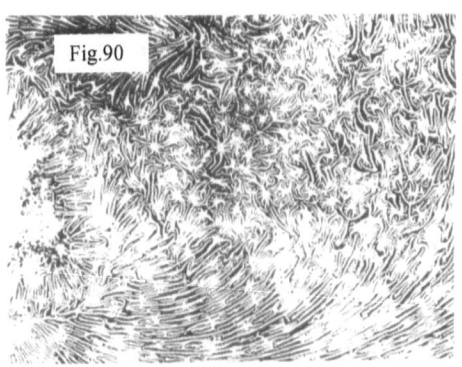

Fig.90

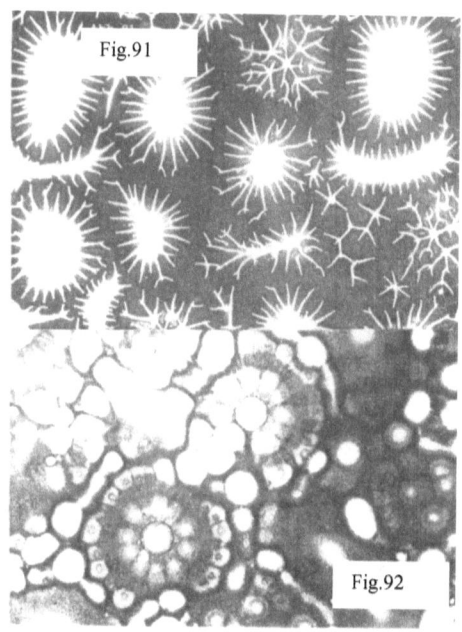

Remember the photographed thermal spheres of figure 3. The event documented in that picture has a sequel: The thermal spheres soon form patterns by mutual displacement; they squeeze one another into new structures, their impulse fields accumulate in certain spots. When we take a look at figures 90 to 92 we will see this dynamic process graphically before of our eyes.

Energies start to flow (90), displacing each other into central fields (91), and soon create superorders (92) which already remind us of the arrangement of galaxies...

Figures 93 and 94 try to illustrate precondition and final result graphically in a computer simulation :

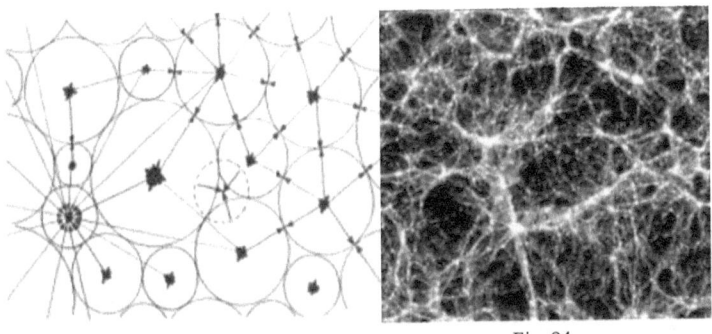

Fig. 93   Fig. 94

The pressure produced by the mutual repulsion combined the atoms into gas molecules and the latter were squeezed into bigger formations in turn. Cold and dark clusters they were, every one of them already a latent star, an embryonic star so to speak ... baby stars which did not shine yet. The astronomers discovered uncountable numbers of such dark stellar children in the universe, and they call them globules. The pressure also makes that the matter is finally arranged in a soap bubble structure since the galaxies accumulate at the boundaries or in the areas of pressure equilibrium, i.e. at the skins of the giant, almost empty space bubbles so to speak – figure 94! (In the first version of this book in 1975, when I came to the conclusion that the universe had to look like lather, I deleted this sentence again because I could not believe it myself. Shortly after the first edition of the book had been published the news was spread worldwide that astronomers had discovered that the matter in the universe was concentrated in clusters and bubbles – a structure which can never ever be explained by gravitation!)[28]

In all these pressure events, there were and there are of course places in the universe where the pressure streaming in from all around comes together without immediately producing a globule because there is not yet enough matter available within a certain radius (broken circle in figure 93). Such a place would not remain empty for long, though. Because all masses which are getting into the vicinity of this place will inevitably be pressed into this centre. Apparently this spot is thus already exerting gravitation without there being a corresponding central mass in it.

Physicists, who derived solutions from Einstein's equations, which Einstein himself wouldn't have dreamt of, constructed very similar formations in theory, placed them far into outer space, and called them black holes. With that they mean spaces curved so much by central masses that even a beam of light is unable to escape from them. Since the effects of gravitation can, however, always only be attributed to the surrounding masses in our opinion, we are unable to comprehend these monsters developed from a misunderstood General Theory of Relativity. According to the repulsion principle, there can never be such a thing as a black hole with central mass gravitation and none such thing has been found yet. But they are very popular at the moment as an explanation of phenomena in astronomy which are not understood. So if something cannot be substantiated with conventional theories, it is just a black hole - and one will not be able to travel to any of those places for the next million years to check if they really exist!

The gravitation effective in the vicinity of celestial bodies, i.e. the universal pressure streaming in spherically, comes predominantly from very distant mass fields – practically from the whole universe. Therefore the total field of the universe appears to be very consistent; all in all the universal pressure is quite isotropic. Central places of pressure, like the "black hole" of our version, are also such preferred places where suns and stars are created. In such a place our sun came into existence, too, long before it had any planets. It also began life as a globule, as a dark baby star, and it must have grown only very slowly because exclusively such matter was flowing towards it which had already formed such extensive fields that they offered sufficient resistance to the universal pressure - i.e. molecules already or at least hydrogen molecules.

In the same way countless other suns were growing. Slowly, over billions of years they were getting bigger and the impulse fields accumulated in them were exerting an increasing pressure against the universe. In turn, they caused new globules between each other - and this process has actually not stopped until today. Still, new stars are born. We can understand this quite casually; we don't need any auxiliary hypotheses for that nor any unbelievable compaction theories on the basis of gravitation nor any illogical mechanisms of revolution... Because young stars do not yet rotate on principle aside from their relative movement towards each other.

At a later time everything had to start moving nevertheless... Although the universal pressure turned out to be essentially isotropic it wasn't so through and through to allow a rigid structure of the sky. In the course of time, a real dance of the stars must have started. In the beginning, it was certainly a dance of random, disordered movements. Gradually at first, again over billions of years, a certain order had been coming into this chaos of movements because everything that had stood in the way had finally been devoured and consumed at some time - incorporated in ever increasing structures...

Now we should continue our conclusions with factual logic. When we are faced with the question where in a star there is the highest pressure we must not answer spontaneously on any account: in the centre! Because this would be wrong! Because the matter of the star is certainly exerting an individual pressure which would have to destroy the star if it was not kept in check by the universal pressure. Therefore the highest pressure has to reign where individual pressure and universal pressure collide. With a sphere, and stars had to take this shape inevitably, this place is on no account in the centre but on the surface.

Certainly this is not understood instantaneously but the correctness of this apparently paradox assumption is confirmed by every standard weight which actually exerts a pressure of, let's say, one kilogram onto the scales on the surface of the Earth only (and only up to a certain depth). When we take this weight below the surface it becomes lighter as is generally known. We also get the same result on the uppermost floor of a skyscraper.

This can also be explained satisfactorily with the conventional theories of the acceleration of free fall. On the surface, it has the value of 9.81 m/sec^2. Towards the centre of the Earth as far as to the theoretical border of the mantle, the acceleration of free fall rises to a maximum of 10.5 m/s^2 and then decreases again. It also decreases the further we get away from Earth. Analogously the same applies to the "attractive force", it appears to be highest slightly below the Earth's surface and then drop to zero on the way to the centre point. But let's now continue our thoughts (which may appear a little naïve): if an object has its highest weight in the mantle area of a celestial body, the pressure can only be so strong directly below the surface of a star that impulse fields get "heavy enough" to enable their mutual tunnelling for the purpose of merging.

When this process of the integration of fields began on the surface of the sun, the energy from modifying the field's surface, which we already know as "fusion energy", was released. The star began to emit radiation...

Of course, this requires a certain minimum size of the star because after all, the required pressure resulted from the universal pressure and from the individual pressure which has to be sufficiently strong. That means: according to the repulsion principle the place of fusion is closest to the point where the two repulsions meet, therefore at the surface of a star or immediately below it!

The sun itself gives us some clearly visible clues: everywhere it breaks up, the surface opens to let us look at obviously cooler areas. For that reason, sunspots are always darker than their environment. Evidence of a different kind is provided by the neutrino research: we know that with every fusion of several fields energy impulses are released which we equated with neutrinos. The conventional theories demand a definite amount of neutrinos but to the astonishment of the astrophysicists the neutrino radiation of the sun seems to be much lower then to be expected on the basis of the theory. Even if observations of this kind have to remain controversial both ways because neutrinos are extremely hard to prove (as a "theory of the last resort" one postulated in the meantime that the neutrinos transform into other particles), we can offer as an explanation for this fact that the fusion processes are in truth not so extensive as one has assumed so far because they only run off at the surface or rather only immediately below it!

It has always been a problem for science to use the theory of gravitation for substantiating the coming about of such a high pressure that nuclear reactions could commence because the gravitational force in the centre point of a sphere is zero as is generally known. Since this centre point would certainly also be attracted by all surrounding masses this is the very place where pressure cannot come about.

The books on physics from our time at school remain discretely silent about this fact but we learned that all celestial bodies react according to gravitation as if their whole mass was located in the centre point. According to the repulsion principle, the gravitational development is also spherical inside the sphere. If we hung a lead into a deep pit it would not point to the centre of the sphere but curve into a circle. Newton could not give us an explanation for this phenomenon and even Einstein does not help us out of this dilemma, though. Neither does he provide a reasonable explanation for the gravitational development inside of the masses.

Which mass should be responsible for the fact that a sphere remains a sphere? The one in the centre point? Is it bigger than the surrounding mass? And if not: how can it hold onto the surrounding mass? One could say the weight of the outer mass rests on it - but this weight is already an effect of the centre-point mass after all, which in turn is too low to cause this weight. How is that?

With the usual theory of gravitation it is really very hard to substantiate logically why celestial bodies are spheres. The difficulty lies in the dependency of gravitation and mass on one another. That means, the heavy mass is the cause and the inert mass feels the effect - but both masses are identical in a celestial body.[19]

Even the tendency of matter to minimum surfaces postulated by the physicists appears as an axiom whose background becomes clearly evident with the repulsion principle. Everything is falling into place automatically, however, when gravitation is replaced by repulsion. While the gravitation theory implies a pressure continuously increasing towards the centre point of a celestial body, the repulsion principle makes the distribution of pressure turn out in a completely different way. In case of the sun, a pressure of roughly 200 billion atmospheres in the centre point is the result of calculations in the conventional way. As a consequence, the temperature in the core would have to be 14 to 20 million degree Celsius - oddly enough the effective temperature on the surface of the sun is only 5512 degree Celsius! This fact is surprising because in the corona of the sun which is the outermost and thinnest layer of the sun's atmosphere, it is possible to measure temperatures of up to 2 million degrees Celsius.

Some very brilliant ideas were developed concerning the coming about of these discrepancies; none of them is absolutely convincing. If one uses the universal pressure and the individual pressure of the sun as an argument and if one considers that the universal pressure is shielded off by the matter up to a certain degree, the zone of highest pressure is on no account relocated to the centre point but below the surface of the star although this expression has to remain extremely relative in the face of the gaseous condition of the matter. But we can conclude that the dark and still dead star encrusted on the surface, similarly to the blocks of land on Earth onto which the universal pressure could have an effect. Between these crusts and the rest of the spherical body it must have gotten hotter and hotter...

The liquid, red hot layer below the continents of Earth came into existence in the same way, and as has been proved, it would be wrong to suppose that the whole interior of the Earth is made of igneous magma. The Earth is too small and the pressure too low, however, to initiate nuclear reactions.

A good model for the pressure ratios in a star is provided by the soap bubble. This analogy is good because according to our opinion the appearance of matter depends on its kinetic content of energy and the pressure in a soap bubble is conditioned by the motion of the gas molecules. At the same external conditions the pressure in a small soap bubble is higher than in a big one. And this explains why for the most part small stars (starting from a certain minimum size, though) shine more brightly and are hotter than big ones.

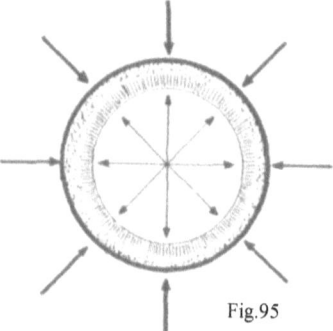

Fig.95

Figure 95 shows the zone with the highest pressure of the sun directly below the surface. In it, the atomic fusions take place, and here heavy elements are gradually produced in these processes. The centre of the star, on the other hand, remains relatively cool.

Even under the surface of the sun the tremendous amounts of matter are sufficient to create higher elements by means of tunnelling through and through the integration of the fields, even if the event itself is extremely rare. Surely several million degrees of heat are not required to fuse protons to helium as has been assumed so far. In the hydrogen bomb, on the other hand, one will not be able to do without temperatures of several million degrees Celsius as in this case there are only small amounts of material involved and one has to enforce what is happening in the sun with ruse and patience.

Currently the sun is in an intermediate phase. It is naked so to speak and only radiates energies which have once accumulated under the surface. Because the fusion processes did presumably not proceed on any account as continuously as it seems but have started over and over again after the cooling-down periods.

We could roughly imagine the events as follows: in the first hot zone created under the sun's shell, the pressure continuously increases because of the fusion energy. Mighty eruptions will break through gaps in the outer skin, and the outer skin created from the scoria of the heavier elements will not be able to withstand the pressure infinitely. It will grow to a certain thickness - the star is getting distinctly darker meanwhile - and one day the star will just blast it off! It will burst like a giant soap bubble and make the star blaze dazzlingly similar to an inconceivable explosion.

But the star only blew off this shell. On its surface, the familiar fusion processes commence again and in the course of time a new shell is developing...

So this is a completely different, new picture of a sun which we see here: the sun is on no account that peacefully shining atomic reactor for which we took it but an extremely changeable star which blasts off tremendous masses of matter from time to time and with that it undergoes something like a real rejuvenation treatment!

What happens with the blown off masses? Do they just fall back onto the sun?

In order to understand these processes exactly we have to consider that the stars do not just simply rest in the universal pressure but that the space all around is polarised by other stars. All these stars are in motion and represent charges. For that reason, there is a giant magnetic field in the universe in which the sun will start to rotate immediately like a cosmic motor when it develops only the trace of a magnetic field itself.

We know that practically all matter that moves relative to its own field provides electric currents. And therefore the elementary processes beneath the shell of the sun produce currents of electrons to an inconceivable extent. When these currents happen to flow in any preferred direction, the sun is transformed into a conductor loop so to speak and we already learned what will happen in this case: the rotation setting in builds up a mighty magnetic field again. A very strong rotational moment is created through this self-induction, and we have to assume that the sun rotated much faster in its beginning than it does today.

When the sun conveyed the blown off shell quickly enough out into the cosmos its rotating magnetic field transmitted a fraction of its angular impulse to this equatorial masses, and while the remaining matter fell back down into the sun these masses remained above the sun caught in a magnetic bottle so to speak - and formed a ring around it.[29]

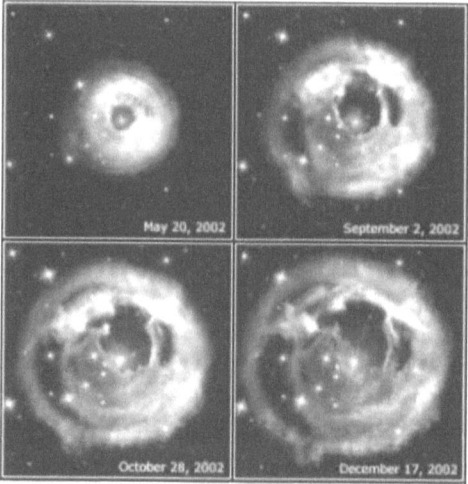
Fig. 96

The remainders of the last ring around the sun still exist today and they become visible from Earth as so-called zodiacal light. It is, however, also conceivable that big alien masses came from outer space and broke apart because of the curving force when falling down onto the sun and survived as a ring.

The process is so plausible that we can go ahead and claim that all celestial bodies have to carry more or less well-developed rings around them. We have known about those around Saturn for a long time; in 1977, the ring around Uranus was photographed for the first time but even Jupiter and Neptune possess rings. Earth itself has something very similar: the Van Allen belts. (Peter Fawcett of the University of New Mexico and Mark Boslough of the U.S. Department of Energy's Sandia National Laboratories pointed out that even the Earth could have had rings several times in its history). And in this case we know very well that they go back to the magnetic field of the Earth which holds the matter in its magnetic bottle.

All these rings consist of dust and large lumps of rock, partially even of ice. Only when the ring's matter still consists of hot, incandescent sun mass, too, such a ring can develop into a planet. We will examine that in the next chapter.

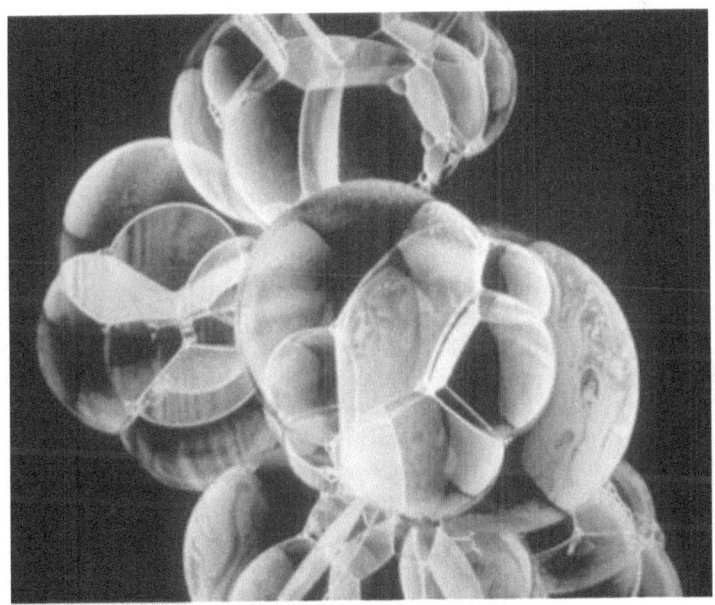

Fig.96a - soap bubble structure

17 Planets

Well, we have been talking about planets for some time and yet only described a ring around the sun. The idea that planets originate from rings is not particularly new. Originally, it came from Laplace and was discussed at length but rejected again later because there were to many contradictions. As it is, the planetary distances and the distribution of the angular impulse remained unsolved. The repulsion principle, however, presents a solution of these mysteries just by the assumption of rings. The theory of Laplace was obviously much too "simple" for the scholars. Later theories (Kant, Kuiper, Weizsäcker, etc.) were more complicated by far and besides they solved the contradictions just as little. Therefore we will adhere to the idea of the rings without hesitation and pursue it further...

Just recently that blast off processes of shells or rings have been discovered by astronomers particularly often. In 2002, a spectacular occurrence took place with object V838 which the astronomers were able to observe live. Figure 96 shows some snapshots of this star which discharged its shell explosively. It clearly demonstrated the blast off process of matter and the formation of rings. The astronomers consider V838 to be a new kind of "changeable" because it does not fit into any of the categories "nova" and "supernova", and one does not know the reason for the ejection of matter and the formation of the ring (allegedly it already has 11 rings). The rings are of different age (!), the oldest one is about 2500 years, the youngest might have just come into existence.

We see that events of this kind are not too rare in the universe. And for that reason, we assume that even the sun blew off its crust from time to time to light up anew. A ring developing from the material of the crust already took away a little of the sun's angular impulse. Since impulses can always only be transmitted from one body to the next the sun had to rotate a little slower as a result.

What happened with this ring subsequently? When the ring is of cold, low-energy matter nothing exciting will happen at all. All particles have the same velocity, and we would see no reason to describe the accretion of these fractions to one single body. But the ring consists of matter from the sun! It is plasma, a material condition of electrical activity of the highest intensity. In this form matter reacts very sensitively to magnetic effects and electric fields -

for the sufficiently well-known reason: repulsion or attraction in the polarised space.

The equator of the sun and the ring don't have the same rotational velocity any more. Since an angular impulse was transmitted, the same velocity would be impossible. And therefore the ring becomes a conductor which moves through the magnetic field of the sun. As we know, this has to lead to various electrodynamic processes. Among other things the ring will not be able to maintain its original position in relation to the equator of the sun due to the occurrence of Lorentz forces and will slightly tilt out of this position. We can therefore explain a phenomenon which has left the astronomers completely at a loss when they discovered it: namely the variations of the orbital planes within the ecliptic. Because this impulse which the ring once received has to be still active in the planets today and is the reason for the planets not moving exactly on one and the same plane. This variation of the orbital plane is symbolised in figure 97.

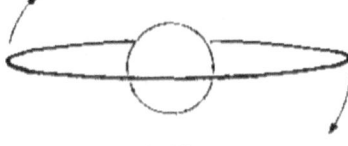

Fig.97

In all probability, all planets developed from a ring around the sun or rather from a series of rings which must have been created one after the other. How could the creation of the planets have happened at that time?[30]

Inevitably, the ionised ring of matter in the magnetic field had to create eddy currents. As the basis for this assumption we already mentioned the Lorentz force. Physicists know a very similar process which is called Hall effect.

This effect acts like a magnetic brake which slows down a section of the ring. For that reason, this section looses its equilibrium with its environment. It receives an acceleration of free fall towards the sun which finds expression in a narrower orbit and a higher velocity Thus the debris races along the inside of the ring shielding off the solar pressure towards the ring and promptly receives the remaining ring matter as a gift from the universal pressure. In other words: when just one grain of dust in the ring is getting slower or faster, it gradually gathers up the remaining ring in the course of overtaking so to speak.

We can still track down this effect in the rings of Saturn. This ring consists of many individual rings with nothing in-between. The moons of Saturn are to blame for this. They slowed down particles in certain places and these particles immediately swept part of the ring empty in order to be flying along with an inner ring as bigger chunks up to today if they did not fall down into the Saturn straightaway. The rest of the rings remained stable because they consist of cold matter, dust, and ice.

In comparison, a ring around the sun will not be preserved for long. Very quickly, it accretes to an individual body due to the electrodynamic interaction. In doing so, the matter is already cooling down a little. It rolls along between solar pressure and universal pressure as it were and with that we come across another effect which we want to call the rolling effect (figure 98).

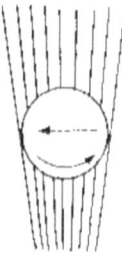

Fig.98

The rolling effect causes the rotation of the growing planet and is easy to comprehend when we consider the field lines of solar pressure and universal pressure. The lines are denser on the side facing the sun. This means increased resistance. For that reason, the planet will always turn the same side towards the sun in the beginning which already means a rotation as we know it from the moon. This angular acceleration remains constant and therefore the rotational velocity has to increase continuously. The moon, in comparison, will always be fetched back into the Earth's shadow because of its pear shape, that is the reason why it moves back and forth a little (libration).

The planet in creation, however, increases its rotation constantly. If it has a rotation which goes into the opposite direction for electrodynamic reasons this rotation will be slowed down gradually and turn into counter-rotation - a process which is obviously not yet finished with the planet Venus...

The material composition of a planet results from the nature of the sun's matter at the time of the ring's formation and thus reflects the ageing of the sun. The content of heavy elements will be low with the oldest planets whereas the youngest ones will receive the greatest density. In addition, a certain selection will take place upon collecting the matter for the ring. First, ionised gases (hydrogen) will come together preferably forming a relatively inhomogeneous, loose ball which will sweep through the ring matter just like a wad of cotton wool and acquire a skin of higher elements. There is no reason to assume that a solid core (of iron?) had built up first and that lighter elements and gases settled down later only because of the gravitational effect of this core. Besides the ring might have been gathered up in a different way with each planet because the composition of the matter was different. This happened relatively quickly; certainly the whole birth of a planet did not take longer than a few centuries. At the moment, astronomers are watching the birth of a planet from a dust ring with star KH 15D at a distance of 2400 light years – and the sensational event is happening over a period of months up to a few years![31] According to latest insights, geologists acknowledge a maximum timeframe of up to 20 million years for the birth of the Earth – which is still astonishingly short from a cosmic point of view (Science, vol. 295, p. 1705).

Now we are getting to an important station in our reflections. Because we should ask ourselves: does this just created planet remain in its orbit for ever and for always? The answer is: no, it is moving away from the sun!

There are at least two reasons for that: firstly, an effect occurs which is similar to the one that takes place between the Earth and the moon. Two celestial bodies circling each other cause a friction, so to speak, through their field contact to each other, i.e. they decelerate one another. This leads to an increase of the pressure from the sun because the falling body opposes it with less motion. For this reason the moon constantly drifts away from Earth. Originally it was much closer to it.

The tidal friction as a cause also applies to a perihelial planet, it is also gradually moving away from its central star. Secondly, there are remarkable facts of the matter already implied in our knowledge about repulsion: the universe is expanding! It is expanding because it is pressing itself apart and while doing so it obtains all its energy from the simple fact that it is standing in its own way. At the same time, however, the pressure, i.e. the universal pressure has to decrease incessantly as a result of this expansion. This is manifested in a continuous modification of the gravitational effect as was already suspected by the physicist Jordan and others.

Roughly regarded, as a consequence of this progressive easing off of the universal pressure all celestial bodies are moving away from each other, and that means that our planetary system is expanding, too. The celestial bodies, which are restricted by a gradually decreasing pressure after all, are expanding in the same way. The sun is expanding and every single of its planets is expanding. On the other hand we have to think back to our example of the fan wheel: small bodies are less subjected to the universal pressure than bigger ones – that means that galaxies do not expand or shrink at all whereas the space between them grows constantly bigger. And small suns are expanding faster than big ones on which the universal pressure can more easily put the screws.

In any case, a planet is expanding during its whole existence, and therefore the old planets are already giant gas balls with a relatively low density whereas the young ones are still solid little bodies. But we do not want to jump ahead of events but to consequently continue our considerations: the sun got back a large part of its blasted off masses after its first big eruption - apart from that new born companion which has been circling it ever since. For the reasons mentioned above the circles the companion is moving in are getting bigger and bigger and millions of years are passing by...

What does the sun do in the meantime? It develops a new shell, and under it, it pursues its jig-saw puzzle of the elements (proton-proton cycle, carbon cycle etc.) all over again. From the matter that has fallen back it creates even higher elements. And after a certain time its shell becomes too tight again. The game with the ring is repeated.

The result is a second planet whose composition has to be a little different because there already were more heavy elements in the second ring.

The new planet pursues its course within the orbit of the old one and together with it, it moves away from the sun. Again millions of years pass by until a new ring is blasted off... In this way the sun gives birth to one planet after the other in perfect order. Every single one of it receives a part of the sun's angular impulse and with every planet born the sun slows down a little. Today it rotates around itself in about 28 days while the majority of the angular impulse has been put into the planets. But still the sun combines 99% of the mass of the system. And because of this distribution of the angular impulse and this mass ratio, every hypothesis assuming that all planets had come into existence at the same time was doomed to failure. The planets Uranus and Neptune also provide circumstantial evidence: if they had come into being at their current distance from the sun, their weight would have to be only 10 times the Earth's mass at the most – they are, however, 50 to 70 percent heavier, which indicates that their place of birth must have been closer to the sun.[32]

Another interesting piece of evidence for our considerations is provided by the corona of the sun, by the way: in this outer gaseous envelope of the star there are still all the higher elements to be found of which the perihelial planets are composed.

What would a finished planetary system have to look like if it came into existence according to our repulsion principle? Let's list some of the most outstanding characteristics:

1) All planets would have to observe Kepler's laws in spite of their masses.

2) The outer planets would have to be older than the inner ones. Thus Mercury is obviously the youngest one (or rather Vulcan of which we will talk later-on).

3) The existence of heavy elements would have to increase from the outer ranges to the inner ranges of the system.

4) The older planets would have to rotate faster than the younger ones (because they would have been subjected to the rolling effect for a longer time).

5) The orbital planes would have to be tilted away from the sun's equator and deviate from each other since they were created at different times. The creation of the planets on a solar-equatorial plane would have to be recognisable nevertheless (ecliptic).

6) The planets would have to exhibit significant signs of their expansion; older planets would have to be expanding for a longer time and would therefore have a greater enlargement and a lower density.

7) It should be possible to attribute the distances of the planets to a temporally and spatially cyclical process.

8) The orbital ellipses would have to rotate, the movements would have to be in the same direction which corresponds to the rotation of the sun. The proper rotations would have to correspond to the rolling effect.

9) Older planets, i.e. the outer ones, would also have to be bigger

than the younger ones because the eruptions of the sun would become weaker as a result of the reduction of the star and what is more, less and less masses would be conveyed into space because of the diminishing rotational velocity.

10) Considering that we do not know the total angular impulse of the solar system at all because we do not know how many planets have been born by the sun up to now, the recognisable angular impulse would have to be mainly in the planetary movement.

Should we really still be surprised that our planetary system corresponds rather exactly to the listed points?

Our sun did not always shine so evenly and pleasantly as today. It must have been exploded, so to speak, in more or less regular intervals only to begin its game again, a little smaller but brighter and hotter.

These hypotheses are on no account absurd. For a long time astronomers have been observing stars in the universe which do very similar things. Only in recent times one discovered in addition that especially young stars have remarkably violent eruptions for which one has not yet found any explanation. One example for this is the already mentioned object V838 as well as AFGL 490 in the constellation Giraffe or Camelopardis. Inside the cloud L1551 in the constellation Taurus there, too, is a star which ejects enormous masses of molecules. The measuring results point to the fact that the ejected matter spreads around the star in a discoid. The astronomers still rack their brains about this phenomena which cannot be put in accord with the present ideas of the creation and development of stars. A short while ago a case became known in which a star MWC 349 in the constellation Swan (Cygnus) was surrounded by a gaseous disk. And the data of object AFGL 961 point to a similar picture, too...

Until now one hasn't known why the outer planets of the solar system have preserved their original atmosphere and the inner ones have not. Now it seems quite possible that the inner planets were also subject to such eruptions as can be currently observed in the universe and that the gaseous envelops were just blown off.

Why hasn't anybody (apart from Laplace) come up with the idea actually that planets could have come into existence in this way? According to the conventional gravitational theory, there are too many contradictions. For example, repulsive energies occur with the observed eruptions which can be explained neither with the centrifugal force nor with the radiation pressure. The repulsion principle, however, fills the gap. Because everything that is now added in explanation is the individual pressure of the star which - not least of all - pushes the ring away – and later the planet.

But now a word concerning the distances of the planets to the sun: when examining the origination of light (chapter "Hydrogen") we already found that atomic fields shield off the universal pressure from each other. We named this process "shadowing". A certain quantised regularity results always from the interaction between universal pressure and individual pressure as it finally came into effect in the wavelengths of the produced light. It seems to suggest itself to suppose such an effect in the interaction of big fields as well. Let's take a look at figure 99:

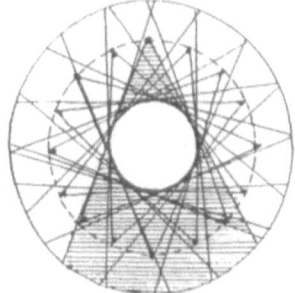

Fig. 99

Even the sun casts a pressure shadow as we want to call the zone which is mainly filled by the pressure from the sun. When we use a circle of headlights as a symbol for the universal pressure streaming in from all around and when we place the sun in-between as a sphere casting shadows we get a "quantised" picture of the pressure distribution around the sun. That means, the zone of the "black", empty hole in our figure 93 was still marked by a certain pressure isotropy but the pressure does not proceed as regularly any longer when there is a celestial body. The field produced around the body is divided into areas of different pressure. For the same reason, every electrostatic field is divided in such areas which are restricted by "equipotential surfaces". In astronomy the term is also known as surfaces on which bodies can move without any expenditure of force. We will transform the term into "equipotential spaces".

We will therefore divide the space around the sun into equipotential spaces. This means that for getting across any of these spaces the same work has to be expended every time. In aphelion, a longer distance is therefore overcome with the same expenditure of energy than in perihelion.

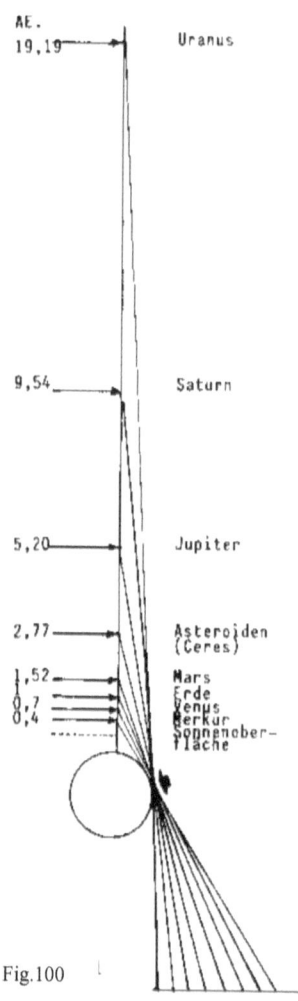

Fig.100

If one regards the universal pressure as a pressure stemming from far-away masses and if the vectors of this pressure starting out regularly from an imaginary circle located in infinity are applied in such a way that the shadowing effect reveals the equipotential spaces and if we take the borders of these areas as a clue (figure 100), to our astonishment we will get amazingly precisely the medium distances of the planetary orbits to one another! Therefore the planets move in principle at the outer limits of the equipotential spaces.

That the energy required for crossing these areas of different distances is every time the same means that the expansion of the planetary system did not take place gently and gradually. Every single one of the sun's pressure shadows reaches a little farther into space all of a sudden when the star diminishes. And of course that is exactly what happened from time to time. This forces us to conclude that the planets always made some kind of quantum jump up to the next border of an equipotential space when the sun was changing its size.

Asteroiden = Asteroids, Erde = Earth, Merkur = Mercury, Sonnenoberfläche = surface of the sun

And this clarifies the last problem of our model: the strong and differing inclinations of the rotational axes of the planets towards the ecliptic which indicate clearly that of the same intervals at which the sun made new planets the planetary spheres were catapulted through the universe as if seized by giant fists...

As we are going to discuss in this book we could probably resolve the last great mysteries of the Earth's history into easily comprehensible processes by means of our concept: the reversal of the poles and the ice ages, series of catastrophes of a cosmic dimension, the collapse of the magnetic field, and many more...

Figure 100 does not provide a correct allegory for the scale of the events which we let unfold in such a simple way in our mind's eye: in this figure the sun is extremely exaggerated. Related to the illustrated planetary distances it would be just as big as the head of a pin. The whole planetary system (for lack of space, Neptune and Pluto were not included in the figure; but their distances can be determined in the same way as well) could just be accommodated in a hat box - but in order to reach the next fixed star we would already have to walk for about 8 kilometres...

The regularities of the planetary distances have come to the attention of the astronomers for some time now. They called their law - as already mentioned - the Titius-Bode law of planetary distances. After the paradox of the angular impulse, this law was the second, big obstacle for all theories about the origination of the planets. None of these theories could explain why the planetary distances could be calculated by means of a simple formula. Even both the asteroids and the planets Neptune and Uranus were discovered with the aid of this formula. Only Pluto does not fit completely into this mould.

Only the repulsion principle provides the explanation why the planets had to take exactly these distances and not any other. Moreover, the pressure relations around the sun revealed by the planetary orbits provide powerful evidence for the repulsion principle.

In figure 101 we put the lines of the Balmer series of the hydrogen spectrum into the pressure shadow and its equipotential spaces. We shouldn't be too surprised to find quite similar distances here. This confirms at least that the processes in the microcosm as in the macrocosm can be explained just in the same way by means of the universal repulsion of matter.

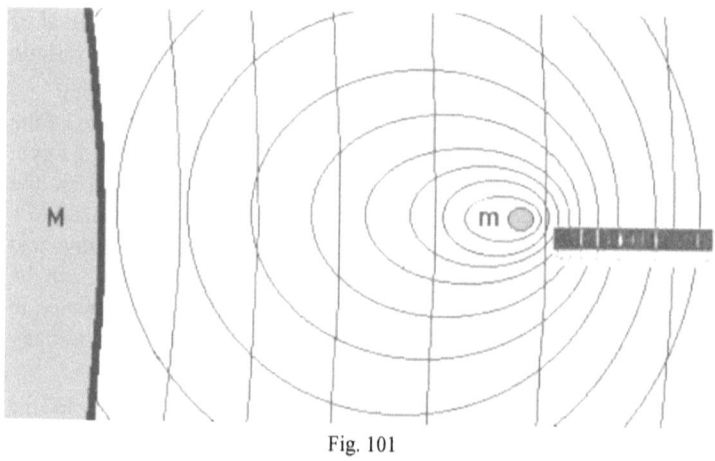

Fig. 101

18 Communication

Just like the celestial bodies stipulate each other's path and, so to speak, take notice of each other in this way the individual fields of matter, the atoms, run a kind of news agency among each other. The principle of action and reaction makes every energetic information move from atom to atom - in a variety of definitely recognisable paths and ways.

What finally comes out of this communication of the atoms - the image of matter – is determined by us, the perceivers, by the brains and the sense organs of the living things which are nothing but receiving atoms themselves, governed by quite practical considerations. Perceptive organisms answer with reactions which are determined by the messages. The possibilities for this reaction are on principle limited, that means, the answer is always the manifestation of the question. Thus the wing is the answer to air, the fin the answer to water, photosynthesis is the answer to light, and the phenotype of an organism is its response to its special environment...

All this is possible because T.A.O. possesses the simple ability to transmit information in form of impulses. On principle there are only these few forms of impulses as we described them. And therefore different contents of information have to result from the temporal coding of these impulses. After all, it only matters what the recipient makes of them – the recipient "understands" the message because it has to comprehend it and because of that he becomes part of this message himself. It does not perceive, it does not really understand but it repeats the process, imitates it...

And because the atoms are forced into this behaviour because of their pure existence and their situations in relation to each other, because they therefore behave just like environment, like space and polarisation demand them to, their behaviour has to appear to us already reasonable, determined by desire and force. In this behaviour, there is not only variety, colour, and shape of this world but also the root of consciousness and intelligence.

We already know the basic pattern of any message of this world. There is only a simple shove in the T.A.O. matrix. By moving through time and space an impulse field develops, the atom, indicating a certain energy content and state of motion. And in addition there is this compulsion to transmit the impulse, this inability to put an end to the motion of every impulse from atom to atom, from impulse field to impulse filed. When we now try to imagine such an impulse field three-dimensionally (figure 102), we have to be aware that we can only do this in a roughly generalising manner, without being entitled to perfection or absolute correctness.

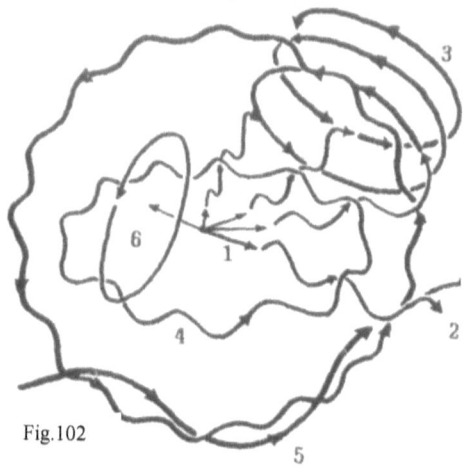

Fig.102

The basic impulse creating a centre and producing waves (1) determines the spherical field and in a broader sense the atom. It must be possible to track down this basic impulse already, to prove it by experiments. After all, the structure inside the atom is not a "nucleus" but nothing else but a high-energy electromagnetic field. The physicists Kopfermann and Schüler carried out experiments which pointed to this structure. They called it hyperfine structure, and we now know why they had to make their discovery. It means nothing else but the perpendicular (radial) component of the electron wave (4) which makes a transition into the finestructure outside the atom (2). The two structures are distinguished by their spatial quality; understandably the hyperfine structure is denser and of shorter wavelength than the finestructure. Both structures reveal their special effects in the spectrum of the light.

Quantum physics tries to attribute these effects to the behaviour of the electrons and thus sets about it the wrong way. Because these structures are the cause whereas the electron waves already mean an effect of these fields. And a material particle or a corpuscle is nowhere to be found.

The effects of the finestructure are based on the polarisation processes in the space as we already described them: they cause magnetism and electricity, but also have an effect on other electromagnetic impulses by splitting them up through their spiral rotation. Light passing through magnetic fields therefore exhibits several neatly arranged lines in the spectrum - and the physicists call this the Zeemann effect. In the same way the behaviour of the hyperfine structure is expressed but conditional on dimensions it affects the light of shorter wavelength, like X- or gamma radiation.

Similar phenomena occur in the electrostatic field as well, in this case we speak about the Stark effect. On principle, both effects prove the existence of these structures and we comprehend how and why they exist.

New impulses - triggered by electron waves - stream away from the field (3), we call them by the collective name light. Depending on which areas these impulses are created in their temporal sequence (frequency) changes as well and it is logical that X- and gamma radiation have to come rather from inside of the atom whereas heat waves (5) are only produced in the outer areas but are in return allowed to jolt the whole atom.

Superposition of oscillations create new oscillations and patterns (6), similar to the Fourier oscillations. They characterise the atom, determine its valence, its possibilities for contact and bonding. And we should not forget: all of this is created in one single pulsating field. For that reason, this is not a small machine, not a something which can be dissected into individual functions but an inseparable unit of existence, and its effects can be substantiated by a single cause: the existence of T.A.O..

Every spatial and temporal correspondence in the succession of impulses (frequencies) marks the places where messages are created and understood, that means absorbed. In the hyperfine range, gamma and X-ray waves are both produced and absorbed in the same way. The external electron waves produce and absorb light, and impulses of light of particularly low frequency are called radio waves. As we already discussed in connection with mercury, they are easy to produce - moved fields are already sufficient. We can easily imagine that the whole universe has to be pulsed through by uncountable wave-like shoves but only a small portion of them becomes noticeable to us. They fashion the visible and perceptible world.

Our conditions of encounter apply to all these impulses, waves, and frequencies. Penetration, interference, resistance, harmony, and disharmony, absorption and reflection create the whole reality, the cosmos, including its invisible parts. And therefore the cosmos is an inseparable whole. It alone exists, and there is no other universe anywhere else, a Hereafter or Other World for instance, a realm of spirits and souls, because the universe itself seems to be one single big soul in which everything is contained what human brains can detect or think up.

In their oscillational patterns, atoms carry an unequivocal programming which determines their physical behaviour. But of course without any objective of their own. Yet atomic structures and molecular bonds are not produced merely at random but the new things which can originate through them, beforehand without any obvious probability, often gives us practically thinking observers quite the impression of randomness. Because our concept of randomness is defined as the product of the calculus of probabilities within the framework of a logic full of prejudice. But if we really designated the events of this world as "random", we would not get to the heart of truth.

Buddhists have a better word for all events in the material world: co-incidence. It expresses that everything which happens coincidentally arises causally from programming, from compulsion and necessity. The significance of the occurrence is not immanent to any event but it is only created in the relationship between originator and perceiver. It is created by the brains of the world and only refers to these brains or to the creatures who want to find a meaning in the cosmic events by virtue of their thinking.

Transformations occur between all messages of matter. Irradiated light waves make whole areas of the atom oscillate via the electron waves. Therefore, in the case of absorption, the atom emits other waves on its own, like for example heat or electron waves,. Depending on the type and state of the atom every kind of wave can be transformed into another one in this way. Light changes the frequency, heat transforms into light, including X- and gamma radiation, electron waves (electric current) changes into light, and so on.

Basically every transformation is possible when frequencies correspond to each other and certain encounters take place. But all these mechanisms run off statistically, it is a game of the quanta, and every attempt to watch the game will immediately change its rules. Because we are a result of these quantum mechanisms ourselves – and can therefore never be a neutral observer but only a participant!

It is remarkable that every place where an impulse propagates is absolutely solitary. It only releases this single sequence of impulses. No other wave could start from the same point or use the same path within an atom if the spins did not evade each other. This corresponds to the exclusion principle by the physicist Pauli and is actually a (Nobel price awarded) matter of course.

The vibrations of the atomic field also influence each other indirectly. Thus, an atom - excited by light waves – can increase or reduce its ability to transmit electron waves. Even thermal vibrations disturb the transmission of electron waves. We say: the resistance of the conductor against electric current increases. By comparison, in the electrolyte the supply of heat reduces this resistance since the mobility of the ions is increased. On the other hand, the lack of thermal vibrations can make the electrical resistance fall to zero as is the case in superconductive elements and structures. "Structures" for the reason that the variety of atomic configurations which admit superconductivity - even those which are organic – is conceivable.

Fundamentally, nearly all mutual influences imaginable are possible and for every kind we will also find examples by experiment.

That way the physicists had to discover their many effects and phenomena. Many of these effects caused particular confusion, especially those in which waves apparently reacted with particles and therefore one never quite knew what one was actually dealing with. One of these contradictory phenomena is the photo effect the interpretation of which helped Einstein win the Nobel prize.

We would like to describe the effect from our point of view right away: When we expose a metal plate which is highly active with electron waves to short-wave light, electron waves will emerge from the plate. Obviously a transformation from light into electron waves is taking place. Since the energy of the light is determined by its frequency (every shove transmits a certain partial amount), it is absolutely plausible that this also determines the frequency of the electron waves and thus their energy. This results already from the congruence of the wavelengths which are the prerequisite for the transformation after all. Since the number of light waves determines the intensity of the light, it has to make sense immediately that the number of electron waves is also determined by it. There isn't any contradiction in our concept.

But if one considered the electron to be a particle which converts the energy of the light into motion, the intensity of the light would have to influence the energy of the electron. Observations, however, revealed that this energy was always only connected with the frequency of the light whereas its intensity seemed to determine the number of electrons. Since one did not doubt in the electron being a particle, there was only one way out: light had to be a particle, too. Einstein was its godfather and called it photon.[33]

With that he showed science a way that had to terminate in the dead-end street of dualism.

But because of the little difference between our idea of waves and the real wave (in which energies oscillate harmoniously whereas a sequence of impulses really transmits individual shoves, i.e. quanta) we understand why both light and electrons have to act like particles. Photons correspond exactly to light pulses, and these are nothing else but packages of energy which we could certainly also call energy particles if the word particle did not convey the impression of substance.

As expected, events similar to the photo-effect also unfold in the space of the hyperfine structure of the atom, admittedly among the X-ray waves, though, and in this case the physicists had to come across the so-called Auger effect. For the most part the electron waves excited by it are not ejected from the atom but cause further X-ray waves with characteristic frequencies which exhibits a process analogous to the photoelectric effect.

The structure of the atomic field leaves the mark of its own apparent regularities on the transformations. When an electron wave in the outer area absorbs energy, only the inner next electron wave can release energy again. The transformed light has therefore a shorter wavelength than the irradiated one.

In comparison, X-ray waves react on the inner areas of the atom. Transformed X-ray waves are therefore inevitably produced in areas farther outside and always have a longer wavelength than their cause (Compton effect). This all is so irresistibly logical that we don't have to loose many words about it.

Every electromagnetic wave leaving a field radially gets into the geometry of the space. That means the wave is expanding (figure 103, 103a).

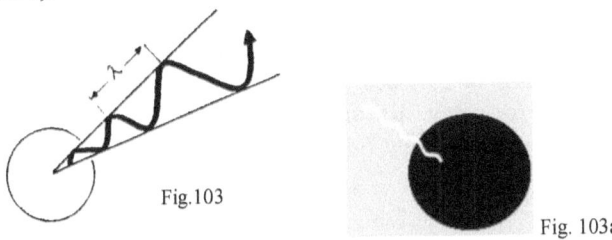

Fig.103

Fig. 103a

Its wavelength becomes longer, as the figure shows, its frequency lower. Thus a red shift sets in. The known red shift of far-away galaxies, however, cannot only be attributed to this effect called gravitational red shift but also to the Doppler effect which occurs because of the movement of the galaxies. There can be no doubt about the expansion of space for that reason...

The geometrical field relations (namely the spherical influence of the repulsions on one another), which could be paraphrased quite well as curvature or expansion of the space in Einstein's sense, generally change the light and the electromagnetic processes respectively. The corrections in the calculations which are for that reason always necessary correspond to a large extent to the corrections which result from the General Theory of Relativity. Due to these facts, Einstein assigned some mass to the light because it looks exactly as if the light was loosing energy under the influence of gravitation. Since the acceleration of free fall reflects exactly the geometrical relations of a field, the loss apparently made by the expansion of the wavelength corresponds in turn exactly to that energy which would have to be expended to raise the light quantum against the acceleration of free fall.

Within 45 meters, the frequency of a gamma ray is reduced by about a factor of $5 \cdot 10^{-15}$. In short, this can be described as the consequence of the fact that the variation of the amplitude of a wave will always be proportional to the distance from the point of excitement because of the spherical spatial conditions of a gravitational field. Seen from this point of view the mass of the light is immediately revealed as purest fiction. One can therefore not confirm Einstein's General Theory of Relativity with the gravitational red shift.

Light waves are also bound to the structure of every field in tangential direction. We could see this most clearly with the diffraction of the light. A process definitely corresponding to this diffraction also takes place in a spherical field which is getting continuously denser in direction of the centre. Then a light impulse will find the same orbiting conditions as a moved field (figure 104).

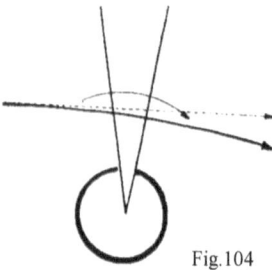

Fig.104

We already know that these orbiting conditions depend on the velocity among other things. Therefore the deflection of the light, for example in the field of the sun, is very small, but still detectable. The fact that this deflection exists finally helped Einstein to his triumph and made the professional experts no longer doubt the correctness of his theories. We will come back to this in the chapter "Relativity".

From our point of view, the curvature of space does on no account result immediately from the mass of a field but also from its size as such. Therefore, very big stars with slight surface curvature exhibit surprisingly little gravitational effects without exception. The physicist helps himself out of this paradox by assigning a correspondingly low mass to these stars. That in turn leads to absolutely absurd density values. With regard to its gravitation, the giant star Betelgeuse has, according to the opinion of astrophysicists, a density which would fall far below any vacuum that could be produced on Earth. We know that this bizarre result can just not be correct.

The inverse conclusion is just as inadmissible: the assumption of a black hole because of gravitation. Since light can easily escape the sphere of influence of a tiny atom there is no reason to assume it could be held by a "singularity" (whatever this is meant to be). And only with the assumption of a central gravitation would it be possible to cook up a theory of the black hole - Einstein's General Theory of Relativity achieves just plainly absurd results in this case.[34]

The mass is a pure operand, it does on no account express exactly the amount of any substance. It will never be able to do so because there is no substance! For that reason, masses can never be so big and at the same time of so small a size that they would not let the light escape. But we have to call to mind that we discovered at least real Empty Holes after all: the repulsion principle causes places in the universe where there has to be no mass at all - and yet matter is flowing towards these places.

The repulsion principle which we described within the T.A.O. matrix of the universe suggests to doubt all physical postulates and axioms. Just the assumption as such that everywhere in the cosmos the same laws of nature apply would be hardly justifiable and not secured by anything. We can imagine that physical or chemical processes run off according to other rules and at other velocities in other regions of the universe where the pressure distributions are different. As it is, the velocity of light pulses is not standardised either on any account because it always depends on the fields in the space. A perfect vacuum does not exist anywhere. Such an "empty" state could never exist in the universe at all. Every so-called vacuum is in truth filled with T.A.O. in which impulses can fluctuate at any time and therefore particles can be created which could be called virtual rather out of embarrassment than for any logical reasons. The vibrations in the vacuum can be proved, for example, by means of the Casimir effect (figure 104a):

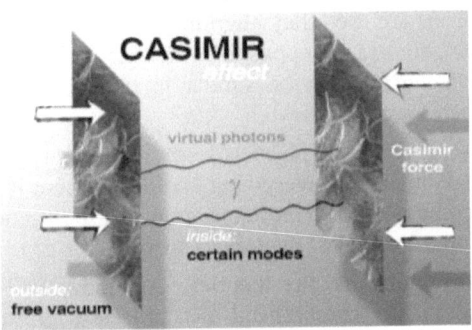

Fig. 104a

In 1997, the Casimir effect was established in a measurable way by an American researcher. Casimir calculated in 1948 that two metal plates which were brought close together in a vacuum would have to be pressed together without any external reason. The cause would be that not any "quantum particles" could come into existence in the narrow gap between the plates but only those whose wavelength would fit into the gap. In this way a lower number of particles would be produced in the gap than in the surrounding space whereupon the plates would have to be pressed together from the outside. The theory for this says that according to the principles of quantum mechanics no "real" vacuum and no empty space in the true sense of the word is possible. One rather assumes that the vacuum contains mysterious, fluctuating fields which are responsible for the Casimir effect.

The effect is a confirmation of the repulsion principle. After all, we discovered that the impulses in T.A.O. cause the repulsion, the universal pressure because of the increased requirement for space. Even in the vacuum around and in-between the plates the impulses in the matrix occur and the plates are shoved together. The explanation of the quantum theoreticians is therefore really comprehensible.

We know that disturbances and encounters continuously take place in the vacuum. One has to see it as it is: fluctuations, oscillations, and impulses within T.A.O. are virtual. The creation of a stable "particle" is an extremely rare event. If we wait long enough maybe a proton will come into existence between the Casimir plates ... (Heisenberg would not be happy about this at all).

By the way, the effect is too strong for gravitation to be the cause. All explanations of the phenomenon have yet another problem: when corrugated plates are used they align in such a way that the peaks of the corrugation are exactly opposite each other. This could be caused by the fact that a polarisation similar to that of a magnetic field occurs between the plates as well.

In any case, the nuclear physicists are increasingly forced to part with the image "matter is everything and the vacuum is nothing". It seems to become more and more apparent that the vacuum contains everything and the world of matter is a special state of it!

There is no doubt that the theories valid today will not always sufficient by far to comprehend the processes in the universe completely. Again and again physicists and astronomers observe phenomena which will absolutely not fit in with the network of their explanations. Not least of all the disastrous tendency to universally generalise observations within our limited range of experience is to blame for that. Material processes all over the world, however, don't have to proceed unconditionally in the same way in the stars on any account. An example for that: one was able to identify about 50 to 60 types of molecules in the interstellar space. Some of them are also found on our Earth but one also discovered cyano-acetylene chains which are so exotic that it would be impossible to produce them in any laboratory on Earth, not at any price...

19 Asymmetry

We already made the facts about the creation of more complex atoms clearer by explaining how protons and helium, maybe even deuterons, combine to form new total fields. As a rule this is only realised in the nuclear reactors of the stars but cold encounters are also possible. Up to the iron atom, atoms are very stable but basically it goes: the more individual fields form a total field, the more instable the structure will get.

That's because firstly the repulsion of the protons and alpha particles increases with their number, and secondly more and more neutron fields are integrated as weakly oscillating spaces and the curving force (strong interaction) decreases with the increase of the total size of the field. One possibility for an instable nuclide to maintain or regain the harmony of its oscillations consists in simply eliminating disturbing impulses. They are discharged and, understandably, can be identified as electron waves. Such a radiation is called beta particle radiation.

Ever disappearance of an electron wave shakes the remaining field in a drastic manner. The oscillation of its inner area leads to an output of energy in form of light of extremely short wavelength which is know to us as gamma radiation. Now and then the highly energetic state also lifts one of the primary fields across the barrier whereupon it is immediately expelled from the bond. It should not be surprising in the least that a field catapulted out in such a way is revealed as helium atom. Radiation of helium is called alpha particle radiation. This frequent occurrence of the helium field is understandable because heavy atoms consist mainly of helium. But even protons and neutrons get ejected, and one already makes use of this experimentally in high-energy physics. The whole process in which the atom strives for a more stable constellation is called radioactivity, and it is not extraordinary if only for the reason that the stable atom is practically the exceptional case according to the principle of a matter which repels everything around it whereas one can generally assume that all matter will decay again in the end...

If we wanted to smash an instable nuclide, we would require a field which is not too fast, as big as possible and of low repulsion in itself - as we know from the example of the fan wheel. A slow field of neutrons fulfils all these conditions. Shot on a nuclide it is briefly added to the nuclide for the time being but disturbs the structure that is unstable in any case in such a manner that the atom decays into two mostly unequal halves. In doing so, more neutrons, at least two or three, are released. We have to consider in this case that the protons we are dealing with can have lost their oscillation. These neutral fields can in turn trigger a fission. Since they constantly multiply during the process it will lead to the familiar chain reaction with its enormous expressions in energy. To be exact, these energies do not come from the atoms themselves, as we know, but actually stem from the cosmic pressure.

The disintegration halves are again atoms which can be reintegrated into the classification of elements. They halve their original amount of energy into new spherical fields with a now bigger total surface. Therefore a new equilibrium of forces has to be found with the environment, with the universal pressure, something that - as we also described already - happens in shoves until the universal pressure has the fields under control again, so to speak. It's these enormous shoving energies that lend the devastating effect to the atomic bomb.

The game of forces in increasing and diminishing the surfaces of spherical fields leads to the circumstance that both the so-called mass deficiency takes effect and an apparent increase in mass becomes noticeable. An element can therefore even transform into a higher element through decay. In this up and down of the decay series, regularities can be found again which have to be understood merely statistically, though, and never take place with a precision of one hundred percent. Even the regularity of the decay results from statistical distributions. The attempt, however, to use this regularity for measuring the time, e.g. by means of the C^{14} method, is extremely dubious for the reason alone that the gravitational effect has certainly diminished continuously because of the expansion of the universe and that the probability of decay has increased in the course of time.

From time to time alpha particle radiation is able to disengage hydrogen radiation, which is often pure, from nuclides. Events of this kind prove therefore on principle that really all atoms are composed of a few basic fields. By means of these "standardised" fields one can manipulate the matter in the same manner as with a modular construction system. When a helium atom is shot at nitrogen, sometimes a hydrogen atom is released from it whereas the helium field settles down. The result is an oxygen atom.

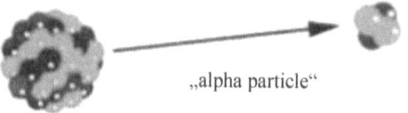

„alpha particle"

Fig. 104b

Hopefully we did not forget in the meantime that these "particles" consist of invisible impulse fields and are not small spherules as illustrated in figure 104 b. These impulse fields behave similarly to drops of mercury or a liquid of a similar kind. Fields of protons do not settle down on each other but mostly create overlap integrals up to the size of helium fields. These are only absorbed by an atom if they have come very close to it. The probability for a hit is thus very low. For one single transformation it is necessary to shoot off about 500 000 alpha particles. Meanwhile high-energy physics already creates artificial elements which are not found naturally, at least not on our Earth. The possibilities in this respect are only limited by the symmetries which are connected with the produced atoms (even mass-numbers). Accordingly there are areas of stability alternating with areas of instability.

Radioactive decay works only as regular as a clockwork over longer periods of time. Statistical variations are quite the rule with weak preparations and short periods. For that reason, there aren't any exact clocks based on decay anywhere in the cosmos. In principle, it is impossible to foresee when an atom is emitting an alpha particle. Basically all types of atoms decay at one time, even the stable ones, but the half-life value of stable atoms is much too high to be comprehensible by human standards. Even helium atoms do not live infinitely, and the proton does not have the privilege of immortality, either. This first and simplest of all impulse fields will decay presumably into an anti-electron and several neutrinos sooner or later. The half-life value of a proton, however, is calculated with about 10^{30} years - no reason for us to get nervous...

In addition, every decay is compensated by the formation of new structures, and in the stars, even in their crowns of radiation, higher elements are constantly produced. All in all it is a process which makes a possible end of the universe take place in an unimaginably distant future. But a proton is not able to pulsate in all eternity if only for that reason that it is ceaselessly distributing shoves and impulses to the universe and in doing so looses energy which in turn contributes to the formation of new protons in other places, though...

Despite this constant renewal we have to notice fundamentally that the cosmos is obviously heading for a state which it already had at one time: chaos. It is, however, allowed to ask if it will ever reach this state. Because it is just this endeavour which is at the same time responsible for the existence of our world. A fact which has received attention only lately since the previous statements of thermodynamics barred the way to such insights. In this connection we point out to the examinations of the Nobel price laureate Ilya Prigogine which deal with the non-equilibrium and dissipative structures demonstrating that the Boltzmann principle is not universally valid.

Processes of self-organisation of matter, the entering into orders, have their driving force just in that physical parameter which seems to exclude all this at first glance: in entropy. Energy in the cosmos cannot flow off indiscriminately, it creates orders in the struggle for space and path, in the interaction and counteraction, orders which already mean a perceptible image to us, actually an endless series of images which only resemble one another for short periods of time. Just as the fixed stars are changing their places in reality, the cosmos changes its whole image, too and there will be scarcely a state among it which we can justifiably call "end".

All atoms are - at least in our range of experience - apparently in a state of equilibrium with each other at least at first glance. When we take a closer look the whole activity of the matter is revealed as a game of electricity. Only because matter keeps its balance always on the edge of the equilibrium it creates both inorganic and organic structures, and it's especially the latter which are struggling for an equilibrium with their environment as long as they exist.

We already met the ionised atoms in the crystals or in the electrolytes, and we know that they are polarised impulse fields. But actually all atomic fields of this world are polarised. But when they are combined to molecules we don't notice it - like for example in the common table salt. In order to produce the polarisation effect distinctively the equilibrium between the atoms has to be disturbed first. This is mostly done by "ionising" radiation or electromagnetic processes like electric current or heat. Depending on the dose, all radiation which we find with radioactivity is ionising because it is able to make the atoms they hit loose their energetic equilibrium - generally this happens in two ways:

1) by strengthening an atom. In that way it has more energy than the other atoms and repels them more violently. We are talking about a positive ion.

2) by weakening an atom. It moves a little closer to the unweakened atoms, and we call it a negative ion.

In this case, positive and negative have an almost analogous meaning even if it is only to express that there is more or less energy available. After all, strengthening means that by supplying energy the electron waves oscillate farther away from the centre and weakening means that they move closer to it. Of course it looks as if electrons were given to one of the atoms and were taken from the other, and therefore the particles theory talks about exchanging electrons. This makes things only unnecessarily more complicated than they are.

Atoms strengthened or weakened in comparison to their environment form clouds of ions. They do not act neutral any longer but can be influenced electromagnetically. The result are repulsions and attractions depending on the available polarisation. As it is, ions are always created in pairs because the strengthening of one atom has to be always on the expense of the other. As to be expected the two ions are soon adapting to each other again (recombination).

Since the equilibrium of matter can be disturbed so easily we find ions practically everywhere. Near the ground we find about $10^3/cm^3$ in the air, i.e. a vast amount which is produced by the radioactivity of the Earth. The gases, normally very bad conductors for electron waves, turn into good conductors when they are ionised. This goes without saying when we think of the processes in the electrolyte. A gas whose properties are significantly determined by the existence of positive and negative ions is called plasma. This plasma is quasi neutral since the ions balance each other. Matter at temperatures of several thousand degrees, for example star matter, is always in the state of plasma.

Since strengthened and weakened ions always occur together at the same time, a strange effect takes place in the plasma. The lost equilibrium results in a separation of the ions (strengthening according to point 1) and immediately afterwards in a reunion (weakening according to point 2). The plasma therefore performs oscillations - to the very confusion of the physicists since these processes cannot be explained very plausibly with the theory of the electrons.

Oscillations of a very similar kind are also possible in chemical processes. Especially in molecular biology, these oscillations (chemical clocks) play a dominant role.

The plasmatic state is also contagious, so to speak. All matter coming into contact with plasma also looses its equilibrium and starts oscillating immediately. For that reason, plasma cannot be kept in ordinary containers but can only be contained in magnetic fields (stellarators).

Because of the oscillations, extremely strong electrodynamic effects arise in the plasma just as permanently demonstrated by the sun. By means of the to and fro in the plasma the magnetic fields constantly change poles. Therefore the multifarious phenomena on the surface of the sun can be well explained by means of plasma physics, as for instance the polar appearance of sunspots in pairs. In every place where the plasma atmosphere of the sun is torn open by magnetic fields we are looking at matter which is up to 2000 degrees Celsius cooler than the outer shell. We already discussed the cause of this in the chapter "Celestial Bodies".

The ionosphere of our Earth also consists of plasma which oscillates at several megahertz and represents temperatures of up to 3000 degrees. Radio waves which oscillate slower than this plasma belt are reflected by it (the fan wheel principle again). Only impulses which oscillate faster than the plasma will penetrate it.

Beams of protons or other fields, i.e. ion beams, also exhibit all phenomena which we know from electron and light waves: diffraction, refraction, and interference. This could amaze us if we believed in compact matter particles.

Electron waves also get into the space geometry when exiting the atomic field. They suffer an increase of wavelengths and a loss of frequency just like the light. Every field (magnetic or electrostatic) provides the electron wave with the usual, already described orbital conditions. Therefore it always leads to distinctly curved paths which revolve around the magnetic field. In particle accelerators (synchrotrons) one can accelerate electrons almost up to the velocity of light but not above it – and the supporters of the Theories of Relativity love to present this as a proof of the Special Theory of Relativity. We will soon discover that it isn't.

We already noticed that a body cannot be accelerated above the velocity of light because the T.A.O. matrix determines every kind of motion[2] structurally. This applies both to impulses and bodies because they all propagate in the same way. The properties of the matrix depend in turn on the pressure ratios of the space, and these are determined by the surrounding masses. Just as we have to assume that even the gravitational constant is conditional on the orientation in space[35], i.e. that it turns out differently according to its position in the universe, we must not see the velocity of light as an absolute quantity on any account for that reason. If we thus say even an electron wave cannot be faster than the light, it is in fact absolutely correct – but it is easily conceivable that the light itself will break its own high-speed record sometime.

Even if all conceivable forms of impulse are possible in T.A.O. and probably even exist, the apparent waves significant for the material events have, with only a few exceptions ("neutrinos" and the like), a definite spin. We already illustrated this in great detail and also considered how this spin interconnects with the spins of other impulses by either creating matching spins itself or by admitting only matching spins. The visible, perceptible, or measurable reality is actually the product of a destructive game of interferences of impulses– we live in a world that is left from the incessant process of extinction! This constant process of extinction represents a "vacuum energy", exactly that fluctuation of particles which both induce and extinguish themselves incessantly in the vacuum. It is a kind of struggle between matter and antimatter – a struggle between "left-hand" and "right-hand" so to speak. That the vacuum does not remain vacuum can be put down to the fact that antimatter cannot exist any longer starting from a certain complexity of the atoms due to interruptions in the symmetry. Only with the spiral impulses is a distinct separation into normal impulses and anti-impulses still possible. It is also still perceivable with proton fields – thus there can also be some kind of anti-hydrogen. Even many "particles" can occur as anti-particles or, like neutrinos, be their own anti-particle (if the theories of the quantum physicists demand it). But the anti-electron, the positron, differs only in the spatially opposite polarisation of the "charge" after all – so it is to be regarded as anti-matter only because of a sloppy definition. This definition is not relevant anymore for heavy, complex atoms. For example, there is practically no anti-iron atom since the surface of a heavy atom can have both right-hand and left-hand polarisations, even both at the same time in different places. Two iron atoms which could penetrate and destroy each other without hindrance would be out of the question. Thus anti-matter is restricted to simple particles and impulses only, and we know what to think of the fairy tales in which one dreams about complete anti-universes. Real anti-matter, by the way, would be negative matter with negative energy – but this is absolutely impossible, anyway.

Therefore we see that matter is not dominated by symmetry from the outset but the idea of the symmetry of matter has always been haunting the minds of the scholars (more out of esthetical motivation than for physical necessity). At first glance it really looks as if one could integrate all the many particles in a pattern but then one realises: already at this stage there isn't any symmetry. If suddenly a particle appears which does not fit into the desired pattern at all, it is classified as "strange" particle, like for instance the K mesons or the hyperons.

The whole matter is getting even more uncomfortable when the hoped-for symmetry of matter seems to be obviously violated as a whole. Most of the time these violations result from unsatisfying theories only: thus negative charge adheres to low masses while positive charge resides on big masses. This astonished already Einstein and made him suspicious (we, however, know the reason: there aren't any positive or negative charges, after all).

When the spin of the electrons was discovered, naturally one had to believe that the probability for left-hand and right-hand rotation was the same. Therefore it seemed quite peculiar that all electrons obviously have the same spin. But more annoyance is yet to come: when a substance emitting electrons is put into a strong magnetic field, for example the cobalt isotope ^{60}Co, in such a way that almost all presumed nuclear spins are aligned by the field, one will notice that all electrons are always emitted in the same direction. This must catch the quantum theoreticians by surprise because according to their assumption the nuclear spins (even parity) can adopt two different states ($+1/2$, $-1/2$), and the impulse of the electrons would also have to point in the direction of the nuclear spin because of the reciprocal orientation with the nuclear spin, that means an inversion of the nuclear spin (from $+1/2$ to $-1/2$) should also result in an inversion of the electron impulses (odd parity).

Therefore the expected inversion process would consist in the electrons being emitted into every direction of the aligned spin. This, however, can never be observed. Apparently, of two processes which develop from one another because of the spatial inversion, only one has been realised in nature. For that reason, one is talking about a violation of parity and notices with astonishment that the probability for electrons to follow a left-hand twist is higher than to follow a right-hand twist. This absolutely correct observation is on no account shrouded in mystery, though.

We know why the spin of the electron waves is defined by, let's say "left-hand": because of the uniformity of all proton fields. All electron impulses of this world exhibit inevitably the same twist. With that the assumption that left-hand and right-hand rotation are of the same probability is already wrong. But also the experiments in which one wanted to inverse the spin of the electrons cannot demonstrate the hoped-for symmetry at all because the electrons emitted by the radioactive cobalt are strongly influenced by the magnetic field. Since magnetic fields causally come from electron waves the spin of their finestructure has the same one-sided definition as that of the electron waves. When we put the beta particle radiating cobalt into the magnetic field, despite the spin of some imaginary nuclei an effect occurs which is similar to the so-called HALL effect (figure 105): in the magnetic field the electron waves are subject to the already discussed Lorentz force as so-called charge carriers and are aligned to a predefined side.

The radioactive cobalt transforms into nickel by means of beta particle decay and all emitted electrons have always and without exception only left-hand spin! Because of the Lorentz force there is therefore only the direction allowed by the magnetic field for the emitted electrons. For that reason, the expected inversion fails to occur of course. The hoped-for symmetry proves to be a false hope because contrary to a particle impulse the spin of the electron wave (and in the end it is certainly responsible for the charging effect) has - even parity, and therefore it cannot be expected from the experiment of Madame C.S.Wu (figure 106) that it will reveal a violation of the parity or that it contradicts a symmetry which cannot be there at all.

By the way the experiment was repeated by the physicists Yang, E. Ambler, R.W. Hayward, D.D. Hoppes and R.P. Hudson - always with the same result.

Only the spatially inversed electron, the positron, would be emitted in the opposite direction. It is just not possible to simply inverse an electron and expect that it will now behave differently.

The spiral of figure 107 preserves its spin in anti-clockwise direction even if we turn the book on its head. The direction of the electron emission, however, results only from this spin. The attempt to get electrons out at the other side is approximately as if one turned a clock upside down and expected its hands to rotate counter-clockwise now. But we can of course hold a clock any way we like - the spin of the hands will always remain the same!

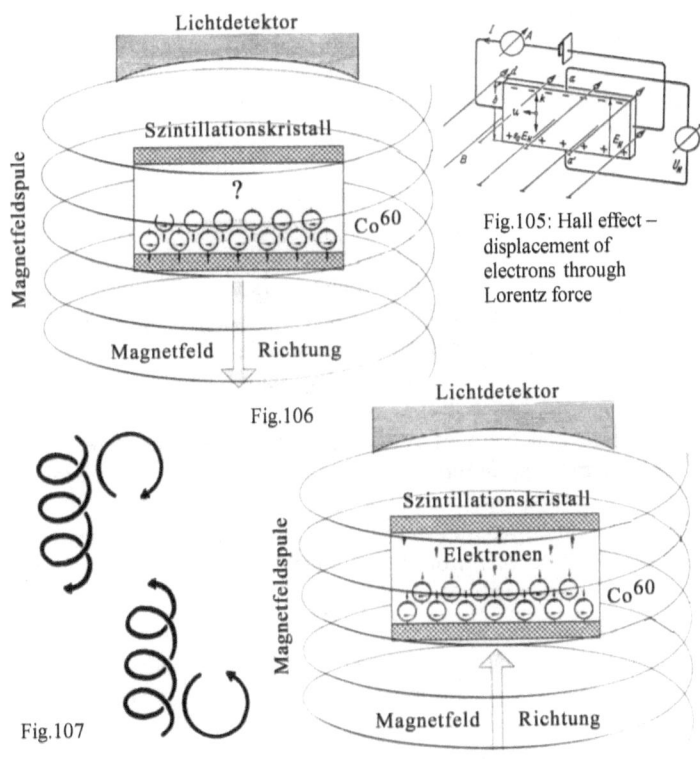

Fig.105: Hall effect – displacement of electrons through Lorentz force

Fig.106

Fig.107

Magnetfeldspule = magnetic field coil
Lichtdetektor = light detector   Elektronen = electrons
Szintillationskristall = scintillation crystal
Magnetfeld = magnetic field   Richtung = direction

It is almost unbelievable that physicists really conducted the experiment in the described way and were astonished about the preferred direction of the electrons.

As we already described, the so-called weak interaction is revealed in all processes depending on electron waves. It is therefore not amazing in any way if the parity appears to be violated in all events assigned to the weak interaction on any account. Matter cannot be inversed exactly by means of charge reversal. For that reason, anti-matter can never have properties analogous to those of matter - unless time is also inversed simultaneously with charge and space. But that is impossible. The invariance against the inversion of charge and space, which can be observed, also demonstrates that nuclear reactions are irreversible on principle although recognised theories allow for it (especially quantum mechanics which is still too much committed to classical mechanics). Although quantum physics is dealing with reversible processes without any exception, all interaction processes have to be irreversible because of this asymmetry if only for the reason that the arrow of time cannot be reversed because a causality from the effect to the cause would be absurd. Even if there are apparently retroactions to the cause, time is not reversed in them. That even quantum physicists are infected by some kind of intellectual paralysis when they establish superluminally fast tunnel effects is proven when they talk about impulses which exited sooner than they had entered – although the velocity of light has nothing to do with time. It's true, Einstein postulated the constancy of the velocity of light but this refers to the constancy of its magnitude – he did not determine the magnitude itself. If it turned out that light is a little faster than had been measured so far, it would not shake the Theories of Relativity in the least. In this case one would just have to calculate with the new value.

When one operates with the incorrect concepts plus and minus und their reflections, the apparent violation of the holy parity also occurs in the disintegration of mesons by means of charge reversal. It is interesting to note that there is no symmetry between a particle and its anti-particle from the outset. When the one has a right-hand spin, the other has a left-hand spin - but both are moving in the same direction! When, however, the direction is mirrored as well, nothing changes at all and no anti-particle is created. That means even a mirrored right-hand helix remains a right-hand helix in the world of the mirror. From that we understand in all clarity how ridiculous it has to be to search for symmetries of such kind in our matter![36]

Just another interesting question: is it possible to steal an electron, an atom, or even only one single tiny impulse from the universe? The answer is No! If someone put his hand into our world from the outside and took away an atom, this atom would in fact disappear from that place, the universal pressure, however would immediately invade the suddenly empty area in a shove and this tremendous shove would propagate like a sphere. It would be nothing else but a gravitational wave and it would cause exactly the energy which represented the stolen atom.

Upon its disappearance even one single impulse would cause an impulse of exactly the same magnitude. The repulsion principle makes it plain in a simple way: nothing can be taken away from the cosmos. Logically, its amount of energy remains forever constant. The physicists therefore had to discover the principle of the conservation of energy (or of the impulse)! Even impulses which seem to interfere away without a trace are in truth streaming away laterally as neutrinos (neutral current). We have to be aware of the fact that even the destructive interference of impulses has to lead to the same propagation of energy as if the impulse had been stolen. In that way every impulse will reappear somewhere in T.A.O. without any exception, as a particle, as a wave, or at least as a neutrino.

When the energies, the spins, and the situations of encounter are known, all material events become well predictable. For that reason - although based on other models - physicists know all about what will happen in the various shoving processes. But predominantly this knowledge has been worked out empirically. When looking for a particle demanded by theory one will usually discover it on bubble chamber photographs which have been existing for a long time and which have been examined thoroughly again and again. Long since, concepts like positive, negative, spin, and mass have not been sufficient any longer and therefore one is just introducing new, sometimes quite bizarre definitions which do not lack a certain humour: peculiarity, charm and anti-charm, beauty, truth, ... the colours red, green, and blue along with their complementary colours ... or spatial concepts like upward or downward and so on...

Well, an "untrue" particle ... that would probably be the most applicable designation for that impulse event which we are only permitted to call an atom for reasons of tradition. Heisenberg once wrote in the face of the fact that obviously all the different elementary particles can spring from each other: "These facts can be interpreted in the simplest way by assuming that all elementary particles are only different stationary states of one and the same matter..."

Fig.107a - NGC 4622

20 Galaxies

Let's describe in a few terse sentences how the cosmos obtained the image it presents today: in the beginning, light quanta especially rich in energy were produced by disturbances in T.A.O. and from them sprang the protons. They formed nothing else but plasma, this absolutely dynamic condition of matter which soon was set into motion - and thus the protons squeezed themselves to centres of energy, the stars. These stars pressed one another into new centres, the stellar groups. And those soon displaced each other to form new superorders, the galaxies. And these galaxies again displaced each other into new systems, the hyper-galaxies ... and these into open clusters and open superclusters and globular clusters and globular superclusters and so on...

This went on as far as the cosmos goes, up to those borders behind which the chaos presumably still reigns today...

If it really happened in such a simple way, the creation of matter and of the universe? How can we know all this? The answer is: we don't know – and will never ever learn. What we can know is that there can never have been a real beginning of the universe for logical reasons, that we live in a world of change and that we do not know from which image today's image of the universe developed. But if we absolutely want to believe in a beginning of the universe we should at least acquire some theories that are reasonable and plausible. The theory of the Big Bang isn't in any case.

Therefore, we will not rack our brains uselessly but turn our attention right away to the first thing that comes to mind when we think of the wonders of the cosmos: the galaxies. Actually one expects of a galaxy that it is expanding as well because of the total expansion of the universe. But considering the fact that, on the whole, even a galaxy forms a field again, united and strengthened by its main magnetic field, the understanding is gained that stars are pressed into the galaxy. For that reason, galaxies contract, i.e. they are shoved together by the universal pressure.. For the same reason, atoms rich in energy are getting smaller instead of bigger within a certain environment after all, as already learned. And the galaxies repel each other in the same way as the atoms. All observations made by astronomers are quite in accordance with the truth, and almost without any exception, they are inconsistent with the theory of the Big Bang. The universe expands like a gas which drifts apart because of the motion of its atoms. We will see that these observations are interpreted with a lot of imagination by the scientists – after all, it is possible to theorise very casually in this special field because who would travel to the next quasar to see for himself if everything is as the astrophysicists claim it to be. Little wonder that this field is teeming with black holes...

Of course the freedom of unverifiability is at our disposal as well. The repulsion principle, however, will provide a more logical explanation for many a mystery of cosmology than the hypothesis of the Big Bang. Even the astronomical realities appear completely different now. Thus, for example, the centre of a galaxy is not necessarily the birth place of new stars but mainly the grave of old ones which are practically building up an enormous hyper star there. From this hyper star matter flows in the same way as from any other star – back into the galaxy again in the form of individual atoms and as gas and plasma respectively - building material for new globules and stars.

Thus every galaxy has its cycle of living which postpones its final going up in the hyper star for a very long time but not forever.

The shrinking of our own milky way has a pleasant side effect: the diminishing of the gravitational constant[37] (the expansion of the universe reduces the universal pressure) is slowed down by it and with it the expansion of the planetary systems is slightly delayed. Nevertheless even the sun and with it all the planets in the centre of the galaxy (which, seen from the Earth, lies behind the constellation of Sagittarius) will disappear some day.

There are examples to be found in the cosmos for all intermediate stages of this diminishing process of a galaxy. The variety of forms of the galaxies ranging from spherical cluster shape to the ellipsoid of revolution are explained by it. The causes for the rotation of the galaxies are absolutely the same as for that of the individual star: electrodynamic effects of their magnetic field with each other or in the superdimensional magnetic field of the universe itself.

Understandably the transmission of their rotational moments to each other through the field of the universal pressure takes place from the outside to the inside. This explains the fast motion of the outer stars which appear to be practically advancing the rotation of the galaxies, to disregard Kepler's laws and to create spiral arms.

The latter are therefore not dragged behind without exception but point into the direction of rotation now and then, as is the case for example with the stellar vortex NGC 4622 (figure 107a).

All these peculiar characteristics of a galaxy - sufficiently verified by observation - have remained unsolved down the line so far. According to the repulsion principle, many of these mysteries can be substantiated in a surprisingly logical manner. For explaining the unexpectedly high velocities of the outer stars of a galaxy (and the being too slow of the inner ones!), the astronomers have two solutions at the ready: the so-called Dark Matter or the Modified Newtonian Dynamics (M.O.N.D.).[38] None of the explanations is comprehensible and none of them is necessary.

Moreover, the arms of the spiral galaxies prove that their form is not the result of gravitation due to rotation because in that case the elementary shape of the galaxies would have to be the bar - which is absolutely out of the question of course. It is more logical that the spiral arms were dragged out because the drive of the galaxy came from the universe and the impulse was transmitted from the outside to the inside.

Fig. 107b

Faced with figure 107b one has to ask oneself what the starting position of the galaxies at the beginning of the rotation might have looked like. With a rotation from the inside to the outside it has to be a bar – and besides none of the galaxies would have completed an entire rotation. All previously presented hypotheses about the development of the galaxies are therefore unbelievable. There are even theories which postulate the formation of galaxies before the development of the stars by claiming stars could only come into existence inside of galaxies. But that these big vortexes originally "rotated out " of an originally homogenous distribution of stars is actually apparent at first glance (in exactly the same way as proton fields "rotated out " of T.A.O. because of the encounter of the impulses).

If the expansion of the universe had not already been discovered, we would have to demand it. But what we do not know exactly is the average velocity of this expansion. The corresponding figures are corrected year after year; in principle, however, this remains without any meaning. It is a uniform expansion, in which galaxies move away from each other like raisins in the yeast dough. It cannot be attributed to an explosion but results from the pressure which came about when T.A.O. started moving[2]. Since we know that the curving force intensifies the illusion of "gravitation" and since this curving force also concerns the total field of the cosmos, the velocity of the expansion has to increase continuously – because the radii of the fields increase and the surfaces get flatter! But with that the repulsions predominate more and more – and as a result we have an accelerated expansion as it was discovered with amazement by the astronomers.[39]

In the chapter "Proton", we already implied that there was a solution to the mystery of the quasars. For them and for the radio galaxies there is, however, yet another solution: a proton flying at the velocity of light would not appear as a stationary field to a stationary observer but as a sequence of impulses distributed over the distance covered. With that even the proton becomes a wave which can certainly be subject to Doppler shifts. In the same way as the light of far away galaxies shifts into the range of red wavelengths, protons and atoms of fast moving galaxies shift into the wave range, too - for us relatively stationary observers they become light!

When a galaxy has superluminal velocity relative to our milky way, and there is no reason not to assume this, the "image of light" it transmits shifts into the range of radio waves whereas its protons occur as hard X radiation. When complete galaxies shift into these ranges of the spectrum we don't see them directly any longer. That's why they give the misleading impression as if relatively small objects (they are probably much farther away then previously assumed) would emit incredibly high energies in radio and X radiation. Thus quasars are presumably nothing else but galaxies with extremely high Doppler shift. Pure roentgen galaxies have to be put into the same category as well. But of course it is possible that they are phenomena which existed billions of years ago and to which we won't find any parallel in the present at all.

The previous theories about age, structure, gravitation, and stability of the stars along with their classification in the spectrum are not plausible in all probability. It is likely that the truth is just the other way round; old stars are actually young and young stars have been in existence for billions of years... But one could easily do without theories which can neither be confirmed nor falsified even in the future!

Since one had calculated up to then that stars can only remain stable up to max. 120 000 times the sun's mass, one had to learn otherwise in July 1981 when the super-sun R 136 A was discovered in the 30-Doradus nebula. This sun has obviously 300 000 times the sun's mass, and thus it doesn't give a damn for the theories of the astrophysicists. R 136 A has a diameter of about 150 million kilometres, which means it would fit exactly into the orbit of the Earth. It shines 100 million times brighter than our sun, its surface temperature is nearly 60 000 degrees Celsius which is not particularly much in relation to its size. It's possible that R 136 A is a hyper star as we expect one to be in the centre of a galaxy.

Actually R 136 A should have collapsed to a black hole a long time ago if the relativists had their way with their theories. That it hasn't done so demonstrates that something can't be right with the theory of the black hole. For us, R 136 A is no particular mystery. We know that even the mass dependent, space curving gravitation as defined by Einstein cannot exist as (to be exact) potentially infinitely great force. There is, however, the curved space and the "real" holes between the stars as those places in which globules like to come into existence. By the way, they only become visible if they stand in front of a bright gaseous nebula.

Incidentally, relative superluminal speed of galaxies also means that we won't learn anything about them which is in the range of the visible light. For that reason, the night sky is black which makes it possible to solve Olbers' paradox as well.[40]

There still is chaos outside of the farthest galaxies, as we even suspect, this will also be the place where the expansion ends. Or where it doesn't. Of course the far away galaxies do not fly into this chaos at superluminal velocity because they are not faster themselves than our own galaxy. The high relative velocity only comes about because of the great distance.

The theory of the Big Bang begins to sway considerably when one finds a galaxy which has an impossible direction, i.e. which dashes along perpendicular to the other galaxies. Already in 1980, the first of such galaxies was actually tracked down but yet there are other obvious indications. For example, beyond the constellation of Virgo one discovered an enormous cluster of stars which is sucking in whole solar systems, among them our own milky way, at a speed of 1.6 million kilometres per hour. The diameter of this super-galaxy is about two billion light years according to NASA information! NASA scientist George Smoot explained that because of this star cluster there were grounds for the assumption that the matter of space has never expanded explosively and monotonically.

The so-called "proof" of the Big Bang, the isotropic thermal radiation of 3 degrees Kelvin[41] is possibly explained - as we already demonstrated - by means of the waves coming out of chaos which still arrive at the Earth exhibiting an extraordinarily high Doppler shift. Moreover, these waves should differ considerably from any terrestrial radiation. As it is, they would of course exhibit both right-hand and left-hand spin, i.e. have a peculiar polarisation (which has to be verified yet). We certainly know that in chaos the decision for right-hand or left-hand spin should not have been made yet.

The Doppler shift of background radiation provides us with a possibility to roughly calculate the size of the universe. Because originally it has been extremely hard gamma radiation after all as it is required for the creation of protons or as it is finally created during the decay of them.

Wavelengths in the heat range are in an order of magnitude of 10^{-2} cm (0.01 cm). Gamma radiation of extreme hardness is in an order of magnitude of about 10^{-11} cm (0.00000000001 cm). Protons can be compared to a wavelength of ca. 10^{-12} cm.

In order to turn gamma radiation into heat waves we have to expand it approximately by a factor of 10^{10}. Calculated in light years, the result is thus a distance of 10^{10} light years, i.e. 10 000 000 000 light years. We could claim already that chaos would have to be about 10^{10} light years away from us - which would be a little over-hasty, though.

Einstein calculated the radius of the world with

$$R_E = \sqrt{\frac{3c^2}{4\pi\gamma p}} \approx 10^{10}\,light\ years$$

Using Hubble's constant the event horizon due to the expansion is calculated with

$$R_H = \frac{c}{H} \approx 1{,}77 * 10^{10}\,light\ years$$

From a cosmic viewpoint these are still good correspondences – at least concerning the dimension if one acknowledges that Hubble's constant has undergone several corrections in the meantime. At a dimensional distance of about 10^{10} light years there lies therefore the area in which galaxies exceed the velocity of light. We could now say the visible cosmos has approximately a radius of 10^{10} light years (at the moment the average value stated in the specialised literature is ca. 14 billion light years).[42]

If the background radiation was really absolutely isotropic - superficially thinking - one would have to assume that we were coincidentally in the centre of the world. Therefore one mistrusted this background radiation as a test in California proved in which one tried to measure this radiation exactly by means of a U2 equipped with microwave antennas. With that one expected to find differences in the range of thousandths of degrees. This endeavour, however, proves also that one does not take the Theories of Relativity too seriously because if one had done so, one could have saved oneself the test. In the meantime, one has in fact succeeded in determining and measuring the absolute state of motion[43] of our galaxy relative to the background radiation. According to the Special Theory of Relativity, this should not be possible at all. But obviously it is exactly that way as we assumed in our hypothesis of repulsion: spheres of light propagate absolutely in the space and motions can be measured relative to the light.

However, now we have to consider as well that when looking into the distance we also look into the past at the same time. That means nothing else but that the event horizon of the universe was at the distance of 10^{10} light years calculated before already about 10^{10} years ago. In other words that means that today we exist in a background radiation which was produced 10^{10} years ago! With that, every project to determine our location becomes an act of pure stupidity because not a clue at all can be found as to our momentary location. At best, the isotropy and the absolute propagation of the radiation spheres make it obvious that we have in fact a relative motion compared to them but that our true position in the universe cannot be ascertained. Where should the "centre" of an endless universe be?

But when the universe already had a radius of 10^{10} light years 10^{10} years ago the theory of the Big Bang drops completely out of the running. It can never have happened! Even if our cosmos seems to end after 10^{10} light years this value does not mean its real expansion at all. Because it has continued to expand for 10^{10} year! Where are its boundaries today?

We don't have to write down this number any more. It becomes meaningless because it is unimaginable. At best it will give us an idea about infinity itself, about the immensity of the universe, which we would so like to restrict. But instead of new boundaries we only find new conditions for which there are new words ... and all these words finally lead to the one word which is without boundaries and free from characteristics because boundaries and characteristics are not contained in it: T.A.O. - which does not know any sizes nor any distances at all as long as no standards are applied...

Thus the question for the size of the universe is meaningless and was asked senselessly. The universe is neither small nor big because all scales are relativised to our thinking, to our mind, and to our very own logic! But that means also that concepts like infinite or restricted are also just rooted in our thinking and don't have any universal validity!

Let's turn our attention again to the background noise of the universe, this time looking at it from the aspect that we could possible be perceiving pure "matter" – that is to say a Doppler effect of matter: in an infinite, homogenous universe every straight line of sight which is drawn in any direction must eventually terminate at the surface of a star. According to that, every point of the sky would have to have about the same surface luminosity as the solar disc. According to Boltzmann's law, the result would be an isotropic irradiation of ca. 4000 degrees Kelvin onto the Earth. Luckily the stars have never heard of Einstein. As we mentioned, after about 10^{10} light years, they simply exceed the velocity of light and in this way they are stealing away from our universe.

Will we really never again get to know about them? We have to realise that the expansion of the universe itself does not take place at superluminal speed on any account. The impulses of the galaxies farthest away make traces in the universe which remain independent of the movement of the galaxies and are expanded by the high velocity. In this way even a star flying at superluminal speed can leave its track in the universe (figure 108).

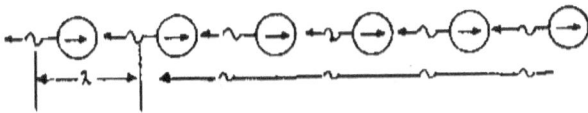

Fig. 108

After all, light is composed of impulses independent of each other. Thus even a body moving very fast leaves its naturally extremely stretched trace, which sets out on its voyage at the velocity of light in the universe. In the course of time this stretched wave arrives at our place and is identified as radio wave or heat.

An oscillating proton with the maximum frequency of 10^{17} oscillations per second would have to cover far more than 300 000 kilometres in this second in order to leave a light wave - i.e. it would have to fly at superluminal speed. Well, the background radiation consists of considerably longer radio waves, though. Therefore we can imagine the velocity at which the galaxies beyond the cosmic fringe are moving!

Well, electron impulses or light shoves are exactly that "stuff" of which every vibrating atomic field is created in principle, holding its own against other fields. What is flowing in to us from the farthest galaxies and regions of the universe is nothing else but the universal pressure which, all in all, forms the field of the universe - and what was measured with a radiation of 3 degrees Kelvin is its temperature - one proof that every apparently empty space is filled with this universal field...

In this giant field of force, which stands there like a colossal colourless crystal, the "images" of our world develop, and our brains create the three concepts which are sufficient to comprehend the function of the materially and spiritually detectable: energy, space, and time.

Countless books have been filled with theories and hypotheses in order to explain the beginning of this world. The most bizarre and obscure assumptions have been made, the most fantastic speculations and far too complicated theories have been flowing from the thinking brains of the scholars and philosophers - but the "truth" is certainly very simple...

Figure 109 shows the Andromeda Nebula[44]. This galaxy with a size of about 200 000 light years in diameter is about double the size of our milky way...

Fig. 109

21 Entropy

The ancient Greeks composed the events of this world of four elements: earth, water, air, and fire. Today this must appear to us as magnificent intuition since these four concepts contain in fact the four states of aggregation of a matter which is only able to cause the diversity of nature by means of these different qualities. These four basic properties are called: solid, liquid, gaseous, and plasma (however, the ancient Greeks were not able to predict the Bose-Einstein condensate).

In principle, it is possible for every element to adopt any of the four different properties. For doing so, the content of individual energy and that of the environment is always decisive... and it is always revealed as a game of the temperatures. Though basically there aren't any "temperatures", actually we can only speak of different states of motion. It is also gravity, inertia, and acceleration to which the different states of the elements can be attributed. The lighter an element the faster it changes into liquid or gaseous states and the harder it is for the element to solidify.

When solid, all elements can become crystalline provided they are pure. As a liquid they adopt a variety of viscosities which range up to the superfluidity of helium; their melting and boiling points are different and faithfully follow the energy content of the atoms, i.e. the periodic system of chemical elements. Nothing in this behaviour of the matter is unexplainable to us, it is well substantiated by the states of motion and the resulting distances of the atoms to each other which immerse their fields more or less into one another. Even the electrical and with that the chemical behaviour agree with the different states of aggregation, and the appearance of this world depends on these states, its quantities and structures and its harmonies, disharmonies, separations, and bonds or deformations...

In the end, originator and moderator of these states is always the universal pressure which constantly duels with the individual pressure of the atoms. The more an atom remains unbonded, the more it determines itself and the less it is subject to the dictates of the environment. Big gaseous stars remain predominantly stable for the reason that their matter is available as plasma which binds itself by means of strong electricity. Yet a steady current of single atoms which we know as cosmic radiation is flowing away from every star or every hyper star. At some time these atoms fall back to low levels of energy again by yielding impulses. They are then available as new building material for molecules, celestial bodies, or organisms. Each of their yielded impulses means a new disturbance of T.A.O. and prevents that it will ever get deadly silent and cold in the universe.

Because of this uninterrupted circulation of the energy absolute rest can never occur. We should therefore reconsider one of the most desolate basic postulates of physics, the entropy, and see if this vital activity of the cosmos is really flowing towards a deathly stillness in the end.

To put it very simple, entropy is the opposite of energy. Just as energy can represent the physical parameter of a system, entropy is also a concept for the physical parameter of a physical unit. Energy outlines the state of motion and the degree of order, entropy that of stillness and of disorder. Other such quantities are for example pressure or temperature.

If one wants to express the state of a system as a certain quantity one has to create arbitrary magnitudes for the entropy and determine an initial point. But with the creation of the concept entropy the thoughts of the physicists became somehow double-edged and no other explanation but that of entropy has divided physics so drastically into two camps - provoked by the formulation of the Second Law of Thermodynamics by Claudius. Conventional dynamics collided diametrically with thermodynamics; Newton's edifice of ideas developed the first rift ... his dynamics (as reversible process) was replaced by the discovery of the irreversibility. With that Newton's static universe lost the aura of respectability of the divine machine and its credibility...

Not all of the physicists could get used to this new idea for the irreversibility of the processes seemed to forbid the establishing of any order. But the assumptions of both camps, both those of the energeticists and those of the thermodynamicists, span a yarn which missed the essential: this universe is not created by the opposites themselves but by the unsteady and unstable state in-between these extremes.

On the one hand, it had been formulated quite correctly that energy in the cosmos could never be lost, on the other hand, it was suddenly claimed that the cosmos was heading incessantly and inexorably for the state of the lowest quantity of energy, namely the maximum entropy - the greatest stillness, the least warmth, the big, deathly chill...

But evidently this distressing conclusion had been done a little too overhasty because one examined certain physical phenomena in a far too isolated manner and did not have a comprehensive general view of the events. One of these phenomena is the dispersion of a gas into every available space until complete uniformity has been reached. The cause of this is known: it is the immanent content of energy or motion of the atoms which intensifies their repulsion towards each other.

We can say that the growing entropy of the gas has its roots in an energy which is inherent to the gas itself. The internal energy of a gas is demonstrated by the pressure, which the atoms exert on each other, and their state of motion which we call temperature. When we compress a gas slowly enough, however, this kinetic energy can retreat into the interior of the atoms and the increase in temperature which would ensue from fast compression does not arise. When a gas is expanding slowly the energy emerges from the inside of the atom to the outside again - and again the original temperature is maintained. So if we postulated blindly that compression and expansion of a gas were irreversible processes we would be only half right because the gas does in fact not return to its initial point but it remains energetically unchanged. Only when a gas is compressed quickly, the temperature cannot be transferred to the interior of the atom and as a consequence it is lost to the environment. This process is really irreversible. It goes hand in hand with an increase of the entropy and a corresponding decrease in the energy within the system concerned. Since the dispersion of the gas takes place just like that we are immediately tempted to draw following conclusion: only processes in which the entropy grows and the energy diminishes can take place on their own. And the inevitable conclusion would be that all physical processes had to be irreversible since energy which does not return has to be expended even for the retarded expansion of the gas as described above.

But this consideration is one-sided. Only if there were no adversaries for processes of this kind, i.e. no factor which retarded the expansion so to speak, our conclusion would really apply. With that it would be ruled out that orders spring into existence on their own, so to speak, because everything has been incessantly heading for disorder... Hence, something like a universe should never have come into existence!

On the other hand, if we found an energy which was available at any time and in any place to retard certain material processes sufficiently and to reverse these now reversible processes at any time, our train of thought would have to be different, we would say: apparently even processes take place on their own in which the energy increases and the entropy decreases...

With that we would of course behave as if we were observing a gas in a compression basin and just negated the pressing and retarding piston in order to put just any automatic energy in its place. And that is exactly how the physicists behave actually when they talk about reversible processes which are, strictly speaking, theoretical wishful thinking anyway. Because even the periodicity of the planetary movement, for instance, is on no account reversible since both place and time are variable. The expansion of the cosmos, i.e. its loss of order, is superimposed on all movements of the celestial bodies - but that is just what keeps the course of the stars going!

But this automatic energy mentioned above really exists: it means nothing else but the universal pressure! When we take the most powerful effect of the universal pressure as a starting point, i.e. the gravitation, we can easily discover one of those orders which come into existence all on their own so to speak, namely in the atmosphere of the air which gets thinner and thinner when getting upwards, denser and denser when getting downwards and obviously does not expand uniformly as we expect it of a gas. Without doubt an equilibrium developed here between the endeavour for minimum energy and that for maximum entropy bringing order into the gas atoms which went to certain areas depending on their gravity. But that in addition to that energy is released which works and causes the measurable (and utilizable) gravity (the weight) of the atmosphere is the pleasant side aspect of the events which forces us to suspect a significant difference between theory and reality...

The freedom to do so is provided by the repulsion principle. Because if the extremely low mass of an atom was the scale for its gravitation, we could not expect the identified automatic effect. Every order which the atoms enter into would have to appear like a miracle. But if we realise that atomic events take place under pressure practically all the time, which keeps at least many processes reversible on the one hand and is expressed in significant forces like the curving force and the electricity on the other hand, the creation of orders becomes natural and will in fact appear as if they are caused by themselves...

It is just like the production of a jar on a potter's wheel: if we ignored the hands of the potter we would probably have to wonder very much why the lump of clay was suddenly forming into a jar - as if lead by magic forces from the inside. We would invent many theories to clarify the mystery but they would all remain insufficient. But if we discovered the hands of the potter as a force which keeps the clay under pressure, the jar would suddenly cease to be a miracle. Then it would not make any sense anymore to ask how great the probability was for the clay to become a jar.

When the probability to enter into orders is only determined by the individual atom itself, it is surely very low or actually zero. But luckily there are many other atoms which already limit the possibilities of the individual, for example, to be able to occupy any place it likes.

The probability of orders in an atomic bond depends first and foremost on the state of aggregation of the matter. White and black sand, once mixed thoroughly, will never find its original order again on its own, the sand will remain grey. Two liquids of different weight, however, once shaken thoroughly, will soon separate again into two layers with one lying on top of the other. In this case the probability of the liquids to form an order becomes immediately extremely high because of the gravitation, i.e. the universal pressure, so high that this order can only be prevented by the supply of energy.

It is no question that liquids are best in a position to obey existing forces promptly. Even the course of events in the electrolyte or in the accumulator was already governed by great determination and order.

How great the tendency of the universe under pressure towards order has to be is first revealed in the formation of molecules and crystals and subsequently in the creation of stars and galaxies. The sometimes organic function of molecules stands out against these orders in a marvellous way but the marvellous is just the balance of our interpretation. Even the above mentioned jar remains a thoroughly meaningless accumulation of clay molecules as long as the user of this jar does not give it a property – exactly the purpose to contain liquids...

Again we realise that setting up concepts like energy and entropy sets us limits in the same way as values like positive and negative do where there aren't any limits at all in reality. A similarly wrong limit is set when making differentiations between organic and inorganic molecules. The two are absolutely equivalent to each other and the organic molecule is by no means the rarer phenomenon.

The rocks of our Earth contain approximately 100 million times more organic substances than all organisms living today taken together. If we cut a rectangular block with a length of 100 kilometres and a depth of 10 meters from the rock of the Paris Basin, this cut-out would contain two to four million tons of organic molecules.

Entropy is the expression of striving for an equilibrium within a system. In a closed system, this tendency will finally result in an irrevocable decline of energy into lower forms. In order to transform lower orders into higher ones, it would be necessary to supply energy to such a system. But this is only possible when the system is open, i.e. when the exchange of energy with the environment can take place.

If this problem is considered only unilaterally, for example only relating to heat, i.e. from a thermodynamical aspect, the second law of thermodynamics seems to be an insurmountable barrier for every automatic entering into orders. As already said, the cosmos itself would be impossible. The truth is, however, that there are not any closed systems at all in the framework of our world, yes even the world itself is open. That is to say at least it is open to a different state of T.A.O. In addition every atomic action is also open towards the inside, so to speak, because atoms themselves are not closed systems and have to be considered as open energy reservoirs. From that we can deduce that the second law of thermodynamics cannot apply with all strictness when one views the actions and effects of nature. With this interpretation many a barrier of improbability is falling down. Even if oxygen and hydrogen (both are gases) exhibit no probability to become liquid or wet, their merging is called water! And water is already a developed order. We know how spontaneously this order is created. There are uncountable orders of this kind, always creating the improbable again and again, springing into existing of their own accord, so to speak - from repulsion and attraction at the force of the cosmic pressure -; the whole inorganic and organic matter practically consists of them.

The development of life could not be explained with regard to the law of entropy since organisms have a lower entropy than their environment. But the increase in structure in the universe proves that there has to be another "law" than that of the increase of entropy. This motivated in particular Ilya Prigogine to search for the principles of self-organisation in order to find an explanation for the noticeable variety of alterations in nature. But research in this field is still in full swing.

Remember our figure 2. It shows a dissipative structure as does figure 3. When systems are prevented from reaching the thermodynamic equilibrium by the pressure of the universe but are brought a long way off the equilibrium through the constant supply of low entropy, macroscopic structures develop spontaneously. This principle is responsible for the creation of all complex forms, even for the creation of life as such.

The existence of the dissipative structures demonstrates that in the course of the constant decline as it is described by the law of entropy, something new develops, something new is created, something new in the sense of innovation. Created by the pressure from the universe, far off the thermodynamic equilibrium.

22 Primordial Molecules

Among the primordial elements we already found the unconventionally shaped carbon atom with its many possibilities for attachment. The first molecule which we discussed in detail was water but there are many other molecules which came into existence in the same spontaneous way as water, most of them with the assistance of carbon. We know some molecules of this kind as methane (CH_4), carbon dioxide (CO_2) or in connection with nitrogen as ammonia (NH_3). These molecules are stable final forms of various intermediate constellations. As everybody knows, there is, for example, also carbon monoxide (CO) but it oxygenates finally to carbon dioxide.

When the first higher elements took shape the first simple molecules developed from them immediately as well. We know the architect of these molecules as the universal pressure, which brought the atoms together in general at first – and then it was up to them if they prevented or maintained a bonding. After all, with the Fourier oscillations, the atoms already carried the corresponding programmes to do so.

When the cosmos in its process of eternal modification began to develop a new appearance, it did the first step towards life in accumulating atoms to conglomerates which we want to call primordial molecules: water, methane, ammonia, carbon dioxide... These are the compounds which are still the most frequent in the universe...

Every biologist knows the experimental biosynthesis which Stanley L. Miller carried out at the Biochemical Institute of the Columbia University in New York in 1953. He filled a glass flask with methane, ammonia, water, and oxygen and sent electric charges through this mixture for one week. In doing so he imitated the atmospheric conditions presumably predominating on the primeval Earth. Promptly some types of molecules developed in the flask which proved to be organic compounds like they are also found in the living cell. So to speak as in the accumulator, i.e. driven and controlled by electricity, new atomic associations were created in the mixture which we know as glycine, alanine, aspartic acid, and glutamic acid. The continuation of Miller's experiments soon revealed that with the aid of similar set-ups nearly all kinds of molecules developed of which one had believed up to then that they could only be produced by living organisms. In a gas volume of 3 litres, about 100 milligrams of amino acids, of which living structures are composed, as well as adenine, guanine, cytosine, uracil, and thymine, the building blocks of the nucleic acids, were created in this way within 7 days. More recent experiments showed that these amino acids can also come into being in the dark nebulae of the universe.[45]

But what can be produced by such processes above all, however, are proteinaceous hetero-polyamic acids which already show a tendency to organise when coming into contact with water. As it is, they already develop a double-layer membrane, i.e. a cell wall, and they can already reproduce in a simple way.

Of course it would be going too far to already designate this simple kind of information molecules as life. But what has to attract our attention in particular is the development of a wall, the creation of semipermeable membranes, to be exact, because it is precisely this characteristic - later supported by lipide molecules - which is the most important thing for life at all. These walls - and it might be necessary to emphasise that they result from atomic affinities just like any other form of molecule or crystal - have been more important for life than, for example, the genetic code which even came into existence at a much later time.

But we want to talk about these walls when the time is right. Prior to their significant emergence, many other, no less significant things were happening.

At the very moment when the primordial molecules came into being and existed in the water of the oceans and in the atmosphere, the first organic molecules developed - just like in Miller's flask - which had actually nothing to do with life, yet. Many theoreticians think that the aerosphere did not yet contain any oxygen at that time. But there is no rational reason to assume that this was the case. Already, we cannot imagine that the development of the primordial molecules took place without oxygen, and there must have already been a sufficient amount of it at that time. It separated from the water vapour of the atmosphere – exactly in the same way as it still does today. As it is, the plants were on no account involved in the emergence of oxygen nor are they in any way today...

The irradiation of the sun must have been much stronger at that time since the Earth was much closer to the sun and the sun burned more intensively than today for some time. So the chemist "nature" had a lot of energy available in form of light and electric discharges from tremendous thunderstorms or the heat from the volcanoes to stir, to shake, to heat up, and to cool down matter like a giant jig-saw puzzle in order to create again and again ever new, ever varied situations of meeting and bonding. In this way the building material of life was produced by itself so to speak, that is to say molecules, which are wrongly rated organic although they are created in quite an inorganic manner. And therefore this building material is still available in surprising amounts here on Earth even today. Of course, it is impossible to tell if this building material has already been utilized before and now represents traces of former life or if it has never been used by life at all. In any way, there must have been enormous amounts of these molecules in the water of the ocean back then. Their creation was not yet bound to cells - and so the whole ocean changed certainly soon into something like a single giant primitive cell which bubbled away while being bombarded by the sun, struck by lightning, and churned up by magma; a primeval soup full of energy, a hodgepodge of acids and bases ... fighting a constant battle against one another as well as incessantly creating new molecules through interaction with each other...

In Miller's flask the amino acids were created with both right-hand and left-hand spin. Of course, every molecule has a spatial reflection - and therefore both kinds of molecules must have developed in the primeval soup. Today we know that only one kind has emerged victorious. Nature had to decide for one kind and not without immediate cause. It is inseparably connected with the development of photosynthesis.

On the other hand, when amino acids are produced in the laboratory, a mixture of both forms, ones with right-hand spin and ones with left-hand spin, will always develop. The two types can only be separated under great difficulty and the selection of one type, which took place without doubt, has to appear the more amazing. This selection was effected in a specific way: whereas amino acids are only available with left-hand spin, nucleic acids have a right-hand spin (this only concerns the optical and electrical polarisation; spatially the nucleic acids are also left-hand helixes). But all this has its special reasons...

Molecules are spatial structures. They create impediments or resistances or are suited for each other. With this property, they determine a certain, limited framework of possible accumulations and attachments. Today we know about 25 amino acids (contrary to popular opinion there are actually 25 and not 20 amino acids) which constitute life but at former times there must have been far more. And in addition there must have been many other structures of that kind of which life did not make use subsequently because they were not stable enough.

All these molecular structures took shape, reacted with each other, and disintegrated again in endless chains of reaction, and we have to conclude that in this ocean all possibilities of getting together and cohering were already tested by the molecules without exception – in an aimless and unsystematic manner. After all, there was no definite plan and no example.

What is more, however, molecules are not only spatial structures in which electric and magnetic moments have a creative effect; firstly, they are energy accumulators because they always carry the energy magnified by their bonding. And secondly and above all, they are always the material equivalent of an event which shaped them. This is already a suggestion of memory, some kind of notes about the environment which intervenes, influences, or destroys and in doing so is recording its actions in analogous molecular conglomerates.

This means nothing else but that every molecule represents the substantially manifested reaction to certain environmental actions, to light, to heat, or even to other molecules. Just like atoms "understand" each other so to speak by imitating and repeating each other, molecules also understand each other within the framework of action and reaction. Every molecule which finds inclination or resistance with the other orientates its actions to that - this must appear as if it was aware of its environment. Of course, this is not yet an "ego", not a personal consciousness but it only means a mere reactive perceiving of its environment. But the step from this simple kind of compulsion and necessity to the conscious intention of a living thing is not so enormous as we tend to believe.

Neither is there any independent inner self-awareness of the self in living things. Just like any kind of awareness the form of the "ego" familiar to us is created by perception, in the human being finally by perceiving the self. This is basically the same perception which is already practised from atom to atom, from molecule to molecule, and with the admitted bonds we already encounter the principle of impediment which will be so important for comprehending the functioning of the brain because with the it will not be possible anymore that just everything can happen - but only the permissible ...

It certainly seems very odd, and we will only comprehend later what we already say now: a molecule becomes aware of its existence because there are other molecules which influence it. But we have to concede of course that this perception is simply, informally, purely topologically forced ... this is not yet recognising but the way that eventually leads to recognition is only an unexpectedly short one as we will soon see.

When we dissolve a crystal in water its atoms separate from each other. Although they retain their programme, i.e. their specific properties and possibilities for bonding, they won't find to each other again because of their movement. When we restrict this movement by evaporating the water, for instance, the atoms will crystallise out again - simply because they have to. They will form a new crystal which will be similar to the original one.

In order to guide the atoms in the water to each other again we can also give them the opportunity to recognise their place faster. What can we do? We hang a thread with some solid atoms of the same kind attached to it into the solution or put in little crystals so carefully that they won't dissolve. This means: we contaminate the solution with the idea of the crystal so to speak. What happens then? Atoms moving along "recognise" the offered hold (the valence or the polarisation of the motionless atoms) and promptly settle down. Soon a new crystal develops, formed according to the idea inherent in it which was "comprehended" by the atoms, so to speak, when the thread or the small seed crystals were there. As it is, the thread contains the work programme for the atoms which they continue in themselves. And with that it becomes obvious that none of the particles alone would have led to a crystal; both, thread and atoms, had to work together.

Even molecules carry programmes. But as long as they lack the idea (the thread), there won't be any new orders developing any time soon. Well, there is nothing on this threat which would make us expect a complete crystal if we were unknowing of the connection.

Yet it comes into existence. In this way we could cause a lot of crystals, and depending on the type of atoms or their arrangement they would all look different.

In certain appropriate situations which depend on temperature and pressure almost all elements of this world develop crystals. And crystals already have one significant property: they complement each other and are renewed again and again. This is the first form of growth which there is to discover.

What's sauce for the crystals is sauce for the molecules. They also love to crystallise but they can also be destroyed again by the same environment which formed them. The chemist speaks of the law of mass action and some think therefore that life could not have originated or even begun in the water because water would have taken the molecules apart again immediately after their formation. That is quite correct if we don't consider that even molecules had to come into existence which resisted water by simply turning an insoluble side towards it.

The true adventure of life, however, began with another invention which was just as inevitable as irreplaceable: catalysis.

With the crystal thread, we already became acquainted with a kind of atomic initiating catalysis. The atoms of the thread exerted force on the atoms in the water; therefore they were not doing anything at random anymore but settled down. One programme prevailed.

The programme of a foreign atom in an atomic bond can be so strong that it overpowers the other programmes. A very small amount of manganese introduced into ozone makes any amount of ozone immediately disintegrate into oxygen. How does this happen? The easiest way to understand it is perhaps the following: the oxygen atoms which get in contact with the manganese adopt the manganese programme, i.e. the oscillations which are typical for the manganese. Altered in that way, they are naturally not suited for each other anymore, their three-unit molecules break away from each other spreading the programme at the same time.

Thus catalysis can separate, but it can also assemble, and it causes these effects especially in the molecular range. And we are right in concluding that atoms with strong programmes, that is for example metal ions, play a leading part in it, too. They act as pole reversing agents so to speak and make the flow of energy possible in places where it would not take place without it. We already found something very similar in the battery or in the transistor, and this principle multiplies the possibilities of encounters and designs tremendously...

The various amino acids and other molecules soon agglomerated into further structures in the ocean. They convoluted and coiled apparently indiscriminately and at random but chance did not have a say in it at all. Because every new form was causally forced by electricity and spatial conditions.

Just like the thread in the crystal, these structures became the trigger for the formation of further orders because of their specific surface constitution. By holding and gathering molecules which would never have met each other otherwise (we could also say: would never have recognised each other) or by bringing molecules to the same levels of energy and by establishing oscillational harmonies they combined these molecules to make new, more and more complicated forms. Such initiating molecules are called enzymes. In principle, their function is simple:

Let's assume the enzyme provides a possibility to settle down for two molecules which are unknown to each other and which would never find each other on their own. Both settle down on the enzyme. A rough extent of accordance is already sufficient for settling down; it doesn't have to be absolutely perfect. After all, it could hardly be expected that enzymes and molecules have such matching surfaces that they fit without gaps because the surface constitution is only one of the criteria, and especially the role that electricity plays in it must not be overlooked.

The two molecules, settled down on the enzyme, are now pressing two spots together which otherwise would never have found each other in the confusion of wandering about. These spots are adapted to each other through the new distribution of energy of the enzymatic bond. The two molecules now link in this place which leaves its marks on them – because now their impulse behaviour and the form of their oscillation, respectively change with this bonding - and it results in their not fitting the enzyme anymore. Freshly combined to a new molecule they fall off the enzyme again. As a rule, falling off has predominantly electrical reasons. Because when the molecules adopt the programme of the enzyme unambiguously, the partners are polarised alike and as a result, repulsion takes place... We see that very complicated mechanisms are beginning to work here, now.

The enzyme itself is released again - always at the ready to repeat its game with other molecules; although with certain restrictions because it has lost energy which has to be replaced for the time being. But it should soon be able to find some structure somewhere from which it can take away a little energy upon separation...

The combined molecule, however, is not so easy to separate anymore. Water alone cannot separate what enzymes have joined. This is among other things a matter of the energy balance. Only other enzymes are in a position to reverse the process again. For that reason, enzymes surely came into existence before there was anything like cells or life at all. But they were not really immune to the destruction by water themselves. Thus they disintegrated again, developed anew, disintegrated again... But in the short span of their life they formed solider structures, whole chains of energetic molecules which could certainly not help it to become aware of their environment in which they were pushed around and pressured.

Still, something like a concept did not yet exist in this effervescence of the molecules. But actually neither did anything unintentionally because every action had its precise preconditions after all. In this elementary piracy of catching energy and chaining it down, carbon was the ringleader. And there was yet another atom which was quite unsymmetrical and which therefore always rubbed the wrong way and was captured as a troublemaker: the hydrogen atom.

Carbon atoms have a strong affinity for hydrogen; wherever carbon left a possibility to settle down untaken, a hydrogen atom would soon turn up to occupy it. The chemist says carbon gets saturated with hydrogen.

We immediately comprehend all these proceedings when we know the principle of the polarisation of space. Everything had to develop exactly in this way and nothing else could happen.

Well, as we know, energy wants to transform into entropy. But suddenly this was not so easy at all anymore because the enzymes broke through the energy drop in a drastic way. Because they charged the settled down molecules with fresh energy and incessantly refuelled themselves with stolen energy. Well, it did not go downhill anymore just like that as the entropy would have liked it to but again and again the energy was pushed back so to speak, lifted up to new launching paths again; and it was practically the energy itself which put up these obstacles. This is like a centipede constantly falling over its own feet. And we must not fail to notice that energy was constantly resupplied: light, electric current, and heat as well as cosmic radiation and radioactivity continued to take effect over millions of years...

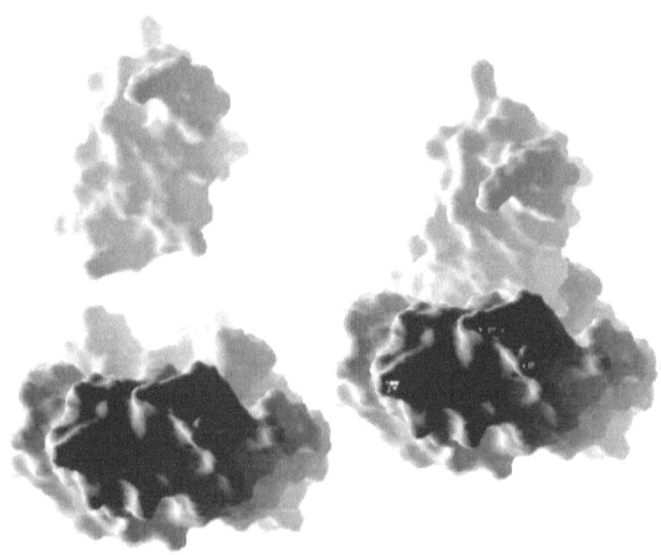

Fig. 109a: Spatial adaptation of two molecules

23 Organelles

For the survival of the enzymes it was important to find molecules which they could break down in order to compensate the loss of energy and to postpone their own decay. Already in the beginning, there surely were various molecules suitable for this purpose. They were robbed of their energy wherever they were found. This was already something like "eat and be eaten". We find this principle already on the molecular level. And the original variety of the primeval soup was certainly reduced again a little by these battles of energy. When too many energy suppliers had been decomposed, the corresponding enzymes soon dissolved again - and that was already a control mechanism as we still find it in the cell today.

Another molecular control circuit soon consisted in the products created by the enzymes stopping their own production by deactivating the energy suppliers and with that making other production processes possible again. This promptly led to a molecular evolution, to a real explosion of combinations. Today we still know about 2000 different enzymes on this Earth but at that time their number must have run into the millions - because actually every complex molecule was somehow able to be an enzyme for other molecules.

And we are repeating it intentionally: just as the atoms didn't have any choice than to coexist with each other and to react to one another because they got caught in a competition for space and energy, the molecules were also forced to make connections whether they liked it or not if they couldn't successfully prevent them because of their structure. Huddled together as they were, bonding must have been the most likely. (The teleological mode of expression using terms like competition, battles, games, find and rob, feed, have a say in, etc. must not be misunderstood! It is used for stylistic reasons only.)

The driving force behind events, was on the outside; the environment forced and pushed, shaped and designed. If one regards a molecule in an isolated way, as a little machine so to speak, one will find it immediately difficult to explain - just as in case of the atom. But neither the atom nor the molecule have ever been little machines which acted of their own accord. Each of these formations only followed the paths which were opened for them. And therefore we have to regard the whole closely related chemical game of the molecules homogeneously as an inseparable whole in order to realise that both a relentless, comprehensive initiating causality and a multifariously connected interaction prevailed in the procedure of these reactions.

Enzymes didn't go in search of energy under any circumstances. And besides it was absolutely unimportant if they disintegrated or not. Even the specialisation of certain molecules to choose one or the other enzyme as a mediator only resulted from the coincidence of adequate conditions which just occurred inevitably – which had to occur at some point in the course of time. And they were not in a hurry!

Thus it was the co-incidence which played the important role and on no account mere accident because we must not take any calculus of probability as a starting point; there was definitely never and nowhere any intention to create exactly this or that amino acid compound.

Everything resulted from the interaction of space, structure, and electric potentials. These potentials, nothing else but differences in the states of oscillation, here left-hand, there right-hand, here a little more, there a little less, were exchangeable. An energy flux took place from molecule to molecule.

Groups which put this exchangeability into effect on the plane of the electron waves are called oxidation-reduction systems. They are equally easy to reduce and to oxidise, which means they are enzymes which bring along or carry away oxygen. Oxygen is known as a very aggressive atom. Wherever it finds a lower potential and a matching oscillation it settles down and "oxidises" the corresponding substance.

This would have turned out badly even if the adversary hydrogen, which oxygen is taken in with beyond all measure, did not have a say in it, either. Therefore molecules could get rid of oxygen again when they made it meet with hydrogen. In doing so, water was spontaneously produced, and the released energy was available again to start the game - actually a battle - all over again and to keep it going over long periods of time.

Maybe it would have remained this way until today if those molecules had not come into being which don't love water in the least. We are talking about fat-like molecules, so-called lipids (syn. lipoids). Do not love water means that they don't make friends (bonds) neither with the oxygen nor with the hydrogen of the water molecule. In his short experiment, Miller already revived preliminary stages of these fats which are not keen on contact, like formic acid, butyric acid, etc. These are very simple molecules made of carbon, hydrogen and nitrogen. They created complex structures with other elements, as, for example, with phosphor, which is found in great quantities in the water of the ocean, and turned their hydrophobic end away from water. At the same time they settled down on each other offering water the smallest possible surface. If they had not also formed an alliance with protein molecules befor,e they might have floated on the surface of the water forever and ever. So, however, they sank down and developed spherical enclosures which suddenly enveloped everything that just happened to get into these enclosures.

We can produce such enclosures artificially as so-called coacervate droplets; even heated amino acids already show a distinct tendency to form into systems upon contact with water by developing an enclosure, a membrane wall, which causes a selective transfer of matter. But the lipids could do it even better. Because they were not averse to anything and everything, certain substances like enzymes and proteins could pass through the skins of the lipids without hindrance. On the other hand, there was also water inside the enclosure and therefore such skins developed without any exception as a double membrane which was insoluble from both sides. Between the water inside and the water outside a pressure relation came into being (osmotic pressure). When the pressure outside was higher the skin was squeezed - it shrank - when the pressure was lower outside, the skin expanded.

In addition, many lipid skins were semipermeable, that means some molecules or ions could only pass through in one direction. And exactly this property depended greatly on the osmotic pressure. In this way molecules could accumulate inside the enclosure and increase the pressure until it burst (plasmolysis). In many cases, however, the supply of molecules was running out before that happened whereas there were still enough lipids available. As a consequence the enclosure became too big for the prevailing pressure inside. And now something happened which we already discovered in a similar form with the atoms which opposed the universal pressure with their changed surfaces: the pressure outside acted upon the surface and squeezed it towards a new equilibrium, that is to say into two new enclosures which distributed the halved volume among the increased surfaces - and therefore they could and had to grow again until the process was repeated.

With that it becomes apparent that this preliminary stage of cell growth and cell division went off absolutely uncontrolled in the beginning. It resulted exclusively from the complicated pressure conditions. Only the amounts of the substances involved initiated division and further growth. There wasn't any genetic code, any governing molecule which issued any commands, and it has basically remained this way until today.

That means it was not necessary to write down the idea of encapsulation, the invention of the enclosure as such in order to preserve it for the future; it was and is immanent to the substances involved in order to be fulfilled again and again when these substances and the required environment occur. And only the occurrence of these essential conditions later ended up in a pattern and defined itself in a code.

The basic idea of the enclosure - i.e. the cell - has existed until today only because we are surrounded by a cosmos whose force or repulsion puts this idea into effect in the same way as any other form of matter, no matter if crystal or rock... And this environment, into which this "patent of enclosure" was born inevitably, has in addition remained the main cause for it up to today ... and because it has done so, because the primordial ocean of those days even distributed itself to the organisms later-on and was preserved inside of them, this basic principle of life has been working for billions of years already.

Every living thing depends on this great event of the enclosure because life is indeed a wall phenomenon. Every organic unit is encapsulated by such enclosures. A cell is on no account a shapeless droplet of plasma in which molecules seem to know miraculously where they have to go to but it is criss-crossed with uncountable shells and skins which, similar to the road network of a big town, stipulate the directions, open only certain paths and at the same time fulfil a regulating and controlling function...

This is a considerably meaningful insight for it shows us that every command headquarters inside the cell would be nothing without these skins, shells, cisterns, passages, and permeabilities. Therefore the primary object of life is on no account the genetic apparatus. It could not accomplish anything at all if it did not exist within this phenomenon of the enclosure which is basically always able to sustain itself and reproduce even without the genetic code as long as the right conditions are preserved. The genetic key only takes part in securing these conditions - but it was created only much later as an independent something which only became effective when it had been integrated in these lipid shells. This did not happen accidentally but many intermediate stages had to be coped with until it was ready. We will get to know them in sequence at least superficially...

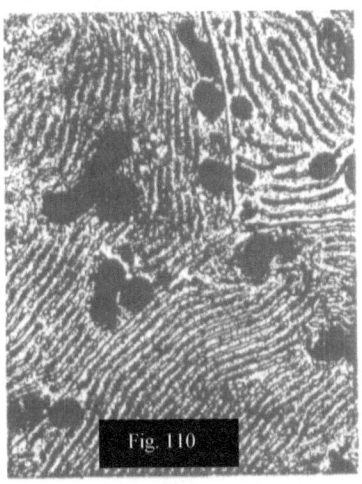
Fig. 110

The biologists gave the network of enclosures inside a cell the name endoplasmic reticulum.

Figure 110 provides us with a view of three adjoining cells of the pancreas. We see the perfection which this enclosure system managed to make and immediately understand its directing and organising function. Of course, the figure shows a cross-section. We therefore have to imagine the enclosure to be spherical. Hundreds of spheres made of double membranes nested into each other. Here, it is not possible that everything just flows as it likes, systematics and force already prevail. In the following, we will abbreviate this endoplasmic reticulum with "ER".

At that time, enclosures of this kind already enveloped a variety of enzymes which could sometimes react and specialise more specifically for that reason. Not everything that was possible developed here but only very particular molecules were created since the building material had already been selected by the membranes. All this still took place in an unsteady manner, in short attempts and finales, and it happened only now and then that a system divided and grew in such a way that its function was preserved. This function was determined by the enclosure itself, which had already obtained some exceptional properties through the integration of very particular protein structures and which let only certain substances pass.

Of course there were many different enclosures. They let building material enter and finished products exit but nothing was produced on purpose, everything reacted completely automatically and unconsciously. If the molecules were available and if they carried the correct "programmes", they just had to react to each other...

And thus production started spontaneously and in a carefree manner, regardless of the fact whether the products could be used for anything. But exactly these random products could be welcome to other shell systems as building material, after all.

Everything took place in incredible orders of magnitude. The whole ocean was rapidly filling with these small protein factories. And presumably mechanisms got into their stride which were lost again for the most part later-on, which were not successful - and which we cannot discover anymore today for that reason.

Internal force and external necessity soon resulted in an extensive interaction of all these enclosures. What one of them discarded could be useful for another one. Because of that a further selection soon took place since many enclosures produced useless things, others did not receive any building material at all and perished. Only those which were useful for one another lasted permanently.

We must not misunderstand the word "useful"; none of these enclosures had the task to produce exactly this or that. They just did it and that was very convenient for other systems. The indisputable impression of coincidence results only from the function: thus, for example, water is on no account a product of coincidence and it was not created to drive mill-wheels, yet it can be used for this purpose. And when we follow conventional theories and transfer the events into the ocean, into a kind of primeval soup, we must be aware of the fact that this is only an allegory for every other place where there was enough water and material available – maybe even on other planets...

Of all these wall systems which stood at the beginning of life we want to select only the most important ones. Already at an earlier date – from a cosmic point of view several thousand years are a piece of cake - the activity of the chemical processes became systematic; certain forms of molecules used themselves like standardised building components and created this and that...

This was absolutely bound to happen inevitably. Everything that was found could be given a try just as well. Some things lasted permanently but a lot were destroyed again - and very seldom such a molecule developed into something which became standard.

One of these standard molecules was adenine whose other important functions we will get to know in the next chapter. In this phase of events, adenine combined with one sugar and one phosphoric acid molecule forming a structure which was of no better use for the time being than to act as an energy transporter. And one of the shell apparatuses specialised in loading these adenosine monophosphates with energy. This happened by hanging further tails of phosphoric acid onto the molecule. When only one was added the molecule transformed into adenosine diphosphate (abbr. ADP), another phosphor tail completed it to adenosine triphosphate (ATP). It was the bonds of these little tails which carried the energy (as everybody knows it was obtained through the incident of bonding and the surfaces modified by that).

Well, this ATP was an extremely interesting molecule. Like a master key for a cylinder lock system it fitted a variety of enzymes and could be used as a universal energy supplier. Above all the ATP could have already been created outside of every enclosure, and therefore it had been that universal energy depot from the beginning which came exactly at the right moment for the enzymes as the kind of molecule which had to be broken down so that it could be robbed of its energy.

So there were uncountable enzymes which broke the ATP down to ADP and gained from doing so. And in the same way there were enzymes which regenerated the ADP back to ATP. Later-on they did the same within small, interlacing shell systems. They obtained their energy directly from bringing oxygen and hydrogen together in several subsequent catalyses, i.e. from taming the oxygen by means of redox systems. The biologist knows this series of reactions as respiratory chain, and we comprehend from this expression alone that oxygen must have been one of the energy suppliers.

The first small shell systems allowed ADP and phosphoric acid to enter them and discharge finished ATP. In this way they became tiny molecular factories, filling stations for enzymes - and we know these filling stations as mitochondria (mitochondrion). Even today, they are still important occupants of every cell, and they had existed without doubt even before cells came into being which encapsulated and carried along the ocean including its contents later-on.

Such a mitochondrion is called organelle. And in the same way as these, organelles with other functions soon developed. They were still individual systems within this single giant cell, the primordial ocean. Each of them specialised in certain products using the products of the others for that purpose. Apart from many developments which were lost again, maybe because they were not useful for anything at all, some organelles have remained integrated in their interaction and have also been preserved until today. We know them for instance as dictyosomes - made of lipids, it is a place of production and a storage vesicle for substances of all sorts whose signalling effect was to transfer them into hormones later ... but also plasma liquids, mucus, and secretion or glues were created in whole dictyosome complexes which are nowadays called Golgi apparatus.

Even lipid vesicles which did not produce anything at all but only collected superfluous products, waste products so to speak, were useful in the events. Today we find them in the cells as vacuoles. Like inflated balloons inside the cell they prop it up and provide it with the required stability (tonus). At that time, however, they swam along and simply existed, just like so many other varieties of the organelles. They all were more or less important and interchangeable with each other, and again maybe everything would have remained this way if the multifarious game of the molecules and lipids had not invented something else, the importance of which is only beaten by the chromosome: the centriole.

Well, at that time, there weren't any centrioles yet but only quite independent organelles. What did they do?

In all these events full of electricity it would be really astonishing if there had not been some kind of accumulator as well; a molecular structure created solely for the purpose to collect electric energy and release it again by radiation. These organelles became charged ion containers whose function - which the biologists still find quite mysterious - is not so hard to understand. These little bodies – which we also know as centrioles today - did nothing else but grow and divide but they did so on a purely electrical basis.

We know from the accumulator that certain molecular arrangements can exhibit strong electric potentials. And thus ions came together in the centriole which caused the continual growth of an electric field. The spatial polarisation of these little fields could turn out both left-handed and right-handed. But above all they could only grow up to a certain size because they were mono-poles. Basically their components repelled one another - and just as we could see with the radioactive atom the simple structure noticeably lost its stability while growing and broke into two pieces. And these were growing again until they broke apart once more.

This process contains a fundamental factor for life: it is life's clock! The growing and dividing of the centriole subsequently determined the growing and dividing of the cell itself. But that is not all: its electric field also brought some order into the processes within the cell; it polarised the interior space of the cell and directed correspondingly charged molecules onto particular paths.

At the time, however, at which we are at the moment in our minds, there weren't any cells in the customary sense if we disregard the fact that the organelles themselves were practically nothing else but little cells of their own accord which also carried their own genetic codes (but we are not yet that far).

Thus in the beginning the centriole existed thoroughly as an industrious piece of work of nature, it collected ions, it grew and divided, and it continued collecting... At the same time it manipulated through electricity in a special way which we will come back to again later-on.

Everything we described previously, existed to an incredible extent. And again thousands of years passed by before a change occurred in this system. Maybe the biologists are missing the chromosomes or the ribosomes and many other components of life on our list. But they didn't exist yet, they were all created much later! For the time being there was only this vague interaction of the organelles and that had surely nothing in common at all with those processes of life which we are acquainted with nowadays.

Still neither idea nor goal existed. A quite aimless exchange of energy took place. Only the first principle of reproduction was born: division. Nevertheless it was some kind of life because substances were exchanged. Recognition and force already existed, and all that was lacking for completion were programme and strategy. Consequently it was an activity quite free of information...

Well, in our considerations we didn't go into the environmental conditions in detail, in fact for one reason: they are obviously not so important as some biologists assume. Miller's experiment has been modified in a variety of ways, substances were replaced, temperatures changed, different forms of energies supplied, but the result was almost always the same. Only time made a difference. The more the experiment was prolonged, the greater was the number of molecules created and the more varied was their interaction. This authorises us to take relatively great liberties in reconstructing the process without having to go into details. Only some rough conditions had to be fulfilled; one of the principal demands was the reducing characteristic of the mixture. Then of course the availability of water and of primitive molecules was important as well as observing a certain temperature range which could be very extensive in addition.

Concerning the energy it didn't even matter at all in the beginning in which form it was supplied. We know after all that in principle there is only one kind of energy: the impulse. Just any energetic manifestation consists of the same impulses and every temporal sequence could be transformed into other frequencies through the atoms.

For that reason, we don't have to assume that life began with the precision of a Swiss clockwork and that a devilish randomness must have been at work. Not on any account because the basic tendency for life is already immanent in the matter, in its variety of the atoms and in its specific behaviour.

We already emphasised the various possibilities for a molecule to absorb energy. For the time being the transmission of energy via the electron waves was probably common. Molecules also communicated their motional states to one another through heat waves. But all these forms of energy costed something, they always had to be paid with a weakening of the system. Suddenly another possibility to gain energy arose which was, however, delivered frankly and free domicile...

A very frequent element in sea water - as on Earth in general - was magnesium. It could therefore not be avoided that every now and then magnesium atoms were included in the growing molecular structures. Unexpectedly a form of molecule was created with that which was able to absorb the weak impulses of the light and to transform them into electron waves.

The molecule which received its energy from the light in this way is called chlorophyll due to its colour which comes about because chlorophyll absorbs only the red fraction of the light but cancels the one in the green range. Soon these new structures also encapsulated themselves into shells together with their appertaining enzymes, and in there they produced one of the primary nutrients of the world, glucose, by using water and carbon dioxide; the organelles created in this way are called chloroplasts.

The glucose produced by them serves as a transmitter molecule of the energy obtained from the light for other organelles which soon adapted to this comfortable nourishment. They returned the favour with substances which the chloroplasts could make good use of in turn. The circumstances accompanied by these events, that is to say the selection of particular left-hand molecules demonstrates in what a causally combined and linked manner these first beginnings of life were taking place. After all, the light waves brought along a uniformly standardised spin which is to be attributed to the spin of their creators, the electron waves. Electron waves in turn are predestined by the similarity of all protons, they all oscillate in the same direction. That's the reason why those molecules had to be left-handed which matched the spin of the light waves. If they have the opposite optical activity, the gratis energy cannot be absorbed. Probably even right-hand molecules of the chlorophyll developed from time to time but they didn't make any sense because either they reacted much too weakly to the light or not at all. With that the polarisation of all molecules integrated in this kind of energy gain was determined. When a molecule possessed two possibilities which were the mirror image of each other, only that one was finally preserved which could be integrated in the transmission of the left-hand spin. And thus the symmetry was also broken in the world of the living. The probability for left-hand and right-hand spin was suddenly not the same anymore. Scientists have been puzzling over that until today but there is not any riddle to solve at all.

The decision of life for a specific type of molecule was already hidden in the nature of matter itself which only permitted this one possibility!

This generation of "left-hand" energy brought a huge advantage to half of all the organelles existing at that time. Structures oriented to the right were still dependent on the absorption of already existing molecules after all. Maybe they also ingested food with left-hand polarisation but they weren't able to do anything with it because it didn't fit in anywhere in their own reaction process. With that their extinction was sealed because even the ocean was not an inexhaustible energy reservoir without making use of the light.

Even when they didn't have any chlorophyll on their own, structures with left-hand polarisation, on the other hand, still received food in form of left-hand bonds and still remained in the metabolism of the giant primordial cell.

All molecules which shaped life subsequently have remained left-hand coils until today and have been polarising the light accordingly. With one exception: when molecules came into being as a mere reaction to the existing ones, as it were as a pale imitation or an imprint of them they automatically had to turn out right-handed. These molecular mirror images of the events actually turned up. They had nothing to do with the metabolism itself but were only the transcript of the activity so to speak and with that pure informational molecules. As we will soon see this storing of information is to blame for us being able to think about these past events...

With the activity of the chloroplasts a new, extremely important molecule came into play: the glucose. It is a type of sugar, and wherever oxygen was not available directly, this glucose was a welcome energy supplier. Other organelles converted glucose to ribulose-5-phosphate in several steps by means of phosphorylation only to generate energy (pentose phosphate cycle) and just threw away these ribose molecules. For the time being they were of no use for anything, waste as such, which soon accumulated in the ocean... But nothing really remained waste for long in this primeval soup.

Well, let's imagine again what we would have found in the primordial cell of the ocean at that time: different kinds of amino acids, indiscriminately combined amino acids as enzymes or whole enzyme complexes, metal ions as co-enzymes, lipids and lipid shells, certainly even some without content, organelles like mitochondria, dictyosomes, chloroplasts, furthermore glucose, ribose, simple protein molecules, and already even more complicated structures as well as the easily developing molecules adenine, guanine, cytosine, thymine, and uracile, the energy storages ADP and ATP and in addition several types of fat...

This ocean was a chemical laboratory of giant dimensions although we should assume that the more significant course of development rather took place on the surface and in the shallower regions. At first, the sea must have exhibited a play of all colours and with the development of the chloroplasts it must have become bright green. It might have looked like a giant pot of pea soup.

Can we say that this soup already lived? Yes, it actually did, because with the chloroplasts this primordial sea had already created some kind of meaning: the recognition of light! And already the chlorophyll molecules turned - obeying the spin of the electron waves - the most favourable side towards the light, in the same way as the lipids already recognised water and arranged themselves accordingly. This is an act of submitting to a certain situation which - although forced down the line - gives the first implying impression of intelligent behaviour.

Without doubt this complex, tremendous procedure of reaction up to the development of organelles took longer than Miller's experiment in the flask. But neither should we overestimate the duration of this process since all reactions took place at an uncanny speed - and after all things had basically not gone far yet.

Figure 111 shows us two kinds of mitochondria. We see clearly what a complicated apparatus of enclosures these organelles are which still produce the indispensable ATP in our cells.

Fig.111

When we bear in mind that the ocean of those days was certainly not a motionless stretch of water - submarine volcanoes and storms ploughed through it, currents developed because of differences in temperature - we will understand that this laboratory of nature remained inimitable, that procedures were going off which would be found most difficult to duplicate even in the most modern chemical laboratory because of their complexity. And who would like to stay put in front of his test tubes for a couple of million years?

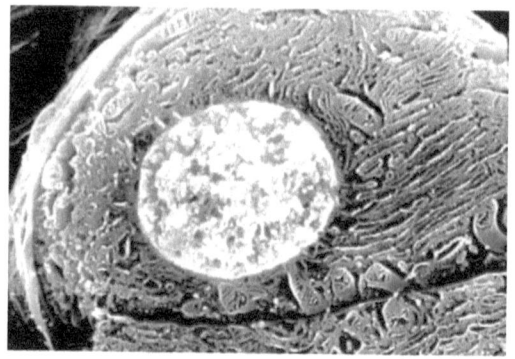

Fig. 111a: Cross-section of a cell with ER, nucleus, mitochondria, and plasma membranes.

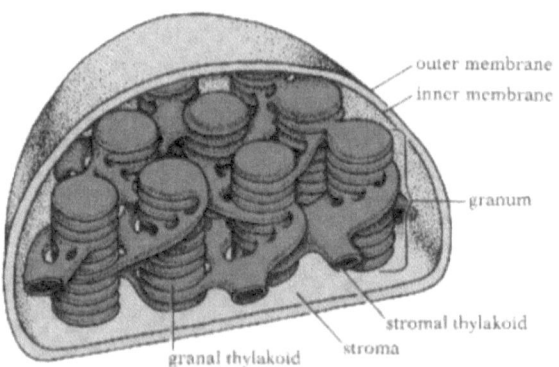

Fig.111b: A Chloroplast

24 Information

In biology everything is more complicated than it seems, a scholar once said and there is no objection to that because the abundance of players and actors in the biochemical evolution is unmanageable in their quantity. All conventional theories often abstract the events very deliberately, even simplify them too much because many of the molecular partners have not been discovered yet after all. Especially in our present time, the discoveries follow in rapid succession; further details and functions, new enzymes and hormones and substances with up to then unknown properties are continuously deciphered. The problem with that is, as mentioned, only the quantity of the events and their incredible combinations. In our further descriptions we will also be unable to avoid simplifying the sequence of events tremendously reducing them to the most essential because of their interlinked complexity. This preface is meant for those biologists among our readers who might consider the following descriptions to be a little too inexact or even too simple.

Now let's try to reconstruct what must have happened further in the primordial ocean. In doing so, we are aware of the fact that we cannot discuss many molecules which are introduced as spatial and electrical mediators in all the various phases. For one thing because then a comprehensive account would hardly by possible, and for another because we still have not identified many of these molecules at all. But we know that they exist. That should be sufficient for us because their precise description is not necessary for the fundamental comprehension of the creation of life.

The molecular life in the ocean, concentrated on the variety of types and forms of the organelles, left several kinds of waste right-away. There was the useless centriole, only an adornment of the scenery so to speak, there were the base molecules which were of no use at all because they were rotating right-handedly, and the already mentioned ribose was swimming around between them. Even the already produced protein structures and amino acids were mostly without a function yet, created for no particular purpose. They merely existed and constituted the environment - creating urging, compelling, or compliant little necessities...

Well, we already know form the first chapters of this book what great significance the polarised space holds for the encounter of two bodies. It also decided with the molecules if there was an attraction or a repulsion. In their entirety, the amino acids in the ocean were soon all left-handed (after possible other forms had been sifted out) but they all possessed very characteristically defined ends as well. At one end there always was an NH_2 group and at the other end an oxygen atom could be found in the residual group most of the time. We know the affinity of oxygen and hydrogen for each other. It was therefore the obvious thing that the oxygen ends and the hydrogen ends of the amino acids found each other and linked to form chain molecules. Of course, the enzymes always helped them along diligently, and they brought amino acids together which would otherwise not have found those ends which were inclined to them. Their OH_2 compound (just think of H_2O!) was firm and stable. In this way, two amino acids formed a dipeptide (this special kind of bond is therefore called peptide bond), three formed a tripeptide and so on. More than ten are called a polypeptide.

Their bonds entailed that the specifically different parts of the amino acids remained free and that always a spiral (alpha-helix) developed at the same time because the oscillations of the hydrogen and oxygen atoms involved a moment of rotation (as far as it would go so to say).

And now we comprehend perfectly why a spiral shape had to be the result of it. Of course this had to happen with all peptides. Through this arrangement of the residual groups of the amino acids which jutted out on all sides, the peptide obtained a very compact, spatially characteristic appearance, which certainly differed from peptide to peptide (figure 112).

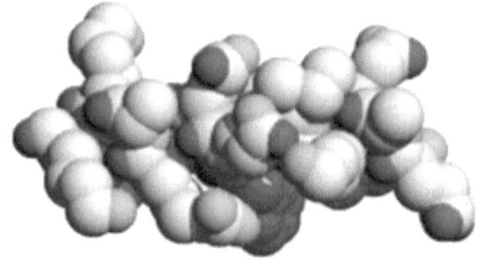

Fig. 112

Peptides are helical, coiled protein structures as well. But there was also a subsequent reaction to the formation of peptides: the right-handedly oscillating base molecules, which had been only waste until then, pounced on the left-handedly oscillating hydrogen groups of the peptides and clang on to them but not too fiercely since they could not get close enough to the hydrogen. Soon various base molecules - indiscriminately mixed up at first, of course - attached alongside a peptide - and therefore helically as well...

Now it happened that always three of the tiny compact bases found enough space on one single amino acid. There were, however, four bases which were equally suitable: adenine, guanine, cytosine, and uracil. They all had a different structure, and only when they combined in an ideal way did they fill the space perfectly. In doing so they always occupied a section of that specific part of the amino acid as well. When, for example, one guanine and one adenine molecule clang to the amino acid, there was just enough space left for one uracil molecule; when there already were two uracil molecules, perhaps only one cytosine molecule fitted in. And so on...

Since all amino acids polarised to the left, it could never happen that for example one amino acid took the place of a base. Only the right-handedly polarised bases were downright attracted. As a consequence of the many molecules swimming around or rather tossing and turning about, a selection was made by electrostatic means which reflected very specifically the sequence of amino acids of the peptide like an imprint. This was a series of co-incidences which did not have a meaning yet.

The loosely bound bases extended their ends into the water, and prior to that these ends had been linked with the ribose phosphate molecules which had already been available as waste. And now again one of those grave co-incidences took place: it happened that one little ribose head always went to lay down at the little phosphor tail of the other base molecule and promptly bonded with it since again hydrogen and oxygen met. We notice that nearly without any exception, the "love" of two kinds of atoms for one another is responsible for the creation of life!

When all this had happened, and consequently the ribose phosphate chains had threaded on all bases accurately, the whole ribose chain including the bases fell off the peptide - namely for electrical reasons. For one thing, the settled down chain received the polarisation from the peptide and attraction had to turn into repulsion, and for another, a weakening of the whole molecule resulted from every further bonding. The entropy struck and the first victim was of course the weakest of the links within the whole complex, which was exactly the base-peptide linkage which was not strong enough anymore after the whole structure had reached a certain length to compensate the energy sapped by the riboses. Since the energy drop inevitably ended in favour of the oxygen of the amino acids it literally pushed the bases away now, which had been so welcome at first (they were oscillating as right-handedly as the oxygen itself).

This game of the electricity is immensely complicated but can be intuitively comprehended with our interpretation of left and right. Both effects of the electricity, the electrostatic one and the magnetic one, must have played a role in this molecular activity. It was just the interaction of both phenomena which made it possible that attraction turned into repulsion and vice-versa.

Remember the electrically traversed conductors which attracted each other electrostatically but repelled one another electromagnetically. For very similar reasons the peptide spiral disengaged from the ribose-base spiral. It was now weak in energy and possibly no longer able to repeat the game but it was certainly still available for other purposes. The other spiral, however, came off this process strengthened by the ribose. It was bursting with electrodynamic power and went on its journey...

We call this spiral ribonucleic acid, subsequently abbreviated RNA. This RNA spirals became (still as individual strands) the first form of genetic coding which nature made use of. The first more complex organisms on Earth might have laid down their genetic information exclusively in RNA strands. And up to today the genetic effectiveness of the RNA has gone far beyond what the biologists, who want to see only a messenger and transmitter in it, believe it to be capable of. We are entitled to these claims for the reason that nature has never taken back any of its evolutionary steps. If the RNA was a real information carrier once with immediate effectiveness on the genetic make-up, it is so still today as well. It was therefore not only the precursor of the DNA which developed later but also the originator of this bigger carrier of the genetic make-up to which the main work in processing genetic information is attributed today.'[46]

What else did the RNA bring about in the course of the reactions, apart from being the first "note pad" of life? Because it was after all a faithful copy of the causing peptide, even if the sequence of the amino acids was now coded in a certain succession of bases. Actually the bases themselves also matched each other quite well. In fact in such a way that the head of one adenine molecule always fitted the head of one uracil base, and in the same way the guanine fitted the cytosine. We know the reason: here, too, oxygen and hydrogen came close to each other but they were on the left and on the right of the molecule's head each and for that reason alone the bases would have never found each other on their own. But now there was a thread of rigidly anchored parking spaces (similar as in our example of the crystal), and immediately the corresponding bases seized these spaces. In this case, it was also a rather loose association because oxygen and hydrogen atoms did not come together in just the right way. The head of the molecule (nitrogen and hydrogen) protruded a little and thus prevented too tight a bond. Let's take a look at figure 113:

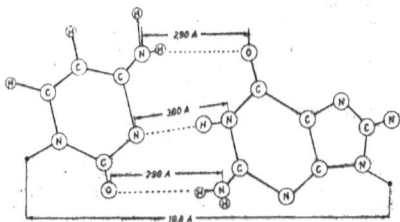

Fig. 113

Although this kind of depiction, generally common in chemistry, does not provide us with a particularly clear idea of how compact and spatially filled these molecules actually are. Again, carbon makes a strong annular structure possible, very similar to the one we found with benzene, only this time nitrogen atoms are involved. These are the so-called purine rings. When we try to do justice to the spatial image of these bases at least on the two-dimensional plane it looks approximately as shown in figure 114.

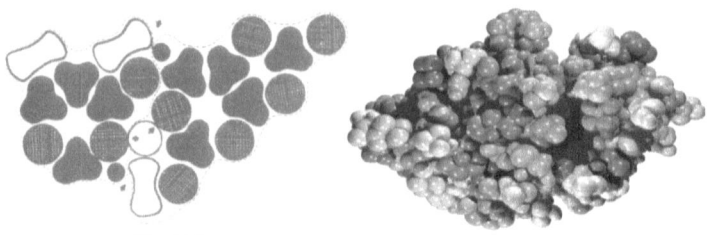

Fig. 114　　　　　　　　Fig. 114a

Here we can see better how hydrogen and oxygen hold the two structures together. In a very similar way but under different spatial conditions, adenine and uracil (or thymine) combine with one another ... In principle, all chain molecules of nature fold several times; their spatial constitution will then look quite complex (114a).

Since exactly the same spiral composed itself along the "parking spaces" of the RNA spiral again, the game described above repeated itself:

Again ribose and phosphoric acid molecules combined the bases to a chain, and again this new spiral fell off from the template. These two strands, however, were not exactly identical because a base named thymine fitted even better to adenine than uracil. Wherever strand 1 carried an adenine base, strand 2 now carried a thymine base.

This difference did not arise accidentally on any account. Of course, strand 1 was on no account indiscriminate with the peptide which had caused it; all in all its energy content was a little lower and the distribution of energy had to be a bit different as well. Therefore it would be astonishing if the same as before happened in this case either.

The new bases had a somewhat lower energetic quality. They did not only carry the same phosphor tail as the ribose mentioned above but there was also another copy of this ribose which lacked one oxygen atom, and logically it has therefore to be called deoxy-ribose. It was these deoxy-ribose bases which settled down at strand 1 and fell off again as a chain. Although the new chain was also a copy of the first one it could be clearly distinguished from the other by the different sugar and the thymine base. The new strand (2), however, consisted of fresh, unused bases after all - and again a trick was played on entropy which could just disengage strand 2 from strand 1 but had to let further events take their course.

After strand 1 had caused strand 2 as a deoxy chain it was "exhausted" and not worthy of consideration for a repetition of the process. Energy was economised very strictly and uncompromisingly; if any amount, however tiny, was missing, the whole situation would change fundamentally. It could for example happen that very similar reaction processes lead to extremely different results...

What did the now useless strand 1 do? When it got into a lipid shell, it went on its way with it. Most of the time, however, it coiled together with similar strands, actually on the basis of the same classes of weight. We can imagine that these strands - there were three bases for every amino acid of the causing peptide - were immensely compact and heavy. The biologist speaks of a high molecular weight. In addition even these individual strands also carried riboses and phosphor tails at their ends which loved to bond.

Thus, as a consequence, many of the strands combined to long chain molecules of RNA. These long RNA formations still exist today with or without lipid shells. They are nothing else but the simplest kind of virus that we know. Such a small, naked, RNA-containing virus is for instance the Feline Calici Virus (FCV). Also containing RNA, but encapsulated, however, is the Bovine Parainfluenca Virus (PI3).

Viruses are really something like preliminary stages of life. Over millions of years they have been disturbing the development of cells because they have an effect as insidious information bombs. Wherever RNA played a role later they could interfere. Yet these RNA viruses are scarcely more than crystallised RNA, they don't have any metabolism and they don't multiply on their own.

The deoxy strand 2 with the thymine bases, just developed and therefore full of energy, continued the game a little longer. Again adenine came for thymine and guanine found cytosine. And again the ribose-phosphor tails connected the whole to a chain. It was less rich in oxygen, and therefore the repulsion did not take place at first or it was not strong enough to separate hydrogen and oxygen. And as a consequence the strands did not fall apart (for the time being). With that the game was over (or at least its first round). What was left was a double spiral of bases which still carried the sequence of the original peptide and in which there weren't any uracil bases anymore. This double helix is called deoxyribonucleic acid or short DNA.

If we still find some readers at this point of the book, it will be those who are really interested in the details. Admittedly the description of the molecular processes which led to the creation of life is a dull and confusing subject. The reader who followed us patiently up to here shall at least be rewarded with the admission to go on reading ... Even if it is getting more complicated yet and the reader's powers of imagination will appear to be challenged to the bounds of the bearable – the subject will get exciting, that much can be guaranteed.

The famous DNA must have come into existence in the described way or at least in principle in this way, in collaboration with enzymes and other molecules, which we ignored for the sake of simplicity. When such a strand of DNA remained independent with or without lipid shell, it has remained so until today, to be exact as that kind of viruses which just consist mainly of DNA, as for example the naked, DNA-containing virus Bovine Adenovirus (BAV) or the encapsulated Equine Rhinopneumonitis Virus (ERP), and many more...

Later, in a yet to be explained manner, the flood of information of the DNA developed proper little lipid apparatuses, machines of DNA crystals: the bacteriophages - little monsters in the world of living cells.

But what is - for the time being - more interesting for us was the other possibility of the DNA to bond among its own kind in the usual way and to form tremendously long chains. Again a combination of whole knots of DNA took place on the basis of the molecular weight. They surrounded themselves with lipid skins like every other organelle and for the time being they did - nothing at all. They simply existed, a molecular imprint of the events, reaction to actions that had taken place, reflections of countless different peptides and of course of enzymes, too, which were nothing else but protein bodies themselves.

The RNA strands - as already hinted at above - also met in enormous amounts. As the heaviest bodies among the many molecules and organelles they developed - nearly for the same reason as the stars - countless centres of RNA through mutual displacement and repulsion. These centres of RNA, squeezed, spherical, simple structures, were soon encapsulated by lipids and peptides (obviously nothing at all escaped the obsession of the lipids for restriction) and temporarily formed highly inactive organelles which were nothing else but repositories full of information because the base triplets of the RNA contained after all the codifications of a diversity of peptides and molecules.

The individual RNA strands - as a whole, each signified a very particular protein molecule - did not bond tightly with each other but remained separate. Every single one could therefore be fished out of the mixture again. With that a kind of archive, a memory for peptides was created – the first molecular memory of the world!

After some time, everything that had been produced in the ocean up to then, be it peptides, enzymes, or lipids, was put down in some kind of writing in these little memory bodies. We still find this memory today inside of every cell and we call it ribosome.[47] Whoever wanted to remember could make use of this archive - but in those days nobody wanted to remember anything for the time being. And so the ribosomes were accumulating in the ocean and they were waiting...

Of course the strands of DNA were also concentrated information. They had adopted the writing from the RNA which now existed in duplicate moreover.

And now an important point arises in our reconstruction: only three letters were contained in this writing because every piece of information could only find expression in the spatial polarisations (spins) of the base pairs, namely as simple sequence of different states of charge - i.e. left, right, and neutral. How many different words could be formed with triplets of this kind? The answer is easy: 27 (factorial of 3).

So, there was the possibility to put down a maximum of 27 different amino acids in encoded form. However, there were certainly much more than 27 of such acids at that time - but they had to be reduced to 27 because of the codification. In addition, many acids similar to each other must have caused the same sequence of spins on the DNA, no matter if the used bases were different (there were four possibilities after all). But the electricity decimated the 64 words of the four bases to 27 variations of polarisation! The biologist knows about this fact, he says the code degenerated - and so far he has not had a clue about the cause of this strange reduction. We, on the other hand, understand it straight away. It was impossible that more than 27 of the many, many amino acids remained in the game.

Proof has been established for 25 of these amino acids up to now. It is safe to say that the remaining two also exist. Maybe they are used as "punctuation marks" in the genetic code, as terms meaning "beginning" and "end". Whoever had to read the writing needed to know where a piece of information began and where it ended.

The result of the electric degeneration of the code was that several base triplets are possible for one and the same amino acid provided that they cause the same sequence of polarisations. Here is the proof for that: let's just assume that every base has a certain polarisation, right-hand for adenine and guanine, left-hand for uracil and cytosine. And let's now assume that the analogous polarisation triplet for the amino acid alanine would be right-left-left. For this sequence we could therefore place the bases as follows: AUC, GCU, and GCC. Well, the triplets of the RNA have already been deciphered to a large extent and one knows the combinations rather well which are for example possible for alanine. We shouldn't be particularly surprised that they correspond exactly with the combinations above which all mean the same when looked at from an electrical point of view.[48]

When the first 20 amino acids had been found, one discovered that the genetic code used several different "words" for every kind. Since one expected that one single world would have been actually sufficient, one was baffled. We, on the other hand, can say for sure that there have to be exactly three different words for every amino acid (and there have to be 25 of them) which finally amounts to the same electrical information. Such a word is called codon.

We can assume that the degeneration of the code must have been accompanied by an enormous loss of information as well. In the beginning, when the events left their marks in the ocean, countless different amino acids were the triggers but, apart from those 25 which were best suited for the codons, they were all doomed because only these 25 remained clearly distinguishable. And it might be necessary to emphasise how slight the role of chance was in determining this writing. We can convert all known words of the amino acids into electrical triplets, and we will see that they all fit into our pattern.

So it is the spin of the electrons, or to be more exact that of the atomic Fourier oscillations which is important for the script of life. Every two of the bases which stand opposite each other in the codons therefore always carry opposite spins; the counter-word for alanine is therefore left-right-right or UAG, CGA, and CCG. Again, this arrangement of the bases corresponds to the electrical aspect of the codon. With every development of an RNA or DNA spiral, the directions of the oscillations are transmitted primarily. This is a very safe, reliable method. It would probably be much too unreliable if the bases only recognised each other on the basis of their spatial properties.

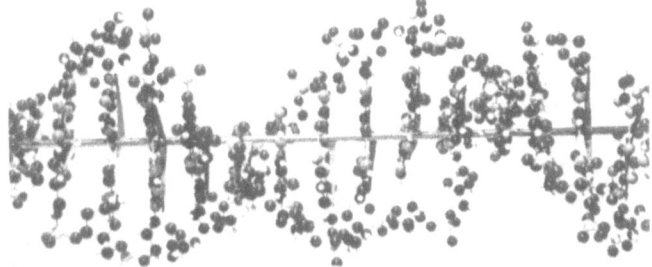

Fig. 115

Figure 115 shows us a model of the DNA double helix. When it was discovered the cheers were many but they came too soon. It just looked as if the machinery of life had been discovered and immediately a glorious picture was painted of this machinery. As the supreme control centre as which it was seen, it had to be sacrosanct! And above all it was believed that the DNA double helix had to contain all functions and characteristics of life without any exception. But this is only true up to a point! For example, none of its codons contains the principle of cell division and it even evoked all the other characteristics, which it caused, only indirectly, like a switch which puts distant mechanisms into motion. We could never comprehend the function of the DNA if it was examined separately. Apart from the fact that those strands of RNA (actually shreds of RNA), which we were "left with" after the development of the DNA, are also involved in the process of life as switches or repressor genes and even pass on the genetic make-up independently (epigenesis).

One of the most interesting partners of the DNA, which does not depend on it in any way and exists absolutely autonomously, is the centriole of which we already spoke. This tiny accumulator of nature does not contain any information worth mentioning at all and still it is almost the most important component of every cell. It is the clock and the motor of life. It is responsible for that effect which has been considered the mysterious power of life for so long. Of course, there is no mysterious power of life because even life is only caused by one single force: the repulsion principle, the pressure under which the cosmos puts itself because of its own existence...

In the electron microscope the centriole reveals itself to be made of tiny tubes (9 symmetrically arranged triplets of microtubules), their interior containing water and ions. Electrically defined there are, for that reason, certainly both centrioles with right-hand and left-hand orientation as already mentioned. After a certain time of growth (in the cell at the end of the S-phase or prophase of division), every centriole separates into one half with right-hand polarisation and one half with left-hand polarisation. At the risk of tiring out the anyhow already exhausted reader we have to analyse this process in still greater detail because it is of fundamental significance: for the time being the centriole can - as a mono-pole - actually only separate into two identical halves. It is finally the repulsion of these halves which drives them apart and makes them move away from each other as far as possible. The electric radiation of these little bodies is so strong that it can be detected in experiments - one talks about mitogenetic radiation. Before the centriole divides, and even still during division, it releases almost all of its energy to the environment and transforms it into a field with like polarisation. The point of time for this radiation arises from the electric resistance of the environment which can be overcome when a certain potential has been reached.

Now the two halves march away from each other in this uniformly polarised field (either only to the right or only to the left). They immediately begin to grow and to radiate again - but this time in such a way that they fit in with the electrostatic field. We came to know a similar process as influence. When there is a uniform field between the centrioles, they have to polarise each other in opposite ways (fig. 38). And for that reason, two differently polarised centrioles face each other after a short time dividing their environment into two oppositely oriented halves. This has remarkable consequences...

All DNA strands show the same helical direction, but on more detailed examination they are electrically differentiated formations - after all they carry different polarisations in their triplets which do not neutralise each other on any account but also find expression in the ribose-phosphor chain of the helix. Well, it would be an extraordinary coincidence if these polarisations spread out so evenly that all in all every individual strand was absolutely neutral. One polarisation will always be predominant and one strand will always be forced to be the counterpart of the other. When one of them is emitting a little more left-hand spatial polarisations, the partner provides a little more of the right-hand sort...

Wherever and however DNA strands exist, they are always differentiated in this electrical way eventually. We can say that every strand carries one dominant electrical information. And that had its consequences, too...

Everything we have described up to now could still take place in the primordial ocean – or in ponds and small local enclosures. Here, the evolution went from the molecular basis to the level of the organelles, and these organelles continued developing for a long time after before they were captured by skin-forming molecules.

These lipid skins, however, did on no account only envelope these single organelles. Again and again new skins formed, and soon they also enveloped finished organelle systems. Skins slipped over skins, and in that way the mentioned ER was created. In between there was a variety of captured organelles and enzymes which were suddenly as if torn away from the land of milk and honey and had to get along with each other. Only in a few of countless cases could this work out, could the encapsulated mini-ocean continue to play its game. Although it was probably only rarely the case that organelles were encapsulated which complemented each other in an ideal way. In the end it had to happen at some time, and in the course of billions of years it surely happened many million times.

In this way, the first, simple kinds of cells came into existence. They were probably very simple in comparison to later developments but yet already pretty complex in their function. And again it would be more than a little strange if some of these cells had not encapsulated ribosomes and a small amount of naked DNA strands as well so that the original ocean, the giant cell, remained complete even within the newly created smaller sphere.

Already this first attempt of life, and of course it was not a conscious attempt but just an unavoidable result of molecular, infinite pre-processes, was such a success that its results still exist today as fossils. Figure 116 shows us some specimen of those first simple cell structures. They are 3.1 to 3.8 billions of years old!

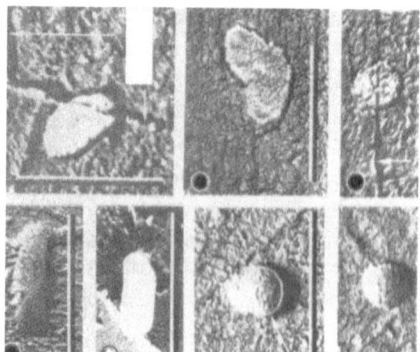

Fig. 116

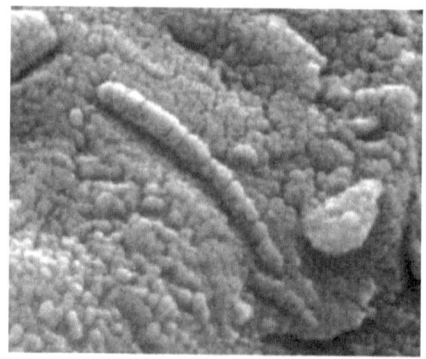

Fig.116a: bacterium on mars?

25 Bacteria

This apparently simple something which was created in our mind's eye in the previous chapter is called bacteria. Although the truth is that it is already an immensely complex organism, it still does have neither a nucleus nor any chromosomes. A few hundred or thousand strands of DNA are sufficient for it; but there already is a centriole, mitochondria, and other organelles and maybe even some chloroplasts. According to that, such a bacterium would already be a plant but usually bacteria make up their own area of life. They can neither be classified as belonging to the plants nor to the animals, there are even some which have mastered both life-forms depending on environment and necessity...

Let's take a closer look at such a primitive bacterium. What was encapsulated in the various shells was at some time determined by mere accident - but it had to be co-incidence if a functioning interaction arose from the encapsulated objects.

What happens now in this tiny, encapsulated primordial ocean inside the bacterium? As is to be expected the same that has already happened outside of it. The bacterium exists in the water, and material which is available in abundance in the ocean penetrates through its lipid skin. The primeval bacterium grows...

But now the encapsulated DNA strands[49] develop a function for the first time. They have a similar effect as the thread in the crystal solution, their polarisations radiate into the space, and there is only one kind among the molecules which is in itself sufficiently polarised electrically to react to these temptations: the nucleotides. Actually, it's those RNA nucleotides, which are particularly rich in energy, that can move in the cell's fluid and which are attracted by the DNA. They settle down on the matching sections of the DNA double helix according to their spins, and as a result the base uracil comes into play again after all (thymine is a deoxy building block). What now develops in the already known way is an RNA strand as we already know it. It adopts a certain length which is maybe determined by the length of the DNA section and then loses just so much polarisation energy because of its own linkage that it falls off the DNA again. And at the same time it takes away so much energy from the DNA that the DNA itself - anyway a slightly weaker partner with lower cohesion - possibly disintegrates.

For sure the biologists will protest now because we are violating one of their doctrines – the sacrosanct DNA - but this should not confuse us for the time being. For reasons of energy it is in fact rather unlikely that the DNA is reacting with molecules as a possibly indestructible structure without being subject to any modification itself. After all, it is astonishing enough that its double helix stays together for a while at all. We shouldn't expect any more of it.

We are rather more interested in what happens with the newly developed strand of RNA. Well, it cannot just swim around in the shell indiscriminately because there are the many walls and skins of the ER, there are mandatory paths (similar to the switching circuits of an electronic component) and in addition there is an electric field which, radiating from the centriole, stipulates a direction of movement to everything that polarises on its own. This is nothing else but electrophoresis, the movement of ions and molecules in the unipolar field (here control and movements are generally caused electrically although locomotive mechanisms are also possible on the basis of microtubules the likes of which can be found most distinctly with the sperm cells.)

Eventually the RNA goes to where an RNA belongs: among its own kind - to one of the ribosomes of which there are vast amounts inside the cell as everybody knows. As we already know these are conglomerates of RNA joined by a little protein. Before one identified the rather plain structure of these organelles, authors had vied with each other in fantastic descriptions of the functioning of a ribosome. For the most part, they described them as little sewing machines, as mysterious apparatuses which assemble peptides. We don't want to go into these bizarre, teleological descriptions any further at all.

Sixty percent of a ribosome consist at least of RNA - and it is that RNA which once caused the DNA and was just kept as a memory. We want to call the new, recently created RNA messenger-RNA (m-RNA) because it acts as a messenger for the DNA. With a little freedom and imagination we can very well picture what is happening here: the m-RNA comes across a ribosome where it is passed through between two ribosome halves into a kind of gorge. Just freshly created, it possesses so much polarisation that it is able to pull its counter-parts in segments out of the RNA archive of the ribosome. When it does not succeed completely with the first ribosome, maybe because the right segments are just not available from this memory or because they don't react promptly, the process is just continued with the next ribosome. This happens quite indiscriminately and takes until the RNA has been completed to a DNA-like double strand in any case. The sections of RNA which are taken out and added on are called transfer-RNA (t-RNA). They fall off the m-RNA immediately for the now already rather well known reason. The process is repeated until the m-RNA is robbed of its energy and can finally merge with some ribosome or other. The t-RNA, however, is practically exactly that piece which originally developed from a peptide. It represents precisely the negative part of the spatial properties of the peptide and therefore that of the amino acid sequence as well. And again it has the same effect as the thread in the crystal solution: crystallising amino acids settle down exactly along their bases in accordance with their original sequences. A new peptide originates, falls off afterwards, folds into new, quite surprising secondary and tertiary structures and has an effect...

What does the t-RNA do? That's easy: after all it is nothing else but the already known strand 1. Therefore it causes a new DNA (!) in the already described way and returns to some ribosome.[50]

We see that both types of RNA are finally settled down in the ribosomes leading to the creation of new ribosomes respectively. For that reason, the number of the ribosomes has to increase continuously in the cell. And a good thing, too, because when the cell divides every half receives a sufficient amount.

We have to define another fact more precisely: the newly created peptide is on no account identical with the one which originally caused the DNA. RNA could not develop on finished peptides because - conditional on their electrical properties - peptides coil into complicated secondary and tertiary structures. So what originally brought the DNA into the world were the peptide segments, maybe only a few amino acids, which had found each other. And further we have to conclude that the original synthesis of the very first RNA was caused by enzymes which did not exist anymore at a later time - simply for the reason that we are unable to duplicate the process in an experiment today.

In the cells living today RNA can only be created on the DNA; the pure amino acids don't synthesise any RNA anymore because the required enzymes which existed in former times had been singled out a long time before any cell came into existence at all. At the beginning of evolution, though, information was selected indiscriminately which created something completely new at a later time - when it took effect for the first time - by combining individual segments, individual codons which - originally caused by di- or tripeptides only - could now suddenly create polypeptides. And only these - giant new formations among all these preliminary stages of life - restructured the beginning development drastically into higher organisms in the first simple primitive bacteria for the first time.

Two cycles developed in the cell: one is the cycle of the heavy, right-handedly polarising molecules: RNA creates DNA, DNA creates RNA, and RNA causes DNA again, and so on... The other is the cycle of left-handedly polarising molecules, of peptides and of enzymes: food brings amino acids, amino acids create peptides, and these in turn develop apparatuses to take the food in or they become food themselves...

Both cycles determine each other. Their point of contact is the t-RNA from the ribosome. Somehow the cycle of the heavy molecules represents the mirror image of the other cycle or should we say, vice-versa? In any case the relationship between nucleic acids and proteins is revealed in the sense of a mutual catalysis: nucleic acids contain the information for the production of proteins and enzymes which for their part produce nucleic acids.

What is achieved by this interaction are chemical fluctuations or oscillations, a swing of life so to speak. These chemical oscillations and cycles also determine the temporal course of the reactions and with that the temporal existence of the organism. Like two toothed wheels these great cycles mesh with each other. But first they had to get into their stride. This certainly happened in myriads of attempts in the first days of life...

A previously unappreciated basic element in these reactions were (and are) without doubt the unipolar electric fields of the centriole because they kept the molecules in motion and forced them into the paths presctructured by plasma. Since the two big molecular cycles polarise differently a distinct separation was the result. This separation is still very obvious in every cell today: therefore we find the ribosomes only in very particular areas of the lipid shells; preferably they are located outside the tubules of the ER and never within them because these paths are occupied and used by the molecules with left-hand polarisation. The electrostatic field enables us also to understand why the RNA strands flow away from the DNA at one time and then flow towards it again. Apparently they are provided with electrical information which dominates in the opposite direction after every reaction. Therefore every to and fro, here and there of the molecules inside the cell can be understood as being caused electrically in the same way as the atomic or molecular movements in an accumulator. Without the centriole - the repository of the ions - all of this would not be possible at all.

Well, our descriptions have been a bit complicated up to this point, and yet we sketched the biochemical processes in a very rough and oversimplified way. Of course, we have to be aware of the fact that without excessive claims for correctness, we only tried to describe a pattern, which exists within an almost unmanageable world of events,. Many of the structures, organelles, and systems involved were simply ignored. Even dealing with the electrical and chemical processes in more detail (transfer of spin, influence, pole reversal, change-over from attraction to repulsion, etc.) would fill a book on its own. Therefore it must be sufficient for us to know that the illustrated processes for controlling, moving, and processing the units of information and energy exist inside of cells and above all why they have to exist. We therefore understand the processes very well, at least in a symbolic way, as the game of a continuously dropping energy which cannot flow as it wants and leaves its paths and traces in form of certain structures in a completely indispensable way, a game which is mainly ruled by electricity. And after all, nature and cause of the electricity are no particular mystery to us anymore...

Now let's assume that there was a time when all this happened for the very first time. Primitive cells with a little DNA developed ... and in some bacteria this DNA suddenly began to cause absolutely new, complicated peptides. There had never been any like them before. Subsequently these new peptides began to thoroughly alter and reorganise the shell together with its contents. As peptides, they had a variety of properties, they produced this or that effect, they became new organelles, new mitochondria, new skins ... that means the whole process which had taken place in the ocean before now started anew from the beginning but this time already with specific, more complicated and more compact building blocks – and above all in the protective envelop of lipid membranes.

This was already something like a systematic effect. Not individual amino acids or simple dipeptides were at work here but finished structures which could complement each other like the parts of a prefabricated house. Totally unintentionally they experimented, created little machines, shapes, and functions and the final result in perhaps a few cases was a completely, newly, thoroughly organised shell which had nothing to do with the original form anymore, a new bacterium with very particular properties. And there were only two possibilities: either these properties had the qualification for the continued existence of the structure or they didn't.

We have to see it the right way: among billions of similar developments only a few had to be successful or just tolerably successful. And in the process, maybe only a part of the unintentionally captured DNA had been scanned and destroyed. Again the next m-RNA set out on its journey, again new peptides were created, polypeptides they certainly were, and their chains became longer and longer, their shapes more and more varied.

All this happened in the sequence caused by the DNA, and this sequence only had to result in something useful in broad outline because the principle of division, yes, even the principle of the cell itself, was not contained on it. This principle could therefore not be destroyed anymore. For that reason, all these first experiments could be repeated until something came of them. The laboratory of nature had infinite time and endless patience... And again several thousand years went by...

Many books on biology give the impression as if the processes inside a cell are extremely precise, as if every minute error has devastating consequences. But this cannot be assumed necessarily. All biological processes sum up statistic events with tremendous redundancy. Thus it may happen that now and again some RNA or DNA end up some place they don't belong. This has little influence. Because the essential point was and still is the overriding result, the observation of the relatively big cycles. Without any doubt everything goes off strictly causally, surely individual molecules always reacted causally with each other but the result was eventually the effect from the reactions of thousands of molecules. It was thus easily possible that a few wrong ones were among them. They were covered up so to speak. The main thing was and still is that the information of the DNA has always been much more extensive than necessary, fitted with tremendous reserves which made an indefatigable repetition of an order possible.

Again we need the right viewpoint: every single peptide, yes, even every single amino acid had its own codon on the DNA. When in the end millions of molecules in the cell influenced each other, there were also millions of codons on the double helix. Every ordinary bacterium already has a surplus of information available which never takes effect.[51] This surplus was fundamental because everything was based on it. Meaningless information was deleted until the remaining bits resulted in the appropriate, although appropriate only in retrospect. Nothing had been intended from the beginning. Therefore we have to find a new interpretation for the DNA. Enclosed in the cycle of the nucleotides it must be an unstable structure like all the other structures of life. As long as the cell lives, the DNA is disassembled (stripped down by the messenger-RNA) and re-assembled (by the transfer-RNA).

With that we are very consciously in conflict with the theories in force. We can, however, concede that it is also probable that the principle of a stable DNA existed as well - in fact obviously with some species of insects and plants. Maybe one had examined exactly these organisms and judged the general by these standards. Of all living beings, however, it is those which developed further that have most probably a dynamic DNA which is regenerated gain and again. Namely in already practised functions - in exactly the sequence which it initiated itself before it disintegrated. As a rule it should regenerate itself in an identical form. But it could also change itself by simply omitting, skipping, forgetting, or loosing information... And that is the crucial point of life whose significance we will make more apparent.

Our second supposition is that the two strands of a DNA differ electrically from each other, namely in their dominant polarisations. Expressed in the customary way, a DNA is always composed of one negative and one positive strand. Actually, this strange doubling was originally an industrious piece of work. It is conceivable that already the identical function of disassembling and reassembling a base spiral would have been sufficient for simple forms of life. And indeed there are viruses with only one DNA strand.

The bipolarity of the DNA strands resulted in the development of an order within a DNA complex. Because of their polarisation the strands turn like compass needles in the field of the cell in such a way that all left-hand strands point to one side and all right-hand strands point to the other side. On that basis, a dipole field develops within this complex (the future nucleus). This order fits completely in with the order which is caused by the divided centriole. When the centrioles situated in the cell's halves intensify their polarisation they have in turn an effect on the strands of DNA. They arrange them in order and pull them towards themselves. In doing so they can tear the strands apart like a zip fastener.

The torn apart DNA halves march towards their corresponding centriole whereas the other molecules march away from them and they will meet in the middle creating a wall which suddenly divides the cell in one half with left-hand polarisation and one with right-hand polarisation. The bisected DNA strands complement each other by adding the corresponding nucleotides, and soon a messenger-RNA will settle down again on the double helix and go travelling...

Well, all of this has to be comprehended in the right way. When we look into a kaleidoscope we see structures and patterns developing continuously which don't make any sense at all. From time to time, however, we discover something meaningful in the pattern: flowers for instance and snow flakes or crystal shapes. While the DNA was scoured in the cell, the cell developed just like a kaleidoscope, often towards the meaningless and destructive. And for sure the process was held up or came to a standstill thousands upon thousands of times. But not just in every case!

Sometimes this molecular motor was running so well that it was sufficient for preserving a structure until the next division set in. Nutrition in form of finished amino acids and protein bodies came from outside. And when nothing else came and when the water was lost, the shell ceased its activity and dried up... that means it crystallised while maintaining its molecular positions. And when this thing got back into water and nutrition again, the process continued exactly where it had stopped.

Many bacteria still play this game today; the biologist says they sporulate. Spores are nothing else but crystallised cells without water. They are able to remain viable for thousands of years withstanding heat and cold without any damage and are immediately revived when the environment is suitable for them. It is exactly because of this cunning that there are still bacteria today as there have been then, and in any possible form, too...

Sporulators are also called bacilli. Everybody knows the role they still play for every organism which they infest aggressively if need by. In the realm of the bacteria literally everything exists which our brain can imagine kaleidoscope-like, every kind of idea has been realised. There are breathing bacteria as well as those which manage without oxygen. Some even adapt completely to the corresponding environment. But all of them are specialised in particular processes of the metabolism or in substances which they cannot produce on their own. And all of them discharge excrements which are as a rule unsuitable or even poisonous for the affected organism – but which can also be useful for the host organism.

Fig.116b:Protozoa *"Hastatella Radians"*

26 Chromosome

Bacteria are actually a dead end of development. No other living being descends directly from them. Their comparative simplicity has ensured their survival for billions of years. But for them, their life is probably without particular impressions, without any special significance. Fortunately for us (some would say: unfortunately for us) they were not the only product of that primordial ocean, though...

When we picture such a bacterium completely without any organelles, i.e. without any ribosomes or mitochondria, only filled with tremendously many DNA strands and one single centriole among them, i.e. pure, encapsulated DNA complexes and nothing else, we see nothing less than a chromosome. There is no question how it came into being. It was only necessary for some kind of bacterium to lose its organelles or for a shell in the process of formation to encapsulate exclusively DNA and one centriole - and a chromosome was born. Of course, the DNA soon caused other protein structures around it which made a stabilising spatial arrangement possible. But to simplify matters we will not go into this in detail.

Like a virus, a chromosome alone is not capable of surviving. It is in fact really a bomb of information but absolutely useless without any working organelles. But chromosomes have a significant characteristic: because of their own centriole, it is unequivocally possible to recognise their orientation as left-handed or right-handed.

Unnecessary to say that the amount of information in them must have been almost colossal. It was latent information, its for the time being unspecified purpose and influence should become apparent only after the events...

Well, back then the developing protein shells certainly encapsulated all sorts of things. At some time they also captured some chromosomes and therefore we still find those structures in the nuclei of the organisms. Concentrated loads of DNA they are, and when such a chromosome came into a bacterium or was encapsulated in a lipid shell together with the necessary organelles, basically the same mechanism took place which had been caused by the individual DNA strands in bacteria but there also ensued enormous differences. Now there was much more information available and it probably came from several chromosomes at the same time.

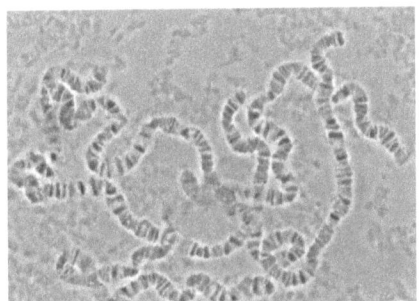

Fig. 117

Figure 117 shows us some chromosomes which consist of thousands upon thousands of DNA strands.

Just like the bacterial DNA strands, the complete chromosomes are disassembled and reassembled in a nucleus. A nucleus is virtually a free, blank space within the ER which is enveloped by a nucleus membrane. The transportation of matter into the surrounding cytoplasm is done through countless pores.

Since the formation and development of the chromosomes in this field practically starts anew from the beginning with every cell division they are not visible in-between the cell divisions. It is easily possible to observe the division of a cell containing chromosomes using a microscope, and the biologists subdivided this process, which they call mitosis, into several phases.

Let's take a look at the single phases of cell division as they take place in almost all kinds of cells all over the world.

PROPHASE (introduction): after the DNA of the chromosomes has been disassembled it is gradually assembled again. In doing so it will again correspond to the production steps of the cell it initiated itself. At first one sees irregularly scattered little granules and strands which soon restore the original picture of the chromosomes. These are chromosomes which are not yet completely finished because every centromere of a chromosome divides and arranges the chromosomes into left-hand and right-hand halves. That means, already at this point the DNA is ripped and doubled. These longitudinally split chromosomes are called chromatids.

Now the centriole located outside the nucleus divides after having beamed forth strongly first. Its halves move to opposite areas of the cell and polarise them in opposite ways. This new order has consequences: the ER restructures itself to spindle-shaped tubules reaching to the left and to the right from the nucleus up to the centriole. It is as if the centriole pulled these structures out of the lipid shell of the nucleus. Inevitably, the chromatids follow these fibres according to their electrical allocation. Next comes

METAPHASE (gathering): the electric power preferably takes effect on the centromeres of the chromosomes. For that reason, the latter fold over in this place and drag the rest behind in a U-shape. All chromosomes now settle down aligned in one plane between the centrioles where they condense and shorten. The fibre paths radiating from the centrioles become more distinct. They seem to pull on the centromeres of the chromosomes but of course it is the force created by the opposite charges that is pulling and which even the lipid fibres have to follow in the end. Next comes

ANAPHASE (migration): now the condensed chromosomes (or rather chromatids) migrate to the cell poles, the spindle fibres shorten, and their structure gradually disintegrates. Next is

TELOPHASE (destination): the chromatids align in a star-shape around every centriole. They have reached their destination and now they descondense, loosen up, and become fully adequate chromosomes. Because of the activity of the m-RNA they will be continuously disintegrated, and while the ER is enveloping them they disappear noticeably. In

INTERPHASE, the amount of DNA in the new nuclei diminishes by 75 %. It does not drop completely to zero because at the same time new DNA is assembled again. New chromatids develop because of the duplication of the DNA - and of course they are not absolutely identical with the old ones. The reassembly of the DNA brings about that pieces of information change their place from time to time, just as if the chromosomes were cut in pieces and put together again while exchanging their sections - which is true in certain respects. The biologist speaks of crossing-over because he already noticed this exchange of information. But up to today nobody has found a really good explanation for that.[105]

While the disintegrated DNA lets its flood of information loose on the cell the DNA content of the nucleus is already increasing again, and a new prophase begins. The created daughter cells soon repeat the game...

A new wall has formed between the daughter nuclei. With that the remaining content of the cell along with the organelles was divided more or less. Figure 118 shows us the course of the described phases as they can be followed under the microscope.

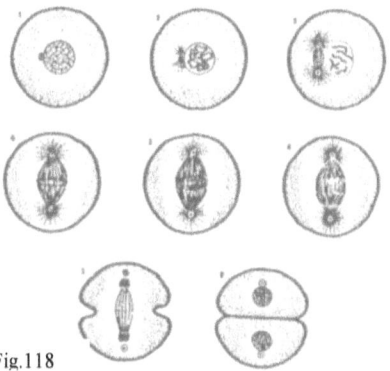

Fig.118

All motional sequences of mitosis have both electrical and spatial causes which we could illustrate at least in a roughly schematic manner. Of course the entire causal molecular sequences are even more complicated. But at least we understand relatively well why the halves of the chromosomes know so precisely where to migrate to. An error is barely possible, but still it happens (chromosomal aberration).

As a rule the system works very reliably. The division of the cell itself is first and foremost determined by the centromeres of the chromosomes and secondly by the own centriole. Evidently, these little accumulators have got well into stride with each other in the course of billions of years. The growth of the cell has been coordinated just as well, and this growth has in turn an effect on the growth of the centriole. A division only takes place if a certain relation of the sizes to each other is exceeded. If the growth of the cells is prevented, for instance by partially removing its plasma, the division fails to occur! Hence this is the proof that the division is not triggered or controlled by the chromosomes or the DNA. Even the centriole – so far totally underestimated in its importance - only divides after having reached a very particular size. Well, actually this is all very plausible and it should be rather astonishing if things were different.

He who has thought up to now that DNA and chromosomes were each reduplicating absolutely identically, falls victim to wishful thinking. As we understand it, the disassembly and reassembly of the DNA is subject to a certain differentiation. Whole sequences of triplets can change, above all there is the possibility to refrain from reassembling useless sections at all, i.e. to delete information. And it's in the nature of things that information which went wrong does not lead to a further reassembly of a DNA section at all.

This fact is of enormous significance because it accounts for one of the most important abilities of all organisms: to gain experience. This ability takes effect especially in the interaction of several cells which are exchanging matter with each other making it possible to co-ordinate functions with each other. It also allows the modification of the DNA on the basis of changing environmental conditions. But with a certain restriction: information can only be deleted, new information is not added! Once a piece of information has been used up and discarded there was no way back. This will remind the biologists among our readers immediately of the laws by Louis Dollo (1857-1931) who already postulated:

- Development is directed.
- Development is limited.
- Development is not reversible.

The mystery about these sentences - and it isn't a mystery at all - lies hidden in the DNA. Already at that time, in the ocean, a certain amount of information was collected and definitely determined which could only be used up until today.[52] From that results for one thing the impression of a direction in evolution, and for another an apparent limitation because when the information of the corresponding creature was used up, its development came to an end. Unable to adapt to new habitats the corresponding organism had to die out.

The irreversibility (new information cannot be assembled, deleted information cannot be replaced) is almost one of the main features of evolution. For example, living beings had once given up their gills and when they got back again into the water habitat, nothing would give them back their gills. Other organs, like for instance the mucous membrane of the pharynx, had to replace the lost gills. Singled out organs were irretrievably lost and often completely different organs which had originally been intended for other purposes grew into their functions. For that reason, Dollo had to formulate his famous sentences.

There are still countless unicellular structures with chromosomes in the nuclei. They are called protozoans. They already possess organelles for locomotion (flagella, cilia) as well as their own organelles for food processing and breathing. They are already little animals, and often there are even smaller animals inside those little animals which - of granule-like appearance – control the metabolic functions (ciliophora).

All concepts of the later evolution which eventually lead to such complicated cellular systems as represented by the human being have in principle already been realised in the protozoans. Thus, apart from the asexual reproduction, which we described as cell division, sexual reproduction (copulation) already existed as well. We will learn more about that later-on. Some of these little animals already encapsulated some chloroplasts. So they are real intermediate stages between plant and animal.

If the DNA had been an immobile, rigid machinery-like structure, these incredible living beings wouldn't have come into existence at all. Because accidental mutations played - if at all - a very small, mostly negative role in evolution and only at a later time.

How comes that such a tiny protozoan already lives, already feels the force and the urge to follow the light ... swims around and survives until it divides? And how comes that one has not discovered the motor of these events for so long? Although the individual phases of life become absolutely clear molecularly and electrically - why do they take place at all?

Even if we have already presented very extensive descriptions and with that not only deciphered the How but also the Why quite well, there are still some fundamental things which have to be said in this respect: we already hinted at it with the stumbling centipede: each of these living molecular complexes is actually only up to one thing: to get rid of the energy it represents. This is not surprising in any way. Just like the river creates an ornate delta around obstacles lying in its way and divides into many water ducts or flows together from many brooks in its endeavour to finally flow into the sea, the flow of energy does not find a path without any obstacles either. The majority of obstacles is caused by the DNA which forces the flow into new paths by triggering new structures again and again. The flow of energy would have run off and dried out long ago if the springs and brooks had not provided new energy again and again ... and thus this flow in the cells cannot come to a stop because new energies are supplied all the time and the DNA always fuels the machinery with new ideas. Therefore it is continually necessary to seek new paths, or rather these paths develop on their own – exactly through the flow of energy. Therefore it is actually the striving for entropy which makes nature come into existence all around us.[108]

The stored fantasy of the DNA is in constant battle with this entropy. Certainly not on purpose; it is not aware of its mighty work itself. Fortunately it came into being at a time when there was a great surplus of energy available on this Earth, and for that reason, it also contains a very great surplus of information.

Wherever energy wants to flow the DNA and all its products get into its way; and exactly these products are still accumulating new energy which in turn is used for building new obstacles...

That the DNA and its fantastic effects could develop was only thanks to the trick with the apparently gratis generation of energy from light. Only one single molecule had to be able to reproduce first - and a planet began to live...

Since obviously all means are fine and everything that was possible could also come into existence, today there are even cells with two nuclei. We find them in the livers of the animal kingdom. They are the ultimate in information, the most differentiated and most efficient apparatus of nature with about 600 different functions.

Well, the chromosome is on no account a repository of commands which can have its way like a dictator and produce exactly this or that edifice from the beginning. It only contains possible plans. To what extent they are really carried out is determined by the environment - which also comprises the interior of the cell, its plasma. So the nucleus does not have a monopoly on heredity. Most organelles - that also includes the mitochondria or the chloroplasts - reproduce independently of chromosomes which is comprehensible because they have been there before (and have their own DNA and RNA at their disposal). What is caused by the nucleus is the building material, the assembly units of production and even that is in principle supplied only by enzymatic control, i.e. very indirectly. The DNA actually carries only the codons for certain enzymes (one gene - one enzyme) but every enzyme brings along its very specific function. This means the nucleus contains also the commands for the production of the "tool".

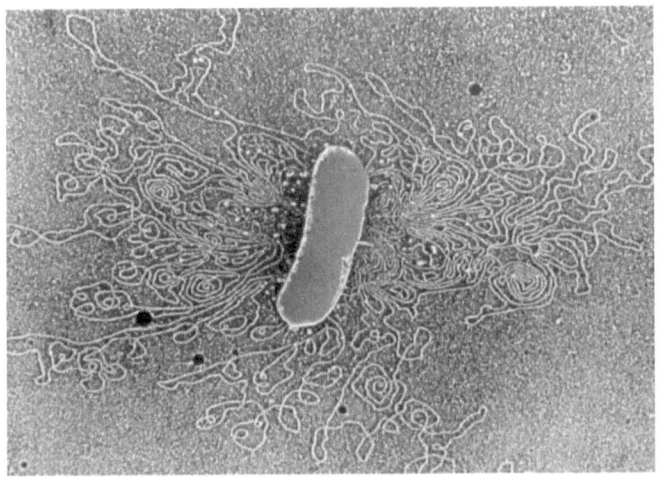
Fig. 118a: DNA coming out of the bacterium E.coli

The plasma of the cell now consists predominantly of these enzymes - and we already mentioned that not everything goes off so precisely. Thus there are remainders of the DNA (endomeres) in the plasma itself which are strongly involved in the overall events. Even the most important mechanisms of life, like division or the ability of the plants to produce chlorophyll for example, are passed down through the plasma... Therefore there is both a chromosomal and a plasmatic transmission of information - but actually that, too, has to appear self-evident to us. It would only be really astonishing if we had truly found the DNA to be that life-creating machine as which it is considered by biologists. But it isn't. Plasma and environment carry the idea of life to a large extent. Living beings, which contribute to the survival of their species, therefore always create very exactly the same environmental conditions for their descendants (in the amnion of the mother animal or in the egg). In this way they enforce structures which are similar to each other. We will discuss later-on how far that had to go.

A structure created by the flow of energy is shown in figure 119: The estuary of the Colorado River at the Gulf of California. The manifold branchings were created by the tidal inflow and outflow of the waters.

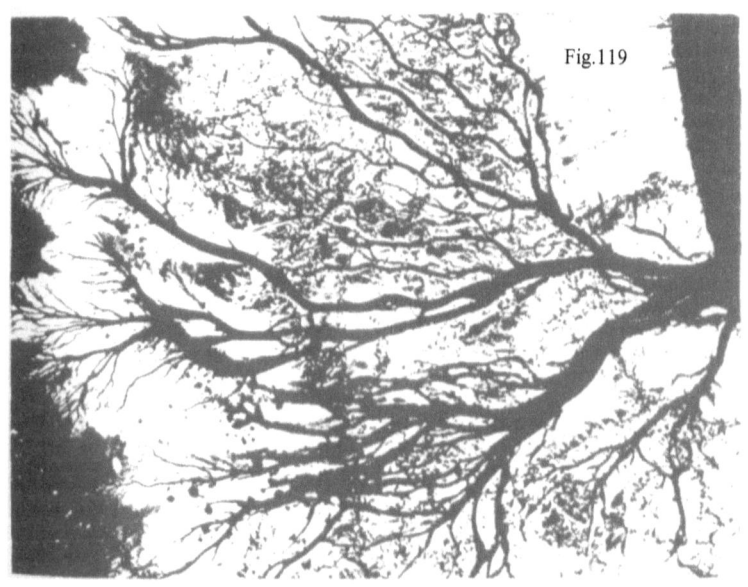

Fig.119

27 Plan

Evolution doesn't have a plan - we already hinted at that. Everything is based on the experiment, on unconscious, aimless trial as we have to emphasise. When it was important for a protozoan to move in a particular environment and when the DNA had just caused straight structures which could do so - for locomotion, for example, pseudopodia, apparent feet, which were created when a cell wall undulated, bulged, and dropped -, this protozoan had "lost" the energetic game! It had to keep its energy whereas those which could not attained the universal objective: the final loss of energy.

Life gives us the impression as if the gain of energy is its priority endeavour - but appearances are deceptive. From time to time even a river is prepared to flow a little bit uphill if it goes downhill again afterwards. And therefore it looks as if an endeavour for experience and knowledge prevails in life. But in the end all these endeavours have only the one inevitable purpose: to find new slopes for the flow of energy.

In this way a simply cell was once created which mastered only a few chemical processes and would have come to rest soon, and now such a chromosome gets into this cell and makes things tremendously complicated all of a sudden. Suddenly new proteins are created, enzymes which connect and separate, molecules which oscillate along with the light, flagella which rotate, and cilia which beat. And nothing came of rest!

This abundance of new reactions had to be mastered and organised first. For that, however, new paths and processes were required as well as new energies, of course ... and so the cilia whirl up nutrition while beating, and so the flagella rotate, and so the chloroplasts turn towards the light - and with them the whole cell.

Suddenly the living being strives for the light which it seems to "recognise" and to sense. When the flagella are located in the right place, the idea was "good". The process continues and the tried situation is passed on as information onto the new DNA. When they are located in the wrong place, the process comes to a stop and the information is lost because it leads to the destruction of the cell. The new DNA, on the other hand, does never again contain a code for the wrong flagella. From now on they are automatically located in the right place. As long as the environment remains as it is there is no reason to change this section of the plan. But the plan changes in other sections, again only by trying accidental structures and that until the protozoan is sufficiently up to the environment. It remains this way for thousands of years, divides and reproduces...

Where is a real plan in that? Nowhere! Neither in the DNA nor in the plasma. Everything happened by co-incidence, by the interaction of favourable circumstances. That which does not work comes to an end. That which works becomes plan and edifice at the same time, technology and engineer in one - becomes manifest reaction, enforced answer to the challenge of the environment. Force governs inside and soon outside as well. Having to live, is the slogan!

There are multifarious theories about the sequence of the origination of the various forms of life. Even if it is essentially quite immaterial which way evolution took exactly, one could toy with the idea when exactly the element oxygen arrived in this world as a donator of energy. Of course there are traces for the fact that primitive forms of life could do without any oxygen at all and that they received their energy by means of fermentation but these living beings still exist today.

On principle one can possibly assume that all plants and animals were growing up in a parallel development and that the plants did not necessarily represent a preliminary stage because oxygen already existed in the water and in the air from a certain time on, long before there were any plants. As we already mentioned briefly, the plants have not contributed much to the oxygen content of the atmosphere up to today. Actually they consume as much as they produce! Odd that this fact does not receive any attention in most theories although every secondary school pupil knows that assimilation and dissimilation balance out each other. Just to remind you: in assimilation, 6 molecules of carbonic acid (6 CO_2) plus 6 water molecules (6 H_2O) and an expenditure of 675 calories produce one glucose molecule ($C_6H_{12}O_6$) and free oxygen (6 O_2). When the plant dies, the glucose is oxidised during dissimilation, and in doing so the oxygen produced before is used up completely, water is separated and carbonic acid is released. The 675 calories go back to the environment.

The whole oxygen of our atmosphere therefore comes from the Urey effect; that is the separation of oxygen and ozone from water vapour in which process the ozone layer in the atmosphere has a regulating effect keeping the share of oxygen at about 21 percent.

As if it was the most natural thing in the world, we are already talking about animals and plants, yet we still have a long way to go on our travel through evolution until we finally come to those multicellular organisms which really deserve this name.

Why did life pursue this almost endless course? Did the ocean alone not offer enough possibilities to sustain itself and its descendants? How came that life also invaded the land and conquered the Earth almost thoroughly ?

Let's again take a look through the kaleidoscope. The probability for every meaningful picture - if one takes the contents of the kaleidoscope, namely the splinters of stained glass, as a starting point - is just zero. Nevertheless such pictures develop constantly. None of them is predictable or calculable. Thus the probability for a protozoan to develop in just the from which it exhibits today is also on no account predictable, and therefore the scholars of this Earth often think such a complicated object as the cell could not have been created by mere accident. But actually its complexity does not play any particular role because already at the sight of a snow crystal we would have to make similar, quite absurd observations. The whole matter, however, appears completely incredible if our various species of animals and plants should have developed from one kind of cell.

This mental problem is primarily based on the wide-spread misconception that all living beings on this Earth were descendant of only one type of primordial cell. But to really believe in this would be utter nonsense. Let's draw a parallel: it would already be impossible to look upon the atom in an isolated way because every single one owes its existence only to its environment ... and therefore one type of cells could never have come into existence on its own but many cells must have developed at the same time, in fact many different kinds of cells!

Many different cells as a starting position multiply the possibilities tremendously. A complex concatenation of arising co-incidences took place for which the chess game provides us with a good comparison as Richard Feynman once demonstrated illustratively: the course of a game of chess is unpredictable. But the abilities of its pieces are determined by the rules of the games - similar to the abilities of an enzyme which are determined by the molecular structure. Not predetermined are the moves - apart from the fact that it would never be possible to make all moves in the same manner -

because they are a result of each other. At the beginning of the game there are only a few possibilities for opening but the variants grow immeasurably already after a few moves, yet they are never endless.

The pieces of the chess game equal the protein structures of life: there were just so few possibilities for opening that the first moves developed very quickly and almost automatically. Therefore these opening moves could be so easily repeated in Miller's flask. Only at a later time does the DNA begin to govern these structures; it determines the pieces and their possibilities for moving - but it does not lay down the rules! Because they are the only established factors in this game, the laws of nature so to speak; and these, on the other hand, are nothing else but the consequence of one single principle which can be deviated from the cosmic pressure: the repulsion principle to be exact. The opponents in the chess battle are called energy and entropy. When all is said and done entropy will always win - but the game has lasted for quite some while...

And this period of moves and counter moves following each other is called Existence, Development, or Life, depending on the perspective we are adopting at the moment. Although entropy wins, the game is not yet done with; it will start again and again from the beginning. Incessantly, its pieces are checkmated but just as incessantly the interaction of DNA and protein molecules supplies new pieces!

Every cell, every organelle, every chromosome was a new variant of the big chess game. For sure there were cell forms of which nothing reminds us today. They did not stand the test of time and have long been extinct. Those which were successful also learned to live with each other. Many transitional forms developed among these primordial forms. Some of them have survived until today. Therefore, there still exist some organisms which stand somewhere between bacteria and viruses, like the rickettsiae or the bartonellas which are also called Great Viruses. In fact, they are already able to divide but can only feed on the inside of bacteria since they do not produce some of the required amino acids on their own.

The described processes are not devoid of the impression to work like a machinery. Nobody quite likes this concept but we have to admit: on the whole the cell is really some kind of machine; this is a fact which we can't ignore. Down the line every DNA causes machinery-like structures and processes. This can be seen most clearly with the viruses in which the parts of the machine do not swim around as in the unicellular organism but remain more or less crystalline. Already this simplest being possibly possesses an obviously mechanical nature: feet for clinging to objects, drilling implements for perforating a cell membrane, capsules and containers for the DNA.

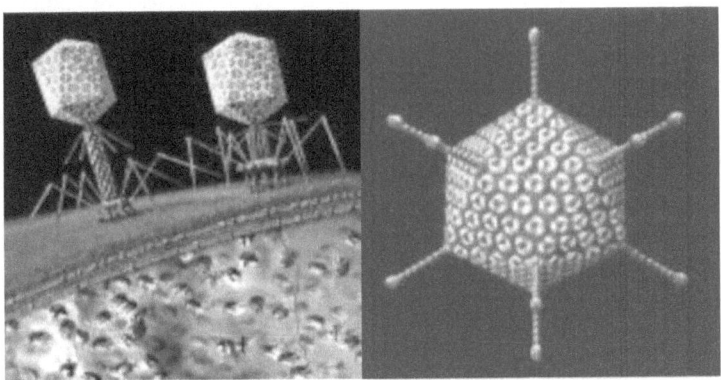

Fig. 120   Fig. 120a

Figure 120 shows us such a machine, a virus on DNA basis: the bacteriophage T4. No less machine-like is the adenovirus of figure 120a. The pictures surely speak for themselves. But we should recall that living beings like viruses are basically nothing else but dynamic crystals, on no account are they more impressive than the crystals of the rest of the world, the so-called realm of the inorganic.

This is not a depreciating assertion. It would be more astonishing if these crystals of life did not exist. Figure 122 does not show us snow flakes or the burlesque excesses of an artist obsessed with symmetry. These are radiolarians, small organisms living in the suspended matter of the oceans or rather their skeletons which were enveloped in jelly-like plasma in life. Such an amazing order also prevails inside of every cell. Let's take a look at the leaf cells of the water weed which demonstrates the endoplasmic reticulum very nicely (figure 121). The dark spots are dictyosomes.

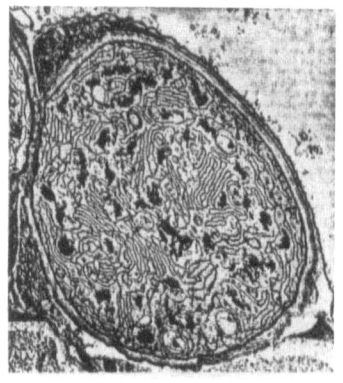
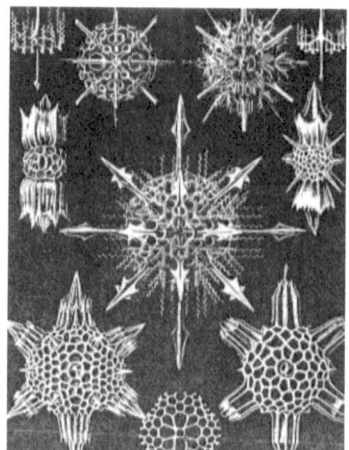

Fig. 121 Fig. 122

But let's resume our considerations a bit: at some time the pattern of DNA disassembly and reassembly was broken in some cells. Thus the DNA was not immediately destroyed in the following and eventually it existed four times in the centre of the cell. When there also were two centrioles to go with them, a division into four parts became the custom right away - a method which has been maintained until today.

The more chromosomes were enclosed in the shell, the greater were the possibilities to create a matching response to the respective conditions by going through the DNA programmes. And the longer took the game since more and more effective intermediate moves joined in. The various positions in the game mean nothing else but colours, shapes, structures, organelles, enzymes, peptides, hormones, and so on...

Every negative experience destroyed the programme of the DNA in the section concerned; in a repetition of the game the moves therefore took place more spontaneously and more effectively. So the programmes could be corrected, for instance in the following manner:

Let's assume a cell possesses one chloroplast at one end which is only working when it is turned towards the light. It supplies glucose which is indispensable for assembling the DNA as ribose. Let's further assume that one piece of information exists several times on the strand of DNA (or on several ones which are active at the same time), information which will finally cause the creation of a rotating flagellum. It does so several times but always in different places of the cell. As long as the flagellum is not produced in the right place, that is to say where it can cause a turning of the chloroplast towards the light, there will be no glucose and the inside of the cell will be running out of nucleotides.

The returning t-RNA cannot create any more new DNA, it will soon disintegrate enabling the development of a new m-RNA which reads the next section of the DNA. Prior to that the wrong flagellum has been carried out but it does not cause any supply in glucose.

In this way a pure RNA cycle develops which causes a series of wrong flagella. This is continued until suddenly a flagellum is located in the right place and turns the chloroplast towards the light. Now glucose is supplied again which makes the production of new nucleotides possible.

The next t-RNA will therefore find again DNA building blocks inside the cell which have the right level of energy and a new DNA is assembled. On the final DNA strand, the meaningless orders of the old DNA will not turn up anymore. When the cell divides the next generation will automatically produce the flagellum in the right place and none of the wrong flagella will be carried out...

Of course, this terse description was again a rough simplification of highly complicated processes. In truth it must be hundreds and thousands of pieces of information which cause a flagellum or something similar. Still this kind of adaptation takes place faster than previously assumed. Naturally it has a particularly strong effect on unicellular organisms; and really, bacteria have an ability to adapt that borders on magic. This is only possible if their DNA, which is not located in a nucleus but freely available within the plasma, has an enormous surplus of information at its disposal.

But we find such spontaneous adaptations inside our own body as well! We are talking about the acquisition of our immunological abilities. Our body's defences are not congenital. Shortly after our birth, our body cannot distinguish at all between own and foreign matter. And yet its antibodies are soon spontaneously able, after an extremely short learning process, to specifically adapt their development to the characteristics of a foreign intruder, no matter what the troublemaker may look like.

This process has been researched by physicians and biologists for a long time. If the DNA is assumed to be static, the process is really inexplicable. One knows that the antibodies, which are adapted to the intruder in a mysterious manner, are created in special cells, the plasmablasts. Actually these plasmablasts should carry the same genetic information as all the other cells of the body. But where do they suddenly get the additional information from which matches their properties exactly to fit to the disturbing antigen? Very simple: they acquire it! Plasmablasts are really specialised in the processing of information, in fact of instantaneous information which is not available from their own repository on any account. It seems reasonable to conclude that the usual amount of RNA is not sufficient for this purpose and that plasmablasts must have a higher RNA content. Actually they contain noticeably more ribosomes than other cells of the body.

When some antigens get to the surface of these special cells they create a specific environment which immediately forces the cell to make a counter reaction. The cell promptly produces antibodies which emerge and glue the antigens together in a wicked manner rendering them inactive in that way. This process takes place in quite a similar manner as we have seen it with the creation of the correct flagellum. And this only works with a dynamic DNA which can change conditional on the environment.

So we obviously still find that elementary DNA process in our body which already provided the great variety of forms at the beginning of life.

There are also less distinct examples for the adaptation of the cells of individual organs to certain functions, i.e. their specialisation. Less distinct for the reason that we would never think that a genetic modification was really taking place in this case.

The biologist thinks the specialisation of the cells is done by repressing certain genes, and he knows several possible processes for it (repression, induction) which in fact exist without any doubt but which are nevertheless insufficient since they cannot substantiate any modification of functions but at best their sequential retrieval. Apart from the fact that these control mechanisms certainly also have their significance we advocate the view that genes cannot only be repressed but can really be deleted irretrievably. For this reason the specialisation of a body cell can never be revoked again.

This is an insurmountable obstacle for the attempt to cultivate the whole body from an arbitrary body cell. It does not work - at least not with higher developed living beings! Only when the specialisation is not very high will a clone grow up to an identical organism (plants, newts, maybe even frogs, possibly insects). Living beings which can be cloned easily (mostly plants) have a static DNA system. This has limited their development from the beginning. We must not judge highly-specialised creatures, as for example mammals, by those standards. For this reason, egg cells are used for cloning as it is usual at present. Since the number of possible divisions at the chromosome is determined by the telomere, cloned living beings have almost ever a shorter life expectancy.

When the genetic code was discovered, one believed it had the same universal validity for all organisms. This is not the case. There are actually some basic correspondences but there are also exceptions from the rule. With many species, the processes of reduction and induction go other, unexpected ways. Often the adaptation to the environment takes places over several generations and often the influences on old processes, which were running well together, had to be exerted very drastically. One single gene doesn't have any significance at all, only the interaction of several groups of genes makes the connection to a certain characteristic.

On the other hand a characteristic was very quickly lost because if only one single gene of one of these groups failed the whole trigger could be rendered useless. Confusing complexity makes the feedback processes of life varied and flexible, but every experience with the environment finds immediately or indirectly expression on the DNA, and without this influence from outside even the DNA would be meaningless. All forms of life therefore carry no inner plan; they develop because of their function and way of life. So organelles and functional structures never developed in the right place by accident but they were enforced if the inner conditions allowed their formation at all. Every cell became the environment for the other and everything it ejected and discharged, i.e. its waste products, became a characteristic signal for the others. In that way, they could mutually influence and control their metabolism. We still find these signals in all organisms as hormones.

In this way, a virtuosic interaction of all cells developed already in the primordial ocean. To us it has to appear perfect only in retrospect because only those cells survived which could integrate themselves into this interaction. Not a trace tells us about the unsuccessful trials and attempts and of the dead-ends of evolution. And surely the vegetative, unconscious existence of the cells in the primordial ocean would have remained that way if a mishap had not caused another fundamental invention of nature...

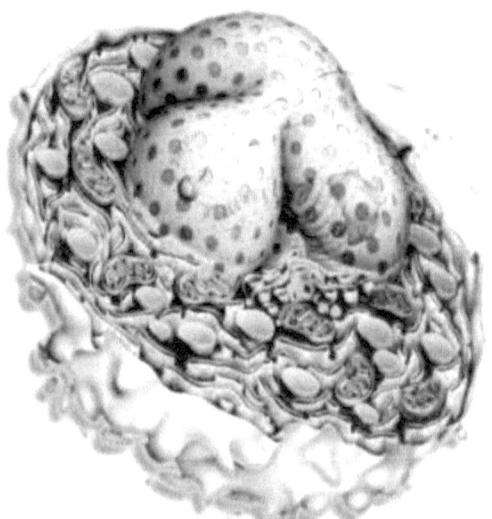

Fig. 123: View into a cell

28 Sex

In the first cells, as we described them previously, a complete, new set of chromosomes developed with every division. Reproduction by means of division was therefore asexual and in principle possible for every single cell. We understood that this division had to be based on a very accurately co-ordinated schedule; i.e. the body of the cell must not divide before the division of the chromosomes had taken place. Such precise processes, however, were rather rare. It was much more likely that this schedule was not kept every time and in every case.

For example, what happened if the body of the cell grew too quickly and divided before the separation of the chromosomes had taken place? All preparations had just been made, the spindle had just formed - and now the cell divided prematurely and involuntarily sorted the complete set of chromosomes to the left and to the right. This was quite a mishap which had to be expected to happen some time in the course of these highly-complicated processes - but at what consequences! None of the two new cells was exactly like the old one. From now on, the interaction of the chromosomes was impossible; there never was a new generation.

Two unfulfilled, crippled cell fragments were swimming around, maybe developed some arbitrary new structures, discharged a little energy - but that was just doing things by halves. When chromosomes and the body of the cell were divided unevenly, soon every half looked completely different. It was possible that metabolic apparatuses did not develop at all, at best the halves still reacted to certain signals, like hormones, but that was all.

For the separated cell parts, there was only one possibility to make up for the error: to come together again! For that purpose it was sufficient when any of the halves became active. But at first, the halves certainly came together purely by accident. They didn't surely do that reluctantly because they were polarised differently after all. When they met each other there was certainly anything but repulsion...

Since it was quite common anyhow to eat each other one of the halves ate the other and the original programme was restored again and began to be carried out as usual. The result was a new cell which could fulfil itself - as originally planned.

Genuine reproduction, however, was not given by that. Well, there was still the principle of division into four parts as well, though. On that occasion, it could happen that two halves turned out identical and the other two, however, divided the chromosomes haploidly. The result were two cells, each of which dragging along half an additional set of chromosomes like an adjunct. It is thoroughly possible that this adjunct - a dragged along, unfinished cell - ended up inside the carrier cell.

And consequently the carrier cell carried nothing else but a germ cell inside! In order to bring these germ cells together the cells had to copulate, i.e. fuse their germ cells in any way. The result was a new cell which again divided into four parts, namely in the same way as described above. Two asexual cells and two sexual ones each were left over and had to fuse again in order to repeat the game...

And this little mishap was the root of sexuality in our nature. We already find this simple primitive sexuality with the protozoans, and as was to be expected, they mastered both kinds of reproduction, the sexual one and the asexual one because after they had lost their germ cells again, father and mother could of course carry out a normal division without further ado.

Once the "unsuccessful " division found its expression in the DNA, which could not remain unaffected by all these processes, this new way was followed permanently. The division into two genders had arrived in the world. This brought great advantages because now different experiences could be combined which led to new programmes and to an increase in the ability to react.

The germ cell-like structure inside a protozoan is called the sex factor. The climax of this momentous "error" was found when a division into four parts became the practice which left a halved set of chromosomes in every cell. By the way, our own germ cells (zygotes and gametes) come into existence in this manner. The discovery of this principle, however, was already accompanied by the creation of multicellular organisms. The whole matter was yet preceded by the combination of several sets of chromosomes which we can easily understand when we simply assume that the corresponding cells just "ate" each other and created something totally new by combining their programmes: an organism, which could have never been managed by the unicellular organisms.

Having two sets of chromosomes is called diploid though the combination of three or four sets of chromosomes also developed and has been maintained until today. We can still find them in a few, extremely resistant plants.

All organelles inside one shell are actually cells within a cell. They are states within a state. They do not only play their own game, which they coordinate with each other, but they also take part in the metabolism of their host cell. One takes, the other gives; one controls, the other is controlled...

Even chromosomes are cells of their own, they already possess cell specific structures, like segments of DNA which are only responsible for automatic control, or their own centrioles. They divide very similarly to the main cell and reform again prior to every division. And now we notice something very important: all processes which we have described up to now, all stages of development up to the chromosome and far beyond have always started anew in every cell since the very beginning!

That means: not the idea or the blueprint as such are passed on to the next generation but also all the conditions which caused the development of these ideas! The original procreation did not take place at some time or other but is a continuous, never-ending process. In every germ cell of our living beings, the complete evolution begins anew! At first every germ cell is only primordial ocean, in which all processes that lead to the development of life are repeated as in a time-lapse. For that reason, the whole organisational apparatus of the DNA disintegrates again and again thus creating exactly those conditions which make it come into existence.

Yes, even the centriole disintegrates and forms anew! Just as if life was sitting on a swing of making and passing...

It is the already mentioned crossing-over which shows us in what a dynamic way the chromosomes are organised. For this phenomenon, biology knows at least two insufficient theories. One of them assumes ruptures of the chromatids and crosswise recombination and cannot explain why these ruptures occur so precisely that the chromatids again match each other when crossed; the other one speaks about copy-choice and suspects the exchange of single gene segments during DNA reduplication but cannot explain how more than two chromatids can recombine in this case. If one assumes, however, like we do, that the whole DNA is created anew and that the crossing-over of strands has to take place already at that stage (they are visible as chiasma with the chromatids), these insolubilities are eliminated.

Our point of view has yet another advantage when we assume that the reduplication of the DNA is done segment by segment and not on the whole. Pulling apart the DNA helix does in fact entail rotations which would have to amount to up to 10 000 revolutions per second with the separation of very complex strands of DNA. On this occasion the circumferential velocities would adopt superluminal speed! This unbelievable figure and the velocities connected with it are, however, reduced when reduplication takes place bit by bit so to speak. Neither is it leading to an objective to establish the molecular basis for the particular order of the disassembly and reassembly of the DNA. This order has been quite indiscriminate from the beginning and was caused by the respective possibilities. It was only important that this order had to be maintained because it were always the same conditions which occurred again and again. When the DNA strands were long, connected chains, a certain sequence in processing the information was given anyway. When the objection is raised that it is odd that it was always only the old and never the new DNA which was read and disintegrated, it should be considered that these strands differ strongly both energetically and electrically.

It is probable that the new DNA is also read but not destroyed, and that the final information materialises only from the interaction of the two DNA complexes. The already indicated phenomenon of polygenes is also a point in its favour.

When doubling the genetic make-up, relatively high precision is important. Billions of base pairs have to be separated and new, matching partners have to be found. Too many errors can be deadly for the daughter cells. On the other hand, little changes are necessary for being able to react to new environmental conditions. In order to comprehend this, our new point of view is certainly very useful.

The exact reconstruction and analysis of all these processes are dispensable for the purpose of this book – apart from the fact that a lot of work remains to be done for the researchers. For us, it is sufficient to know that the phenomena of life, sexuality, and reproduction have actually simple causes but lie hidden in the enormous and quantitatively unmanageable possibilities of molecular reactions. They are not miracles on principle and have nothing mysterious about them.

At least we comprehend on principle in any case that atomic and molecular information could, yes even must have triggered off life in the course of an incredibly long time. Yet, this still happened without any awareness, absolutely under the compulsion of complete, causal events. And it is on no account more difficult to comprehend how one day the wanting and deciding accompanied the could do and must do, i.e. the method of the organisms to do exactly those things which were useful for them: which means nothing else but the development of the drives.

We already got to know one drive: the longing for light for which life itself is trigger mechanism and motor. Only those cells which could follow this drive by creating the right flagella or a light-sensitive organ as an eye could survive. And their descendants naturally exhibited this drive from the beginning. When a sexual cell developed mechanisms to ensure its fusing again, this became a bonus compared to other cells which didn't do so. As a rule (with many exceptions) only cells could prevail which developed the functions that were advantageous in finding the other, as for example the reaction to hormonal signals. And so a dominant importance was already attached to signals of this kind in the very first beginnings. Paying attention to these signals - functionally exactly the same as the recognition of light - promptly turned out to be a new drive – in its most perfect form this is exactly the sexual drive.

And in the same way a drive for food developed as well as that not at all mysterious compulsion to avoid any destruction by developing defence mechanisms or modes of behaviour towards disturbing influences which had to lead to nothing else but to the drive for survival.

Something similar as the drives, preliminary stages of the drives so to speak, can already be found in the inanimate, inorganic range. Some metals, as for instance aluminium, protect themselves (with just as little intention as the cells) against possible oxidation or acid corrosion (which amounts to the same thing) by means of a thin skin of gas consisting of atoms of the same metal. Something similar happens with other substances as well in an absolutely arbitrary manner because the transition from body to environment takes place "softly" so to speak; all elements have soft outlines, and this is indeed an often just as unintentional as effective protection.

Perhaps it would be wrong after all to speak of a drive for survival with regard to aluminium, maybe simply because this metal behaves passively. Only an action with an (apparent) objective becomes a drive but it is the objective itself which causes this action - as we so clearly saw with the light. The root of every drive lies outside of the living being which exhibits it. So when we are looking for the programme of various drives on the DNA we are mistaken. At best we will find a programme for the behaviour which we can misinterpret as drive.

Those behaviours, i.e. the actions which are initiated by the drives, are really laid down genetically was already proved by professor Walter C. Rothenbuhler in his experiments with bees. And professor Erich v. Holst demonstrated that all major drives are composed of numerous minor drives which are genetically fixed in the behaviour.

Fig.123a

29 Concept

Let's return again to the beginnings of cellular life in the primordial ocean. Among the individual cells there was for sure already some kind of interaction and naturally the first signs of rivalry turned up.

But not only the mutual destruction spread but the combination of several cells to cell clusters soon also became the practice. Some things just went better when cells of different function - originally linked by accident - just remained together permanently. Their dictyosomes produced adhesive and bonding materials and also held on to the cells which had been newly created in division.

The mutual assistance, which was made possible by that, revealed itself as further bonus for the continued survival of development to the top. Without this interaction it would never have come to evolution at all. Differently specialised cells which had first exchanged their signal substances through the water of the ocean now took advantage of the benefits of shorter signal paths and soon showed a new drive - that of affection.

Even today, this transition from the individual to the multicellular organism is vividly demonstrated by the aggregation of slime moulds and Acrasia amoebae. When the environment in which these amoebae live becomes inhospitable, they are going through an amazing transformation. First they are just isolated cells and then they fuse to a mass consisting of tens of thousands of cells. This mass immediately develops into different shapes which change constantly. A stalk is created which suddenly contains cellulose and a head of spores. The spores are ejected and spread...

This spectacular example of fusing to a multicellular organism which already reminds of a plant is - as one knows from experiments – actually enforced directly by the environment. It takes place because of the existence of a crucial substance (AMP) and leads to an actually new form of life which makes the intrusion into other areas of life possible because of its increased mobility. It was also practical for many other cell organisms when they stayed together. And when a mechanism had developed which supported this staying together and made the cells grow together, this new principle was also anchored in the DNA and was preserved - again by deleting information. In this way, multicellular living things came into being, and the individual cells developed into organs, and every organ created a specific environment for the neighbouring organ.

At the same time, however, something even more significant happened of course: there weren't any rules concerning the number of chromosomes that were enclosed in a developing shell. Cells were created which had maybe only two chromosomes but there were also others which had perhaps twenty or more different chromosomes. In the beginning these cells only differed distinctly in the nuclei, on the outside they were still quite similar. But each of these structures carried a different programme for the possibilities to react to the environment. Soon there must have been an unimaginably great amount of cell varieties with different chromosome numbers. Moreover, and probably even at an earlier time, there also were independent chromosomes, viruses, which lodged into the cells and provided a further increase of information from time to time. The most important thing with these considerable events was: all programmes, which became responsible for the abundant blossoming of life at a later time, all of them without any exceptions (!), were prepared and determined at that time, in the very first beginnings! These cells or micro-organisms, crammed to the brim with the most diverse chromosome combinations, were the original cells of all (!) species living in the past or today or in the future! So there was not only one universal original cell which divided into other forms later-on but thousands upon thousands of different original cells!

One and a half million species of the animal kingdom and about 400 000 species of the plant kingdom still exist today, and almost every one of them goes back to its own original cell! On principle, all experiences which could be brought to bear later-on had already been prepared for in the ocean as possible future programmes and had been exchanged among each other before they came into effect. This exchange becomes apparent when the whole genetic make-up of a living being is decoded which has already been successfully done in some cases. Thus the comparison of the genome of Thermotoga Maritima - a eubacterium - with the DNA sequences of other organisms revealed a strange result: nearly a quarter of the genes stems originally from bacteria which are called archaebacteria and are less related to the eubacteria than human beings are to daisies. This proves the exchange of genes to a so far unknown extent.

Exchanging, copying, and forwarding genes at that early stage led to a functioning of all organisms according to similar principles down the line later-on. And yet every form of life has its very own evolution within its species. This is the reason why no missing links, i.e. connecting intermediate forms between the species, can be found. And even in future one will never discover real transitional forms because they have never existed.

The only mysterious thing about that is why one has ever tried seriously to attribute the diversity of nature to only one single original form at all. Well, there is a good way to reconstruct the evolution of a living being. Ernst Haeckel (1834 - 1919) discovered this way. It is the fundamental biogenetic law, namely the fact that all stages of a species' phylogeny are recapitulated in its ontogeny, that means that all manifestations of the past, which the corresponding species went through at some stage of its evolution, are repeated in time-lapse.

All species experience their complete evolution again in their embryonic development. We already emphasised that this already begins entirely with the original procreation in every germ cell. But this principle is continued until the living being is born and to be exact even until it dies. In this connection it is very characteristic but also very logical that with every species this germinal development takes place in exactly the same environment in which it once happened and that these environmental conditions are practically maintained by special set-ups and modes of behaviour. Because only the same conditions obtain the same results together with the programme on the DNA.

He who has not yet completely comprehended it up to this point will understand it now: the DNA alone is of no importance. It is not the commander but in a very complicated way it reacts upon itself through the events it triggers, and only this cycle forms the organism, yes, the organism is nothing else but the inevitable expression of this retroaction, it is way and waygoer at the same time.

A DNA divorced from its context would be a molecular strand and nothing else. Because it always was the environment which determined whether a matching form which was just found would be preserved or whether it would be subjected to modification if the DNA allowed. In order to bring about a characteristic modification of the DNA, the environment had to change very drastically, at a time in fact, when it was still possible to affect the protected conditions of the germ's environment itself. Only then were permanent reconstructions possible. When the germ cells had undergone several divisions and were matured to a certain specialisation, the later phenotype of the creature was determined definitely. Therefore there was and is only a short space of time in which it is possible to immediately and effectively influence the DNA even of highly specialised living beings. But all these modifications lie strictly within the framework of information once set in advance ("development is directed") and could only occur until the information was used up ("development is limited"). Pieces of information could in fact be deleted but it was impossible to pick up new ones ("development is not reversible")!

Especially the embryonic growth of the human being provides distinct indications to his own evolution. As an embryo he has gill clefts, and that means the human being was "fish" once but he is not descended from fishes. These only put the same idea into practice which they had to stick with until today. Whatever may happen, it would never be possible that a fish develops into a human being. Once the human being was also "saurian" without being descended from saurians which certainly still exist today; and therefore the human being was once what the ape is today without being descended from this different species in the least. And of course the human being does not look back on the same ancestors as the ape on any account! Because the apes had their own evolution from the very beginning.[53]

The cells of the human beings contain 46 chromosomes. And they have always contained this number. Even when he was "fish", "saurian", or "ape". Neither concerning his chromosomes nor his intellectual capacities has he ever been comparable with these species still living today. He only lived according to the same "concept".

These living concepts were dependant on the environment. For that reason, organic accomplishments which resembled each other tremendously appeared at the same time in the evolution of all varieties of species. The original cells in the primordial ocean also lived according to one single concept but of course in individually different ways. This is the fundamentally new aspect of our viewpoint: the sets of chromosomes of all organisms that have ever lived have never again increased in number since their first encounter in the first original cells, most probably they haven't been reduced either; the genetic sedimentation of information in the DNA always took place only by deleting programmes that had become unnecessary.

This means: it should be possible to pursue a species with 46 chromosomes completely through all the former forms of life, a species which followed every prevailing concept and changed on the outside in accordance with them. Never again in the course of evolution was it possible that the set of chromosomes of the human being was created. Already in the very first beginnings, some kind of jellyfish must have swum around in the primordial ocean which carried the potential higher development up to the human being in its 46 chromosomes. An alteration from species to species has never been possible, as experiments at breeding revealed.

Concluding from its ontogeny, it must have been particularly easy for one form of life to gain a foothold on land: for the plants. This is not surprising at all − because they received their energy directly from the light and with that they saved themselves many actions depending on drive. They relied on wind and water or even on other living things which had come into existence at the same time and lived together with them, like bacteria or insects. The other beings took care of both breaking up the food and the advancement of the chromosomes.

Plants developed apparently passive forms of behaviour which are so manifold and perfect that they appear like a miracle to us. Their "concept" of living was obviously so good that it has lasted to this day. Only the dying forests of our time demonstrate that even the programmes in many plants are exhausted so that they are unable to follow the rapid changes of the environmental conditions anymore.

The palaeontologist Edgar Dacque (1878 − 1945) was the first to notice that the various geological eras did not simply contain all possible forms of life but that there were very characteristic forms of life for every epoch. Thus the late Palaeozoic age was that of the newt. The Triassic involved the concept of the turtle. In the Mesozoic epoch, the land-living animals stood up - it was the age of the giant reptiles. In the Jurassic the concept of flying was discovered, although this idea was much older and had already caused sensation with the flying insects.

Until previously one believed that the Archaeopteryx was the oldest bird on this Earth but in a quarry in Colorado, James Jensen discovered an ancient species of birds to which he attributed an age of 140 million years. Probably even older specimen are to be found because it must be possible to trace back the evolution of the birds without gaps to the first beginnings, and it is very likely that the basic concept of every species was defined very quickly after life remained on land.[54]

Dacque realised that these phenotypic stages did not have any real significance on the descent but that stages of similar forms were only the result of one-sided specialisation of the living things to one concept. This thoroughly corresponds to the processing of information as we assume it. However, we should not misunderstand the word "concept", nothing was ever created by mental intention but it was always only a matter of particular forms of life which had to resemble each other because they had come about according to the same principles of interaction between environment and programme, i.e. between external conditions and internal conditions.

Today we find particularly marked resemblances in this respect between the fish and the aquatic mammals. Two absolutely different living things resemble each other very much - and the reason for that is not too difficult to work out. Prior to the beginning of the Triassic - 225 million years ago - the class of the Thecodontia lived on Earth, small reptiles which already walked upright. Their teeth were already located in alveoli dentales like those of modern human beings. They even had five-fingered hands already... And already at that time there must have been the human being or that what was the human being at that time! It must have looked just like the Thecodontia but with 46 chromosomes in its cells whose programmes had not run out for a long time yet. It developed further; maybe the Thecodontia became dinosaurs, yes, maybe, because the traces of the Thecodontia which we still find today could just as well be our very own!

30 Soma

Let's return to that fourfold cell division which caused sexuality. With that we discovered cells which carried a second cell with the haploid set of chromosomes on or in them. Actually, all that mattered was this sex cell; the original cell was already a luxury in comparison, an industrious piece of work of nature but a very useful one because it developed those functions which transported and nourished the sex cell and led it to its fusion.

When this luxury cell carried an extensive programme, there was no reason why it should not continue to grow until a division occurred again. In this way a body could develop which took on the task to protect the germ and to preserve the environment of the germ and even to rebuild it in later stages of development.

Again we should not misunderstand the used mode of expression: there were no tasks, no-one set them - but nevertheless only those germs were considered for reproduction whose bodies (soma) carried out the right functions. When they were unable to do so, the organism soon ceased to exist. Only a posteriori, from our today's point of view, it seems as if life has consciously and deliberately taken care of cultivating the germ.

Of course it would be simple and tempting to simply speak of accident in all these cases. But if we took blind chance into consideration, all the described events would be very unlikely. The probability increases only to a sufficient extent if we take into consideration that there was a multitude of programmes which - although they didn't mean anything at all at first – still restricted the sphere of influence for chance very much.

The much strained argument, chance could never have created life is therefore to no avail. "How often would one have to shake iron atoms thoroughly", the nit-pickers among the biologists and philosophers often asked, "in order to produce a vehicle?" But they failed to noticed that it is not a question of iron atoms in this case but that engines, wheels, bodies, and gearboxes had to be combined here - and with that their calculus of probabilities was no longer correct!

In the development of life, the separation into soma and germ was the crucial moment. The drive force of the two forms, however, was laid down only in the germ and that means that the often expressed dire thought that the body was only a means to an end and would only serve the conducting chromosomes as an instrument, is quite correct.

It were those two fundamental drives, the instinct for survival and the sexual drive - whose simple molecular beginnings we examined - which caused the phenotype, the body of the living things. Because these drives could only develop as well by means of the functions and activities of the body; the actions they set off, however, finally determined the appearance of the organism.

Even the extremely complex apparatus of the human body serves only as tangible evidence for the purpose to shield off hostile environment from the germ: by recognising this environment and by giving the correct defences, reactions, and modes of behaviour. The gender was determined by a difference in the chromosomes. 22 chromosomes of the human being exist in pairs (autosomes), two chromosomes differ from each other: the X chromosome and the Y chromosome (which is one of the smallest). The X chromosome is carried by both genders. When a second X joins the first, the programme develops a female body; but when a Y is added instead of the second X, a male is growing up.

In males, the production of sperm cells is continuously done from the epithelia cells of the seminiferous tubules by a kind of division into four as we already discovered. In doing so, some of the sperm cells receive an X and some a Y. The gender of the future creature is therefore exclusively determined by the semen of the male since only X chromosomes can be found in the female.

The germ cells of the next generation develop in the female body already during the embryonic stage, again by division into four. In doing so one cell receives almost the entire plasma whereas three of the germ cells simply perish. Every female egg cell is a new creation of the primeval cell. It contains one X chromosome beside the 22 other ones, and now it only depends if the male semen brings along an X or a Y in order to define female or male.

When these processes still took place in the ocean by way of faint traces, they were still conceivable without a body. Later, the body only served for artificially maintaining the primeval world of the ocean. Therefore we should not be surprised that the serum of our blood actually resembles sea water in many aspects. We are still carrying the ocean of that time in our bodies.

But the most significant is still to come: the male semen (sperm) swims through the female body like a protozoan and through paths created especially for this purpose it reaches the egg cell which it infects like a virus by discharging its chromosomes into it. The chromosomes of both partners merge to one nucleus and the programme starts running. It is possible that two cells met already in the same way in the ocean.

The egg cell (zygote) soon lodges itself into the womb by force - like a parasite - and the first thing that happens is the new development of the well-known primeval world, of the ocean in form of the amniotic sac and the chorion in which the growing embryo can swim as if in sea water. Thus a very old and proven form of development of life begins. And now the growing creature goes through all embryonic stages of its phylogeny.

After the formation of the amniotic sac it looks like a primordial, primitive jellyfish, plump and undifferentiated and it subsequently develops a couple of characteristics which the born human will no longer have. Only after a few days, it becomes a newt, a fish, a saurian, a hairy mammal...

It is the embryonic condition which determines the basic form and later appearance of the new creature. An immediate heredity of such fundamental equipment like the organs does not take place at all on this occasion. On the DNA, there is no equivalent for the lungs or for the brain. But a corresponding programme exists for each which has to lead to such organs in the exact implementation of its single steps.

We will understand it much better with an allegory: if we equate the body and its organs with the villages and towns of this world and the enzymes with the corresponding craftsmen who built them, it is only the craftsmen who are passed on hereditarily and never the towns. As it is, all organs, all extremities, and all characteristics are created by the causal succession of events which determine or restrict each other. Organs literally grow into their functions just like the cells in the ocean once specialised without being directed by overriding programmes. Neither accident and nor selection are involved in this.

What is determined by the DNA are the designers of these organs and only indirectly the appearance of the finished creature, its cellular characteristics, its capabilities, and its skills...

And we must not forget that this power of the DNA to determine is in turn dependent on the repercussions of the caused structures. As we already emphasised, it is an interactive process and on no account a stubborn executing of orders from the DNA. If this was really the case, origin and function of the DNA would remain absolutely unexplainable.

There is a stage in the development of the human foetus in which it does almost not differ at all from the foetus of an ape. This shows that the - absolutely separate! - development of the apes went ways very similar to those of the human being but came to a stop at an earlier stage. The same applies to fish, newt, and saurian...

Obviously the same principle applies to all living things which developed higher: a modification of the DNA structure because of the direct influence of the environment can only take place in that short space of time during embryonic development before the egg cells of the next generation are produced. When we think a little about this fact it will occur to us that there has actually never been an evolution of the organisms at all but primarily only a further development of the reproduction methods. Because what mattered predominantly was the development of the germ. The grown-up creature had to be sufficient for the environment only long enough that the germ cells came together again. It got the greatest growth over and done with inside the egg or the mother animal and only during this time had the immediate conditions of the environment already an effect on the next generation.

When the human being is born he has already spent about 99% of his energy and of his programmes. In his life afterwards only the avalanche of information, which he received as an embryo, is gradually coming to a stop. This kind of evolution, which we discover here, is not that of Darwin. In fact, it didn't play any particular role at all when the living thing was destroyed in the so-called struggle for existence, provided that it had already multiplied and that was of course possible very soon. Mutation and "struggle for existence" are therefore truly unsuitable arguments for the evolution.

From that point of view at least the mammals, and that means man, too, get just twice as old as they actually had to in order to preserve their species (including the period for upbringing the next generation). Therefore the ability to survive beyond sexual maturity and the capacity of reproduction is a downright industrious piece of work of nature and by no means a safety factor.

Well, there are even quite distinct confirmations for this viewpoint which will surely not remain unchallenged: if one cuts off the tails of adult mice over generations it will never happen that mice without tail are born, simply for the reason that their embryonic conditions were not affected at all. But when pregnant mice are subjected to the cold, their descendents will promptly get a warmer, thicker fur - which is even maintained for generations to come.

In our introduction we already mentioned the example of the Alpine salamander of which we want to remind you now. We also anticipated the phenomenon of the butterfly wings. These cases are no mutations. In addition, we want to mention that the human being already makes very consciously use of the possibility to directly influence the embryonic conditions. There is a method in which the expecting mother puts a depressurised cabin around her abdomen since one discovered that babies developing under such conditions grow up much healthier and have a higher intelligence quotient.

So there are really acquirable properties which are also passed on - but only within a very particular, short embryonic period. The other common factors of evolution, like mutation and selection, are firstly of secondary importance and secondly in no case suitable to establish a transition between the species. Besides, the number of useful mutations is much too low for such theses.

Let's recapitulate in which our viewpoint differs from conventional theories of evolution:

- Every species looks back on its own primeval cell. All species developed genetically independent of each other.
- Within a short embryonic period the environment has an influence on the programme of the DNA; this is the main reason for modifications in a species.
- At best, mutations modify the phenotype of a species but they will never create a new species.

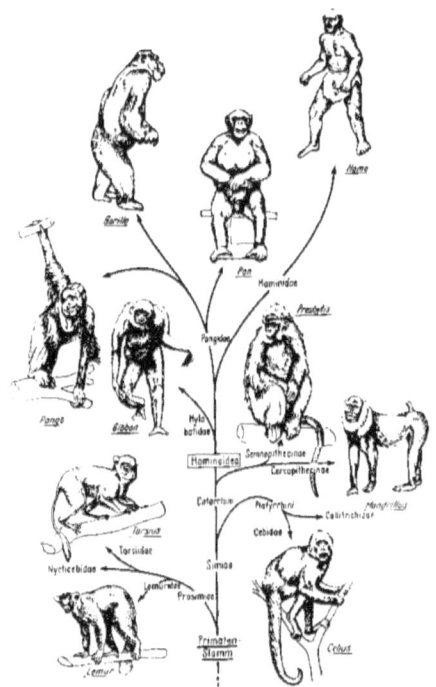

Fig. 124
Primatenstamm = phylogenetic tree of primates

- The principle of selection explains only the disappearance of several, badly adapted life-forms, for that reason, it will never have a direct influence on the evolution in the sense of a further development.
- Selection by means of preferred choice of partners as a result of noticeable features (signals) have a great significance within the species. Of course, it will never create intermediate forms.
- For that reason, there are no "missing links".
- The DNA as programme structure is dynamic and possesses a surplus of information which is utilised in the course of time.

The pictures of descent of the animal and plant kingdom in form of a phylogenetic tree of life are therefore absolutely misleading. Let's just pick out one of these wrong plans concerning the connection of the human being with the development of the ape (figure 124).

The question was at which point of the phylogenetic tree did mankind separate from the ape. This point of separation has been placed lower and lower lately. It would be more correct to show the descent as demonstrated in figure 125.

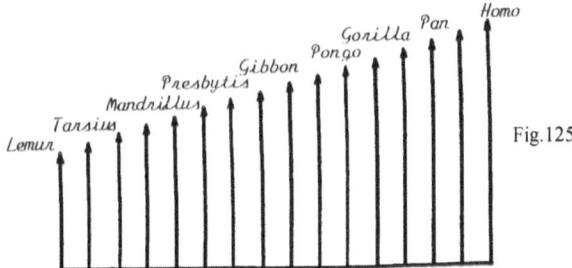

Fig.125

The conclusions which one draws from the comparative analyses of amino acid sequences have to be just as wrong as the usual phylogenetic tree. After all, even inorganic crystals can be classified into categories without being descendent from each other. In this connection it is significant that protein structures or functionally important molecules often changed their places during development without changing the function of the corresponding organ. Amino acid sequences resemble each other for the same reason as whales and sharks; after all they are working under similar conditions down the line!

What makes the events in the organic world appear so alive is the incredible speed in the sequence of events. If we saw the geological changes of our planet, i.e. the inorganic processes which extended over millions of years, in time-lapse, the Earth would also be an extremely vivid thing with thoroughly life-like chains of cause and effect like those in the molecular area of the cell. There, crystals grow according to their strict rules and conditions of selection; some take up foreign atoms and some won't do it at any price (quartz); there, minerals and crystal structures of the Earth's crust form as well as the amorphous and metamorphic structures of the rocks. They melt down to magma and on rising up they solidify again to new forms; there, sediments are created by weathering, they roll along and toss and turn, are polished until smooth, become brush, rubble, and sand; continents drift and pile up mountain ranges; caves are created by dissolving and through chemical processes; the earth caves in creating valleys, karstic landscapes, rugged ranges of hills...

Pressure, temperature, and the programme of the atoms determine the flowing picture, and everything remains always and for ever in motion. Great cycles develop: those of the water and that of the rocks. Metamorphic stones are created from sediments. They melt up to granite and weather back to sediments again. Magmatic cycles encounter those of crystallisation; matters change and what is finally produced in these cycles is the crust of the Earth itself on which we live. The refuse of these processes ends up in the ocean, not sentenced to inactivity but as building material for the cycle of the molecules of life which takes place not unlike the inorganic ones but at a higher speed.

One thing engages with another - and so even life itself has its part in the geologic processes, helping them along or hindering them. What is amazing in all this is only that one found much faster some adequate explanations for the slow, no less manifold and dynamic processes of the landscapes on the basis of the laws of physics and chemistry whereas one has always examined life with a certain shyness as if it was something fundamentally different than the heaping of the Himalayas. But it is basically the same. If the silicon-mineral structures of this Earth were not only information processing but also recognising formations, they would probably have the same shyness in explaining their own kind whereas the molecular processes of the carbon compounds would be no mystery for them...

And here are the two great partners of the two great main cycles "life" and "stage of life": carbon and silicon.

Similar to carbon, silicon is also unsymmetrical and well suitable for a variety of unions. Even the tetrahedron bond of the diamond can be imitated by silicon (in connection with oxygen, SiO).

The cycle of water and that of heat sustain the cycle of the rocks and create the geological structures; the cycle of the heavy DNA and that of the RNA sustain the cycle of the protein molecules and create the living structures. All these cycles cannot be separated from each other, can never be considered isolated from each other. Just as little as the geological changes of the Earth require any "vitalism" does life require any mysterious forces - because these are the same which also take effect in the big picture. And finally the whole game is only powered by one single force – by the repulsion principle within the matrix of T.A.O., the cosmic pressure!

Just like the – under no circumstances - accidental results of the geological history of the Earth's crust, the results of the evolutions (no doubt, we have to choose the plural) cannot be put down to "naked" physics and chemistry. The chemist in the laboratory also causes environment artificially; he jolts and shakes, heats up and cools down, exposes to radiation, to light, and to darkness... Every series of chemical reaction in his glass vessels takes place according to the created conditions, always also following the principle of striving for entropy, the flow towards the lowest energy level, and still or just because of that highly complicated molecules develop, carbon chains, which are very similar to those of life.

The chemists of nature are the surroundings and the environment - in a broader sense the universal pressure. Plasticine put under pressure deforms; with our hands we can work plasticine into the most adventurous shapes which, subjectively, are all absolutely unlikely for the plasticine. If we did not acknowledge the modelling hands, the plasticine would possess wonderful, mysterious properties and we would not know how they had been achieved.

The power for life comes from the cosmos itself. Because it extends around the Earth it works atoms and molecules into living crystals. The diversity of life has its origin in the diversity of its atoms and molecules, which are forced from the inside into certain paths and shapes by the "plasticine of life".

The soma, the body, is a "waste product". It was of so little importance that nature has not yet created a programme for it which goes on and on infinitely. All programmes are limited, they are unable to adapt for very long in the course of a changing environment - because of deficient functioning of the organs. The more embryonic a living thing is, that means, the longer its lifetime extends over that period in which the environment can have an influence on the DNA, the more immortal it is.

For that reason, unicellular organisms are potentially immortal. The same also applies to the unicellular organism in the human being, the germ cell. But it changes the shells around it and every shell dies... Living things whose soma does not yet have such a well-developed shell character, which constantly live in an embryonic state so to speak, have the ability for regeneration which goes up to reduplication. They repair themselves.

This kind of repairs already takes place in the chromosome which represents an independent living thing after all, even if it seems to be a stubborn parasite. The famous hydra repairs itself directly into new hydras when it is minced into small pieces... The same can also be discovered with certain worms, yes with almost all living things of a similar simplicity - even with many plants. The cells of a sponge can be separated almost completely from each other; the isolated cells, however, will immediately unite again to form a new sponge. Even certain organs of the human being are constantly regenerated. The blood, for example, or the mucous membrane lining of the uterus of women

Many regenerations in nature are mostly conditional on the environment, take only place at certain temperatures or are triggered by hormonal signals. Often they are quite planned in advance as one can see with the break-off point of lizard tails; consequently they are an integral constituent of all functions and, as one knows of the endometrium of women, quite important and appropriate. Important in so far as the maintenance and regeneration of an organ is significant for the germ cell itself. The immediate environment of the germ must be in balance with the germ. If it is disturbed, it will be restored.

Everything we said above is not surprising at all; even a crystal tip grows back on its own when it has been broken off. Regeneration means to replace something that was destroyed. The new birth of a human being is noting else than the regeneration of a lost shell. Thus the germ cell is incessantly regenerating a new soma around itself. Seen this way the human being becomes an organ that can be replaced. The actual living thing is called primeval cell, germ cell; that first structure - created millions of years ago - is still living and to the same rules as at that time. It enforced the constant regeneration of the shell which had to change eternally in order to transform the effects of a continuously changing outside world to an always constant inside world.

As logical as this principle is, it has quite dismal aspects for the shell when it recognises its disposable status – because obviously the final destination for it is death. But after all it is also the price that an organism has to pay for being allowed to develop so highly that it could recognise its environment and become aware of it. Only the constant regeneration with death at its end also entailed a further development.

Seen this way, death is something natural and there is nothing mysterious about it. How high we estimate this price is a matter of our subjective interpretation. Lower animals know nothing about death - if we disregard the chimpanzee who is probably able to recognise death as such -, and just as little does our liver learn about its demise. Even we do not learn about our own death but we recognise the death of others. Because we never recognise ourselves but only make out an environment and ourselves in it.

As down-to-earth and unpopular as this point of view may be it has nevertheless also a pleasant aspect: the end of evolution is not by any chance pre-programmed on the DNA. It does not have written the little word "end" anywhere on it. Because the shell was not important enough for the germ even for such an intention. It is probably correct that the programme of the DNA still contains many, many possibilities which have not been used yet and will only come into effect in later generations. Therefore we have reason to believe that the development of our species will not be completed for a long time to come.

Even if the dynamic of the DNA entails a loss of information, as a rule we do not die for this reason; we die of the break-down in the organisation of the organs, and for that there is primarily only one reason: the inner ocean is not maintained forever. Most causes of death are somehow connected with the supply of blood to our organs. If this supply of blood worked continuously in the same good fashion, i.e. if it was not disturbed by deposits and organic insufficiencies, our life expectancy would only be determined by that of the brain cells.

On the other hand the coded intention of death is possible. Since nature has obviously made use of everything that is possible, this course was also pursued. This phenomenon is best know with the example of the salmons which are destroyed by a death hormone after they have spawned. A similar processes was observed with the squid as well. Maybe these animals are really at the end of their programme; it is, however, more probable that their death fulfils an immediate purpose for the germ. This would have to be examined in more detail. It is possible that death leads to an enrichment of the environment with necessary substances, nutrients, or hormones which could not be provided for the descendants in any other way. We find this principle with some insects where the mother animal dies to ensure nourishment for their offspring.

It is gathered from that how indifferent nature is towards the death of the shell, which is used just like that as a means to an end itself. Strictly speaking no living thing in the world dies uselessly - because it returns the original components of life into the cycle of nature: the atoms, especially the carbon atoms which are not available in immeasurable amounts and without which there wouldn't be any life at all.

Lately the number of proves increases that in human cells the amount of possible cell divisions is predetermined by a section of the genome (telomere). For that reason, it certainly seems as if death has found a way to write itself down onto the DNA...

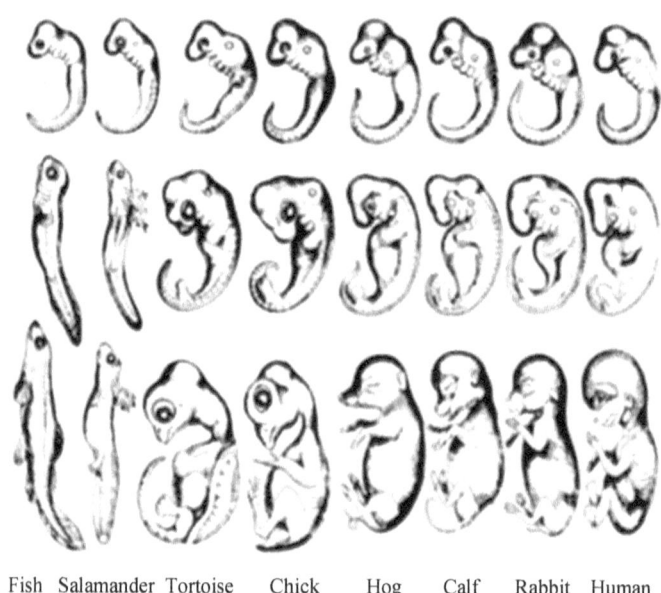

Fish Salamander Tortoise   Chick   Hog   Calf   Rabbit   Human

Fig.125a: Haeckel's law

31 Sensation

A protozoan or a bacterium which just vegetates and lugs an enormous surplus of information in its genes,[55] that is to allow it future evolutions, is neither particularly aware of this latent future nor of its present existence. It perceives almost nothing at all and it doesn't have a "name" for those things it perceives. But in a vague way it already senses its environment - just like one atom already seems to sense the others by the perception of resistance.

Sensing the environment has several degrees. A chlorophyll molecule senses only that which is essential for its function: the light. With that this molecule already becomes a primitive kind of sense organ which selects only a defined range of perception from the environment.

These preliminary stages of sense organs had been in existence before there even was anything like nerves or brains. And already in the early stages there must have been organs which could not yet make out the environment but imitate it in a certain way.

To imitate means in this case to adopt the same condition on one's own which would have been caused by a particular environment. In this way even molecules or organelles are conceivable which do not only recognise light but also cause it on their own. They put their atoms into such oscillational states which mean "light" as a message in the final consequence.

Deep-sea fish use such sources of light but we also know this kind of light from the glow worm and from many species of bacteria. It is cold light, not caused by thermal excitation but through chemical reactions which actually represent an imitation or a reversal of discerning light.

Such surprising functions of and drives for imitation still exist in many organisms even today, simply for the reason that these functions and drives have been made possible by the inner flood of information. It goes without saying that exactly those modes of behaviour, which helped the germ to advance, were specified precisely by this advancement; these drives became an indispensable component of the behaviour. Creating protein structures, turning towards the light, swimming after food, pursuing a partner germ, evading the disturbance... these are all complex behavioural patterns which have also determined the overall appearance of the living thing - by creating organs which supported this behaviour.

But for a long time these behavioural clichés, developed from imitation and reaction, were taking place absolutely unconsciously of course, as unconsciously as a stone falls down or as water flows, or as unconsciously as a motor runs and the toothed wheels of a gearbox engage...

All fundamental functions which served for the pure preservation of the organism have remained unconscious until today - i.e. the cellular functions of the metabolism, the activity of the organs, the beating of cilia and flagella which are still doing their work in our own bodies (e. g. in the bronchial tubes). These are ancient mechanisms working well together. Their immediate cause and link is the DNA in connection with the ribosomes, which practically represent a first kind of memory (archive).

We already emphasised how much it was of advantage for a living thing dependent on the environment to respond especially to very particular and limited sectors of the environment - like light or heat. For the time being there was only the possibility to make the behaviour of the molecular machinery find its place in this sector from the beginning while the basis for this behaviour was of purely physical nature - like for example the spin of the light.

But soon there was also a different path: the creation of organs which specialised in perceiving the environment, just as other organs had specialised in particular metabolic processes or syntheses.

How does "environment" reveal itself? No matter which messages are involved, they are without exception oscillations or impulse sequences to be precise - no matter if light, heat, or sound are concerned. Naturally this simplifies the matter very much – because it was sufficient to develop structures which were able to absorb exclusively impulses and to make a certain choice among them.

Here, every type of atom provides already a different selective behaviour; this also applies to molecules when they integrate particularly characteristic atoms in such a way that they can oscillate and transform captured energy into electron waves. In the chlorophyll it is the magnesium atom which has adopted this very important role. With the incidence of light it supplies electric power and works quite similar to a common photoelectric cell.

Well, we shouldn't be surprised that we find the basic structure of the chlorophyll in all bodies, plant and animal alike, in exactly those places which are in particularly intimate contact with the environment (respiratory and visual function). Its special function depends on whether an iron, magnesium, or cobalt atom is integrated in this basic structure (porphyrin) – the combination with iron is known as haemoglobin.

All these porphyrins are pigments of the body - that means nothing else but that these structures predominantly know what to do with the light; they absorb one portion and reflect another one. Their colour is a result of that. Chlorophyll appears green to us, haemoglobin red, and porphyropsin (the visual purple of the eye) purple.

But all porphyrins are also able to do something else: with the corresponding stimulus they produce light on their own (fluorescence). The chemist can easily prove the existence of porphyrin in other substances by stimulating them with ultraviolet light. They distinctly respond to that with coloured light. The existence of such molecules (the bases of the DNA and RNA already contain such porphyrin rings as well), easily made possible by the special bonding properties of the carbon, permitted the creation of a sense organ in the very first beginnings which probably came into being before all the others: the eye - in the farthest sense.

The simplest kind of eye probably only provided shadow (in form of a pigmentation mark) for a light-sensitive little sector somewhere inside a protozoan. When light fell onto the light-sensitive little mark, the direction into which the protozoan was swimming was obviously wrong. The little creature only had to see to it that this mark remained in the shadow of the pigmentation and the direction was right.

We already demonstrated the inductive connections – repression of cellular processes in case of "wrong" direction - in this way at any rate the protozoan could (and had to) follow the light which was essential for life already (figure 126).

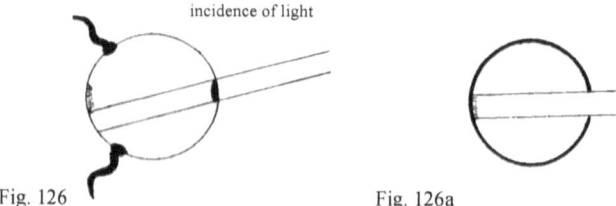

Fig. 126   Fig. 126a

The other way round was also possible: a kind of cave eye (figure 126a), which achieved it most perfect form with the squid and with the human being. But the simple light-and-shadow eye can already be found with unicellular organisms (infusorians) and it had obviously been sufficient for the survival of the species.

What already became necessary with even the simplest eye was the creation of organelles which specialised in transmitting the impulses of those electron waves that had been created by the light-sensitive structure. For that purpose, electric conduits had to be laid, tissues which could store and transmit electric potentials according to the principle of the accumulator.

These structures - already in the protozoan nothing else but cells within the cell - are special formations which can become up to one meter long. These are the nerves, and today nothing incomprehensible is attached anymore to these electric conduits in all living things; their functions have been clarified for the most part. Membranes play a great role in them; they change their polarisation by means of acetylcholine, a molecule that is released from the vesicular structures through electron waves; and with that they change the permeability for sodium ions.

The familiar game of polarisation and depolarisation (acetylcholine is immediately destroyed by the enzyme cholinesterase) transmits the impulses. Synapses - again membranous constructions - hand these impulses on from nerve cell to nerve cell; they determine the direction and the velocity.

The creation of the conduits together with their motoric organs (end plates, synapses etc.) was accompanied by the creation of a place of coordination, a cell which was able firstly to do something with the impulses and secondly to send some out on its own and to direct the received impulses into the correct paths respectively (again the "correct" results are achieved by the effect of induction). In the protozoan, this central place is a simple motorium, a cellular organelle which in principle already works like a neuron (a brain cell). But how does a neuron work?

In order to understand the function of a neuron, we have, like in all cases, to look again for the simplest thing, for the simplest structure which manages to identify impulses, make analogous decisions, and trigger actions. Such a simple structure can be found in the learning matrix as it finds application in computers which can programme themselves by learning. Therefore let's make a little excursion into data processing (figure 127):

 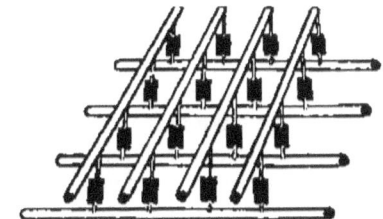

Fig. 127

The illustration shows how a learning matrix is in principle put into practice in the computer. As in a magnetic-core memory matrix (on the left) of an electronic computer two sets of parallel wires are intersected at right angles in such a way that every vertical wire intersects every horizontal one once. (The pictures are from the computer stone age, though, today only integrated switching circuits are in use.) In every point of intersection created in this way there is a memory element, for example a little metallised paper capacitor (figure on the right). Its capacity can be gradually reduced by partially eroding the metallised paper through heat; it is sufficient to subject it to excess voltage for this purpose.

A capacitor which is often subjected to stress in this way has a considerably lower capacity at the end of the learning phase than one through which current is scarcely passed. The distributions of capacitances between the capacitors of a learning matrix thus reflect the added up experiences.

Certain impulse sequences, for example graphic characters, can be recognised by such a learning matrix. One has to provide it with the impulse pattern of a certain letter during the learning phase and index it on a matrix column wire which is thus allocated to that particular letter. When a set of photoelectric cells is used as identification circuit - as the "eye" of the reading device - it is sufficient to connect every line with a horizontal wire (line wire). When the letter A is put in front of the photoelectric cells current passes through all horizontal wires in a way characteristic for the letter A. When in addition an inverse current is passed through a particular column wire, all those capacitors along this column wire will blow because they are overloaded by the voltage of the photoelectric cells. In this way, the voltage pattern characteristic for the letter A is created in the capacitors. When the same is done with all the other letters of the alphabet (or other symbols) by using the remaining column wires of the matrix, one will finally receive a characteristic distribution of capacitance for all letters.

Thus, in the reverse procedure, every letter can be identified again. They are again put in front of the set of photoelectric cells which as a result puts the corresponding horizontal wires under voltage again. Now it is sufficient to scan all vertical wires in order. The letter to be recognised is found where the pattern of capacitance is almost balanced by the voltages. From the learning process one knows of course what the letter assigned to this wire is called...

Let's now try to apply this simple system of the learning matrix to living structures. The wires are nothing else but neural pathways, the capacitors have to be replaced by neurons[56] which can vary an electric capacitance by assembling or disassembling the RNA in the so-called Nissl bodies[57].

This system is even a little more perfect than the learning matrix: RNA polarises to the "right" after all, the material of the cells, however, to the "left ", they already contain the opposite voltage (in electronics: the "earth mass"), and we see that the unilateral specialisation of heavier and lighter molecules in "right-handed" and "left-handed" was very favourable for the later development of organic learning matrixes.

Since we have to stay with the analogy of the capacitors, we recognise that one single neuron on its own has no meaning at all. Isolated, it does not work at all, only in connection with many other neurons will information and message find expression in the neuron matrixes as characteristic distribution of RNA and potential!

Neurons are connected with the perception organs on one side and on the other side with the executing organs (muscular cells) through neurites; this corresponds to the column and line wires. The learning matrix itself is produced by many connections (dendrites) among the neurites. The more complicated the tasks, the denser the wiring mesh. Figure 128 shows us the "capacitor" of the living learning wiring, the neuron.

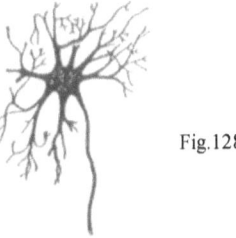

Fig.128

The wiring among the neurons can be clearly seen in the layers of the human cerebral cortex in which they are connected between supply and discharge lines quite similarly as in our capacitor example (fig. 129).

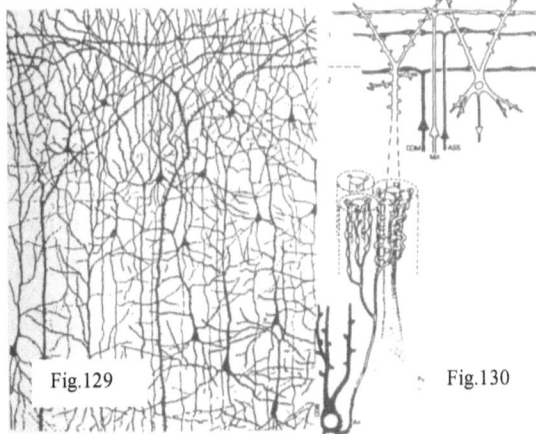

Fig.129   Fig.130

The number of such wirings in the human brain is legion. They are subdivided into discernible units (modules) which can contain up to 10 000 different neurons. Not all of them are only wired according to the pattern of the learning matrix but there are some which are even more complicated and varied but correspond in any case to the demonstrated basic principle. It would also be possible to fashion the learning matrix of a computer more effectively by putting further association lines between the capacitors which make an even finer differentiation of the potential distribution possible. And really, we find an enormous amount of such associative fibres in every brain which chiefly serve for connecting the matrixes among each other and in doing so spread every potential pattern almost over the whole brain. And of course there are also special cells which do not detain the potentials but pass them on into the linked wirings (pyramidal cells – fig. 130).

A protozoan searching for light (or avoiding light) now "learns" to coordinate sensation of light and movement of the flagella. Since every wrong movement has energetic disadvantages, it soon prefers of necessity that direction which keeps the "eye" in the dark (or in the light). When both flagella and eye are switched to the neurons, this preference for one direction finds expression in a certain characteristic distribution of voltage (pattern) in the neurons - like in the example of the capacitors above. We understand: the pattern produced by exposing (or not exposing) the eye spot to the light assigns itself to the pattern of the correct flagellum movement. When light (or shadow) falls on the spot, a new integrated pattern is produced which is assigned to the other flagella or cilia which take the spot back into the dark (or the light). The combination of these patterns activates always only the function of the correct corresponding organs(just as in the learning matrix where a balance of the voltage could only take place with the corresponding pattern). From now on the protozoan does not need to wait for the disadvantages which a wrong direction might bring. Bright and dark on the spot and the assignment by the patterns in the neurons sets the right course automatically.

This fully automatic control is called "reflex". Since all organs are both perception and execution organs, we should not be surprised that every nervous system exists twice so to speak; there are incoming and outgoing lines to the significance of which we will come back.

Well, the discovery of a baser reflex with the protozoan was on no account far fetched. Actually, protozoans can already "learn". For example, we can teach a paramecium to distinguish between bright and dark, to love the one and to hate the other. In doing so we work with the principle of the conditioned reflex by providing new muscular combinations through the assignment of further stimuli. This is very easily done by passing voltage through a culture dish in which the paramecium is swimming around indiscriminately. Further when we separate the areas into bright and dark, the paramecium will still avoid the current carrying sector even when the voltage has been switched off long since and only bright and dark mark the areas. The paramecium has learned, and it remembers the unpleasant voltage automatically since bright or dark, voltage or no voltage were assigned to the potential patterns of the neurons (in the paramecium it exists as a structure called motorium). At the same time a swimming locomotion is also assigned to the patterns which will always lead it away from the dangerous area.

The paramecium already possesses nerves and a motorium, a bundle of nerves, in which nothing but a learning matrix is hidden. Differently specialised nervous end plates which reacted to light, heat, cold, pressure, and depression developed for different environmental stimuli. That way the experience with the environment could find expression in the focal points of the nerves as a process of learning and remembering completely according to the system of the learning matrix.

But often the wirings of the neurons were only caused and created by the environmental experiences. Actually, mainly at that time when the nervous system or its motorium was still in the course of coming into being, and exactly this coming into being could be written down on the DNA of the nuclei and was consequently hereditary to the next generation. For that reason, the descendants received already finished recognition or control patterns which were located in the special way of wiring and could trigger fully automatic modes of behaviour so to speak. Thus there exists a hereditary permanent memory matrix.

Reflexes which are caused by this permanent memory matrix are called instincts; mostly they are already quite extensive complexes of behaviour. Together with their genetic lay-out, animals receive such finished wirings, which contain for example the concept of an enemy (with birds it is for example the shadow of a buzzard) and the necessary fleeing reflexes (hormonal signals, mobilisation of muscles etc.) coded in the matrix, that means their brain already grows with these patterns. When the eye supplies this "matrix of the enemy", the assignment "flight" or "defence" follows inevitably.

Understandably, a great lot of neurons which are wired to a complex are required for that. We know these complexes as spinal cord or brain... First and foremost, brains are permanent memory matrixes. Here, all organic functions are assigned, here, muscular activity is coordinated with the sensory signals - namely according to the simple principle that the charge patterns of all neurons are kept in an equilibrium, i.e. in potentials. This inner equilibrium results essentially from constant willingness for reaction, i.e. latent function and its inhibition. Depending on which side the charge pattern is shifted to, a process of activity is triggered or inhibited as a result.

Fundamentally, an extensive willingness for activity as such prevails which is selected through inhibition to carry out only certain movement processes. All processes of life, no matter of which kind, are based on this passive type of control: actions are not commanded but permitted. This respective enabling of a latent action is practically done automatically through combinations in the neuron matrixes acquired over millions of years; every shifting of an oscillational pattern immediately triggers exactly those functions in the organism which also provide a balancing of the differences in potential so that the equilibrium is restored.

Without exception the entirety of all neurons is involved in these processes. Never does a single neuron decide, because "decision" must be out of the question! Brains do not decide and command, they only combine action and reaction processes which are operating well together and as a consequence they are an integral component of the whole neuronal system, that means for example that the awareness range "seeing" does not exist for a brain without an eye or in other words: the sense organs themselves are the brain, just like the neurons with which they are linked inseparably.

Every new serious area of life and experience creates new organisms with new brains, in principle always according to the basic pattern which we demonstrated with the protozoan. Every new brain did not only work on the solution of new problems in its entirety but it always included the old, handed down brain structures as well, yes, the older structures were always the basic condition for the functioning of the new ones. Through causal connection of growth with action, a certain area of activity can be localised in the brain for certain sensory impressions. Still it is always the whole brain that is occupied with processing these impressions.

The higher an organism developed, the less it was able to regenerate and the more it had to protect itself through its behaviour. Therefore the ability for regeneration has decreased - judged in retrospect - with the increase of complicated nervous systems and is almost non-existent with living things which have a highly develop central nervous system. Cause and effect should not be mistaken in this case: it was the lacking ability for regeneration which forced highly specialised nerve and brain structures into being.

Most animals provide a complex conditioned behaviour which is triggered by signals. But animals learn as well, and through learning processes both by means of learning matrixes and by means of corresponding new wirings[58] – not only when they are still young and growing up! – they develop new behavioural patterns in their brains. This behaviour also remains conditional on signals and therefore appears to be machine-like (training).

What is here so easy to describe, is in principle the same as that phenomenon which evades the immediate assignment to the same pattern because of its enormous complexity: the act of thinking of the human being. And still it is exactly the same processes as we will realise better later-on.

The well-ordered functioning of all cells of an organism finds its expression as balanced charge patterns in the brain. This balance will always be maintained since every sensory stimulus normally finds its equivalent and the easing of tension in a certain reaction. A disturbance of this general equilibrium is expressed as pain, that feeling which is for the time being indefinable and primarily only means disturbance or uneasiness. Only in higher developed living things, which hear sounds and know tactile sensations and can assign pain to other experiences (severe, deep, dull, sharp pain), which stem from all other areas of the senses, becomes pain manifest in a certain quality of sensation and often this sensation is associated with more complex processes (searing, stabbing, gnawing pain).

The kind and degree of feeling pain therefore depend on the development stage of the brain. Even the equilibrium which is suddenly regained after a disturbance is expressed in something like pain (sweet pain, pleasure, lust). From that we see that feelings amount from sensory experience which can be associated quite in the abstract from time to time. When this association is not possible, the feeling as such does not become existent at all but remains only a basic experience for the poles for which we could approximately use the words eagerness and reluctance.

The emotional world of a protozoan or a similarly low developed animal, maybe even of a plant, already consists of these vague contrasts.

Sensation already consists of mere perceiving - of feeling resistances. Already the shifted potentials in the neuronal networks create resistances; currents are either blocked or released - and this is already the effect of a cause which comes from the inside or from the outside. In case of a disturbance the whole progression of functions in the organism is shifted. The elimination of disturbances is not an act of will but is done automatically provided the possibilities are at hand. Hormones are discharged, special enzymes are produced ... soon everything is in turmoil. This "spanner in the works" is felt as resistance, as reluctance, as pain.

That there is "nobody there" who feels is only revealed by the opposite: we feel best when we do not feel our body at all (!) - this is a sensation without feeling and without conscious perception.

Defined and localised pain occurs when other matrixes are also changed by the disturbance of a pattern. From time to time it therefore comes to quite absurd assignments (bright, dark, quiet, piercing pain). These relocations are of course done through the synapses of the nervous system. Pain killers prevent the activity of the synapses by blocking the acetylcholine; the relocation cannot take place and the pain stops...

The organism itself also knows such analgesics which it only uses when it is unable to regain the equilibrium anymore in any other way (endorphins). Many drugs work in the same way, they reduce the ability to feel (to be weightless, not to feel one's body) by blocking every perception of a disturbance. Drugs, which are very similar to endorphins (opiates), are therefore strong pain-killers.

Eagerness becomes only existent - as we just found out above - by the lack of reluctance. There is not any organ that creates eagerness or perceives it but there are organs which do away with reluctance. Lust and pain belong into the same category as sweet and bitter in the sensation of taste. They have the same trigger but different assignments which are experienced full of relish for the reason that they lead to a relief from a drive or compulsion. He who suspects the sexual organs to be instruments for generating lust is mistaken.

Sensation is the preliminary stage of awareness. We all experienced these lower degrees of awareness ourselves: in the first months of our lives of which we can't tell anything. It is the awareness of animals in general provided they do not already have awareness experiences (not to be denied with higher mammals); it can only be defined by eagerness and reluctance and strictly speaking only by reluctance and pain...

The sense organs developed and improved more and more. Eyes differentiated between colours and shapes by extending shapes over numerous "photoelectric cells" through the lenses so that diversely complicated impulse patterns resulted already on the retina. Ears differentiated sounds; heat and coldness receptors distinguished different temperature ranges. In the end, this activity of the senses is always compared with the matrix in the neurons, and only by assigning the corresponding responses (reactions) of the body are the things seen, heard, and felt attributed to their meaning which is evaluated by the fact of how appropriate or inappropriate the experience is for the organism. The same applies to the sense of taste for which substances only became "sweet" when they were beneficial for the body and "bitter" when they were harmful. Some animals, however, make certainly only general distinctions in tasting good or tasting bad since they don't have any words for their sensations – which is also the case with regard to colours and shapes. A bee can in fact distinguish many colours very well but of course it does not known the word "red". By the way, they don't even know the colour either, because bees are red-blind. Red appears black to them. Instead bees can recognise even reflections of ultraviolet light. A variety of flowers which all look just white to us human beings have a tinge into all possible colours for the eyes of the bee...

When we think again of the shadow eye of the protozoan (fig. 126) and visualise how the movement of a flagellum is controlled by the incidence of light we can assume two possibilities for this control. Either the flagellum is always latently in motion and is inhibited by the wrong direction of the protozoan – i.e. incidence of light onto the pigmentation mark – or the movement of the flagellum is only triggered by the right direction – shadow on the pigmentation mark. We already discovered the principle of latent activity and its inhibition in the neurons (the programmes of the DNA are not activated, either, but are released by specific repression) and if we consider which control is the simpler one, the principle of inhibition is the more convincing method in this case, too. For control purposes, it is only necessary to remove the energy from a flagellum, which is potentially in motion, its immobile state becomes the inevitable consequence. On the other hand, a flagellum, which is activated for movement, has to manage two basic situations, that of rest and that of movement. Nature surely choose the simpler way, it designed moved flagella from the beginning and turned off their energy supply as a choice! But that restricted the freedom of decision-making for the protozoan because it cannot activate the flagellum at will but only bring it to a standstill whereas in the other way both possibilities are open.[59]

The neurons of a brain work in the same way. They do not cause anything but connect and continue activities which are virtually available from the outset. Inhibition of correspondingly possible controls creates the specific behavioural pattern of a living thing. We will see that even our consciousness is the product of inhibition and selection.

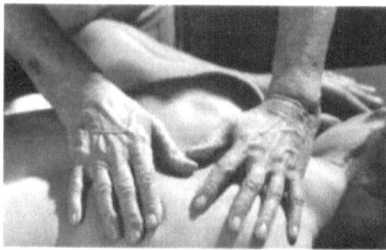

Fig.130a

32 Consciousness

What had to be added to everything we have described previously in order to create consciousness, imagination, and fantasy, was the internal imitation (reflection) of the environment ("outside world").

When we hit a metal cube with a hammer, the cube is put into vibrations which are characteristic for the kind and magnitude of the blow as well as for the place where it hit. The typical vibrational pattern of the cube contains or means the event "hammer blow" in coded form.[60]

Let's now assume that the metal cube possesses the ability to create exactly the same vibrational pattern on its own without being hit by the hammer before. For the metal cube, it wouldn't make a big difference; the vibrational pattern means the event "hammer blow" and manifests this blow in the inner experience room of the cube, no matter if it actually happens or not. The cube, though, could not interpret the event unless a second pattern occurs as assignment - that means, the significance of the vibrational pattern must have been "learned" at one time.

There is a method which can record and reproduce the electromagnetic vibrational pattern in a particularly extensive fashion: holography. A holographic image contains the impulses of the light of an object in coded form without any visible differences in colours and shapes. Only creating a further vibrational image according to the patterns on the film by radiographing the hologram with a further beam of light makes the object existent again - as an image which appears exactly as three-dimensional as its model has been. If the plate or film of the hologram was dynamic and if it did not carry only one hologram but many integrated patterns which could follow one another, several successive images would be possible; a kind of movie would run off...

Metal cubes are not suitable for holographically storing events because its vibrations are gradually wearing out. The hologram radiographed with the laser light is in fact lasting but cannot be changed. In this respect the brains of highly developed living things are capable of doing more. They preserve the codifications obtained by the sense organs as vibrational patterns, sort and define them by combining and integrating these learning matrixes. In order to make this easier to comprehend we can imagine the groove in a phonographic record which - although only a groove - can reproduce a variety of sounds and instruments simultaneously. In addition, all these instruments are integrated in one carrier frequency, i.e. one fundamental vibration, onto which the audio signal is modulated. The system could not work in any other way.

In the neuronal structure there also has to be such a fundamental vibration as well as a material analogous to the groove in the record into which the patterns can be engraved permanently. In the brain and in the neurons respectively, both is realised by the RNA molecules which agglomerate – in a similar manner as with the ribosomes - to Nissl bodies. A fresh, unconditioned neuron contains a lot of (several millions!) Nissl bodies in the ER and in the dendrites. The nerve cell is "conditioned" through the disassembly (!) of RNA molecules. Owing to that the "right-hand" potential in the cell sinks (a similar process as in the capacitors of the learning matrix).

By means of this disassembly but also by means of the specific wiring during growth, countless patterns overriding each other develop which are equivalent to the causing events. These patterns are real vibrational patterns. We know in fact that neurons work according to the all-or-nothing system, that means that only pure impulses are processed, but both the maximum depth of potential and the zero point are never put into effect immediately. When, for example, one neuron spontaneously falls back again to the electric point zero again, it overshoots it several times until it comes to rest.

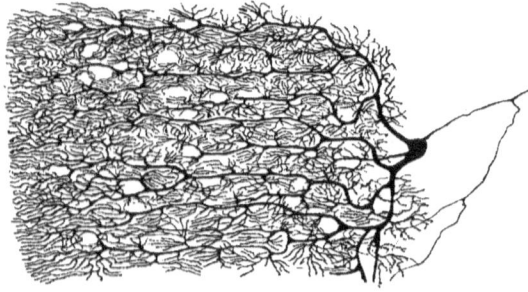

Fig. 130b

In this way the switching system of a brain differs a little from the computer principle in which the impulses are simply switched on and off by transistors. In the computer, the contents of the memory do not influence the appearance (hardware) of the equipment, either, whereas the brain creates and influences the memory by structural modification just like the groove in a record, and with that it becomes an analogous computer despite the digital impulses.

Figure 130b shows us one (!) nerve cell with its dendritic branchlets. Since the dendrites contain vast amounts of Nissl bodies (RNA) we can assume with justification that the vibrational patterns also enforce the development of the dendrites. The software creates its hardware obviously by itself. In addition, the illustration reminds us of figure 119 (the estuary of the Colorado River). The idea that the two structures have absolutely similar original causes suggests itself...

At this point we will not deal with the electrical and chemical causes of signal processing within our nervous system and with the processes in the synapses etc... We can read up on that in biology books because these processes have been comprehended quite well in principle. How the memory and the consciousness come into existence, though, one still has only little idea of. And despite intensive research one could of course not localise a certain region or structure of the brain which is responsible for our conscious thinking – because they do not exist at all. For instance, the name of our neighbour is said to be stored in the temporal lope whereas the brain allegedly memorises his outer appearance in the parietal lope...

Just like every tree has a corresponding bough branching into its crown from every branching of its root system, every part of the body has its correspondence in the neuronal branchings of the brain as well. But that does not mean that the body part is represented only in this place. This section of the brain is practically the address to turn to, the junction of all incoming and outgoing information, and works only like a switching system. When we switch on our room illumination it doesn't mean that the current is created in the switch – actually, however, neurobiologists are regularly taken in by such fallacies when they think there is something like a "language area" or a "visual field" etc. The truth is they only found the "switches" because it is always the whole brain which is involved in the phenomena. The switching station is that place where the instinctive result of the "thinking activity" is transferred into the consciousness by triggering the corresponding actions: it is only there that the neurons become commanders which "spur" the executive organs in the truest sense of the word via the nervous system. The second great error of some molecular biologists is the assumption that the contents of the memory are transformed into some material structure, like a "memory molecule" so to speak.

But there surely aren't any "memory molecules" which could mean something in particular. All theories aiming at that come to nothing from beginning to end. The biologists among our readers will think of the famous flatworm experiments which created the impression, and just with a few researchers only, as if something learned could be passed on by transplanting brain substance or by feeding trained animals to untrained ones. These experiments can be better interpreted with the explanation that the supply of RNA increases the ability to learn as was to be expected. Actually no flatworm adopted the learned matter of its cannibalistic meal; it only learned a little faster. Very similar experiments were carried out on rats. With them, there also was an increase in the readiness to learn through the supply of RNA. This is just logical because the requirement of the brain for RNA is enormous.

We should again emphasise that the brain creates patterns by destroying RNA. These patterns "learn" or remember something. The short-term memory is only a temporally limited continued vibration of a pattern whereas the long-term memory results from the fact that the patterns are determined permanently by the corresponding growth of dendrites and synapses.[61] That means the equivalent for an experience, no matter of what kind a pattern - an electro-magnetic field to be exact - is which remains in the brain structure, where it continues vibrating.[62] With all due respect for the speed of molecular processes, the development of memory molecules would really take too long. We know, however, that we can think at an almost timeless speed and even on different levels of consciousness at the same time.

The essential point of the thinking pattern is coupling the vibrational patterns. When we record two musical instruments onto one groove in the record, they cannot be reproduced separately anymore - provided we are talking about a mono record. It is only one groove, one needle, and one loud-speaker - but it plays back both instruments clearly distinctive from each other (and as for the rest the carrier frequency, which remains inaudible to our ears). On a video tape, image and sound are coupled in a similar way. And that was also the crucial point for the development of thought and the formation of the consciousness: the coupling of image and sound and other sensory impressions.

Many animals demonstrate by imitation that they "comprehend" certain signs and gestures of the others - this behaviour is particularly strongly developed with apes and monkeys. They imitate optical appearances, i.e. postures or grimaces. This process is based on a clearly recognisable coupling: a perceived sight triggers certain body functions and movements because they also belong causally to this sight. That means signals can contain coded events, and that can also mean acoustic signals. Animals "think" in these signals which are not only coupled with the modes of behaviour but also with the images which well up in the perceiver. We still find this principle of imitation in every organism – as unconscious process of the ideomotor activity as well, as so-called Carpenter effect. When we are watching a football player, our own muscles are measurably moving analogous to his pattern of movement. The patterns of movement of the football player (and all other patterns which define him) are "compared" to the patterns in the structure of our neurons; if there are similar patterns, they are intensified and even trigger motor reflexes. We imitate the football player, and therefore we "understand" his appearance, therefore we become "aware" of him because the triggered muscular motor activity has in turn an effect on the vibrational pattern... and this again has an effect on the motor activity... etc. That means the football player triggers a vibration in us which comprises the whole nervous system including the sense organs and the motor synapses – and that is (!) the consciousness!

The human organism has perfected this principle: it did not only imitate optical forms of appearance but also the sound which the observed object caused and for that reason, it uttered the sound when it wanted to designate the same thing (children's language!). In the brain matrix, the associated visual patterns were coupled with these acoustic patterns - and in this way was nothing else but language was created.

Sounds became words. All languages of this world go back to primitive languages which are very similar to each other because they were directly derived from the concepts by imitation. Richard

Fester is even of the opinion that the archetypes of the most important words match absolutely in all languages of the world.

Combining pictures with sounds and words was one revolutionary innovation because with that another tremendous flood of information was created: the intellectual evolution. The pictographic system of writing finally resulted from the imitation of environment by recording it on information carriers of all kinds, and script developed from that.

The more capable of learning a living thing was, that means the more learning matrixes could be laid down in its brain, the more extensive the combination of picture, sound, and symbol became. In the end, there was a creature whose brain had developed the greatest capacity of all, or to put it more precisely, had to develop it in order to survive: exactly ourselves...

Balance prevails in a learning matrix only when all coupled patterns belonging to a vibrational structure have been stimulated into vibration after the vibrational structure was excited by a sense organ. In turn these patterns promptly activate the sense organs belonging to them (repercussion). In the computer, we saw the learning matrix as one plane so to speak; in the brain, many such planes lie above or within one another and they are all connected with each other functionally. For that reason, all vibrational patterns have to be understood three-dimensionally. For simplicities sake, however, we will continue talking about planes, although we know that these planes are practically interlaced with each other.

Because of the inseparable couplings, a word (e.g. "trumpet") or a sound coded as a vibrational pattern – the ear alone accepts only vibrations – makes not only all pertaining acoustic planes vibrate but the optical planes as well which, as a result, - and that is the important thing - simulate (imitate) the picture in the corresponding sense organs (retina). And from there the picture goes back to the brain - but the appertaining plane has already been activated – and the whole process is repeated until a new stimulus comes from outside. The consequence: we do not only "hear" with our ears but also with our eyes in that moment when we identify the sound as "trumpet".

Now we understand immediately the reason why the nervous system exists in two "copies" so to speak. Without this double arrangement there would be no process which created awareness.

The eye does not only serve the physical processes of seeing but also of thinking, i.e. when we imagine something or picture something, the retina of the eyes becomes active (photome, hallucination). In the same way, when we are thinking words, the larynx organs and the root of the tongue are really getting active – or the muscular system when we are thinking of movements...

There are no thoughts without a corresponding parallel function of the organs. Actually, we do not think at all but speak silently or voicelessly inside ourselves and for that reason, tongue, larynx, and vocal cords are really working along. Everybody who observes himself closely can satisfy himself as of this fact, especially when he tries to think something particularly "loud", i.e. intensively. In reality, he is saying it noiselessly but with the corresponding concentration he can distinctly feel the movement of the root of his tongue and of his larynx (this is even perceptible with one's fingers). In doing so he hears himself simultaneously inside because he is making the coupled patterns of his hearing apparatus vibrate at the same time. And in his ear the strings are really resonating measurably! Soundlessly, just like the larynx is speaking voicelessly and the eye is at the same time seeing lightlessly!

We were talking about strings in the ear to depict it more graphically. Actually, it is liquids which are vibrating in the human ear. Nerves react to these movements by means of fine hairs. In the reflection process, these nerves are activated by the brain.

When we try to envision a landscape and look at it from the left to the right with our eyes closed and then touch our eyelids with our fingertips, we will notice at once that the eye balls are really making this movement. Simply because the imaginary picture is not imaginary at all but really appears on the retina - but of course it is not detectable optically because the picture is available as a pattern in the vibrating atoms as if an optical photograph was really impinged on it.

We already mentioned that this image created inside flows back into the brain again. This is important because it serves for identification and only completes the simulation. Since the light-sensitive molecules of the eye have a double function and the impulses of the brain are much weaker than the light of the outside world, they are facing towards the brain. That means, the "film" in our "camera" is loaded the wrong way round for a good reason! We will discuss this apparently absurd design later-on in more detail.

Another thing comes to our attention: it is almost impossible to picture a landscape purely mentally without using the associated words either. We think something like this: "There are mountains ... green ... blue sky ... clouds ... buildings, etc." With these words we conjure the details of the landscape all the more, and not only that we involuntarily also hear the sounds coupled with this landscape - provided we are not deaf and mute!

The brain of the human being, as the one which is the biggest on the world in relation to the body, has set up an incomprehensible amount of learned matrixes - and this mainly in the cerebral cortex which distinguishes the human brain so much from the animal brain. Many of the couplings in the older parts of the brain are on the other hand already wired like a permanent memory because they were created during a chapter of our life when the brain was still growing. These are the first months of our life, and for that reason, these months mould our future personality intensively because these permanent memories are not so easy to erase anymore. They also mould future intelligence and traits since it depends very much on how the wirings (dendrites) were laid out. Short, preferred paths are just as possible as long detours. Conditional on the region in which short, quick connections were created, our gifts, our talents lie in a certain intellectual quality.

Thus because of its flexible learning matrixes the human nervous system is capable of something which is really outstanding of all brain activities: it stores sensory experiences as distribution patterns of the potential by means of RNA and arouses these sensory experiences again even after a long time by sending currents through these patterns. In doing so the sense organ becomes active again - but this time from the inside. The sense organ, however, causes again a distribution pattern in the usual manner which fits the triggering pattern exactly. Therefore we memorise subjects to learn by recapitulating them several times since in doing so we deepen the patterns and imprint them more clearly into the RNA distribution. The sensory stimulus from the brain and the new imprinting following it is called reflection. This reflection also takes place with every normal sensory perception; it makes it possible to find out if something we see is already available as a pattern or not. Depending on the result the sensation turns out differently. When patterns already exist, reflection takes place without leaving a mark, we "recognise". Otherwise there is immediately a new imprint; the seen object was still unknown to us.

All these reflections freshly create event processes from the patterns in front of - actually behind! - our eyes without them really happening. We "remember". If a new imprinting does not take place with new, unknown impressions because of overtiredness or due to a faulty wiring, we will remember wrongly. We know this phenomenon as dejá-vu!

But the game goes even farther: by means of reflection, i.e. by "playing" the pattern, we can simulate sensory impressions that means we can make events happen which do not take place or have not taken place yet. With that we create an inner chamber of imagination in which we can act and foresee possible consequences on the basis of our experience. Our common sense is founded on that.

Mainly the cortex areas of the brain act reflectionally and sensorially. They do not "work" at certain problems and they do not exchange any data as is often maintained. This explanation is only one of many misunderstandings about the functioning of the brain. As strange as it may sound: the brain does actually never know what it is doing. Just as little as the record knows something about the music it carries. The brain is just an apparatus for maintaining the vibrational patterns which are caused by the outside world or by the organism itself and which are conveyed and processed via the senses. All these vibrational patterns contain our whole conception of the world in a three-dimensional hologram (a whole orchestra can already be hidden in one simple groove of a record). Since the vibrational patterns are interlaced with each other we remember so quickly - but always only with the aid of the sense organs! They alone trigger memories through colour, shape, taste, and smell and manifest them by reflection.

Let's again stress the fact: there is no activity of the brain without an activity of the sense organs. The consciousness is created by a continuous reflection process between outside world and inside world, i.e. between environment, sense organ, and brain. No consciousness without environment and none without sense organ. The vibration of the reflection process itself is the consciousness, and it extends over the whole nervous system, actually over the whole organism. The brain alone becomes a dead clod of matter when the sense organs are taken away from it. A brain in a glass of spirit, as is often seen in horror movies, could never think at all and would have not a trace of consciousness.

When one realises that the consciousness is an event from the interaction of the senses, just the vibration between memorised experience and new experiences flooding in, it is only a matter of how these vibrational patterns are maintained in the brain.

Since RNA is destroyed in the Nissl bodies[57] during these processes - the number of the Nissl bodies decreases with growing use and they almost vanish completely when a person is exhausted - the sensory activity has to be stopped or reduced considerably after a while in order to be able to regenerate the RNA. We know this phase as sleep. The neurons produce RNA again overnight. In doing so, vibrational pattern which are far too fine and too cursory are deleted - we "forget"! - and only the rough, distinct patterns remain. The groove in a record also looses information when we fill it evenly with material without smoothing it completely. In this way, unimportant, unpleasant, and badly imprinted things are singled out and removed from the brain, and neurons freshly filled with RNA prepare themselves for the imprints of the next day. For this reason - and actually only for this reason! - our sleep is indispensable.

Withdrawal of sleep would not particularly harm the body but the brain promptly reacts with hallucinations in this case because it tries to do the necessary regenerations during the waking state. Since this regeneration processes trigger reflections themselves in turn - deleting a pattern also means a partial activation of its contents - it doesn't even give us any rest at night: we dream! While doing so, we are acting in a fully simulated environment which can turn out very fantastic from time to time. The dream is therefore not a mysterious process but actually proof for our explanations. When we would try to follow a groove in a record with a kind of filling needle in order to renovate it we would have to be prepared that its content become partially audible.

The vibrational patterns of our brain are delicate and vulnerable. A craniocerebral trauma (concussion) can delete them almost completely; the unpleasant consequence is called amnesia (loss of memory). But also deficiencies in the supply of blood, haematoma, and insufficient provision of energy and nutrition ("calcification") lead to an erasure of whole vibrational areas (loss of speech, paralysis), which can also affect the reflections with organs essential to life (death).

Despite the many differences, the computer remains a good aid to understand the brain. But just as little as the examination of a transistor leads to comprehending the functioning of a computer can the knowledge of a neuron bring us home to the functioning of the brain. The "thinking" of the human being takes place in the whole brain, more exactly: in the whole body, and only takes effect at all by the assignment of speech. We do not only recognise a particular wavelength, which our eyes perceive, on the basis of the available pattern in the brain but also by assigning the pattern of the sonic sequence "red" to a colour. In the same way, the recognition of shape and function is rooted in the assignment of the corresponding word. And all these assignments have to be learned first. As a child we already experienced which sensory impression is called "red" or which shape is designated "table" or "chair". In this way we learned the whole world of concepts of our scope of experience which also includes our own body. We learned the interpretation of perceptions just like walking, grabbing something, or talking ... we couldn't do anything of our own accord. We learned to control our body and its excretory organs in the same way as we learned the ingestion of food - and with that we had even already begun in the womb (suckling reflex).

In the first years of our lives we were taught the meaning of the sensory impressions with a lot of patience by the interaction of assignments (object-word-sound-colour-shape-purpose-etc.), and it was called "training". That way we learned values (good - bad) as well as ethical concepts and moral standards, and everyone of us developed his very own reflected environment inside which is coined by personality and disposition and which has to be attributed completely to the selective activity of his senses ... and these senses never perceive the whole reality. Whatever we carry in us as a conception of the world, it is only a fragment...

By constantly comparing the outside world with the inside world we recognise our environment - and are aware of ourselves in its centre! By assigning one little word to this recognition of physical experiences of the very person which we discover at the centre of the environment, we create the "ego". Even this ego-consciousness is not inherent because we experience our body only gradually and learn to act with it. Animals don't recognise themselves in a mirror since they don't have this distinct "ego"- with the exception of primates who already have a certain genuine ability to learn.

Let's summarise: sense organs are not senders which transmit the picture of the world to a possible receiver in the head but they are integral part of the brain. And the brain is not a receiver, just like a radio, because then the question who was actually listening to the radio would remain unanswered. The consciousness consists of the continuous reflection of an outside world with its corresponding inside world which is available in countless vibrational patterns. Perception and reflection would be impossible without sense organs. For that reason, there is no consciousness without sense organs. Consciousness, "mind", or "ego" are determined by the ability of the brain to maintain vibration matrixes in form of coded RNA distribution. Therefore: no mind without brain!

The little word "ego" designates that person which represents the centre of reflection. The internalisation of the ego is learned in the same way as the recognition of the environment. Consciousness and ego are therefore concrete, comprehensible processes. The principle of reflecting by means of double nervous pathways and "films" in the eyes which are loaded the wrong way round leads to the fact that both the finger hurts where it is and the picture of the world is noticed where it is, namely outside of the head!

Our attention within the whole consciousness is always in that place where at least two strongly vibrating potential patterns correspond or vibrate together because consciousness is not simply an uncertain state of the mind but an incessant process of recognition! Since great areas of the brain are always stimulated simultaneously due to coupling, our perception is complex and associative. Comparison and selection processes are considerably accelerated by that.

Selecting an answer to a question, for example, is done by the corresponding main pattern which is evoked by the momentary sensory activity. Let's assume somebody asks us "What is the capital of Italy?" Since we once learned it, the words "capital" and "Italy" transmitted through the ear make the areas capitals and Italy and of course "what" and "is" vibrate. "What is" is assigned to the concept "question" which in turn is assigned to the concept "answer"; the assignment for capitals and Italy is called - if we know the answer -

"Rome" which is also available as vibrational pattern, namely as language pattern ... and promptly this pattern activates the speech organs: we speak the answer. The brain is thus not a "thinking organ" but a "linking organ" for coded electromagnetic impulse fields, which contain so-called ensembles of concepts. We do not always remember spontaneously. Sometimes it can take a while until the question is "comprehended", i.e. until the patterns belonging to the question are found. And there is always the possibility that another pattern which is dominating at the moment butts in - and we give the wrong answer.

There are people with a good memory and people with a bad one; how good it is depends entirely on the architecture and imprinting ability of the brain. Patterns which are not imprinted or were imprinted superficially and weakly make the short-term memory; we delete them immediately or on the basis of overnight regeneration. Only deeply imprinted patterns, i.e. those which extend over many, many neurons and made great amounts of RNA disassemble, lie deeply rooted in the long-term memory. Only contents which we should remember for all our life are already available in coded form as hardware in the wirings of the dendrites and synapses. It goes without saying that the requirement for RNA is higher in the brain than in any other region of the body.

The similarity of the brain function to holography is evident. What works with light waves in a hologram is done by electron waves in the brain [62]. Drives and instincts from the permanent memories reveal themselves via the cerebral cortex as well as via all other regions. To make "wiring diagrams" of the brain would not make any sense because there are no wirings in the conventional sense. The hologram also contains the whole information in every section... In fact there is a plan for the arrangement of a holographic experiment but none for the creation and codification of the three-dimensional picture.

Maybe this is not entirely comprehended immediately. Many ideas could only be touched here and should be pursued further. But that would already result in a book on its own.

The consciousness of the human being has a high degree of development, and it is not situated in the head because after all we perceive every event exactly where it takes place. But what is situated in and on the head are the eyes and the ears, and these two senses create a large part of our consciousness. Only he who realises how much the processes in our central nervous system are interwoven and linked will also comprehend our complex feeling of ego.

It is of course a little fateful when we want to explain the phenomenon of our mind illustratively attributing everything to physical and chemical processes. But qualitatively this is already possible today. Man lives in the anthropocentric arrogance to be something special but he is only special as far as quantity is concerned with regard to the incredible number of small organisms involved, his cells. Billions of neurons recognise the environment and create the ego. A tremendous expenditure only to ensure the survival of a germ but a great advantage for a creature which is thus able to make something of its life which is far more than the original task. In that lies the meaning of our existence: to recognise the environment and to make it even manifest in doing so because it would not make any sense without the seeing eye and it would be unable to become aware of itself. The cosmos itself only becomes the cosmos by reflection!

How miserable people must appear to us who are still searching for the "meaning in life" in view of these facts. In fact, they looked at the world but have not recognised and comprehended it. Admittedly this is not the task of our brain either which is only to aid in surviving because the body itself is all too vulnerable. The objective perception of reality is also difficult; man contemplates his world, and as a result he gets truths which lie inside himself, and this inside world is coined by selective, limited perception. Therefore man has found only uncertain hypotheses about his world so far. And he never comprised the entirety.

Every brain is a reaction to the environment itself, a grown answer - and therefore it consists of ready answers, unable to ask the right questions. Many people try to evade this dilemma by "sensing" the environment. They meditate about themselves and the world - but even than the result is always only an answer which is thought to be true – without any real "proof".

We could certainly contemplate the function of the brain for a long time. Therefore it has to be sufficient for us at this point to understand in principle how and why such complex structures like the nervous system, the brain, and the living things could come into existence, yes, had to come into existence. Again, neither plan nor goal is to be found in the whole event. Everything arose from the simple beginnings. And what makes the event appear to be so complicated is only its unmanageable diversity and the dimensions of its components. Several hundred billion body cells, consisting of about $7*10^{27}$ atoms, play their game in our body, and one single protozoan already provides an incredible abundance of functions, the detailed comprehension of which leads into immensity. We could imagine the retina in our eye alone as a construction made of millions of such "protozoans", every single one responsible for the perception of a microscopic point of light or shadow or colour. Only the interaction of these numerous nerve cells in this organ creates the miracle of "seeing". But it is of course no miracle, at least none that is greater than the world itself with its atoms, molecules, crystals, stars, and galaxies...

And since we were just dealing with the subject of "thinking" we would like to see now what comes of it if a man like Albert Einstein racks his brain over the world...

33 Relativity

Not only philosophers had their say in working out answers to the questions to this world but physicists as well. Although physics as a pure science of measuring is not entitled to such answers at all and although these answers should not be expected of it, the theories of the "queen of sciences" had always strong philosophical aspects as well; because the basics of physics itself have been of a metaphysical nature down the line and have remained unapproachable to logical attempts of explanations. As a starting point physics has taken axioms and postulates, like "gravitation", "nuclear force", "interaction ", "positive and negative charge", etc.. Many concepts of this kind have been given up, like for example the "material fluids of electricity", because they soon proved to be useless.

At the turn of the century there was particular confusion among the physicists. Apparently radioactivity destroyed the principle of the conservation of energy, and light was for the first time suspected to be a wave which had to be carried by a medium. But nobody really wanted to believe in that – since one had already made bad experiences with the material fluids.

For the first time the velocity of light was measured by means of various methods. It proved to be incredibly high: about 300 000 kilometres per second were covered by this something - but what was actually moving?

Since the views of the physicists were strongly influenced by mechanics, soon the opinion developed that there had to be particles involved, particles of light to be exact; Newton still called them corpuscles, and later Einstein himself invented the photon, nothing else but a particle of light as well.

In the previous chapters, we just consequently and absolutely abolished the model of light as a substantial particle. Of course, other physicists have already done that before. Many theories deal with the ether, and bizarre ideas were constructed about the matter, like knots, tangles, nets, and fields. But none of them answered the question why the ether should "condense" or "tangle" or "harden" in order to carry light and to create matter.

With T.A.O. we brought something similar to the ether back to life, but we lent an absolute function to the T.A.O. matrix which the ether did not yet have.[63] Because of that we could find the simple explanation that the world works "because it exists "... And its functioning principle proved to be immensely simple.

But the significance of our way of looking at things still goes beyond these possibilities. It brings us in contact with the haute école of physics, with theories that make many a person shudder with awe because these theories seem to exceed the horizon of their intellectual faculties... We are talking about Albert Einstein's Theories of Relativity (ToR).

For laymen and private scholars likewise as for many scientists or creators of theories it has become a popular sport to "refute" the ToR. Einstein's theses seem to be an extreme provocation for the common sense; in countless publications it is tried to reproach the genius for an error in his reasoning or a mistake in his calculations[64] or to shake his postulates. But Einstein's theories can neither be refuted nor proved. Up to now they have not been refuted, though – neither have they been proved (even if either has been claimed by opponents and supporters again and again). Neither does it make any sense to search for "mistakes in his calculation" or errors in reasoning in the theories because everything was correctly derived and deduced with mathematical logic – as it is customary in physics. The suitability of a theory – but on no account the degree of its accuracy – results only from the confirmation of its predictions. And we could ask the same question for all theories: does it really correspond to the realities of our nature? This question is particularly burning on our tongue with regard to the ToR. Einstein himself is reported to have said: "As far as the laws of mathematics refer to reality, they are not certain, and as far as they are certain, they don't refer to reality."

In the chapters "Inertia" and "Gravity" we already obtained some results which reminded us strongly of some statements of the General Theory of Relativity (GTR). We will therefore continue our thoughts in the sense of our repulsion principles in order to examine if the similarities with the GTR possibly go a little further.

We should now remember figure 46 which showed us how the pressure shadow between Earth and moon deformed the two celestial bodies and how the tides are created by that. This deformation is produced both by the pressure shadow, as is also demonstrated in figure 44 with the two H-atoms, and by the "curving force" (figure

15), hence by the geometry of the repulsions to each other (after all, pressure shadow and curving force of the Earth manage to deform the originally globular moon by about 1 kilometre – and that at a distance of about 400 000 km).

As we already discovered when examining Kepler's laws and Newton's gravitational formula, the "space" is determined by what is happening in it. When we define it on the basis of the geometric arrangements of the effects which are revealed in it then the space is "curved" – at least it gives this impression. Although the empty space is free of properties, in the presence of matter curving forces still occur which – as shown in figure 15 - distort a ruler and bend or stretch it around the spherical "mass field"- and we could postulate something like a "curvature" of the space. More than ever if we didn't know anything about the forces effective in the space.

Next we discovered that inertia has to do with the arrangement of the internal oscillations of a body and with the resistance upon deformation which atoms put up against a change in their impulse directions or rather with the fact that the influence of a force as well as the transmission of a force (or reaction to a force) can maximally be done at the velocity of light – on that occasion it also became apparent that the acceleration of a body reduces its length in the direction of movement because of the lack of instantaneous influence of a force – which also means a deformation - similar to that which took place because of the pressure shadow. And we should not forget that there are neither inert nor heavy masses in the repulsion principle but only the inertia as such.

The extent of the linear deformation depends on the magnitude of the acceleration. The deformation by the curving force, on the other hand, depends on the radii of the bodies involved and of course on the distance to each other, a fact we have also realised already. The deformation by the pressure shadow is the direct consequence of the geometry of the fields!

The spatially oriented directions of the force and the curving forces lend special properties to the space, which is never empty but filled with T.A.O. and the impulse fields acting therein. The matrix of T.A.O. has no share in these properties as such – it is only the carrier medium of the impulses and impulse fields which are moving through it. These movements are "controlled" by the relations of the forces or the impulse densities ("energy contents") of the fields –

we already saw with the planetary movements how the fields of two celestial bodies influence each other and play - so to speak - ball with themselves and the universal pressure.

We already discussed the concepts space, energy, and impulse in fullest detail. From our simple example of the fan blade we know already that space and energy have a certain connection to each other and that a relation must have developed between them which is fundamental for the manifestation of our reality. The third factor of this universal relationship is time. In these relationships, it defines the velocities and hence the density of events as well as the polarisations or encounters of resistance of the impulses, it determines the frequencies, the vibrations or fluctuations – all these phenomena are events within a certain time, or rather: within the same intervals or separated by them. Maybe we should say interval instead of time, that would be more correct.

An inevitable problem is that we cannot perceive time with our sensory equipment, as we can for example perceive the expansion of the space or the energy of light – but time can only be measured in comparison to other physical processes, movement of pointers, running of sand, oscillation of atoms, etc. This is absolutely not so easy because real clocks measure everything but the "time".

Sun dials only show an angle to the sun. Pendulum clocks and hourglasses measure accelerations. Quartz-crystal clocks change their oscillational frequency when an acceleration deforms the quartz-crystals (Hook's law). With quantum-mechanical systems, the energy level driving the clock changes when the Hamiltonian operator, which causes the acceleration, is changed. When for example atoms are deflected in magnetic fields, the magnetic fields are detuning the transition frequencies. Even atomic clocks are subject to the physical conditions of the space, and naturally they don't measure time but velocities, movements, or frequencies.

And since this is the case, clocks – in fact all of them without any exception – are subject to the influences of the fields. Their operation is influenced by the density of impulses, by polarisations, and above all by geometries – namely by distortions, extensions, or curvatures! It is not an easy life for a "clock" in this scenario which we just created with pressure and shadow and curving force.

We will now take a closer look at the existence of a clock within our multifariously curved and shadowed spaces. For that purpose we design a "clock of light", i.e. a box in which we simply reflect a beam of light back and forth between top and bottom at an increment rate of one second; a good comparison when we think of the tiny spaces in which spherical fields oscillate or electron waves pulsate back and forth. And at that time we had of course already discovered that acceleration changes these spaces and that the atoms have to adapt to these altercations which – since it is not possible in an instant - creates inertia. But it also creates something else, as we will see in a moment: it changes the operation of clocks...

Fig. 131

When we are moving our boxed clock of light we see at once that the distances of the light are getting longer ... but that also extends the increment rate of a second (figure 131 – on the right). Our clock is suddenly operating slower. And since we already realised that this has to apply to all physical or atomic processes because of the internal causes for inertia, we can actually say in general: moved clocks go slower! We could also say: they "age" more slowly because the time seems to go by more slowly.

Of course, such a distinct kind of motion is not necessary to make clocks go slow. Since every kind of motion makes clocks go slower, this applies both to the acceleration of free fall in the field of gravitation and to the curving force which causes the effects of a force as well as an acceleration in the sense of deformation. Hence that means: clocks which are falling or clocks which are being deformed are also going slower. That is to say if our box is deformed to an egg shape on the vertical plane, the distance which the light has to cover becomes measurably longer as well. Hourglasses actually stop when they are falling down, what happens to pendulum clocks is easy to imagine – but the mentioned slowing-down factors affect all clocks. And of course not only clocks but all physical processes.

When these factors are weaker, i.e. when there is less acceleration or deformation (curving force), clocks (or physical processes) go faster. And what we are concluding now has actually been verified by measurement: clocks on the surface of the Earth go slower than clocks on mountain tops because the curving force and thus the deformation are lower on the mountain than on the ground. And even the acceleration of free fall (the ratio of universal pressure to Earth pressure) is lower. We could also say: the clock on the mountain top "ages" faster.[65]

Insiders have long since realised where our considerations are taking us. Already, the General Theory of Relativity is shining through all cracks. But before we jump right into the middle of things let's observe our clock of light for a little while longer. From observing the movements in the cosmos we know that gravitation can economise energy very well and obviously consumes almost none. In fact this is not quite true but the movements within gravitational fields seem to relate to the motto: saving energy at every cost, even if it takes longer. Of course, there is no intention behind it but the effect results because the deformation or acceleration inevitably gets into conflict with inertia and because the energy consumption agrees with the magnitude of inertia. Thus as little inertia as possible, because it saves energy and optimises for instance the movement of a planet around the sun to the force-free orbit, to the apparently eternal revolution.

On the ground our clock "ages" slower – and faster on the mountain top. But then it consumes less energy on the ground than on the mountain where its frequency is higher. Well, we already demanded: as little deformation as possible, as little energy consumption as possible, and everything as slow as possible because the oscillations of the atoms adapt to the spatial modifications all the easier...

On the surface of the Earth this does not work in such an ideal manner. Here the deformation is strongest, the acceleration of free fall is high. The forces of inertia require a high consumption of energy. In fact the clock "ages" slower but at a high cost in energy. That makes the mountain top more tempting. The curvature is weaker, and the acceleration of free fall and the inertia are lower as well... Besides, the clock "ages" very fast – but it still does not have an easy life despite all that because the energy consumption is not that small, neither. In addition there is the catch: somehow we have to get the clock to the mountain top! And when moving it to that place it is possible - as we found out – that it goes slower. Of course, we have to consider as well how long the clock remains on the mountain before it comes back.

We could define the desirable ideal condition as follows: the medium distance between the ground and the mountain top including the deterioration in the balance because of transporting it to the altitude. Therefore, we have to move the clock and to such an altitude that it is ticking, i.e. that it is "aging", as fast as possible with the lowest possible consumption of energy. We are thus striving for a maximum aging of the clock. If we, let's say, throw the clock up in such a way that it falls back after 2 seconds, we have to lend it such a speed that it rises exactly to an altitude of 4.90 metres[66] before it falls back.

In the balance of this mental experiment we see that the clock has aged "maximally" in this case, namely that it has achieved the optimum number of ticks at the slowest possible velocity and with the lowest possible energy consumption. Just the other way round, if we set the clock the task to rise for two seconds and turn back, it would be forced by the curving force and the pressure conditions to carry out exactly that motion which causes maximum ageing: it would rise to 4.90 metres and turn back there.

And for the same reasons a planet finds the ideal orbit around the sun, namely according to the principle of maximum ageing. Because this is the only way that it can - teleologically speaking - sufficiently defy the grip of the curved spaced on its "mass". The planet will thus not choose the direct way over the mountain top – but it will not fly around it either – the resulting way of optimum energy application will be a compromise – for example as shown in figure 131a. Of course, a planet does not "find" anything and it does not "choose" anything either but it is forced to take the easy way which will "deform" it the least – and that is the way between the two pressure forces or the two fields – that of the sun and that of the universe. And for reasons of deformation, an optimum velocity will result between these fields and the planet's own inertia, that is to say one that is as slow as possible – because a higher velocity would already cause a greater deformation again. We could say the planet is idle or lazy, and we could postulate the "principle of cosmic laziness "[67] because the planet presents the way which is easiest for it...

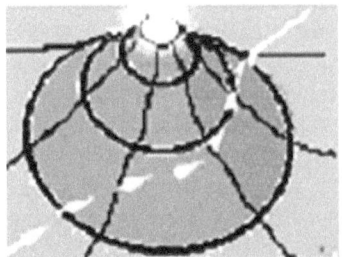

Fig. 131a

When we think of a clock instead of a planet, it will show us the way of maximum ageing because it evades the centre of the temporal mountain and denies the temporal valley at the edge – we could draw two different conclusions from that: either the clock changes its operation (which is the case) or the mass in the centre dilates time somehow – which would certainly be a bold assumption. When we now think of a metre rule instead of the clock which, as we know, contracts because of the inertia, we would measure a circuit around the centre with this metre rule. This circuit would be a bit bigger than the diameter would make us expect. If we did not know about the contraction of the metre rule, we could establish that obviously the space around the centre must have "expanded" – which is not correct in truth. But if we took the expansion of time and space as a starting point, we could soon find out that both effects could not exist independent of each other (E=space/time^2!), that time and space would always expand together (or curve or whatever) – and it would soon occur to us to use the simplified standard concept "space-time". In this way we could deduce the motion of the planets from one single basic assumption, namely from the expansion of space-time - which would be just as adroit as it would be misleading. Because we certainly know that the clock is really and truly going wrong and the metre rule is really and truly contracted. This thwarts the adroit standardisation and makes retardation or acceleration of clocks, changes in scales, and motions of bodies, etc. exist next to each other without any connection. And that in a space which - from a universal point of view - remains Euclidian but in which mass fields let their oscillations loose on each other in a spherical (or "curved") manner.

Well, in fact we have never lost track of the fundamentals of the repulsion principle and still we did not describe anything else but the scenario of the General Theory of Relativity. From that we selected the concepts "interval", "cosmic laziness", and "maximum ageing" and were able to integrate them into our ideas without any problems. Obviously Einstein demonstrated something very real with his GTR to that kind as if he had not noticed the players in a ball game and attributed the puzzling movements of the ball to the mysterious properties of space and time. In doing so he simplified these phenomena to space-time. We did not go so far because we discovered that there are really shortened metre rules and clocks which go wrong – and that this cannot have anything to do with either the properties of space nor with those of time. (By the way, it does not matter if one chooses the one or the other variant, both opinions explain the phenomena of gravitation without contradiction. In addition, in the GTR it is sometimes appropriate to consult both opinions when making calculations.)

For us, the players of the ball game, that is to say the extensive impulse fields of the apparent masses, are the true explanation for the movements of the ball. That Einstein could capture these movements in his equations without knowing the causal background is all the more an ingenious achievement considering that he based this theory on absolutely wrong fundamental assumptions. It is worthwhile to look at it from Einstein's perspective:

The General Theory of Relativity requires a completely new comprehension of space and time. When the physical space has been Euclidian until then (in Newton's mechanics) or at least flat (in the SToR), (almost) arbitrarily curved spaces are admitted in the GTR. In order to put this particular suitability into effect Einstein established a series of postulates. From the SToR he took the space-time concept as four-dimensional differentiable "manifold" and with that he generalised the Euclidian space. This space-time is curved by the presence of energy (e. g. in form of matter). This means that its internal geometry is changed – whatever this means. In any case all physical processes are influenced by this curvature.

Main foundation for Einstein's considerations was actually the postulate of equivalence of inert and heavy masses; this principle of equivalence is therefore an important supporting pillar of the GTR. Einstein discovered that acceleration and gravitation are undistinguishable in certain situations.

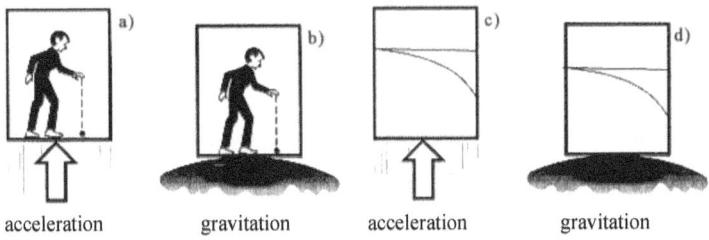

acceleration   gravitation   acceleration   gravitation

Fig. 131b

In an elevator accelerating upward (a), the same gravitational effects should occur as in a gravitational field (b). The passenger is allegedly not able to distinguish if the floor of the elevator approaches the "falling" object or if the object is attracted to the floor by a gravitational field. A beam of light (c) crossing the upward moving elevator describes a curve towards the floor – because of the equivalence principle the same is to be expected in the gravitational field (d).

Interestingly enough, these discoveries of Einstein are downright wrong. The passenger of the elevator is actually very well able to distinguish if he is in a gravitational field or not. For this purpose he only has to drop two objects to the ground (figure 131 c):

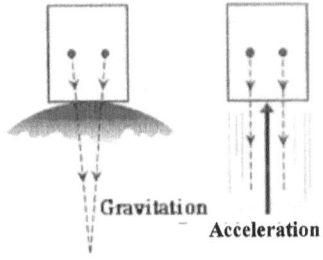

Gravitation   Acceleration

Fig. 131c

In the gravitational field of the Earth, the two objects would not fall down parallel but radially in direction to the centre of the Earth. Unlike the accelerating elevator, leads in the gravitational field would not hang down parallel. When one took notice of this contradiction, one got resourceful with the "excuse" that the elevator would have to be just small enough to make the leads appear to be parallel – for an exact science this is a rather sloppy argumentation.

There is no excuse for the fact that an accelerated, electrically charged sphere radiates, i.e. emits electromagnetic waves, whereas a similar sphere under the influence of a gravity field does not radiate. The equivalence principle thus applies to linear accelerations only in a restricted manner, with rotations (turns) Einstein's arguments fail completely, they are a guess at random – and hit the bull's eye because there cannot be a difference between inert and heavy mass at all since only the inertia exists.

Einstein's inappropriate conclusions prove that his GTR is a theory of gravitation fabricated through and through to lead to a certain objective. It would be a fruitful victim for Ockham's razor[68] for its many postulates alone. Because the calculation method introduced by Einstein, the differential geometry, contains a couple of unproven assumptions.

To start with, the metric tensor of space-time is not determined in the GTR, as it is in the SToR, but depends on the content of matter and energy of the space. This content is described by the energy-momentum tensor. The metric tensor is then determined by Einstein's field equations. Multiplication of the energy-momentum tensor with 8π produces the Einstein tensor, again a postulate of the first water. The next unfounded assumption is the hypothesis of the geodesic, namely the determination that pointed objects have to move on geodesic lines through space-time. In doing so massive objects move on time-like, objects without mass on light-like geodesic lines. A geodesic line is a locally straight curve, exactly the only generalisation of the straight line in curved spaces that makes sense geometrically. It is that path of motion on which no force acts upon moving bodies. Einstein, however, only transferred Newton's definition to the curved space – why (in both cases) no force is acting upon the body, he explained just a little as Newton. It results only from the resistance of deformation in our way of looking at things.

Despite their simple form, Einstein's field equations are a complicated system of non-linear, linked differential equations. Hence, their exact solution is only possible in very few special cases with strongly idealised assumptions. A generally analytical solution is practically impossible anyway. Since the GTR is, however, a theory of geometry, the solutions of the field equations for certain special cases can often only be obtained by geometric considerations.

From the few solutions, one managed to gain some at least very entertaining "insights" about the structure of space and time. Some of the better known solutions are the "Schwarzschild singularities", later named "black holes " by Wheeler and discovered by Karl Schwarzschild (1873–1916) already a few months after the publication of the GTR (today, one rather uses the Kerr metric with regard to the black holes). Based on an examination of stars in a globular cluster carried out in 1939 Einstein himself came to the conclusion:

"The essential result of this examination is a distinct comprehension of the fact why the Schwarzschild singularities do not exist in physical reality!"

The idea of the black holes was therefore not supported by Einstein himself. Neither have any ever been found ever. Yet everybody believes that they really exist. But he who really wants to know can of course travel into space for a couple of light years to check them out...[69]

Figure 131d shows the central area of the Andromeda galaxy (M31) in the visible light, photographed by the Hubble space telescope. The astronomers claim to have discerned a central black hole here with a mass of about 30 million solar masses which is orbited by stars.

Fig. 131d

In any case, the GTR is not a satisfactory explanation of gravitation but only a complicated method of calculation in which it is even impossible to speak of a strict, mathematical derivation at all because of the many arbitrary assumptions. Still, in an astonishing way it reflects a reality which remained hidden to Einstein. When the attractive force of two bodies is calculated by means of the GTR, the result is: no attraction! And that is exactly as it is!

Where is the decisive influence of the velocity of light on gravitation and inertia, which we discovered in the chapters "Inertia" and "Gravity"? We find it in the constant of integration r_s. It is a measure for the mass and has the dimension of a longitude. This constant is therefore also called gravitational mass or gravitational radius or rather gravitational Schwarzschild radius of the central body. It results from Newton's constant of gravitation γ, the velocity of light in vacuum c and Newton's mass m of the central body with the relation:

$$r_s = \frac{2\gamma m}{c^2}$$

This constant and many more which contain the second power of the velocity of light as well as the velocity of light itself are indispensable for the solution of Einstein's field equations. But that should not surprise us particularly.

Many authors assigned a variety of "errors" to the GTR. The spectrum ranges from violation of the laws of energy conservation, the use of mathematically unfounded constants (i= root of -1), violation of causality, use of pseudotensors, the lack of equations for energy up to the fact that the field equations were so general and complex that even writing errors would lead to solutions. Everybody is entitled to form his own opinion about that. Nowadays it is no problem to track down all these authors via the internet...

Einstein once classified his GTR in this way:

"The GTR has nothing to do with reality...!"

But it has. It describes a gravitational cause "from the inside", so to speak, which lies on the "outside" (just as Mach[70] suspected). Even if it reflects reality only geometrically so to speak, it is the best of all the gravitation theories offered so far even if it allows for incredible solutions, like black holes or the initial singularity of the Big Bang and cosmologic constructions like for instance the Friedmann-Robertson-Walker universe. By the way, we would also have to insert the differential geometry of the GTR for the mathematical description of the repulsion principle.

Neither the calculation of the perihelion advance of Mercury nor the deflection of light rays in the gravitational field of the sun are confirmations of the GTR. The ellipses of the planetary orbits revolve around the sun like a rosette, the effect is the most distinctive with Mercury and in the main goes back to the influence of the other planets, to the shape of the sun, which deviates from spherical, and to the solar oscillations (quadrupole moments). In 1966, Robert Dicke and H. Mark Goldenberg discovered the deviations of the sun from the ideal sphere and generated a discussion about Einstein's prediction which has been going on until today. In addition, Rudolf Nedved is said to have demonstrated that the mystery of the perihelion advance vanishes into thin air if the calculations are not made heliocentrically but barycentrically (relative to the centre of mass of the solar system). Moreover, the phenomena of curving time and space in the sphere of our solar system are so minute that one has to calculate with many approximations in the GTR – thus there's no complete denying the suspicion that Einstein prepared his result to achieve the values known at that time.

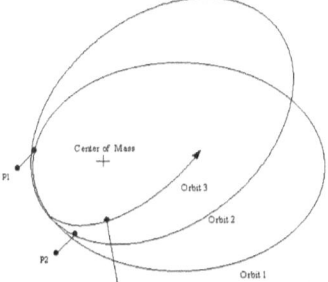

Fig. 131e

With the repulsion principle, the perihelion advance is explained in a similar manner as with the GTR. In doing so, we do not take the expansion of space as a starting point but the simple fact that the metre rule is contracted by inertia. Mercury maintained its impulse of motion by deformation. This does not only substantiate that Mercury is subjected to the field of the sun and to the curving force a little longer but also stands in the way of its own rotation which is therefore very slow. In one Mercury year of 88 Earth days, Mercury rotates exactly three times on its own axis in the same time it takes to revolve around the sun twice. The tidal force of the sun and the impulse of motion of the orbit hold Mercury in this 3:2 rotation.

The perihelion advance of Mercury is already so low that one has to be really astonished at the achievement of Joseph Leverriers (1811 – 1877) who calculated it. In principle it exists with the other planets but it is substantially lower. The GTR fails completely in calculating these disturbances of the orbit. According to Einstein's own calculation, Venus and Mars had no perihelion advance – which was wrong, though. But the magnitude of the disturbances were not yet known at that time – a further indication that the GTR is an absolutely purposeful (teleological) theory.

Even according to Einstein the deflection of the beams of light by the gravitational force of the sun is of course not caused by gravitation but by the expansion of space and time. With the repulsion principle, this effect also goes without saying. The space created by the spherical repulsion forces is logically enough spherical, i.e. curved. All of the electromagnetic propagation processes get caught in this geometry – even the light. Worthless is, however, the "proof" of the deflection of light yielded by Arthur Eddington on the occasion of a solar eclipse in 1919. Aside from the fact that the events surrounding this provision of a proof are suspicious (some authors claim, Eddington had fibbed) and that the lousy photographs produced at that time do not allow an evaluation in favour of the GTR, it could have been a simple diffraction of the light in the vicinity of the sun's surface, especially since the corona of the sun is not homogenous but is composed of several layers. Besides it is very hot, an exact localisation of a beam of light becomes impossible because of that.

Fig. 131f

Figure 131f shows a curved beam of light, as we can produce it on our own by means of two different layers (common table salt and water).[71] A laser beam sent into the boundary area of the two layers is diffracted by the different refractive indices. Similar processes are also possible in the solar atmosphere.

The confirmation of the GTR by means of a radar reflection experiment that Irwin Shapiro conducted with the planet Venus seemed to be much better. The time which a radar signal requires for the distance to Venus and back can be transformed in an effective distance by dividing the time by 2 and multiplying it with c. If light was deflected by the gravitational effect, the velocity of the light would have to be influenced by that as well, Shapiro thought and found in Eddington's text book about the classical General Relativity that the velocity of light could actually change in accordance with the equations of the GTR (which is in contradiction to the SToR). According to the GTR, a radar signal reflected by Venus and travelling by close to the surface of the sun would have to take slightly longer for its journey. After several unsuccessful attempts, Shapiro managed to measure a retardation of the radar signal which corresponded to an apparent prolongation of the distance of about 38 km (over a total distance of about 260 million kilometres!). It had to be attributed to the curvature of space or rather to a reduction of the scale since a retardation of the light was of course out of the question according to the SToR. Shapiro's experiment with Venus (and similar ones with Mars) is, however, no reason for premature cheering. For what exactly did Shapiro actually prove? He proved that a radar signal which was sent to Venus and was reflected there comes back with a little retardation. The reason for retardation can be picked. One could even prove our repulsion theory with it. One can prove any theory with it which predicts a retardation of the returning radar signal for what reason ever.

As one can imagine, Shapiro's experiments and similar ones by other scientists were not so easy. One had to take a bearing on the planets (apart from Venus, Mars and Mercury were also "used") and in doing so their proper movements and also the perturbations by other planets had to be considered. This required complicated astronomical calculations which had to be very exact. He who suspects that this had been accomplished with the ultra-modern, unfailing GTR is very much mistaken because for that purpose, one only consulted of course good old Newton...

Many authors claim that the GTR is a further development of the Special Theory of Relativity (SToR) – which is absolutely wrong. Except for adopting the concept of space-time, the GTR has absolutely nothing in common with the SToR. Compared to the GTR, which gives rise to the supposition of a certain possibility for practical use after all (at least corrections in technical applications are appropriate because of wrongly operating clocks, as for example with the Global Positioning System – GPS)[72], the SToR is only a nice academic exercise since an accordance with reality is not immanent in its system at all. Besides, we will demonstrate at the end of this chapter that the two theories of relativity are so completely different that they cannot even be derived from each other mathematically and are even mutually exclusive.

The "refutations" of the SToR have made a lot of ink flow on this world. The religious war between relativists and followers of a different faith refers mainly to the SToR for the reason that the GTR is apparently too complicated and too uncomprehended for the opponents in the discussion. And common sense has substantially greater problems with the SToR as well. Let's therefore take a closer look at the SToR and let's say in advance that we already found two of Einstein's postulates confirmed in our considerations: the impossibility to exceed the velocity of light in vacuum and the independence of light from its source.[110]

From the properties of T.A.O. we derived an unequivocal definition of light as electromagnetic "apparent wave"- as a temporal sequence of impulses which do not influence each other, at least not when following one another. Since each of these impulses is not "connected" with its source but becomes and remains independent, the necessary motion of the source does not play a role for the motion of the impulses. That means: the impulse is not aware of the motions of the source. But the motion of the source has its influence on the temporal and spatial sequence of several impulses since the distances between the impulses can be shorter or longer. In any case, every single impulse moves at the velocity characteristic for it, which is also the same for every impulse under the same conditions.

At Einstein's time, such a definition was not known. Light appeared to be a succession of corpuscles; and one expected that these corpuscles were to receive the velocity of their source. On the other hand some physicists already had the suspicion that light could be some kind of wave; in this case, however, the question remained unanswered through which medium this wave was moving. Following a tried and tested method, one simply assumed such a medium and called it "ether". The ether was considered to be some kind of fixed something, and for the time being the velocity of light was referred to this medium in which the planets and stars were also moving around. When the velocity of light was a constant quantity with regard to the ether, it had to be expected that the velocity of an observer could be added to or subtracted from this quantity.[73]

Constant velocity of light 300 000 km/s----------->

<---------- velocity of the Earth 30 km/s

When the Earth was moving towards the light of a star at 30 km/s, the velocity of the star light travelling past should be increased by these 30 km/s whereas it had to be reduced by 30 km/s in the opposite direction - in fact always measured from the Earth, simply for the reason that velocities can be added to or subtracted from one another in general after all.

The physicist Michelson devised an instrument by means of which - he thought – he would be able to prove the differences in the velocity of light caused by the motion of the Earth. To his astonishment, however, it was revealed that obviously the light of the stars always passed the Earth by at 300 000 km/s, no matter if the Earth was moving towards the light or was flying along in the same direction.

It is actually not relevant for the SToR if Einstein knew Michelson's experiment or if he didn't because the origin of the SToR lies in electrodynamics as we will demonstrate. But since the general public believes Michelson's experiment had causally to do with the SToR, we will begin our considerations with regard to the results of this experiment and demonstrate that this experiment was unsuitable for any kind of interpretation and that it could neither confirm nor refute the SToR.

If it is impossible according to this experiment to add the velocity of light to or subtract it from other velocities, the light has evidently the absolutely strange property to be independent of both the source and the observer. In the consequence this leads to strange paradoxes, as for example in the following case: a source of light is travelling in a railway wagon, it stands exactly in the middle, and a fellow passenger is asked if the light reaches both the front wall and the rear wall of the wagon at the same time. According to the result of Michelson's experiment, the observer will have no doubt of that because he knows that the motion of the wagon has no influence on the light. Thus he will say: "The light of the lamp reaches the front and the rear wall of the wagon at the same time because it doesn't matter to me if the wagon is moving or not. Probably I don't even know if it is!"

A possible observer on the outside who is able to look into the wagon, however, made exactly the same experience with the light. He, too, sees the light pouring from the lamp at the same time; but he also sees that the wagon is moving and that its front wall is running away from the light whereas the rear wall is coming towards the light. Therefore he will have to say that the light cannot reach the front and the rear wall at the same time.

Both observers have to stick to Einstein's postulate and with that they are getting into blatant conflict with each other. Einstein thought the fiasco could only be solved by assuming that the conditions for measuring the length of the wagon had changed because of its motion and therefore the wagon had to be of different length for the two observers. That means translating the dimensions of the wagon from the moving system to the system of the outside observer results in a foreshortening which makes it possible for the outside observer to get to the same temporal result as the passenger in the train. For that reason, Einstein concluded that moving bodies foreshortened in the direction of movement...

Of course that is not easy to comprehend. But Michelson's experiment seemed to confirm exactly this assumption. The American physicist was probably preceding from following consideration (figure 132).

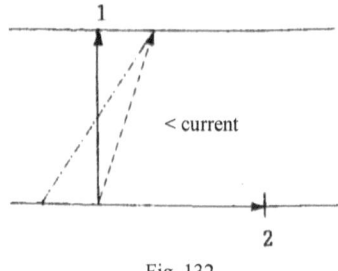

Fig. 132

Of two swimmers which are equally good, one is to swim across the river and back and the other is to swim a similarly long distance upstream and back downstream. The first one has to win, in fact by the time difference of

$$\Delta t = \frac{L}{c}\frac{v^2}{c^2}$$

in case both are swimming at a velocity c and the river is flowing at v. Let's make this more clear by using assumed figures: swimmer's velocity 20 m/s; current of the river 10 m/s; distance 100 m. Swimmer 1 has to take an angle against the current (dotted line) to actually reach his destination. We calculate his velocity to Galileo's addition theorem with

$$t = \frac{L}{(c^2-v^2)^{\frac{1}{2}}} = \frac{200}{17{,}320508} \approx 11{,}54 \sec$$

Swimmer 2 swims the first 100 m against the current and the river reduces his velocity by 10 m/s. For that reason, he requires for this distance

100:10= 10 seconds.

But on his way back the river adds 10 m/s to his velocity; hence

100:30= 3,33 seconds.

His total time is 13,33 seconds. He has lost!

When the swimmers are replaced with two beams of light, the water with the ether and the river bank with the Earth, one has apparently a complete analogy to Michelson's experiment. Measuring the difference in time would have to allow for determining the velocity at which the ether passes the Earth by or at which the Earth moves through the ether. Since the Earth has certainly different velocities at two opposite points of its orbit around the sun (difference 60 km/s), at least in summer or in winter there should be a difference in time at an order of magnitude that can be measured by optical instruments with absolute certainty.

For that reason, Michelson designed a cleverly devised instrument (figure 133).

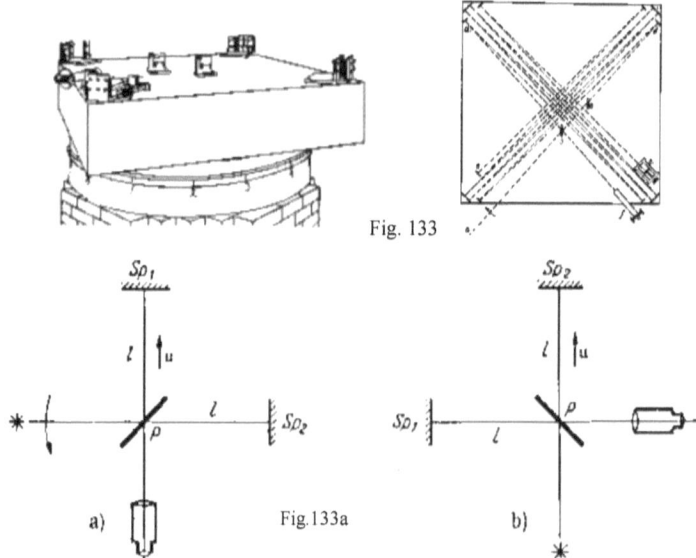

Fig. 133

Fig.133a

a)   b)

By means of a half-transparent mirror (P) he divided a beam of light into two beams moving in two mutually perpendicular directions and reflected them back onto themselves just in accordance with the example of the swimmers. A difference in the optical path lengths of the beams would have to show in the telescope into which the two beams of light were falling. An arm length of 25 metres would result in a difference in the optical path lengths of half the wavelength of green light (500 nm) between the two half beams which would have to annihilate each other away by interference because of that. This difference should shift to the other arm when the instrument was turned and would be proved by the shifting of interference fringes.

The experiment went off negatively. No matter if summer or winter or how Michelson turned his instrument, there was always only a minute shifting in the interference fringes which was far below the calculated value and which Michelson attributed to the influence of the Earth's magnetic field. The light seemed to be equally fast in any direction. Even an experiment with the light of the stars failed. And that although the Earth is moving through space at the incredible speed of 30 kilometres per second...

The physicist Lorentz developed a theory which was based on the assumption that the arm in direction of motion was subject to linear contraction, the so-called Lorentz contraction. Lorentz could actually demonstrate that a system of electric charges contracts exactly by the amount in question in the direction of motion. Therefore, only the plausible assumption would have been actually necessary that all matter eventually consists of electric charges in order to explain the negative results of the experiment.

In our considerations about the inertia we discovered that a moving body is really contracting, and Lorentz's idea was not so bad at all seen from that point of view. In reality, however, this contraction only occurs with acceleration – i.e. for instance on the surface of the Earth - since rotations are always accelerated motions. The SToR, however, refers only to unaccelerated, linear motions. For that reason, we have to look for a different argument. Could it be that Michelson has made a mistake and that the result of his experiment does not have any meaningfulness at all?

Actually, Michelson only wanted to verify the existence of the ether with his light experiment and did not particularly worry about the properties of the light. If regarded as a particle (photon) or as a wave, light was just something which had a velocity just like the Earth. What one has not realised correctly at that time and up to today is the fact that there wasn't any object flying on the path in question in Michelson's experiment and that he shouldn't have expected from the start that the velocity of light could be added or subtracted according to Galileo's addition theorem.

When we define the light as a totally independent impulse, this impulse forms an independent system which is even absolute in the ideal case (vacuum). With that falls Einstein's first principle of relativity, namely that there are no means to measure absolute velocities. Because there are such means! The central point of a sphere of light remains unshakably fixed in space and time; it is really at rest, no matter if its source is moving or not. When it is moving, it continuously creates further spheres whose central points are strung together on the line of movement of the source[110] (figure 134).

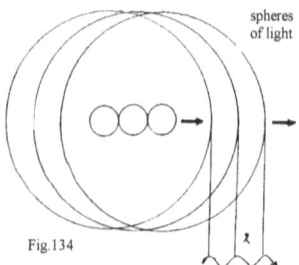

Fig.134

If this was not the case, there wouldn't be a Doppler effect since it is exactly this stringing together of the spheres, which involves the temporal transposition of impulses. To define it exactly, every singly impulse has its own sphere and its own central point. The wave develops from several impulses which follow each other but are not created in the same place when the source is moving. In this case, the frequency of the impulse alters immediately and the motion of the source is distinctly revealed in this alteration. The spheres of light standing absolutely in space can be taken as reference points for measuring the velocity as has even been done meanwhile with the background radiation of the universe and with that one could measure the movement of our galaxy unequivocally![74]

Since a moving galaxy "draws" its spheres of light into the universe, we can establish both this motion and the velocity, which is also called escape velocity with regard to the expansion of the universe.

If we are able to establish the escape velocity of a galaxy because of the Doppler frequency shift (the so-called red shift) why is it impossible for the galaxy itself to establish its velocity by means of its own light? Let's take a look at the situation in a figure (135):

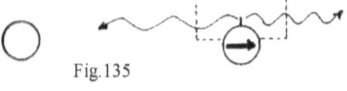

Fig.135

A lamp in this galaxy would distinctly shows us the Doppler effect. This would not be possible for an observer on the galaxy because his moving along with the galaxy would annihilate the effect. After all, he would have to put up - let's assume two - walls (broken lines in the figure), one of them coming towards the enlarged wavelength, the other fleeing from the reduced wavelength. The result would of course be: no discernable Doppler shift on the walls.

The compensation of the spherical shift on the walls certainly implies the fact that the velocity of the impulses has to be different in both directions relative to the galaxy. And it is possible for every light-emitting body to derive its motion exactly from this difference.

Let's put it down again: every single impulse sphere which is created in the universe remains fixed to its place of creation. The Earth moves out of this sphere - the light "is therefore left behind" and on no account does it get the speed of the Earth added to its own like a bullet. This state of "being left behind" corresponds approximately to the expansion in an absolute ether - the idea of a universal sea was therefore not so bad at all. We know what this medium consists of: it consists of the fields of the matter which extend into T.A.O. far beyond the visible....

But why did this possibility escape Michelson's notice? Because his experiment - and similar ones by other physicists - was unsuitable to reveal the "being left behind" of single spheres of light. For example one had to believe that a light signal which is incident on a mirror at the velocity c-v is reflected at the velocity c+v, which is not exactly an assumption that goes without saying. Since the angles of reflection at the mirrors do not correspond to the laws of reflection due to the fact that the light "is left behind", the analogy of the swimmers is absolutely misguided. But let's take a closer look at it again (figure 132):

The swimmer follows a certain direction which results from his destined direction and from the fact that the flowing river makes corrections to his direction bringing him to the right destination. He swims at a certain angle against the current; according to Galileo's addition theorem when reaching the destination a speed is the result which there actually existed relative to the destination over the distance covered by swimming.

With the light, things are completely different (figure 133a): the place of creation of the sphere remains fixed while the destination is moving away. When mirror P is adjusted in such a way that it is hit by the reflected beam, the beam is coming from the place where the mirror was (!) when it reflected the light. When the light is directed from mirror P to the mirror, one has to direct the light to that place where this mirror will be (!) when the light reaches it. It is quite necessary that we visualise this again in more detail (figure 136):

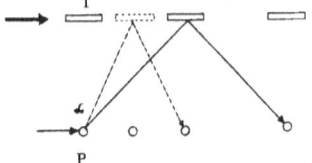

Fig. 136

When sighting at mirror 1, angle α is automatically given once since the image of the mirror needs time to reach P. When angle α is added again, since one has to aim at the future place of the mirror, one has actually used the angle two times (!) for one distance.

Hence the path of the light is: from where mirror P was to where mirror 1 will be. Whereas the swimmer knows only one imaginary point (either start or finish) and is therefore using angle α only once per distance, the light moves from one imaginary point to the next imaginary point – in doing so the angle is applied twice. All in all four times over the whole distance (to and back),. The complicated theory of Michelson's experiment, on the other hand, proceeded on the assumption that there was a regular reflection at the mirrors according to the laws of reflection – it was, however, essentially smaller.

Therefore Michelson's expectations were wrong to begin with. The difference of the interference fringes actually to be achieved had to be much smaller. Since the occurring Doppler effects also annihilated each other again correctly, there was nothing to gain in this direction, either. Neither was there any exciting shift in the interference fringes to be expected when turning the instrument since the speed of the light had to turn out quite the same for both arms.[75]

Michelson only concluded from his experiment that the ether did not exist. But actually his interferometer could not have been able to prove this either. The physicist was well aware of the weakness of his experiment, and in later years he disapproved of Einstein's conclusions very much.

And this experimental weakness would certainly not have escaped Einstein's notice. Therefore it has to be assumed that he didn't care much for Michelson's experiment when he developed his SToR. Because there was quite a different physical problem.

As we already discovered in the chapter "Games", a magnetic field is always produced without any exception around a current-carrying conductor or around a moving charge. And when we contemplate such a charge and don't move it, it will occur to us that exactly in this moment we are rotating together with the Earth at about 1600 kilometres per hour and that the Earth itself is dashing around the sun at 30 km/s... That means, the motionless charge is anything else than that – a priori it is a moving charge – but oddly enough it does not create a magnetic field now. Only when we move it – relatively to what? – the expected magnetic field develops. That is really quite strange.

And it is getting even stranger yet: in 1905, Einstein describes the dilemma in his article *"Zur Elektrodynamik bewegter Körper"* (*"On the Electrodynamics of Moving Bodies"*) as follows: "It is known that Maxwell's electrodynamics - as usually understood at the present time - when applied to moving bodies, leads to asymmetries which do not appear to be inherent in the phenomena. Take, for example, the reciprocal electrodynamic action of a magnet and a conductor. The observable phenomenon here depends only on the relative motion of the conductor and the magnet, whereas the customary view draws a sharp distinction between the two cases in which either the one or the other of these bodies is in motion. For if the magnet is in motion and the conductor at rest, there arises in the neighbourhood of the magnet an electric field with a certain definite energy, producing a current at the places where parts of the conductor are situated. But if the magnet is stationary and the conductor in motion, no electric field arises in the neighbourhood of the magnet. In the conductor, however, we find an electromotive force, to which in itself there is no corresponding energy, but which gives rise - assuming equality of relative motion in the two cases discussed - to electric currents of the same path and intensity as those produced by the electric forces in the former case." *(Translation by W. Perrett and G.B. Jeffery, 1923, Methuen and Company, Ltd. of London)*

Although modern relativists have long since admitted that the Michelson- Morley experiment is unsuitable as a secured basis for the SToR to be exact, the fact that the motion of the Earth does not have any influence on the phenomena of electrodynamics is a bit more hairy for the opponents of the SToR. In contrast to the laws of Newton's mechanics, the Maxwell equations[76] of electrodynamics do not fulfil Galileo's principle of relativity, they do not behave invariantly towards the Galilean transformations. Therefore one believed that the Maxwell equations were a feature of a special inertial system (the "ether system" to be exact), and one hoped to be able to prove it by means of a variety of ether drift experiments. But since all of these experiments were unsuccessful, one finally set about modifying the laws of mechanics ("relativistic mechanics"). It is also possible to describe the correlation like that: When the principle of relativity applies to this effect that all inertial systems moving uniformly against one another have the same rights, then a set of linear transformations which contains, however, a free parameter yet applies between these systems. This parameter has the significance of a velocity which has the same value in all inertial systems. When it is set to "infinite" one gets to the Galilean transformations, when it is equalled to c, one gets to the Lorentz transformations. It turned out that obviously the Lorentz-invariantly formulated laws of nature are more suitable.

But we know (on the basis of the repulsion principle developed in this book) that the moving charge of which we have talked previously, is already generating an electric field around it when still in a motionless state. This electric field lasts beyond the range of perception as "continuation" of the matter field, is polarised and moves along with the charge (the centre of the field) (fig. 21a). This field is continuously regenerated by impulses. When the causing charge is motionless relative to the motion of the Earth, it is impossible to establish the motion of the Earth neither by means of the charge nor by means of a succession of spheres of light which pulsate away from a stationary lamp because Doppler effects always annihilate each other through the measuring process (fig. 135). If the central points of the spheres are fixed absolutely (light) or fixed to the Earth (E-field) in this case doesn't make a big difference when one tries to measure the different properties in drift experiments. It's funny that the deformations of the electric charges occurring absolutely because of the high velocities are explained with the SToR although it is just a "normal" phenomenon. [77]

In order to achieve a magnetic field we therefore have to move the charge relative to its electric field. As described in the chapter "Games", in doing so we "blur" the polarisation into a different direction, and these are exactly the lines of force of the magnetic field. And since we know that every material phenomenon is of an electromagnetic nature, we could not find any reason for having to integrate the electrodynamics of moving bodies into the Galileo-Newton principle of relativity by force by means of a theory which relativises time and space because it has never stood outside of it. And of course it would be a mistake to apply the Maxwell equations absolutely uninhibited to the electromagnetic fields of electrodynamics as well as to the spreading of the spheres of light. Both is in fact an electromagnetic phenomenon but after all so is every grain of sand of this universe, too!

The difference between light and other electromagnetic phenomena can be explained like that: when we compare the universe with the ocean, the light is the play of waves on this ocean; material electromagnetic fields, on the other hand, are the play of waves in the swimming-pool of the luxury liner which is crossing the ocean...

The velocity of light can turn out thoroughly differently relative to the observer. The absolute impossibility to exceed it is given because it depends on the carrier matrix (T.A.O.) and on the fields in the universe with the "vacuum" - provided that it really exists –just determining the upper limit. We already described this in detail and demonstrated the causes. Relative superluminal velocities are, on the other hand, quite possible as the black night sky around us proves. It has always been odd that Einstein's Special Theory of Relativity only applies to linear motions. Rotations are excluded. It is easy to prove that the circumference of the universe revolves around us at several times the velocity of light when we are turning around unhurriedly only once...

It is interesting that even intelligent people are infected by a kind of mental handicap when they come in contact with the SToR. Nigel Calder describes the following thought experiment in chapter 15 of his book "Einstein's Universe":

Einstein inferred another curious effect concerning the speed of light. When the speeds of objects approach the speed of light you cannot add them together in the obvious way. Picture two galaxies rushing away from Earth at seventy-five per cent of the speed of light, in opposite directions. Simply adding the speeds would suggest that they are travelling away from each other at 1 1/2 times the speed of light. In that case, you might think the one must be invisible from the other, because light passing between them could never catch up. But it is easy to see that they are still in contact, in principle. For example, one of them could send a message to the other, if need be by way of the Earth. The speeds of the galaxies relative to the Earth do not affect the speed of a signal.

Sitting on the Earth we could receive the signal from galaxy A that reads: "Warmest greetings on Einstein's birthday. Please pass on to galaxy B". So then we send off a message that reads: "Galaxy A sends you greetings on Einstein's birthday." We know that it can eventually get to its destination because we can also *see* galaxy B. But even if we and the Earth were not there (or were asleep when the message came) you can still imagine galaxy A's message whizzing past the Earth's position in space without any intervention on our part, and eventually arriving at galaxy B. So adding the speeds gives the wrong answer: the speed at which A and B are moving apart must to them seem *less* than the speed of light, otherwise no such message could pass.

What is the explanation here? We have to figure out what the speed of galaxy B seems to be from the point of view of galaxy A. If that came out at something greater than the speed of life, then the two galaxies would indeed be mutually *incommunicado*. To find the answer, the relativist divides the simple sum of the speeds by a certain factor, (...) which takes account of the slowing time, as judged by us, in the two galaxies. – End of quote.

Only for relativists can this example be a challenge to start brooding. Since the relative superluminal speed is forbidden to them, they can only solve the problem by means of tricks in calculating. But although Nigel Calder is not exactly an opponent of Einstein, he should have seen how absurd his mental experiment was – apart from the fact that the SToR would not be applicable in the universe anyway because of the existing gravitational effects, it would not have to be applied either since a signal sent into absolute space by galaxy A is travelling at the speed of light and can therefore catch up with galaxy B which is flying at 75% of the speed of light without any problems! Of course with the corresponding Doppler modification... Besides the Doppler effect offers galaxy B the possibility to determine the relative speed between the two galaxies. Since galaxy B can measure its own absolute speed by means of the background radiation [74], it is also possible to calculate the speed of galaxy A. And with that we can finally consider the SToR to be an aesthetical hobby.

But since it is so much fun to reduce the SToR to absurdity piquantly enough by means of the GTR, here is something else to think about:

Since the GTR seems to be closer to reality and since we found it even confirmed in a certain way (because at least the geometry of the gravitational effect is quite correct), we should also verify if the SToR justifies its existence at all in our world governed by the universal pressure or if our world is compatible with "Einstein's universe" (GTR) at all. But let's leave aside the usual subtleties about the inertial systems and establish straight away that the gravitation does not occur in the SToR at all. But why not? Because the incompatibility with reality (or with the GTR) would immediately come to light. In fact for following reason:

First of all let's make a note of the point that in the GTR even photons are subject to a red shift due to gravitation because of the equivalence principle: when we send a photon to the ceiling in an elevator which is uniformly accelerated upwards, it will arrive there red shifted because of the Doppler effect. According to the equivalence principle, a frame of reference in the sphere of influence of gravitation cannot to be distinguished locally from a uniformly accelerated frame of reference. For that reason, this red shift must also occur in gravitational fields. In the Special Theory of Relativity, however, such a red shift can never occur. Let's take a look at following diagram for that purpose (fig. 136):

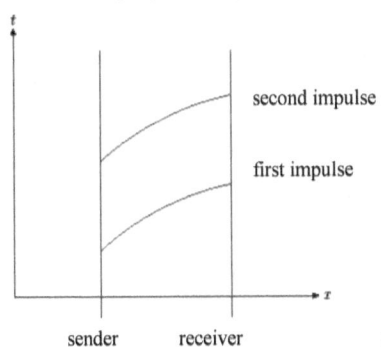

Fig. 136

We see the emission of two light pulses in the coordinates time (t) and path (x). The curvature of the two lines shows the assumed effect of gravitation on the impulses. The second impulse has to move on a curve which resembles that of the first impulse because the situation is static, i.e. it does not change in the course of time. With that the second curve corresponds exactly to a temporal displacement of the first curve. The temporal difference between two impulses and with that the frequency of the light is thus of the same magnitude with sender and receiver. Hence the existence of a red shift is impossible. Since the red shift has been proved in experiments meanwhile, though, our considerations show that the definition of the temporal distance in the SToR is doubtful in the presence of gravitation which can only be due to the fact that the temporal difference at the receiver would have to be calculated in a way different to that at the sender. With that, however, the geometry of the space would also be different in both places according to the GTR since the measurement of time in space-time corresponds to the measurement of length in common spaces. Thus the flat space of the SToR does not correspond with reality in the presence of gravitational effects. The absence of gravitational effects, however, is just as unthinkable within our universe as the existence of an absolute vacuum...

The GTR allegedly comprises the SToR as special case in two respects:

1. With an empty space the GTR results in the space-time structure of the SToR (Minkowski space). An empty space, though, does only exist in absence of the universe.

2. In freely falling frames of reference, the laws of the SToR apply locally. A spaceship orbiting around the Earth, for instance, would be such a freely falling frame of reference. According to the equivalence principle, astronauts should not be able to detect the existence of a gravitational field. But they are! For the same reasons which we found in the elevator (figure 131c). Two objects hovering above one another in the spaceship would move away from each other as if guided by a mysterious force since different orbit parameters would apply to each of them.

Relativists have many calculating tricks at the ready to preserve their dearly beloved SToR into the world of the GTR. The very smallest inertial systems of all patched together or insignificantly weak gravitational fields and suchlike.[78] They like to mark the SToR as excellently supported by experiment and come up with experiments which do often not hold out against a closer analysis, though.[79] If one demands proofs, on the other hand, they are the first ones to point out that one can never prove a theory but confirm or refute it at best.

It is popular to cite the SToR in connection with charged particle accelerators. But the impossibility to exceed the velocity of light applies also for accelerated "particles" because the "dominos principle" of the T.A.O. matrix does not permit a faster propagation of the impulses. If we had issued the postulate of the constancy of c on the basis of these insights, we could provide the fact that it is impossible to accelerate electrons up to c as a proof for the T.A.O. matrix - apart from the fact that there can also be other reasons for the behaviour of the electrons are also possible (the speed-dependent increase of inertia with electrons was already examined by W. Kaufmann in 1901).

And what about the muons and the much stressed argument of their extended life time because of the high speed? Let's take a look at it:

In the cosmic radiation, certain "particles" are found as components of the penetrating radiation that arrives on the surface of the Earth - and this is exactly what they are expected not to be. One knows them from laboratory experiments, actually they are "heavy electrons"; their correct name is muons. They are unstable particles and decay with a half-life value of ca. $1.5*10^{-6}$ seconds.

In the year 1941, when B. Rossi and Dr. B. Hall carried out an experiment with these muons, they believed to know the following about these particles:

- Muons are produced in proton-proton collisions at great altitudes (15-30 km).
- After a very short time they decay into one electron (or positron) and into one neutrino and one antineutrino.
- Since they are produced by cosmic radiation, the main component of their motional direction in the atmosphere is pointing downwards. Their velocity reaches almost light speed.

Based on these assumptions following considerations were made: it is possible to note the impact time of a muon with detectors and observe its decay. This decay of the muon which is retarded and thus coming to rest is recorded. The temporal intervals between impact and decay can be determined statistically with a sufficiently high number of muons; hence it is possible to establish how many of the muons are lost through decay when they travel a certain distance during a certain period of time. When the number of impacting muons is measured on a mountain top and afterwards at sea level, there shouldn't actually be any muons left at sea level because they don't exist long enough for such a long distance.

The experiment was carried out, and the result revealed that far more muons were left than had to be expected. From that it was concluded that muons lived in a "dilated " time because of their high velocity, and the experimental evidence of the time dilatation had been provided. But the credibility of this evidence stands or falls by the nature of the observed muons.

When muons are approximately flying at the velocity of light, half of their initial number decays after about 450 meters because of their half-life value. Of the remaining half, another half decays after another 450 meters, and so on. After a distance of about 2000 metres only 17 to 25 muons are effectively left when 568 muons per hour were detectable in the beginning - as was the case in this experiment. Theoretically we won't find any more muons after 4500 meters. From a relativistic point of view, however, this distance may be incredibly extended. A difference in altitude of 2000 meters should not make any difference at all. But above all: the mass of the muons would have to increase eminently as defined by the Theory of Relativity, in fact from 207 electron masses to 1467 electron masses - that would be nearly the mass of a nucleon already. This mass corresponds to a high energy which has to be picked up. In the cited experiment iron plates of a certain thickness were used which only admitted muons of a very particular energy content for measuring. This was done in the same way both at 2000 meters and at sea level, in fact with meticulous precision. But already the question arises if such heavy particles really have the same speed over the complete distance they cover or if they are also subject to a continuous acceleration like every falling body. That this is the case seems to suggest itself - but then a completely different family of muons was measured at 2000 metres than at sea level! That means even when acknowledging the StoR, the experiment can be doubted. But the SToR is not responsible for accelerations at all.

The solution of the problem is probably even more simple. In order to refute the experiment, it is sufficient to prove that muons can come into existence in different ways and at different heights. Well, there really exist several disintegration channels which lead to the muon. All of them can be found in cosmic radiation. Not only muons are created through proton-proton shoves on any account but pions and kaons as well. These two particles also decay into muons but after different times. The ("positive") pion has a half-life value of $1.8*10^{-8}$ seconds; the kaon (it occurs regularly together with muons) lives on average $8.56*10^{-9}$ seconds - and in addition there is also a neutral kaon which decays into a positive pion after $4*10^{-8}$ seconds. The pion in turn - see above - can decay into muons. All times mentioned are half-life values; we did not list all the other particles which are also produced in these processes of decay because they are of no importance here. We see: in truth the matter is not just as simple as the gentlemen Rossi and Hall imagined it to be. The possibilities to get muons are more numerous than they thought. And for that reason, muons are also a main component of cosmic radiation at sea level.

The stumbling block of the much stressed "muon evidence" is therefore called KAON (also named K meson). Well, there is a particular explanation for this kaon which provides us so willingly with muons - in fact also on the surface of the Earth: it is a so-called strange particle. Strange because it would actually have to be stable according to the particle physics' principles of conservation, and according to the "principle of conserving the strangeness " it should on no account decay into muons. It happens nevertheless. But with that its half-life value is a most unreliable value. It should also be mentioned that kaons are created wherever and whenever high-energy mesons collide with nucleons.

Why, actually, did the physicists Rossi and Hall not take these peculiar events surrounding the Kaon into consideration? Very simple: they carried out their legendary experiment in 1941. The kaon (K meson), however, was not discovered until 1947 by W. M. Powell.[80]

In a very indirect way, the muon evidence can also be duplicated in the laboratory. The results with regard to this are, however, very disputed. The authors Georg Galecki and Peter Marquardt[81] went to a lot of trouble in this respect to pick this and other proofs for the SToR to pieces but of course that can also have been a waste of effort. In the repulsion principle we also discovered that moved clocks or clocks in the gravitational field go slower. And we also realised that atomic oscillation processes are clocks, in a certain way. So when muons distribute their energy over a longer distance due to high velocity because their wavelengths are "extended" and therefore create the impression that they would "live" longer it does not automatically provide evidence for the StoR – it simply proves that clocks in motion are just as unreliable as hot or cold clocks, un-oiled and defective clocks or clocks going sloppy for any other reason. How should we find a standard for the "right" operation of a clock at all? It has nothing to do with time. Time is an operand which can neither be prolonged nor dilated nor curved.

If one puts two modern atomic clocks in two airplanes and flies off with them into different directions, both clocks will go wrong but to a different extent, namely depending on the direction of the flight - which does actually not correspond exactly to Einstein's theories. One celebrated the result of such an experiment conducted by J.C. Hafele and R.E. Keating in the year 1971 as confirmation of the Theories of Relativity – but it is only confirmation for the fact that atomic clocks, just like any other material or electromagnetic field, are subject to inertia against the absolute matrix of T.A.O.[82] Our observations only differ from the postulates of the ToR with respect to the propagation of light which we consider to be absolute. An indication to that is provided by an effect which is called aberration of the stars and was first described by Bradley in 1725.

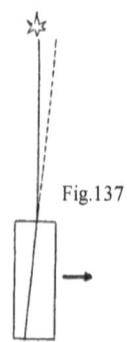
Fig.137

When we look at a star through a telescope, we don't see it in the right place because the light traverses the moved telescope diagonally (figure 137): since we expect the star to be in direct line behind this diagonal, we see it in a wrong place. Because at the moment of its incidence in the telescope, the light becomes nothing else but a beam in the clock of light. The aberration proves that the light is actually left behind while the bottom of the telescope is moving on. By means of the light, the telescope indicates the motion of the Earth and with that it is in contradiction to the StoR. But with this explanation one actually wanted to prove the StoR insofar as that the aberration is independent of the motions of the stars and therefore also independent of the relative motion star / Earth and that the Earth is obviously "immobile" in the sea of ether. We will therefore examine the issue a little closer in the chapter "Remarks".[83]

We see that the Theories of Relativity are hard to confirm or to refute for the reason alone that they predict a series of verifiable facts which can also be explained exactly without ToR when the paradigm is changed. And in fact, it is impossible to really prove the ToR. Einstein himself knew that very well when he said: "No experiment will be able to prove my theory, but one single one can refute it!"

Since electromagnetic fields always have to be spherical (spherical waves) after all according to the Special Theory of Relativity, one should also expect this of electromagnetic effects, for instance of a magnetic field. The magnetic field triggered by a moving charge, however, disappears for the observer who is moving along with the charge. In the same way, the charge itself should be invariant (absolute); but charge density and current density turn out to be variant, i.e. conditional on the motion. Until today one has not found one's way out of this dilemma.[84] For those who still can't make head or tail of it, here is the simplest examination of the Special Theory of Relativity based on the existence of the DOPPLER effect (figure 138):

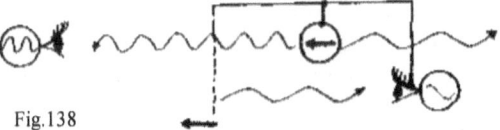

Fig.138

For us, a moving source of light coming towards us shifts the frequency of its light into a higher frequency (blue shift). For an observer moving along with the light, it still has the same colour since he causes an inverse Doppler effect with every way of measuring he might undertake because his measuring instrument is receding a little from every impulse. But exactly that could not happen if the impulse had the same speed relative to the measuring instrument as relative to the stationary observer! It follows conclusively from the running-away-from-the-impulse of the measuring instrument (or the running-towards-the-impulse on the other side) that different impulse velocities occur depending on where they are measured from. When a mirror is used instead of the measuring instrument, it will in fact receive the original frequency but will dilate it because of its motion. When the observer moving along takes a look in this mirror, he is moving against this dilated frequency and transforms it back into the original frequency. It doesn't help either when he directs a vertical beam out by means of the mirror and observes it. The frequency compensation will also take place in this case.

If the Special Theory of Relativity applied, the Doppler effect would not be able to occur at all. After all, the increase in frequency of a source of light coming towards us occurs because the first impulse is not so far away from the source of light when the next one is created as it would be with a stationary source of light. This implies conclusively that it has experienced a reduction in speed relative to the source.

Michelson's experiment was repeated again and again with different arm lengths and even with laser light.[85] These many repetitions and verifications show how hard it was for the physicists to believe that nature should resort to such bad tricks in order to withhold the absolute state of motion from us. Their mistrust was not quite unjustified.

Since clocks moving relative to each other are going slower according to the SToR (and also in reality), one could conclude that of twins moving relative to each other the respective other one is ageing more slowly. Responsible for this is the "time dilatation"[86] or "time stretching" derived from the Lorentz transformations. Already in the year 1911, Langevin pointed out a contradiction in this conclusion, that in fact each of the twins sees the other age more slowly since it depends only on the relative motion between the twins according to the SToR and not on who had been accelerated before. So, which of the twins is really younger?

This contradiction known as "twin paradox"[87] has in the meantime been solved by an experiment carried out by Professor Thim at the University of Linz. He could prove by means of a microwave interferometer that the "transversal Doppler shift" which is also based on the time dilatation does not exist at all although this phenomenon known as "relativistic Doppler effect" had been assumed as certain up to then. The measuring results were published and presented at conventions in Germany and the USA, the last time in May 2002 at the IEEE Instrumentation and Measurement

Technology Conference in Anchorage, USA.[88] It looks as if the SToR had been refuted unequivocally for the first time (?) by experiment.

And here is the promised comparison of the two Theories of Relativity:

The SToR deals only with uniform motions without forces. Every observer has its own space and his own time. Clocks have to be synchronised individually. Space and time depend on velocity. The ether was explicitly dispensed with, the speed of light is constant, and there is no gravitation. The space is always absolutely normal, i.e. flat. The SToR does not explain anything and does not produce anything. It is not applicable in the presence of a universe. The formulas of the GTR are not created in the "borderline case" of the SToR (observer velocity = 0).

The GTR deals only with nonuniform motions with forces. Space and time are the same for all observers and all clocks are always synchronised anywhere from the beginning. Space and time remain constant. The ether is explicitly demanded again.[63] The velocity of light is variable, namely depending on gravity. In the GTR, everything revolves around gravitation which is determined by the space and its curvature, and the space is always curved. The GTR does not explain anything, does not produce anything, but is applicable as a calculation method in the presence of a universe. The formulas of the SToR are not created in the "borderline case" of the GTR (flat space, no forces).

The two theories have nothing to do with each other, they contradict each other in almost all parts, the GTR can therefore never be a generalisation of the SToR. But at least in a geometrical way it describes a physical reality which we hope to have demonstrated distinctly enough with the "Principle of Existence", the T.A.O. matrix, and the repulsion principle.

As predicted in the chapter "Mass" we are now turning our attention to the famous formula $E=mc^2$ and with that we will finish our short digression into the world of the Theories of Relativity. We learned enough to comprehend the derivation and significance of this formula. We certainly understood that there is only the inertia (inert mass) and that it has to be attributed to the fact that the transmission of power cannot accelerate a body instantaneously because the impulse fields of the atoms have to pulsate through the matrix of T.A.O. according to the "domino principle" and that in doing so the motion causes an alteration in the paths (oscillational spaces) - just as in the clock of light shown in figure 131. We could equate the resistance caused by that with the Lorentz force because in the end all matter consists of electromagnetic fields. The deformation (as shortening) of moved bodies which we discovered in the chapter "Inertia"– it also played a significant role as distortion in our considerations about the GTR – was already contemplated by the physicist Lorentz as a possibility to explain the negative result of Michelson's experiment. For the extent of this shortening or contraction, Lorentz determined the factor k

$$k = \frac{1}{1 - \frac{v^2}{c^2}}$$

in which v is the velocity of the body and c the velocity of light. We could also calculate this factor out of our clock of light which represents the relation of the alteration in distance in dependence on the velocity. For that purpose, the familiar theorem of Pythagoras is already sufficient...

If we want to know what length a moving body has in a motionless state we have to insert this coefficient of correction k and transform its linear measure to the motionless state. This is the well-known Lorentz transformation. As we have seen this factor results from the simple fact that bodies cannot be accelerated above the velocity of light because the impulse velocity within this body is limited by c. The extent of the retardation of a moved clock can easily be calculated with k as well. This is actually called "time dilatation" – and, as we know, it is nothing else but a clock ticking "differently"...

For the relation between acceleration and force, Newton established the equation $F=ma$ or $a=F/m$, i.e. the acceleration a is proportional to the exerted force F and inversely proportional to the mass m of the body – which means, of course, the inert mass. The bigger the inert mass of the body, the more difficult it is to accelerate it.

Now let's imagine a particle on which a uniform force is acting... When it is in a motionless state, its subsequent motion is defined by $F=ma$. But when it is already in motion, it has the velocity v because of an acceleration (according to Newton) of $a= F/m$ and it is moving faster and faster due to the imposed force. But Newton didn't know about these oscillational modifications of the atoms similar to the clock of light as a cause of inertia. His equation $a = F/m$ could not be quite correct for that reason. The impulses of the particle react of course slower and slower with increasing acceleration (we could also say their time is stretching more and more), and the magnitude of this internal retardation (and with that the increase of inertia) has the extent of the Lorentz factor so that we have to "correct" Newton's equation as follows

$$a = \frac{F}{m}\left(1 - \frac{v^2}{c^2}\right)^{\frac{3}{2}}$$

One can see from this equation that the velocity of the particle at the speed of light does not increase anymore, even if more force is exerted because $a=zero$ if $v=c$!

Also in the chapter "mass" we came across a formula which expresses the energy content of the moving particle, namely its kinetic energy, with $E=1/2mv^2$. This definition also goes back to Newton who postulated that a work W is exerted on a body when a force F is acting on the body with the mass m over a distance s. He attributed the value $W=Fs$ to this work. When substituting F for $F=ma$, $W=Fs$ corresponds exactly to $1/2mv^2$. The greater the expenditure of force (Fs), the greater $kinE = 1/2mv^2$.

But again we have to correct Newton's equation by the Lorentz factor, and instead of $F=ma$ we now write

$$F = \frac{ma}{\left(1 - \frac{v^2}{c^2}\right)^{\frac{3}{2}}}$$

and the work done now equals

$$W = \frac{mc^2}{\left(1 - \frac{v^2}{c^2}\right)^{\frac{1}{2}}} - mc^2 \qquad \text{with Newton it was only} \qquad W = \frac{1}{2}mv^2$$

383

The Lorentz factor has the effect that W becomes infinite if $v=c$, which makes superluminal speed impossible. But if work lends a greater inertia to a body, the inert mass has to contain energy, exactly $E=1/2mv^2$ - and of course this also has to be corrected by the factor k, which results in

$$E = \frac{mc^2}{\left(1-\frac{v^2}{c^2}\right)^{\frac{1}{2}}}$$

so that because of this definition the equation looks like

$$E=W+mc^2$$

That means, even if $W=zero$, i.e. if neither a force is applied nor a work is done, the particle still has an energy of

$$E=mc^2 \ !$$

The "mass" of a body is thus considered to be a measure for its energy content (just as our simple example with the fan wheel has revealed). This does on no account mean that mass and energy can be transformed into each other just like that. Because apart from the fact that $E=mc^2$ is only a fictitious quantity and has rather a symbolic character, a complete transformation of "mass" into "energy" is only conceivable in the reaction of matter and antimatter. After all, we demonstrated that in truth masses cannot be involved at all when we described the energy by means of the transformation of the field surfaces and the universal pressure which was changed by that.

Einstein's paper in which he presented these relations in 1905, was titled "Does the Inertia of a Body Depend Upon its Energy Content?" Though this formula is not included in this three-page treatise, in which he made the proof dependent on the claim to be proved (anyhow a method of evidencing that is usual in the ToR and by means of which the arguments are defined by "measuring regulations"). Because in its correct derivation it stems from Max Planck, and he actually referred to Poincare's quantity of motion of radiation...

But that is a completely different story![89]

Fig.138a: Albert Einstein is leaving the scene.

34 Planetary Evolution

Everything must have a beginning, some scientists think and have tried to calculate the age of the universe and of the Earth in many attempts. But in truth there is no reliable method at all which allows to take an exact look into the past. The theory of the Big Bang is easy to refute by the composition of the cosmic radiation and the background radiation which should actually have been proof for it.

Since matter would have had to consist completely of hydrogen at first after the Big Bang, the composition of the cosmic radiation, however, corresponds to a great extent to the chemical composition of today's universe, matter could not have been created in a Big Bang at all. If these radiations stemmed from current star processes, though, they would have to change constantly which has not been the case either up to now![90]

A Big Bang would consequently also have a completely different kind of expansion and propagation of the universe than the one which could be proved so far. If an absolutely perfect uniform expansion was already a piece of evidence against the Big Bang, actually the latest insights are turning against it as another extreme. Because the expansion of the universe is not in the least uniform as the astrophysicists Margaret Geller and John Huchra (University of Harvard) discovered after closely studying three-dimensional computer analyses of the universe. It looks as if the universe was composed of giant bubbles on the surface of which the galaxies are "floating"; these bubbles, however, could rather be explained by many explosions than by one single Big Bang, the scientists think - but the most probable explanation was presented in the chapter "Celestial Bodies" (fig. 94).

We should not overlook that the hypothesis of the Big Bang has especially the figures of the scientists to contend with because it cannot explain the existence of star formations which have to be older than the universe. The quasar APM 8279+5255, at an alleged distance of 13.5 billion light years away from us, contains three times more iron than is available in the rest of the universe. From the thesis of the Big Bang and according to the Hubble relation, the age of the cosmos is calculated with roughly 18 billion years (the value, which has been revised again and again, is today about maximal 15 billion years). This period, however, would be too short for the development of such tremendous amounts of iron in this quasar. And the spherical stellar group M5 (NGC 5904) seems to be more than 20 billion years old if one is to believe the astrophysicists...

We should be sceptical about such particulars; the age of the universe is constantly corrected from publication to publication - this is a Big Bang of figures and numbers and nothing else...

Isn't it easier to say that the universe has always existed? We have to understand "always" correctly: where there aren't any clocks there isn't any "time" either. Although we realised that time is an essential building block of the world we have to be aware of the fact that this time does not have a magnitude. There isn't any universal unit of time nor any quantum of time. There isn't any universal measure of length, either. Of course, we can try to interpret everything as quanta but nevertheless the universe doesn't have any size as long as we don't measure it with arbitrarily chosen scales. "Little" or "big" are human concepts just like "beginning" or "end". Isn't it ridiculous in view of these considerations to search for the beginning of the universe? There is no beginning. But that doesn't mean that the universe has always looked the same.

When we assume that the universe crystallised out of a chaos like a dissipative structure, these transitions from chaos to the current sight of the cosmos have surely taken place slowly and gradually over billions of years. On any account, it was not a "bang".

Well, we already discussed the development from chaos via the stars to the galaxies in all detail in the previous chapters. We also saw the creation of the planets already in a completely new connection. Of course, it would be interesting to know when this had actually taken place but the particulars about the age of our Earth vary from 4.6 to 6 billion years - and it is another question whether they are credible. To use radioactive decay processes as clocks is on no account as reliable as some people think. For one thing, the radioactivity has presumably been lower for cosmic reasons in times past (higher universal pressure), and for another the continuous alteration of the gravitational forces must have had its effect on other natural events, too. Therefore there isn't any measuring method covering very long periods of time for sure. That's not the end of the world. If we have to identify a person inside a room which the person has left long before, the knowledge how long he has been in this room is of no use, either.

For that reason, archaeologists, astronomers, and palaeontologists had to correct their figures again and again to a great extent. And they haven't finished yet. We will therefore look into the matter of rough and big epochs of time which can be easily gathered from the nature of our planetary system in principle.

The primordial products of the first blast off of solar matter of our mother star can still be found today in a kind of shell around the whole planetary system which extends rather annularly than spherically into the universe. Surely, it should be visible from other stars when illuminated by the sun. It is possible that thousands of such annular shells exist in every galaxy. In our milky way alone, several hundreds of them are very well known. For other reasons they were called "planetary nebulas", a prophetic name, because we don't have any doubt that these nebulae are connected with the creation of the planets.

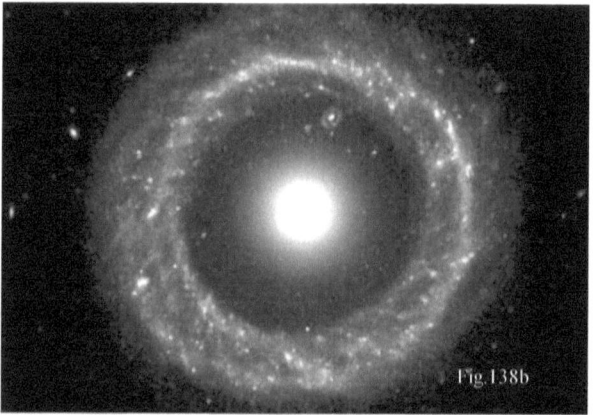
Fig.138b

The show piece of an annular nebula can be seen in the constellation of Harp (M 57=NGC 6720). This nebula, which can already be made out with good binoculars, really stands there like an especially ordered model of our viewpoint. Also with the binoculars or with an amateur's telescope we can find other models in the starry night sky: the Owl Nebula in the vicinity of the Great Bear (M 97=NGC 3587), the peculiar Dumbbell Nebula in the constellation Vulpecula (M 27=NGC 6853) or the beautiful Helix Nebula (NGC 7293) which likes to show us its composition in chemical analysis: hydrogen, helium, oxygen, nitrogen, and neon...

In the centre of these annular nebulae there is in all cases a central star, a nova, which has partially exploded without any doubt. About ten thousand of such annular nebulae in our galaxy prove the process of a planetary birth. For that reason, planetary systems are not exactly a rarity although not an ordinary event either in a galaxy with about 100 billion stars.

All these visible nebulae are traces of a solar eruption as we imagine it to be. The spheres or rings are still moving away from their central stars at high speeds. Already the second blast off process of our sun must have developed the main mass of the comets. They orbit around the sun in long-stretched ellipses in the Kuiper belt and we would have never learned about them if some of them had not been fetched again by giant planets. They were pressed into the shadow of the planet by the universal pressure (in the old mode of expression: "attracted" by the planets) and now they visit their sun, from which they all come, in more or less regular temporal intervals.

Comets are always spectacular events for astronomers. In their composition, they reflect the very first matter of the sun which could not have been rich in heavy elements yet. For that reason, all primordial molecules which we know are found in the comets, i.e. all those atomic fields which could not prevent bonding with each other, like for example water frozen to ice.

Comets are the icebergs of the universe. The pressure of the sun tears a giant tail of gases out of them which always points away from the sun. It distinctly demonstrates the game between sun and universal pressure. Comets often suffer the fate to be ripped apart or to dissolve in a shower of meteorites.

The range of still unknown planets still lies within the sphere of the comets. The Bode-Titius law of distance, whose cause we demonstrated, gives rise to the expectation that at least one planet is still undiscovered which would have to orbit the sun in about 675 years (Transpluto). Since the big intrasolar planet Neptune shows significant perturbations in its orbit there is generally little doubt about the existence of this tenth planet. It is probably a giant gas ball similar to Neptune, built from matter of the sun's childhood. Hence an ice planet which rotates on its axis in less than 10 hours and has most probably a ring which should consist mainly of ice particles... In the meantime another tiny planet ("Quaoar") was discovered outside the orbit of Pluto which – just as Pluto itself – could be a runaway satellite and must not be mistaken for the predicted tenth planet.

Between this hypothetical tenth planet (named "Planet X" according to Percival Lowell) and Neptune one celestial body, which did not originally belong to the planetary family, steps out of line. At least many scientists think so and they believe it is an run-away satellite - maybe of Uranus - or comes from the asteroid belt in which there are many other remainders of a destroyed planet. This escaped moon is in fact the smallest planet with its diameter of about 2,400 kilometres but because of its density it actually fits between Mars and Jupiter (but even better between Earth and Mars). Anyway, today it travels in its orbit outside of Neptune's, in fact in such an eccentric way that it is sometimes coming close to Uranus.

Pluto is the name of this unconventional fellow, the coldest among its kind. It was found accidentally when one was looking for a planet which perturbed Neptune so much that it was travelling a little faster at one time and then slowed down again. The cause of this perturbation is not hard to understand (figure 139):

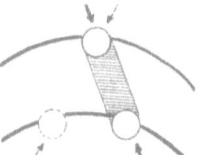

Fig. 139

Two planets shadow off the pressure of the universe from each other and replace it with their own, lower pressure. For that reason, the universal pressure repels them towards each other. Since the inner planet runs faster, it becomes even faster at first and then a little slower whereas the outer planet behaves the other way round. That way one knows exactly if a planet is disturbed from the internal side or from the external side. In the present case, however, Pluto had not been the much sought-after troublemaker but the invisible "planet X" which has still not been discovered. Pluto is accompanied by a satellite which is half as big as Pluto itself (Charon) and one could almost speak of a double-planet system.

Neptune itself was exactly found in the described way after the same perturbations had been noted in the orbit of Uranus as well. As is to be expected, Uranus, a giant planet of low density, contains very few heavy elements and resembles Neptune. Of Neptune, eleven moons are know, but it has probably more.[91] Uranus possesses 21 (or more) satellites and of course one ring, like all the other planets. The showpiece of a ring is presented by Saturn, the next planet in the row. At least 31 satellites orbit around this giant ball, which, like Uranus and Neptune, rotates rather fast - for reasons well known. Among his satellites there is the biggest moon of the solar system, Titan - a frozen ice giant world. Another moon even has an atmosphere of carbon dioxide, methane, hydrogen, and helium, just like Saturn itself which is mainly composed of hydrogen and helium - just like the sun. Another moon displays distinctive volcanic activity.

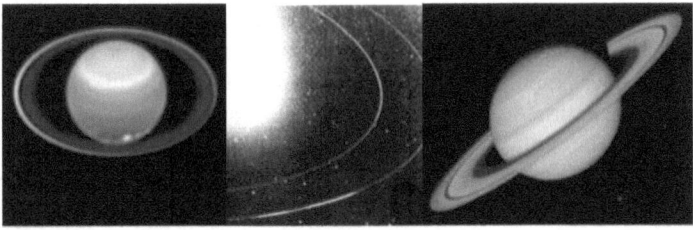

Fig. 139a   Uranus   Neptune   Saturn

There are old legends and reports which attribute the creation of life to Saturn ("The First", "The Sower"). This is not an absolutely far-fetched thought because Saturn must have passed through the region of the ecosphere once. Carbon is already available in vast quantities on it. One of its moons is a giant diamond of crystalline carbon. But even if there ever was something resembling living molecules on Saturn which captured its satellites but at a later time, it has long since vanished without leaving a trace. The atmosphere of Saturn has minus 170 degrees Celsius. Not a pleasant place to live.

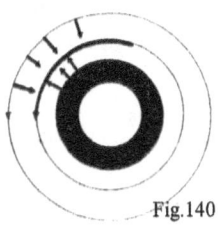

Fig.140

The ring of Saturn consists of more than 100 individual rings made of dust and ice particles. It is extremely thin, namely only maximal 150 metres thick and thus represents a big mystery for the astronomers. It extends over an area of 290 000 kilometres in diameter with Saturn hovering in its centre with a diameter of ca. 120 000 kilometres. Oddly enough, the ring behaves like a

391

rotating record: inner rings and outer rings have the same angular velocity as if the ring was a compact disc (figure 140).

That is surprising because the ring consists of particles which are after all independent of one another and thus must have chosen their velocity according to the distance from Saturn. Actually the inner rings would have to rotate faster. But kindly enough the ring of Saturn demonstrates the effects of the repulsion principle. That is to say the mystery is solved quite quickly if we consider that for the inner rings the universal pressure is shadowed by the outer rings. In turn, the pressure from Saturn has a weaker effect on the outer rings – because of the shadows of the inner ones. Newton's equations loose their validity here. Because suddenly the universal pressure triumphs on the outside - only those rings would survive which turned a little faster than the results of the calculations. On the inside, on the other hand, the pressure from Saturn prevails, and only those rings which turned slower than "intended " were not pushed away by it. If we were still obliged to "gravitation", we would of course be faced with a brain teaser, though.[92] Astronomers already constructed the most peculiar auxiliary hypotheses, like for example the conjecture that the rings were somehow linked with each other like the spokes of a bicycle...

An effect similar to the bicycle spokes, however, should actually be seen. Because universal pressure and Saturnian pressure have pushed chunks into the ring from both sides ... in fact until distance and speed of the chunks were "right ". So the ring must have broken up transversely several times whereas the wrong speed of other chunks caused the longitudinal gaps by means of a pick-up effect as it occurred with the creation of the planets. That the ring did not pick itself up completely may be due to the fact that a continuous retardation over the whole area was never possible. Because unlike the ring around the sun, this matter is "space cold" and possible electrodynamic processes did not take place. A partial retardation, however, has occurred several times by the influence of the satellites. Therefore the ring is subdivided into four (latest observations discovered seven) main rings. Between the individual rings, there is nothing but a gaping void.

The unexpected thinness of the ring - in relation it would almost have to be called wafer-thin - is explained by the pressure relations according to our hypothesis. In addition it would have to be a bit broader on the outside than on the inside for it reflects exactly the geometric course of Saturnian pressure and universal pressure. What keeps it so thin is nothing else but the curving force which becomes immediately effective when the ring exceeds a certain thickness (figure 141).

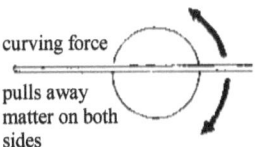

Fig. 141

The curving force caused this ring by breaking a celestial body falling onto Saturn into a sphere of dust. The ring at the level of the Saturnian equator had to survive because the pressure distribution around the quickly rotating star could on no account be uniform. As is to be expected the force of the planet directed against the universal pressure is weaker in the area of the equator than at the poles. Thus every planetary ring will only be created perpendicular to the equator (which does not mean that it will remain there forever).[93] The higher "repulsion" above the poles will displace matter, the curving force will make it fall onto the Saturn apart from a small ring. Once the ring has come into existence its position can also change because of the fact that pole displacements take place on the planet at a later time although only to a limited extent.

The next giant in the row, Jupiter, also carries a ring - although not such a distinctive one like Saturn. It consists of finer material but is a little thicker, as to be expected. Since the ring system is very dark it does probably not contain any ice because Jupiter as the biggest of our planets is already nearly a little sun on its own. It emits substantially more heat then it receives from the sun. The universal pressure, which finds a lot of surface to work on with this big ball, is to blame for this generation of heat.[94] Since the rolling effect is furthered by size and age of the planet, it is not astonishing that Jupiter rotates the fastest - in less than 10 hours. The giant is home to the second biggest satellite of our system, Ganymede, and at least another 59 moons. Compared to Jupiter the Earth looks like a pea next to an orange - and the sun like a cart wheel.

If life should have already started on Saturn in any form it must have continued on Jupiter. But on no account did little green men migrate in a spaceship, it is more likely that the transmission of living molecules was done by means of panspermia, that means for example in form of bacteria wafting through space. These are only marginal thoughts, though, and before we loose ourselves in fantastic speculations we rather turn our attention to another spectacular event of which the next planet in the row was most probably affected.

It must have been a very big planet - already rich in iron and nickel - which once travelled in its orbit between Jupiter and Mars. And it was probably hit by a tremendous meteor because it shattered into several thousand fragments and thousands upon thousands of smithereens. Today the asteroid belt lies in its orbit. The biggest known asteroid, Vesta, measures 834 kilometres in diameter, a considerable chunk but still a tiny thing among the celestial bodies. Another one dashes through space like a giant needle (Eros). But the biggest fragments at all were flying away - hither and thither in all directions. Some were captured by the planets and have remained satellites since then. The shapelessness of them all is a clear reminder of their having shattered as cold matter. They are rarely spherical but mostly asymmetrical, potato-like structures.

There is little doubt that the asteroids once formed one single planet. That is to say their orbits all intersected in one point which is of course the one where the catastrophe must have happened. Only the cause of the disaster will never become completely clear. The collision between two celestial bodies is in fact quite a rare event but not completely improbable. All celestial bodies are struck by meteorites and comets again and again. Huge impact craters speak for themselves. The fact that even the Earth was hit countless times by giant meteors is substantiated by its scars: tremendous craters in Australia, Arizona, and Siberia. But those meteors must have been dwarves compared to the giant which once smashed the asteroid planet into pieces. Yet it couldn't have been hit directly because two celestial bodies of approximately the same size will break each other apart because of their curving force before they fall into each other. If there had already been living things on the destroyed planet, they could even have predicted the end of their world – provided they already knew astronomy.

Maybe the first intentional migration of life from planet to planet took place here... But there is another, even better explanation for the incident. Namely that his planet just burst like a soap bubble when it changed its orbit. In its composition it must have represented a transitional stage from the giant gas planets to the denser and more compact spherical bodies. Maybe that was the reason why it was not stable enough to keep its own pressure inside because the outside pressure (universal pressure) became continuously weaker after all – but going into a new orbit happened suddenly. The gas planets, affected by the same fate, simply expanded up to ten times, yes even twenty times their size. Probably that planet already had a hard crust under which the pressure was growing too much. It had to end in disaster, above all if the planet was very big. Maybe even nuclear processes began under his crust, just like in the sun. The result was an enormous atomic bomb in space.

This was a short review of the old planets. Now let's talk about the younger ones which are of much more interest to us for the reason alone that we live on one of them.

We already demonstrated how it came to the creation of the planets. The youngest of all planets, which was closest to the sun, practically still flying in the annular range of its creation, was called "Vulcan". At least that is what it was baptised by the astronomer Dr. Lescarbault who first spotted it in 1859. In 1878, it showed itself to the astronomers James C.Watson and Dr. Lewis Swift; in the years 1966 and 1970, Dr.H.C. Courten still discovered remainders of the planet and afterwards it disappeared without leaving a trace.

Probably it fell back into the sun; a stillbirth, so to say. Maybe it was even only a chimera, a series of illusions.

In any case, there is no doubt about the existence of Mercury, the youngest among the still existing planets. Created at a time when the sun had already developed great amounts of heavy elements, it presents itself as an incredibly heavy fellow and exhibits the highest density of all planets. The high ambient pressure squeezes it into a tight ball which is smaller than Jupiter's moon Ganymede. Hence it is a planetary dwarf which presumably consists mainly of metals. It is unbearably hot on its surface. We already threw a light on the peculiarities of its rotation. It has a bit of an atmosphere; it is furrowed by scars and craters, it is naked and empty. Active volcanoes don't exist yet. Any kind of life is impossible. We already describe its eccentric orbit and its peculiarities when we examined the GTR.

Well, let's speculate a little: one faraway day, Mercury will adopt the orbit on which we find Venus today. And then it will look like this planet, will swell up to four times its size. Its skin will become thinner and not withstand the pressure below in some places. Giant volcanoes will erupt and envelope the whole planet in dust, carbon dioxide, and water vapour. In the same manner, several hundred degrees of heat make Venus a hell at the time being, in which horrible storms are raging.

Our Earth looked just like that once when it was still closer to the sun, in the orbit of Venus. By the way, the volcanoes of Venus were not discovered until 1984. Volcanoes are extremely important for structuring the planet into an animate celestial body. The causes of volcanism are not hard to find. When something like a cool skin or crust has developed, an enormous pressure builds up beneath it on the otherwise cold planet. This process transforms matter into magma. Chemical processes release carbonic acid, oxygen, and water, and this water is pressed out of the volcanoes together with lava and gases - first and foremost of course by the universal pressure which holds the planets like a vice (figure 142).

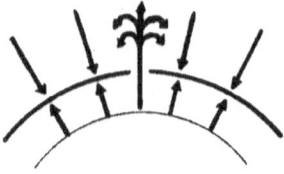

Fig. 142

Almost the whole amount of water on a planet stems from the volcanoes. Even today, the few still active volcanoes of the Earth deliver enormous quantities of water into the aerosphere which is built-up and maintained by volcanic activity, by the way

For that reason, volcanoes also created the atmosphere on Venus which is up to 100 times denser than that of the Earth. Only when the volcanic activity abates will this layer of gas become thinner and more similar to the Earth's. Since Venus does not yet rotate fast and therefore hasn't almost any magnetic field, portions of the atmosphere are constantly lost into the universe.

Apart from a low content of sulphuric acid, the atmosphere of Venus resembles in essence the primitive atmosphere of the Earth. It is therefore likely that Venus is at the beginning of a development which will lead to an animated planet quite similar to the Earth...[95]

With the birth of the next planet, Venus would be burned bare by the sun and at the same time make a giant leap through the equipotential space of the gravitational field. Its rotation will increase, the volcanoes will create a new atmosphere, and life, as far as it has already existed, will have to begin anew. In the slightly cooler region, the water vapour of the air will fall down as rain over decades; floods will come over the planet just like those which the Earth already experienced. For the Earth made this "jump", during which its poles possibly reversed, at least twice, but probably even three times. There is good reason to assume that human beings already experienced the last of these leaps.

After that the newly shining sun will relocate its reactors gradually below the surface again and at the same time radiate more weakly. And Venus will freeze over almost completely, i.e. experience an Ice Age. The traces of such catastrophes can still be found on the Earth today. One has tried to attribute these immense traces of catastrophes to a variety of causes, as for example to the impact of comets – which must of course have taken place in addition. But the main cause for these scars is the sun itself, and every planet is went through a similar series of catastrophes.

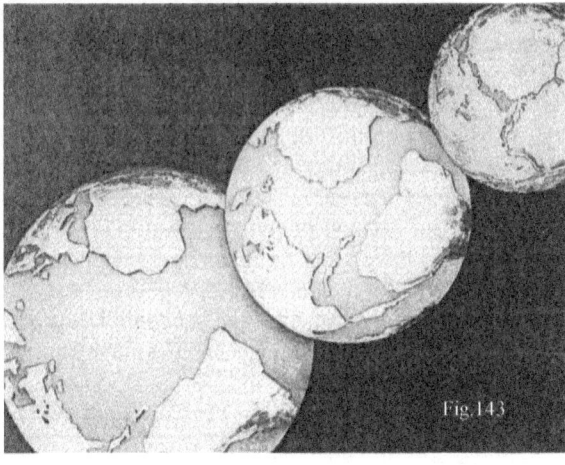

Fig.143

On Earth, the primeval soup, in which the first chemical process of metabolism began, soon covered almost the whole planet. Venus will look just the same one day, too. Today, it is definitely already infected with bacteria through panspermia. It is therefore not necessary that the "concept" of life has to be born anew on it.

Because of the expansion of the Earth (figure 143) the available water of the ocean had to spread over a vaster area. Land became visible. Once it was one single big continent. It gradually broke into big pieces which drifted apart on the layers of magma currents (continental drift according to Wegener) after that. Life never had to "conquer" the land because it was left lying there, so to speak, when the water receded. Shallow waters, zones of ooze, shelf seas, and pools, half sea and half land, became the first playgrounds of evolution. The primordial ocean was conserved in the bodies of the cells, and now it only mattered whether those functions would develop which would preserve this captured ocean further.

From various concepts created in the sea in those days an evolution of its own developed; from countless primitive organisms with different numbers of chromosomes a variety of species developed in constant interaction with and to each other - a fireworks of life was spreading.[107] Indefatigably, the gathered "programmes", which had been accumulated indiscriminately in the primordial sea, were tried and used. We have to see it in the right way: these were not drafts of predetermined properties or functions but these were programmes for numerous possibilities – only the rules were contained in the code, not the game and not the players. Just as the atoms contain the rules for chemical reactions in the impulses of their shells or their surface structures and on no account the programme for special molecules - and they nevertheless create the diversity of the molecular universe - the genetic data collections[96] of the primary cells only contained virtual possibilities of organisms which could come true because of endless reaction series and endless reaction times. And so everything practically developed at the same time and side by side, adapted to one another from the beginning: plants, insects, animals, and not least that special primordial creature which already carried the programme for the development to the human being.

From the beginning there must have been symbioses which are still working today - between animals and animals, plants and plants, animals and plants. Life was spreading like a giant infection, and as in a kaleidoscope functions and modes of behaviour were unfolding for which there always were two simple possibilities: either they proved their worth and continued to exist or the didn't make sense and went down. Even everything that adapted too well was doomed because it didn't have any more prospect to submit to changes in the environment. The most successful were probably the average, rather primitive organisms. Still, evolution consisted basically of the incessant passing away of failed constructions.

The behaviour of an organism also became an absolutely integral component of all biological functions early on. Physical imperfections could be compensated better that way. And what mattered further in particular were the signals which one put up for one another. The more distinct they were, the sooner the continued existence was secured.

Evolution research shows that life moved on only slowly and late from the purely material adaptation of the organic functions to the more practical modes of behaviour depending on signals. They already required a certain quality of the nervous system. And it took millions of years until suitable sense organs were developing. But as soon as eyes had come into existence which could recognise colours the plants began to blossom and the animals were getting colourful - and they were doing it more and more noticeably, more and more colourful and more and more flashy...

In the resplendent, garish world of optical and acoustical signals, it was always the stronger, more distinctive signal that was more successful because the modes of behaviour were still primitive instincts, motor reflexes, and life was still quite subconscious...

And just because this development mechanism was so trivial, so scarce even, that the particularity of the signals developed unerringly from the useful which still gives expression to its archaically founded significance for us by making us feel they are "beautiful". Because even all this supposedly beautiful was created without any plan and was only determined by its usefulness.

For that reason, the beautiful is anchored down with the useful in our feeling. Sun rises, for example, are beautiful because the rising of the sun was also the rising of our life... Only he who denies the (currently often forgotten) function of the "beautiful" is faced with a "miracle", the mystery of aestheticism.

Well, we will get even more speculative and give fantasy a little more leeway when we try to recapitulate the history of the Earth – knowing quite well that we won't be completely able to bring light into the abstruse darkness of the past...

When the Earth changed its place upon the birth of Vulcan or Mercury and the flood came over it, the already existing Venus changed its place, too. For the already existing cultures on Earth, Venus was already morning and evening star and was watched attentively. Legends from the Realm of Ogyges tell us that the planet Venus "changed colour, size, and shape " - to be found in Augustinus' "Civitas Dei". "And from that came a night on Earth for nine months during which the volcanoes of the archipelago went into activity..."

It were the ancestors of the Mayas, who noticed the connection between the alteration of Venus and the catastrophe on Earth. As a result they developed a cult about Venus, started their own Venus calendars and didn't stop watching the Venus - assuming that future cataclysms would be announced by the morning star again. Which was certainly not completely wrong.

Almost all global catastrophes of the Earth, floods or ice ages, have their origin directly in the activity of the sun which was on no account always shining so evenly as we believe today. Every new eruption was preceded by a period of cooling; and it is therefore not surprising that according to latest findings the deluge, which was noted down in almost all historical records coincided with the end of the last big ice age. The newly inflamed sun melted away the ice, flood disasters had to be the consequence.

Ever since the Earth was created the sun had done its cosmic striptease at least three times, and the traces of three major, global changes can therefore still be found on the Earth today.

The course of the evolution across several planets is a fascinating but unprovable perspective. But we will continue our speculations nevertheless. Although we find Mercury today as a dead planet it will not remain like this forever. For now, the sun stands there - after the last successful ejection of its shell - fresh and shining. But its intensity will diminish continuously because a new shell is forming below which the atomic reactor will retract. That way, Mercury will come into the area of life one day, and there will be a time when volcanoes will cause an atmosphere and oceans on it as well. So the event of life will start again there. And when Mercury gets into the orbit of the Earth one day - which will have been travelling in an orbit far away from the sun for a long time then - it, too, may have survived three global cataclysms - provided the sun continues its game for some time... And maybe these cataclysms will be preserved in the legends, fairy tales, and stories of creation, too.

Every planet has its own evolution and contributed its share to the development and continuation of life. In certain phases of their existence, all planets were going through similar stages and conditions. For that reason, we could already prophesy the next "apocalypse ", although the exact date would be hard to define. At some time the sun will be getting colder again, a new ice age will come over the Earth - and mankind will have to realise that its planet is lost. Perhaps the Ark of a future Noah will be a spaceship.

A new inflammation of the sun will burn away any possible life on Venus but cause a flood on Earth. Venus and Earth and all the other planets as well will make their "jump" through space, a giant leap which will nevertheless take many weeks and days - if there are still days. Nothing will remain as it was. Life will migrate to the next, inner planet, as it has presumably already happened several times before.

This lends a new background to the theories of Erich von Daeniken which should not be unwelcome to him who had his problems with the credibility of these theses. For it answers the question where his "Gods" could really have come from. Other stellar systems are definitely much too far away. However, we don't want to discuss how convincing these theories are in detail,.

Fire and water are the elements of an apocalypse; and fire and water are found as the cause in all traditions about such apocalypses. People also noticed the changes to the other planets during such a catastrophe in former times. In the Sumerian tradition, the Gilgamesh Epic, Ishtar, creatrix of mankind, who is represented by the planet Venus, is expressly mentioned and stated as the cause of the flood. It is therefore no surprise that countless Cromlechs and standing stone observatories were erected all over the world to closely observe Venus as well as sun and moon.

Even the story of the sinking of Atlantis tells about deviations in the orbit of the planets word-for-word. Thus Plato makes his Critias report: "There is a story which even you have preserved, that once upon a time Phaethon, the son of Helios, having yoked the steeds in his father's chariot, because he was not able to drive them in the path of his father, burnt up all that was upon the earth, and was himself destroyed by a thunder-bolt. Now , this has the form of a myth, but it really signifies a declination of the bodies moving around the earth and in the heavens, and a great conflagration of things upon the earth recurring at long intervals of time..."

The myth of the planet Phaethon in Greek Mythology is a clear indication of the solar eruption which preceded the catastrophe and brought the devastating fire over the Earth. Similar tales can be found all around the globe, as for instance in the Völuspá, the Pregermanic Song of the Gods: "...from the South came the sun, companion of the Moon, threw his right hand over Heaven's rim, Sun did not know his halls. Moon did not know his might. Stars did not know their places..."

Moreover the altered orbit of Venus gave rise to the biblical legend of Lucifer's Fall, the most beautiful and strongest among the angels, who had tried in a heavenly revolution to throw the Creator God from his throne; that Lucifer was once associated with the planet Venus is proved by a passage in chapter XIV. of Isaiah who reports: "How you have fallen from heaven, O morning star, son of the dawn! You have been cast down to the earth, you who once laid low the nations!"

The Popol Vuh relates how the frightful God Huracan flooded the Earth and that at the same time a big fire was seen in the sky... Similar reports with distinct indications to the Venus can also be found in the Books of Chilam Balam...

Where does our Earth's moon come from? Oddly enough, the oldest calendars of our planet, those of the Maya and their ancestors respectively, do not care about the moon although the periodic cycle of this satellite must have really been inviting for measuring time. They used the sun and Venus for determining the intervals of time. Was there an epoch without a moon? Mercury doesn't have a moon. Neither does Venus. And when the Earth was at Venus' distance from the sun, it most probably didn't have any satellite, either.

Just as all planets would fall at the same speed in free descent, they all covered their equipotential spaces almost at the same time and at the same speed. The transmission of the impulse in the system, however, took place from the inside to outside. The alteration in the planet's locations could therefore be noticed most distinctly with those planets which were closer to the sun. In the process, Venus must have become smaller optically since the distance from Earth to Venus certainly had to increase. The outer planets moved off in the same way but they had been much harder to observe from the beginning.

It suggests itself that the bursting of the asteroid planet coincided with its jump which in turn coincided with the jump of the Earth. On this occasion a big fragment must have intersected the orbit which the Earth was about to take. Even if the supporters of Newton's formulas think this to be improbable and the theories of capturing have had weak foundations up to now, we assume it is very likely that such a fragment became the satellite of our Earth. Its density of 3.34 (Earth 5.52) ranks the moon exactly between Mars (3.95) and Jupiter (1.33). For that reason, it certainly comes from this region (in which the asteroid belt lies nowadays) and therefore has to be older than the Earth.

Determining the age of samples from the moon did actually reveal a higher age. Besides the capturing of a satellite is on no account unthinkable according to our repulsion principle. The process of an encounter of this kind is shown in figure 144:

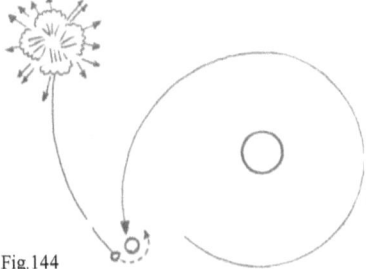

Fig.144

At a speed of far more than 100 km/s the satellite chunk must have approached the Earth. Actually, it was on its way to the sun but it came too close to the Earth... For a short time they were flying next to each other, and this time was sufficient for the curving force of the Earth to change the direction of the moon. It was falling around the Earth ... and in this way it is still falling today at a speed of about 105 km/s.[97]

Initially it was much closer to the Earth. Since the curving force affects and deforms both bodies it causes the tides and impedes both rotating and falling around one another. This results in a predomination of repulsion ... and thus the moon is continuously moving away from the Earth again. For the same reasons the planets have to gradually move away from the sun.

In the same way as our moon, all other satellites of our planetary system were captured. If there had ever been something like a preliminary stage of the moon in form of a loose accumulation of matter close to the Earth, it would have been dissipated into a ring inevitably. The curving force looses its strength only at a certain distance (Roche's limit). For the same reason, every theory which wants to know that the planetary system was created from one single cloud of gas is absolutely absurd. Only intensely ionised matter, i.e. only that of the sun itself, could create planets. What happens to non-ionised, cool matter is most distinctly demonstrated by the ring around Saturn...

In all probability our neighbouring planet Mars once carried an abundance of life. Today it shows which fate could lie in store for the Earth... Without doubt, one can see that Mars must have carried enormous amounts of water which it has lost in the meantime almost completely.

At a time to come the Earth will also loose its complete water - except for those deplorable remainders which are still bound as ice in the poles of Mars. When the volcanic activity ceases - a consequence of the sinking universal pressure - the Earth will shrink considerably because it will have conveyed enormous amounts of hydrogen and helium into the universe. The oxygen released from the dissolution of the water will seize the metals in the spreading deserts; the planet will rust away so to speak and present a picture as it is already displayed by Mars.

Prior to that, the population of the Earth will have made its contribution to the devastation of its planet as well. The groundwater levels will sink, fountainheads will dry up, rivers will run dry... Finally even the oceans will evaporate because less and less water will be flowing back to them in form of rain. Mercilessly, the sun will decompose the remaining clouds into hydrogen and oxygen. Carbon dioxide will enrich the atmosphere (carbon monoxide oxygenises to CO_2) - and what was is left in the bitter end is a nitrogenous carbon dioxide atmosphere exactly like the one on Mars today.

Strangely enough there are legends on Earth which tell about an epoch with two moons. Could it be that this tradition does not refer to the Earth? Mars has two moons! Do these stories possibly come from Mars and were they brought by fugitives who had to emigrate to the Earth? This thought is indeed extremely fascinating. Will history be repeated and mankind - at least a small part of it - emigrate to Venus when Earth will have become uninhabitable?

These thoughts are on no account so fantastic as they may appear at first glance. There are too many peculiar indications, like for instance old drawings on stone with connecting lines between Earth and Venus - or are they lines between Mars and Earth? After all, we must not forget that Mercury has not always existed. Were Daeniken's Astronaut Gods Martians? This question probably elicits a slight smile, although perhaps unjustly so. We have to consider that all these events are separated by inconceivably great periods of time. The dying of the Earth will not take place before it has reached the orbiting range of Mars. But first, the Earth has to cope with an apocalypse, namely the jump into this orbit.

Today we could already send a spaceship with crew to Venus. How far will this technology have progressed when Earth comes into the region of Mars? But maybe this is of no use at all, maybe evolution and civilisation have to start all over again. In any case, one thing is very strange: mankind's desire for space travel. It seems as if we had a foreboding that we would really need this knowledge one day.

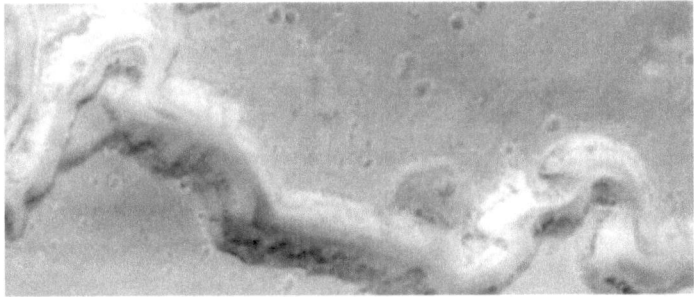

Fig. 144a: Dried up riverbed on Mars

We want to leave it at these suggestions. Because there are not any real answers to any of these questions. The question if life did or did not exist on Mars can still not be answered even after the NASA experiments and space probes. The experiments cleverly thought out on Earth produced absolutely astonishing results, just as if the laws of our chemistry would not apply on Mars. Only one thing has been known for sure since then: there must have been water on Mars, a tremendous amount of water... [98]

Mars is considerably smaller than the Earth. But it is also older, colder, and dried up in addition so to speak. For that reason, it must have shrunk to its current size, an effect which temporarily precedes the final expansion of the planets. The absence of oceans on Mars reveals enormous differences in elevation, mighty mountain ranges the likes of which could be found on Earth if there wasn't any water. There isn't any more oxygen in the atmosphere of Mars. For that reason, the sky does not appear blue but red. Reddish is therefore also the colour of the reflected sunlight, and because of this colour, Mars was given its name.

In older times it was also known under the name Chiun. Among other indications we find clues in the Bible that the symbol of Chiun was worshiped and was tantamount to a god. So here is another connection which is worth thinking about.

Despite all speculation, we should not completely deny the indications that the evolution of life was not restricted to one single planet. It is not exactly necessary that the primordial ocean we deserted was located on Earth. It is, however, probable that evolution started on almost every planet and that only a mutual influencing took place. The "concept" of life, maybe accomplished up to the bacterium, leaped from planet to planet, starting from Saturn down to Mars.

In any case, one thing seems to suggest itself: just as Mars seems to be the planet of our past, the planet of our future shines down on us in the morning and the evening sky: Venus!

When time is concerned, these evolutionary leaps from planet to planet are hard to classify. Maybe the connection with solar activity provides a possibility to choose our ice ages as clues, provided the scholars will one day find plausible figures. Over and above that, a drastic wandering of the poles must have taken place at least twice, most probably, however, three times (maybe even another one when capturing the moon). A change in the magnetic field was of course also connected with that. Actually, there are distinctive traces of such events.

Of course, we don't know at all if the sun did not have any great eruptions in-between, either which did not lead to planets. It seems that there were more than three ice ages - and interim ice ages. For that reason, we have to be very careful with specific conclusions. There is no reliable means to identify the rhythm of the sun; but we have to assume that these periods are getting shorter and shorter while the intensities of the explosions diminish. What is finally left is a rhythmically fluctuating little star, something similar to a pulsar maybe. One could therefore ponder the fact if pulsars did not cause their eruption intervals exclusively by rotation but fall from one eruption into the next under the enormous pressure of the universe, i.e. if they were not pulsating actually.

One of the most essential features of the planets (and stars) is their characteristic magnetic fields. Initially it was assumed that the Earth had a core of iron and nickel which caused the magnetic field.[99] This assumption was extremely unrealistic as Mars demonstrates which only has an extremely weak magnetic field. Contrary to all expectations a surprisingly strong magnetic field was discovered with Jupiter as well as phenomena similar to the Van-Allen belt radiation.

There is - as we already know - a simple cause for the creation of magnetic fields: rotation. It is crucial in this respect whether the surface of a celestial body causes sufficient polarisation, i.e. "charge". The atmosphere which - as we can easily notice during a thunderstorm - is able to build up enormous voltage potentials always has a say in this. Planets without any atmosphere or with slow rotation never develop a strong magnetic field. The magnetic field of Mercury only achieves one hundredth of the Earth's field intensity because its atmosphere is extremely thin and its rotation is very slow. Because of the extremely slow rotation of Venus, its magnetic field is merely not worth mentioning although all other requirements are fulfilled, as for example dense atmosphere, electric polarisations, and possibly even electron convectional currents below the surface.

The magnetic fields of our system correspond very well to the character of the planetary surfaces and rotations. That the poles of the magnetic fields do not coincide with the poles of the rotational axes is also to be expected from the direct connection with rotation. The reason for that is to be found in the temporal interval between cause and effect. Magnetic poles always lag a little behind the causing rotational poles so to speak. In addition a self-induction process of the following kind takes place: as is to be expected, the Earth as moving conductor causes an ordinary magnetic field, like the one we already demonstrated in figure 19, since the equator rotates faster. This magnetic field, however, is getting into conflict with the magnetic field of the sun. It is repelled by the solar pressure ("solar wind") similar to the tail of a comet (figure 145).

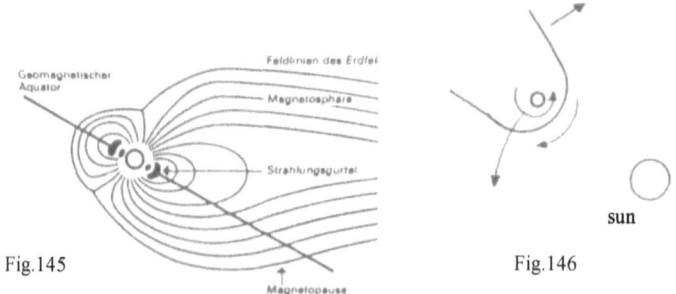

Fig.145　　　　　　　　　　　　　　　　Fig.146

Geomagnetischer Äquator = geomagnetic equator, Feldlinien des Erdfeldes = field lines of the Earth's field, Magnetosphäre = magnetosphere, Strahlungsgürtel = radiation belt, Magnetopause = magnetopause

At the same time it is set into retrograde rotation because it always points away from the sun. As a consequence the Earth itself, especially the ionised magma layer below its crust, becomes a moved conductor in the magnetic field. Opposing currents are inducing each other and will become strong enough in the course of time to make the initial magnetic field break down. The moved conductor, however, remains and builds up a magnetic field again on the basis of its rotation but this time with reversed poles. This game is repeated in intervals of several thousand years as a magnetic field constantly changing poles (figure 146). Even the sun itself, which quarrels with the magnetic field of the galaxy, performs the same game for the same reasons. From time to time, namely every 22 years, its magnetic field flips.

The periodic pole reversals of the Earth's magnetic field have already been confirmed by palaeomagnetic examinations of the rocks. For the geologists, who have several contradictory theories about the creation of the magnetic field at the ready, this is not a problem which can be easily solved. Geologic, namely gravimetric examinations brought another mysterious fact to the light which is of course immediately resolved with our repulsion principle. According to the conventional opinion about gravitation, one should expect that gravitation is slightly higher above great masses of our Earth's crust, i.e. above the continents and mountain ranges, than above the oceans. Measurements have revealed, however, that it is mostly just the other way round. This is exactly as it should be according to the repulsion principle. Because bigger masses cause a stronger counter-pressure to the universal pressure, above them the acceleration of free fall must therefore be lower. When we take, for instance, a look at a gravimetric map of Europe, massive mountain ranges like the Alps or the Carpathians stand out because of distinctive gravitation minima (figure 147 - black areas). Above the oceans, however, particularly above the deep places where there are certainly thinner rock formations, unequivocal gravitation maxima often prevail (vertically hatched and chequered areas).

Maxima Minima
Abb.147

These phenomena are called Bouguer anomalies. Up to now they have forced the geologists to the assumption that of all things the masses of rocks were less dense under the mountain ranges than under the oceans. But this is a fallacy for sure because there is no reasonable indication of the fact why the geological layers should be different and thinner exactly and accidentally under the folded mountains than only a few kilometres away. On the shown map the acceleration due to gravity has been measured in gal (after Galileo)

(1 gal = 1m/s^2). The determined values were arithmetically brought to the same height in order to compensate for the differences in altitude of the measuring points. When we examine the map closely and compare it with the given terrains, it is a significant point in favour of our repulsion principle.[100]

Let's turn our attention again to the evolution - because the evolution of the planets is closely interconnected with that of life. As we could demonstrate, life is on no account based on chance but on the co-incidence which rests on the behaviour of the atoms and molecules. Certain conditions are required for that purpose, like the existence of the right elements and of water as well as of the availability of a particular temperature range which we don't have to narrow down very strictly at all. Bacteria survive the low temperatures of the cosmos as well as heat up to almost 200 degrees Celsius quite well. We also survive and even enjoy a sauna at about one hundred degrees for some time. This is to say that the conditions on Earth are already extremely different from place to place and still life has found an answer to any kind of environment, that is to say organic functions which take account of the respective conditions and requirements.

Scholars often think it would be exaggerated and downright chauvinistic to demand the special conditions on Earth as prerequisite for life in general. But would bees behave chauvinistically if they supposed that other bees somewhere in the universe would also feed on honey? Not at all, because otherwise they wouldn't be bees. For that reason, we don't manifest chauvinism on any account either if we apply the criteria elsewhere which we used to define life here. Since the creation of the planets was absolutely not accidental but a process which has to take place in a similar way with many other suns we can conclude that life will come into existence and take place wherever there are approximately the same conditions.

Presumably, life is a cosmic matter of course which can also be said for space displacement and repulsion of the fields. Carbon will play its dominant role everywhere, and everywhere the spins of the light and the electron waves will determine the angular moment of the molecules.

Therefore life does not only exist over the expanse of the universe in all probability but things should even look quite similar everywhere. The same "principle" reigns as the only rigid "law of nature" somewhere else as well. Certainly the similarities do not only concern the atomic or molecular activities but also the organic ones.

As a mere consequence of functions, even the outside appearances of living things have to be similar down the line. Eyes are always determined by the way of seeing, and the look will always go where the being is moving to or where it is reaching for. And a mouth or jaws will always be in a position where hands can reach or where eating is easily possible, whereas excrements which are of no use are just left behind. Ears grow in that place and point to where the things heard make a practical sense; wings what fly will be wings and fins that swim will exactly be fins...

When we consider life on this Earth extensively we will discover that actually every possible form has been fulfilled. The strange and eerie apparatuses of an insect and the charm of a mammal baby are worlds apart - and yet there are all conceivable intermediate forms between these extremes. Everything that is imaginable was invented by nature, every method of locomotion, of seeing, of smelling, or of hearing.

Some scientists thought that nature had invented everything but the wheel. But they underestimated life too much, one should remind them of the dung beetle or of the fruits of the angiosperms which are round as a ball... and of a species of lizards which bends into a wheel and rolls downhill when it is in a particular hurry... Many things roll in the kingdom of animals and plants and many a thing turns like for instance the flagella of many unicellular organisms which – suspended in a motor-like turning device - actually rotate.

Enumerations of this kind could be continued at will. Whatever we can think of, whatever we ascribe to human inventive genius - nature has known it for a long time and is making use of it.

What should, what could actually be different on other planets, if everything that can exist already exists here?

The cause of evolution to the living things lies primarily in the nature of matter. It is forced into orders, literally pressed into crystals and molecules by its own pressure of existence... And it is exactly from making space, from this apparent intention, from the constant urge to escape entropy, that the flow of energies develops ... this constant striving for the downfall in which so many ways around are hidden.

The ways around have to be "accepted" and these ways around mean life. This is only a word for one state among all the other states of matter, in no way less likely than the so-called inorganic or crystalline state of a virus between living and not living. In the end, life is only a definition created by human brains, framed by arbitrary values and criteria ... but actually the whole universe is alive; nothing is really dead in its ever changing activity.

Of course, the thought that buses sound their horn and music boxes blare on another planet somewhere in the expanse of the universe is somehow disconcerting. Just because one should think that one edition of our insanity called civilisation should be enough... But one may see the Earth as one likes - it is on no account unique! Because the same game is played somewhere else, too. The Andromeda galaxy is almost a twin of our own. Are we to believe that the similarities only go as far as that?

What will we ever learn about each other, we, the fulfilments of a cosmic principle? Unbridgeable spaces and times separate us. Exchanged signals are on their way for thousands of years; and the question is if living beings anywhere don't have greater problems in their worlds than to wait for a telephone return call for one thousand years... But communication across the universe is therefore not completely impossible. Researching genius and inventive talent have already accomplished things which had been thought impossible a while ago!

35 Purpose

There are animals which look like flowers, flowers which imitate animal shapes, plants which look like stones. There are also stones in the form of plants, for example the chondrites. Many a "tree" in the ocean is an "animal". Many things animal reveal themselves to be a plant...

In comparison: submarines and fish are both equally streamlined. The tools of the insects can also be found in our tool cabinet. Flying animals or flying seeds use wings according to the same principle. All eyes see according to the laws of optics. All legs carry something - a body as well as a table top...

What strikes us as a great thought at first glance, namely the immense diversity of nature, is revealed as a small number of concepts on closer inspection. If one disregards the manifestation, the functions of the animal and plant kingdom are reduced to metabolism, reproduction, locomotion, and recognition. As it were, plants move by means of the flight of their seeds and the spread of their growth; animals are moving their germ along with them. The basic idea is always the same, the manifestation is different. Astonishingly the whole diversity of nature serves few purposes.

We also find, however, exactly the same in the inorganic realm. In the end, all diversity of the world can be put down to the simplicity of one principle which is inherent to the atomic. Should we really be surprised by that? Or have we only considered the world from the wrong side so to speak? Is it not possible to dissolve every crystal into those conditions which its atoms impose on each other? Why should the existence of living crystals be harder to comprehend? Where is the impediment to our realisation, which way of looking at things forbids us the natural insight into the nature of all things living?

The cardinal error of our thinking arises probably from the fact that we suspect a meaning in everything we observe. In this way every way of living can be reduced to the purpose of conserving the germ, and this is the incomprehensible part for us because we do not instantaneously realise that cause and effect coincide because we are just too closely attached to the thought that cause and effect stand opposite each other. But this is not the case. Running water digs itself a bed. Water is the cause, the bed is the effect. The bed itself, however, is in turn cause for the flowing of the water! And in this way a river is created: from the common ground of cause and effect it preserves itself and does not stop flowing...

A bulldozer and a shovel excavator require a road. They are able to make this road on their own. And for this purpose they can use the same piece of road again and again by digging it off behind them and filling it up in front of them. There is a road and a something which moves but the road doesn't lead anywhere. Nevertheless the system is incessantly kept in motion. It is just the same with the germ of life. It has to move (because its definition is conditional on movement after all) and this is the only purpose it fulfils. Just like the river finds its bed - because there is no other way - the germ also recognises its path apparently: a result of necessities which go around obstacles like the course of a river goes around hills and rocks.

We probably have to admit that we suspect a mysterious purpose in everything of which we don't know the cause. Nobody would suspect that the purpose in the occurrence of tides is to cause floods. Nobody will believe that the laws of free fall have a specific objective. As soon as causes, although often only apparently, are comprehensible through laws and formulas, one will immediately accept the pointlessness of the event.

Why do we suspect a purpose behind the laws of life? Flowers blossom just as unintentionally as the pebbles in a creek roll along, but with the latter we know at least why they are round. If we did not know this, however, we would under no circumstances ask why they are round but for what purpose! It is actually like this: when we have identified the cause, we have found the purpose as well! And for that reason, we finally know for instance why flowers blossom: because it turned out that way. And as long as the conditions inside and outside of their existence don't change, they will keep on blossoming. Cause and effect, the two are separated wrongly and are thus promptly mistaken for each other. Since a way has been found, life is taking it in order to find it again and again ... just like the river follows its course or as naturally as a body falls to the ground...

We already demonstrated the significance of the signals for this world. Whenever the signals turned out stronger, clearer, or more colourful they fulfilled their purpose better which was actually never intended. For it isn't as if flowers had possibly realised that it was more advantageous to blossom more distinctly and then were doing so for that reason. But those plants which could not do so were simply overlooked and that is the reason why they don't exist anymore. Yet this is not an accidental selection, just as little as the occurrence of distinctive, colourful blossoms was accidental because all this always happened on the basis of already existing internal conditions: the genetic data collections and the repertoire of latent chemical reactions.

That those internal conditions completed the external conditions to a good way was not blind chance either, but co-incidence. Thus, life is not a game of dice at all. A river has to flow, and in doing so it keeps its freedom only in the framework of an overriding law: it is in any case going downhill. The flow of energy is restricted in the same way. It flows in cascades and meanders, accumulates now and then, continues to flow... Its reservoirs are the cells, its valves the molecules, its floodgates the cellular walls and the membranes, its supplies photosynthesis, oxygen, ATP...

Its path curves and winds, finds many forms and intermediate stages and finally it creates us. And we unjustly look at these intermediate stages with astonishment, falsely imply that they do not only have meaning and objectives but characteristics as well: they are beautiful or ugly, good or bad...

Well, it is exactly the signalling effect which entices us to make such evaluations. Blazing signals that mean to distinguish oneself from the accord of the world and to appear to be extraordinary. We still carry the memory of all these signals in us which have ever been of significance to us - they have already triggered certain behavioural patterns during our evolution -, because we have taken part in and have lived through all stages of development. For that reason, we instinctively react to colourful blossoms just like insects. They attract us as if by magic but we don't know why... and for this kind of feelings we invented a concept of its own: "beauty".

The most causal fuel of life, light, immediately lends a tinge of beauty to things which are neutral in themselves: what would a diamond be without its sparkle, what would any jewel be without light, the glimmer of gold, the gleam of water falls, the glittering of the stars, the blue of the sky, or the red sky in the morning ... they are all playgrounds of the light - and therefore "beautiful" to us. Even colours are games of the light. Whenever we see something beautiful, we see light in some form...

What life builds up and defines and preserves in us are order and symmetry. Wherever we find order and symmetry as a spatial function, we see beauty because of that: crystals, snow flakes, radiolarians, honeycombs...

And our life is filled with creating orders and symmetries. Almost all scientists sort their knowledge and search for hidden harmonies. Even their theories only meet with approval if they contain elegance and symmetry. Bright, easily visible colours are the traffic lights of our life; wherever there is colour, our eyes are pleased. Light, orderly forms, structures, and all colours of the rainbow strike a note with our behavioural patterns, our drives, our sexuality, etc.. They make something beautiful and therefore they are means of expression in art and architecture. If man does not find things which are appropriated for a certain purpose beautiful from the beginning, he will soon attach his values to them - and this process is called aesthetics. For that reason, we create works of art and buildings (pyramids, cathedrals, monuments) as objects of "beauty" whose purpose has often been lost. And even the work of art without any function still contains the purpose to be only beautiful or to contrast with beauty, to emphasise through negation by bringing us a lack of light, order, and colour!

We act in exactly the same way with purpose and especially with meaning. The insignificant provokes us in the same manner as the non-beautiful; and just like we find beauty where it doesn't exist at all because seen objectively there cannot be anything like beauty, we will promptly find a meaning where there isn't any. And again there is a confusion: we confuse the why of the cause with the why of the meaning. But the meaning of a river can only be to transport water - and that is also its cause. Thus the meaning of life lies indeed in transporting and losing energy - which is of course also its cause. The meaning of life can therefore be only life itself. And when we say the meaning of life is the realisation of the cosmos itself which only manifests as such through seeing and recognising, we are now as ever caught in the incriminating circular argument - for even this meaning is only the cause of a total event which was just unable to leave life out.

Of its own accord, the cosmos does not intend anything, it exists of its own accord because it exists! Everything only makes sense actually if thinking beings attribute a meaning to it enticed to do so by causalities which they discovered. They think: after all a road has to lead somewhere. But as we can see with the excavator and bulldozer system, this is probably an illusion. For that reason, there aren't any right ways or wrong ways; we cannot look for and find anything in our environment which we do not carry in us ... for "our world" is absolutely based on reflection.

A river bypasses every mountain. It seems to recognise the right way but appearances are deceptive as we immediately realise. Our sense organs and our brains also serve for recognising the way - and again appearances are deceptive: we believe in the freedom of choice[59] but the way is just as forced as that of the river. Still it remains unpredictable because it only exists from moment to moment just like that short piece of road of the excavator system.

Everyone who would have us believe that the future lies perceptible in store somewhere, fantasises. Providence only comprises the functions of a system, i.e. its internal conditions; from them it is at best possible to make a few conclusion for the future but mostly surprises are the result. That is what makes life truly fascinating: that it reveals neither aim nor meaning. And therefore it is neither mysterious nor unexplained because it only hides from us what it doesn't know itself.

Thus we can suddenly look at connections in a much simpler way than the scholars ever allowed themselves to do. Postulated values, like beautiful or ugly, good and bad, divided the world into cause and effect, body and mind, sender and receiver, matter and God, waves and particles; and the scientists sitting on these halves quarrelled with each other without comprehending that everything belongs together...

36 Mind

Where in the events of this world as we depicted it should we localise something like "mind"? Isn't is so as if we didn't need the hypothesis mind anymore to make the world comprehensible? Did we not realise that matter is a hypothesis anyhow because it does not exist as substance, as primary matter at all?

We saw that the development of drives, feelings, and the consciousness lies within the functions of matter. No-one was ever talking about an extra mind. We didn't discover any planner, any creator nor any will. And thus there is no connection from the only cause to the apparently planned, created, wanted either. What we are confusing with mind is information. The world is an informative event; causalities are mutually dependant, they place information. The terrain of a river bed contains information in the same way as the sequences of the DNA.

What we also like to mix up with mind next is knowledge. But knowledge also reveals itself as badly considered concept because it can only mean a collection of information. There is no knowledge about the things – if only because of the fact that we do not recognise things immediately and absolutely. Every experience is selected by the senses and reduced to information. To know and to believe are in principle the same. Even if we don't have to believe in a creator, we believe in this world because all evidence lies within its boundaries.

This has plagued the philosophers since they thought: this being confined to the connections of the consciousness, this relativised "recognition" which is inevitably coined by the inside world, this lack of absolute values and indications. And it has plagued them in particular because they have always tried to explain values which are completely abstract, like "luck" for example. Luck and mind and many other concepts, even information and knowledge are synergetic blends from other effects.

Stars in the sky form constellations, squares, triangles, the signs of the zodiac - but do they really form these figures? Of course not, because the connection lines are only thought. For the most part, the stars are located on different planes and don't have any relation to one another.

This seeing of connections, whether they exist or not, this discerning of orders or categories, this linking process founded in us on the material plane without exception, these are "mental" events. Because we have to realise that mind cannot exist at all as a substrate, which would be opposed to matter. We don't have to accommodate the mind by force, either, as was done by the physicist Jean E. Charon, for example, when he banned the mind of the world into the electrons - a really funny undertaking!

When watching the characters on the cinema screen we don't suppose to find a mental event behind it. But why do we do so when we picture a landscape with our eyes closed? When a pea whistle whistles, there is nothing mental about it in our opinion, so why should it have a mental background when we say the word "abracadabra" or whistle a little ourselves. When a computer calculates the orbit of the moon, it seems natural to us because we programmed it after all. Why does it surprise us that we can discern the environment when it has programmed us itself?

The simple function of a "supernatural" matter creates illusions: gravitation or charge... and even mind belong into this category! A lot of people won't like to admit it. But is it really so important to desperately single something out of all the trivial functions which make us equal to the animal and plant world in order to distinguish us from them? All products of our mind - including the possibility to be wrong – can also be found in the plant and animal kingdom. And the latest generations of computers already confronts us seriously with the question if there are not only slight differences between them and us which will have disappeared completely one day.

Some will say: a computer cannot feel. Why do they dare make this statement? What do we know about the feelings of a computer - and what does it know about ours? What do we know about the feelings of our fellow human beings but the mere assumption that theirs may be similar to ours? Nothing at all. Is this world not full of allegedly mentally ill people only because they feel and think differently from us, so very much differently that we lock them away? What do we know about their feelings? Nothing at all. And does it not remain an open question which of the two sides has to be called insane actually?

Feeling, thinking, and consciousness ... they differ from creature to creature, from genus to genus, from species to species. What connects us human beings with one another are conventions like language, writing – that is resolutions and agreements. Still a certain difficulty to comprehend the other remains because we will never learn if he experiences the colour red really in the same way as we do...

All these are mental events – intended as a collective concept and to be used that way. A book contains information but in the end it is a collection of letters. And thus mind also consists of a collection of informative facts.

We already talked about the basis for aesthetics. Superficially, it appears to be a mental process as long as we don't take a closer look. But other mental events also reveal that we are not what we want to be. One of these apparently unexplainable feelings is sympathy (syn = common, pathein = to feel, to experience). In the same way as we carry the environment in us as a reflection so to speak, we carry selected ideals as reflections of this environment in our psychophysiological reaction patterns. The system of combining these patterns is both surprising and simple, obvious and determined by symmetries: we like people who like us or who are similar to us. We like somebody rather when giving and taking balance each other or when there is a spatial proximity to somebody. Not least, the association with pleasant things determines the degree of our affection: we like people with whom we associate pleasant things. And of course, the physical attraction (aesthetics) has some say in it. All these criteria are transmitted by signals. The body language is a main transmitter; just think of the different feelings of "sympathy" which only the arms of a person can evoke when they are open, folded, extended, stretched, held out, defensive, inviting, bent, lowered, or raised... Other signals can be colours or shapes. They evoke behavioural patterns which feign decisions between appearance, typification, positivity, negativity, ambivalence, aversion, and affection etc... Just like all the other patterns, the behavioural patterns for "sympathy" react to their associative trigger signals. "Pleasant" people (or objects) provide these signals, "unpleasant" people don't.

It is no coincidence that esoterics consider the human being to be a "resonating body " in an ocean of vibrations. In doing so they do not restrict "body" to a mechanistic conception of the world but view the human being as a being both with a material and an immaterial, a so-called "ethereal" body, the "aura". This fascinating word conceals nothing else but an energetic complex of energy which vibrates at different frequencies in the neuronal network of the brain. A separation into immaterial and material is absolutely unnecessary because both mean just as fundamentally the same as energy and matter.

Let's briefly talk about strong emotions like love and hate. Is not love at least a noble and pure product of the mind? And how about hate? How could these strong signs of emotion only be explainable from the material? Should we not spare these emotions, compelled to define something like mind or soul after all?

We should not. Because we already discovered a kind of love which is without any doubt of a material nature: the affinity of oxygen and hydrogen for one another. This is the quantum of love so to speak. All other atoms "love" or "hate" each other in a similar way, too. We know the cause of this behaviour: it is the spatial polarisation which creates either harmony or disharmony. And one fact has to come to our notice moreover: that atoms love mostly atoms which are not like them - i.e. which oscillate in the opposite direction. If similarity is the prerequisite for affection, we come across the opposite here. Obviously we are dealing with a different automaticity in this case.

The behavioural patterns provided by the sexual drive are stipulated organically, they are triggered and controlled by hormones. We should not confuse that with "love". Everybody knows that there is a little more behind love. But upon closer inspection even this more reveals itself only as a product of sums of various processes of the consciousness which are again explainable organically and chemically.

Ugliness or beauty are only differentiated by our behaviour and this was born of experience and memory in turn. Ugliness becomes existent by what frightens us and meets with rejection. But we have to be aware of the fact that we have learned to be frightened. We were taught what had to be ugly, hideous, dreadful, and useless - just as we were taught all the other values of this world. As a baby we were chirpily crawling in the dirt. "Dirt" had not been defined as hideous, useless, and negative yet. Just as impartially we took hold of all objects unrestrictedly, no matter if dirty or clean, ugly or beautiful... And above all without the faintest clue as to any rights.

We only learned at a later time that something can belong to you or me. The concepts of having, ownership, and possession are learned assignments for certain impressions of the senses. Wanting to have something is one aspect of this knowledge, not liking something, the other...

While we grow up we learn primarily that we belong to somebody - namely to our parents. We are thoroughly handled like property. From that two things have to develop: firstly we want to continue to belong to somebody because this conditions protected us and was quite pleasant - and we create gods to which we belong and which have to protect us in return. Any inclination of the human being towards religiousness is rooted in that. Secondly we want to be owners, shields, and protectors ourselves as well, however, because this status is obviously also marked with pleasant feelings - after all it had been practised by our parents. That this can be a misapprehension is perhaps confirmed by many people. Because to possess is one thing and to obey is quite another. As a child we trusted our owners and obeyed. In that way, the order of superiority remained preserved. As an adult we find trusting not so easy anymore and for that reason, obeying neither. But what we want nevertheless is to possess in every respect and thus also to possess a human being - as fateful as this may sound.

Obviously half the motivating force for love is striving for possession, the other half deals with whether a human being is worthy of being possessed and with the perception processes associated with that: signals, affinity, ideals, attractiveness, eroticism, and so on. In addition there is the fact that other people also want to possess "us" - which we don't find unpleasant at all for the reasons mentioned above.

Consequently there are always at least two people involved who want to possess one another or already believe to do so. Just as with sympathy the decisive factor for this desire is of course the applicability (co-incidence) of the correct signals. We find these signals predominantly in the sexual field. But not only in this respect does the other one signalise something which we are not. Paradoxically though, because we are looking for a second self, for a mirror image. As a result we find something which we take for a reflection. We have to believe in this counter part because we do not know the original of this image. Because our life is marked by the struggle for our own identity.

Who does really know what effect he has, how he looks or how he is experienced by others subjectively? We never find identity in ourselves because we are looking out of us and discover our ego in the centre of the world which just remains concealed to us. So we have at best an idea, a mirage about ourselves. And therefore we will never be able to comprehend ourselves to the extent to which we can grasp the phenomenon of other people. In comparison, we can imagine other people quite well, conjure up their appearances, see them in our mind's eye, and dream of them. Their visages and figures created equivalent matrixes in us.

If such patterns of meaning are strongly developed, we already "possess" this human being to the highest possible extent.... But woe betide if we meet anyone whose identity remains concealed to us just like our own. Since he doesn't fit into the previous patterns in our brain (the "everyday people"), his signals have a stronger effect. They make him stick out of the crowd and we cannot retrieve the mental image of his appearance from our mind - we don't "possess" him yet. For that reason, we promptly see in him - like in an empty mirror - everything which we would like to find in ourselves. And then it can happen that we are lost. We fall in love and the consequence is: we have to possess this human being in a real form because he does not exist in us in an imaginary form, i.e. because he cannot be replaced by imagination.

Everybody who tried knows how immensely difficult it is to picture the face of a beloved person in ones mind. And above all we rarely dream of this person and if we dream of him he mostly doesn't have a face. Because it was not saved in us. The mystery of this person was maintained, we therefore did not grasp him entirely. For that reason, we will unfortunately often also see mostly much more in him than he really has to offer. And when it becomes apparent on closer inspection that he has a concrete identity like anybody else, it often happens that all love is lost.

The more human images are stored in the chamber of our imagination, the less likely becomes the "danger" to fall in love. In a certain way inexperience is the precondition for a strong ability to love. Unscrupulous people don't fall in love so quickly and so impulsively anymore for just that reason. For them, only a few people give new and strong signals; all other people remain trivial and easy to classify into the patterns of their imagination. In comparison he who loves projects onto the other what he believes himself to be, in fact until the real nature of the other one conquers this image. Suddenly the other one is anything but oneself, a circumstance which is often hard to cope with when it becomes apparent. The other person's being different which was reason for increased attentiveness and for the compliment: "You are not like the others", ends in the judgement: "Your are just like all the others", and one cannot understand anymore why one ever said to this person: "I never want to loose you!"

Our languages go immediately back to the examinations and the experiences with this truth of life. What do they reveal about us in this case? To grow fond of somebody, to come to love somebody, to love somebody, to like somebody, to estimate somebody, to find somebody nice... Here language becomes were clear for it expresses exactly in what love is rooted: possession. Not caring for somebody, not being fond of somebody, not getting anything out of somebody ... no less informative, this means the opposite.

The apparently immaterial feeling "love" can thus be explained indeed with considerably more trivial behavioural patterns like striving for possession and identity. These are quite old properties and they have probably been of use to us throughout evolution.

On the other hand, acquisitiveness, combined with antipathy and tangible identity, account for hate, an even more distinct and more persistent feeling because the enemy is easier to recognise, his characteristics easier to comprehend - for he often takes something away from us - and we know for sure where we stand with him. But even hate and aggression are fundamentally products of our experience as well and were thus learned. The education of human beings contains so much aggression and suppression that one has to wonder to find something like love in us still.

Other "mental" properties of mankind, intelligence and common sense for example - which are on no account only found with the human being – can be explained as purely "material" functions of the brain as well and can be easily understood in principle. Still we are confronted with an anthropocentric overestimation exactly in this field whereas the truly remarkable accomplishment of mankind, the creativity, rather comes from intuition than from reason. We should also talk a little about that as well in order to round off our digression about the mind.

The attention of a human being, i.e. his present consciousness, is always coupled with the reflective activity of one or several of his senses (=vibration between brain and sense organ). But that doesn't mean that other areas of his brain are idle in the meantime. The RNA in the neurons cannot be stored just like that because it is a dynamic structure just like the DNA and therefore has to be broken down and recreated and increased again and again. That means we are already forgetting while we are thinking; while parts of our brain are structured with new contents, other parts of the brain are regenerating again. This causes an unconscious thinking process, a sorting of contents, a vibration of patterns in incoherent areas. It is often maintained that the human being uses only a tenth of his brain and the rest is idle. This is completely wrong for sure. Why would evolution have wanted to equip us with such a wastefully abundant and excessive amount of brain when thriftiness and carrying out the base necessities has top priority? Surely the complete brain always works as a unit on combining the perceptions.

All neurons as well as all nerves and end plates are particularly rich in mitochondria. This reveals an especially high requirement for ATP. Enzymes do not continuously break down this ATP into ADP, and the released bonding energy turns into electric current, into electron waves - but of course not so totally directly. We already discovered an atom in the chlorophyll which has specialised on electron waves: magnesium. Therefore we should not be surprised that we also find plenty of magnesium ions in the nerve cells. They play a central role in all processes which exploit or produce electromagnetic impulses (light, electric current). Even the cold light of the glow worms and deep sea fish is only created in collaboration with magnesium ions. In the nerve cell they transform the arising thermal vibrations of the decaying ATP or RNA molecules into electric current, i.e. electron impulses. For that reason, there is a significant difference compared to the learning matrix of a computer: the capacitors of the nervous circuit also contain little power generators, batteries so to speak, which are required above all to supply to the great energy consumption when reassembling the RNA. But they also send out current impulses into the other neurons which modulate these impulses depending on the amount of available RNA. With that our brain is a rather complicated analogous computer. The game of its neurons never ceases, and there is of course also a coupled connection between the mainly active patterns which are just creating consciousness through the sense organs and the ones working unconsciously.

For that reason, thinking takes place in multiple layers, develops on many levels at the same time ... and suddenly the currents sum up in some matrix or other and stimulate the corresponding sense organ. "It is thinking inside of us", we should say and we do: "It occurs to me ..." What occurs to us is firstly surprising because our consciousness has not been at all where the solution was found, and secondly it is quite useable most of the time. As is to be expected, such processes work even better when the sense organs are switched off or muted, for instance while we are sleeping, and intuition often copes with the problem overnight which could not be solved during the day...

One of the most interesting and distinctive mental abilities of the human being is humour, although animals also have received a bit of it. The absolutely astonishing, the punch line of a joke, always results from the discrepancy between inner truth and external reality. Our brain does not have any response to such surprise attacks on the basis of the occurrence of uncoupled patterns - the internally simulated event is brought to the wrong plane of expectancy, the presented solution is found somewhere else. Because it cannot think of something suitable, it feels duped, led up the garden path, and reacts with a behavioural atavism which is actually a threatening gesture - laughter. It serves for venting the bottled-up tension. The whole body is involved, the muscles of our stomach, our back, and our face are at work, we bare our teeth ... in short, laughing is a drastic expression of our embarrassment. And we do the same when our brain does not quite know what to do with physical impressions of an unusual kind which it receives for example when we are tickled.

The originally aggressive character of laughter only arises when we laugh at someone. Laughter restores the balance and is therefore experienced with relish. Something very similar applies to crying.

A punch line becomes only possible if the extrapolation apparatus of our inner chamber of imagination is very well-developed and simulates or continues complex plots. Humour is therefore a particular expression of our intelligence. Even animals laugh in their own way, but only the human being can really almost die of laughter. Humour has been integrated in the working principle of our brain from the outset because it can be deceived much too easily. In comparison, behavioural patterns, like for example fear, are primarily learned. Fear is - so to speak - the pain in advance of an event whose imaginary continuation makes us become aware that we will get hurt. Fear is therefore a pure product of our experience. Of course we also find fear in animals and this proves that animals can also gain negative experience. With the lower animals, however, fear is already inherited as a mode of behaviour or well developed as a conditioned reflex. In the latter case the corresponding behaviour is perhaps not accompanied by a feeling of fright at all.

Well, we could certainly continue in this manner to describe and analyse human thinking. We could substantiate the easily feasible deception of our visual sense with the pregrown patterns which are already concealed in the retina of our eyes. Because our organs of sight aren't actually purely optical instruments as for instance cameras. Their functions go far beyond the mere reproduction of the environment. By means of complicated nervous circuits, they transform the events into abstract structures and patterns which later fulfil the requirements of the processing and storage method in the brain. We could also analyse such subtle emotional activities like envy, joy, sadness, amazement, depression, or awe, and dissect them into the components inheritance, moulding, and learning - but this would lead us to fathomless digressions. We would have to go into the broad fields of behavioural research and psychology.

At this point it should be sufficient for the comprehension of a universal principle that mind is not the opposite pole of matter nor anything with which matter forms a vague kind of community: Never was there anything to unite because there were not any opposites. Mind is a material manifestation; a collective name for material information. The loudspeaker of our radio is constantly emitting mind of this kind, and it would never occur to us to expect a symphonic orchestra inside the apparatus. Why have we been looking for mind, for soul, for Od in our heads for centuries ... or for the super-ego, the "unconscious", the super-self, or for the subtle body?

The truth is that all these things don't exist for real and they have never been necessary. Even if there are vehement protests by those people who feel deprived of their mind, we have to clearly underline it again: our mind results from nothing else but the combinations of some determined behavioural patterns which were born of a supply of learning and fixed matrixes which, although very great, is still limited. In them a hierarchical order prevails: courses of locomotion are composed of patterns of locomotion, even thinking subordinates itself to the rules of sentence construction and logic.

This restricts our mental work considerably for it never contains reality itself but only creates simplified hypothetic realities in which we act. The intellect is also subject to an evolution which is accompanied by the organic. This could not be avoided for the reason alone that the old must always be involved upon the construction of the new. Both developments are therefore marked by a certain degree of non-conformity and imperfection; both evolutions do not exactly keep up with the course of time - a fact which has already carried off many forms of life before.

But, as we realised, this is probably the price for everything. In return we get a world like it does not take place at all. Outside of our brain, our conception of the world does not exist after all. And every brain produces a different kind of world. All of these universes are codifications of emotions whose originators are at best wavelengths, impulses, and proportions. Seen that way the cosmos as we know it is actually an informative one, consequently it is a "mental" one. No wonder if our consciousness gets caught in this discrepancy between truth and reality and thinks the universe is based on something higher, intellectual, or spiritual. But the truth is that it has just as little spirit as we have. But we could also say the universe is spirit because in the end "spirit " is also only a word for the immaterial substance of matter for which we have arbitrarily chosen a different word, namely T.A.O....

So our opinion places us between the materialists who want to see the world as a series of material causalities and the idealists who attribute an intellectual plan to the same event: Providence, destination, meaning, ...

We also discovered a succession of causalities as well as the interaction of external and internal conditions. But neither the atom nor the DNA work strictly as causality machines because they are subject to a network of causality and not to linear causality. This entanglement makes the events appear as if by mere chance although they are a series of real co-incidences: the co-incidence of successful conditions - if one will rate the world as success. It is an evolution step-by-step but the word evolution is already incorrect; nothing has really developed "higher", every stage was equivalent to the next as a precondition, even its set of orders was always higher. For this is the motto of the game: the fluid transition from quantitative orders (that of the atoms, of the molecules, of the impulses) into something qualitatively higher ("life", "consciousness") which receives its energy from the preceding set of orders.

In that way order is added to order and every step is reduced in quantity and raised in quality above the creation of the consciousness until it reaches that order which we call society. This hypothesis proves itself if we take into account that the populations of living things increase proportional to the simplicity of their structures both referred to the present and to a period of millions of years. And we understand from natural history that a new order was always found at the expense of an old concept. This mechanism has not ceased, and for that reason, we have to see the current extinction of the animal kingdom all around us and will not be able to prevent it.

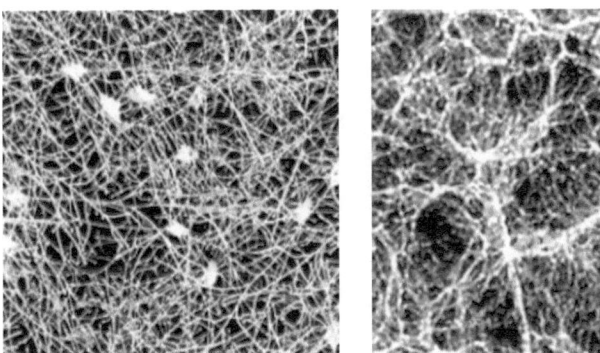

Fig. 147a: A symbol for the universe in our mind. On the left the network structure of neurons, on the right the cluster structure of the galaxy arrangements in the open supercluster behind the constellation Virgo.

Life uses many ways; they are ways of the moment, without destination and without beginning because the ways have come into existence at the same time as the waygoer. Many instructions develop the organisms, although without plan and without planners because they are outlines of the moment, created at the same time as the constructions. And old ways and old constructions are always dragged along; schemata are persevered which are often meaninglessly and cumbersome, only determined by freedom in as much as they don't know what lies in store for them ...

The scholars could not reckon with that for a long time: that the ways of entropy have to lead via new orders which are hidden among the coincidences as necessities and systematically demand new ways because they are in each other's way (and the universe in its own) ...

All ways are open and still there is a main direction; a direction only and not a destination. The times are endless, and still there is an end but it is only the end of an image which will be wrapped up in a new one!

37 Perfection

Is evolution a precision machine? Could we claim that nature was perfect - and that we were its crowning glory? To believe in this would demonstrate once again that overbearing self-arrogance of mankind who, in their unrestricted modesty, take every single person for the very image of a god. Unfortunately the truth is quite different.

For perfecting our conception of the world, it is necessary to correct the adopted perspective of some believers in miracles. Just the very organ of our optical sensation, the eye, is actually an absurd thing and on no account as sun-like as Goethe would have had it: the light first has to pass through the supportive layer, the blood vessels, and the nerves before it hits the optic nerves, and even they are hit from behind. We would never come up with the idea to put a film into the camera the wrong way around - nature did so because the development did not permit something absolutely new. It also had its good points: reflection and consciousness could only develop on the basis of that - as we already described in detail. The price for it is an apparatus whose mere optical quality is easily outdone by any toy telescope.

A tremendous luxury of nerves could compensate for many a physical imperfection; but this coin has a dark backside: neuroses, psychoses, epilepsy, schizophrenia, and so on. The error rate of our organic body is terribly high. Clinical dictionaries are filled with the names of thousands of different diseases which go either back to errors in the genetic programme (hereditary diseases, cancer) or simply to the fact that many things about us are not designed to the optimum.

Every tenth person would miserably die of his appendix if it was not cut out as a precaution. As early as during the embryonic development, the growing organism goes through a hard test which is only passed by those who pass which are reasonably suitable. About 5 % of all embryos are eliminated from the beginning, are stillborn, or die shortly after birth. Another, not inconsiderable percentage is given deformities and defective functions like metabolic disturbances for their arduous way through life. And we don't know at all how many fertilised eggs perish shortly after their lodging because their programme fails already after a few hours. The rate of failure is in any case enormous. Only if the programme proves its worth until the birth, there is an, although slight, prospect that it will function trouble-free for some decades.

He who walks through the hospitals of this Earth will never be tempted to glorify the human mammal with the upright posture. There isn't much left from the impressive and noble conception of man as it is depicted in art and culture. What comes to light here in the form of ulcers, necroses, pustules, boils, eczemas, oedemas, and disfigurements seems to come rather from the kitchen of the devil than to be the product of a determined development with the very image of God at its end.

Damaged intervertebral discs, hernias, varicose veins, flat feet, haemorrhoids, and vestibular disorders are the direct tribute for our better (over)view and the free use of our hands. A great number of constitutional diseases occurs with the human being only because he is a human being: a conglomeration of ideas, often inadequately combined... gullet and trachea intersect, urinary and seminal tracts are together, and birth takes place through a bone channel of all things which is unable to dilate. The child is cruelly pressed into a foetal cylinder, and when it finally comes into the world, it is the most helpless baby of the world, unable to do anything at first, a croaking bundle of flesh which even has to learn first that suckling at its mother's breast is a pleasure.

If we choose the most reliable parts of several automobiles, i.e. the motor of one, the wheels of another, the gearbox of the third, and so on, it is hardly to be expected that the new combination of these parts will be the sum of their reliability. Because they are not suitable for one another and will rather hinder than support each other. And yet this newly created automobile will still draw ahead of all the others if it has headlights in the darkness - and the others have not. With them it will just see the way better... And thus the visual animal man has seen the way sufficiently better in order to continue to exist whereas designs which were objectively more successful fell by the wayside.

A typical example for a wrong track of nature is demonstrated by the dolphin which - a bundle of intelligence - has so much to cope with in an environment inappropriate for it that the cultivation of cultural needs did not occur despite its giant brain. Would it not be better for it to be a fish like it even was for a short time during its embryonic development than to struggle as a mammal under water? But the complete adaptation was denied to it; there is no way back in evolution which can also consist in an increase of errors. Which becomes so apparent now and again that we speak of an involution as if we really thought nature had done a retrograde step. But exactly such a retrograde step would really be a step forward, a real attempt to repeat the experiment - though that has never happened so far.

The formula was much simpler: what went wrong, went down. And everything that was successful, has remained an experiment in an endless series of experiments over millions of years, an eternal experimental stage - and never perfection itself. This certain degree of half-measure and, with regard to the feeding principle, also of cruelty is to be expected in a world which only exists for the reason alone that its opposite would be impossible, and which therefore creates structures out of necessity in which we want to see creative orders almost by force. Because we only can or have to think within the framework of our own subjective experiences - as practically minded living things which create orders on their own by laying brick on brick in order to live in the construct....

It has not always been that way, though. Once naturally available caves were accepted for this purpose, and presumably the world must have been more self-evident at that time. Not one animal racks its brain over origin and demise of the world. It was exclusively our thinking which separated physical and mental; it destroyed our being one with nature... And soon there weren't any wise ones anymore among all the learned.

There are at least two obvious indications for the thesis presented in this book that the creation of the organisms was preceded by a nonrecurring accumulation of information with the creation of the DNA and the chromosomes and that all following phenomena have rooted in the gradual exploitation of these programmes,: for one thing the incredible stubbornness of the programmes which still leads to rudimentary organs today, and for another the existence of indestructible viruses which speak or understand the language of living cells.

Viruses could only have developed at the time when the DNA itself came into being. This can be definitely substantiated chemically: never after the existence of the primeval soup could conditions occur again which would have led to the development of viruses containing RNA and DNA. And without doubt, the development of the DNA must have been preceded by the generation of energy through photosynthesis, just as the respiration of the ATP circulation must have already existed before that.

After the development of the DNA there were two possibilities: firstly the invariable scanning of the preset succession of steps, i.e. the undynamic pattern without the disassembly and reassembly of the DNA while the chromosomes were even preserved in-between divisions, and secondly the dynamic DNA which could gradually specialise in certain functions by eradicating the errors. Nature certainly made use of both possibilities. We expect to find the first one predominantly in the world of the insects where the rigid string of programmes leads to the metamorphoses, to the strange fact that an insect represents actually a succession of completely different living things.

For that reason, the chromosomes of many insects remain visible even during the interphase and become only partially uncoiled (puffs). These rigid control system of the insects' programmes is very easily misled and falsely employed. A locust which had its antenna torn out will sometimes grow back a useless leg in this place. Since it was impossible to write down experiences on the DNA, variants have only been produced by means of a gradually prolonged exploitation of the programmes; for that reason, the life of an insect is going through the most bizarre stages.

It also has its advantages: insects are not very susceptible to mutations. That's the reason why they tolerate radioactive radiation considerably better than those living things whose control is done by means of a dynamic DNA which also repeats its own development in every generation of a species. Whereas insects have remained almost unchanged over millions of years and the word evolution can only be applied to them with a grain of salt, the dynamic structures have incessantly carried out drastic modifications. The reason for that could only lie in a flexible control which "improved" the DNA during a short period of embryonic growth, for one thing by eliminating everything that was useless, and for another by adding the use of certain sequences as regulator genes which evoked a temporally useful scanning of the genes and by creating repression (repercussion of surplus products) and induction (stimulation of genetic effects through available signals, food molecules, or hormones). The genetically effective use of surplus RNA shreds as an initial form of data processing will still be found today as well...

If the geneticists continue to adhere to their dogma of the rigid, sacrosanct DNA, they will end up in a dead-end street. Because they fail to notice, for example, that the regulator genes must have come to their function in some way and that it could not just have fallen from heaven.

The interaction of all genes is entangled so variedly that the control of evolution through mutation will completely loose its credibility. This theory is just not reasonable anymore. Apparently this takes the wind out of the sails of those scholars who spitefully referred to the always negative effects of the mutations and thought (absolutely correctly) that this could just not be the way things went. For that reason, the vitalists and idealists should have been right... Because evolution was in truth running without a motor.

We, on the other hand, clearly presented this motor, and one should just not make the frequent mistake which kept so many natural sciences from making any progress: laying down dogmas which are not substantiated in any way! And above all one should not judge the chromosomes of the human being by the standards of those of the fruit fly because the differences are far too great in principle.

Many biologists thought for a long time that every single body cell contained the complete plan for the body. That may be true for many living things, like plants and many species of insects. Maybe even for certain lower animal species, like for instance frogs, which make one suspect that they follow a rigid DNA in their growth via intermediate forms (tadpoles). In case of highly developed living things the specialisation of body cells is done on the basis of a dynamic DNA which really changes. It would therefore not be possible on any account to clone the complete human being from a single human skin cell. We know a high degree of specialisation in our bodies which even destroys the whole plan. We are talking about the red blood corpuscles, which loose their nucleus completely. They develop from normal cells containing a nucleus, the proerythroblasts, via the macroblasts and normoblasts, which still contain a nucleus, to nucleus-free normocytes; after that they live for about 100 to 120 days and during this time they absorb oxygen or carbon dioxide ca. 175 000 times.

Erythrocytes demonstrate most distinctly that a chromosomal and genetic alteration can take place as a result of specialisation. Our DNA is therefore certainly manipulated and influenced by the immediate environment in the course of our growth. The "complete programme" can only still be found in the so-called "stem cells".

So to speak we are growing from inside out, every stage of our growth forms the precondition for the next one. And in every phase the cells are virtually forced to change their programme and in doing so to commit themselves to a certain function, or more exactly to restrict themselves. Just like the occurrence of the nucleus in the blood corpuscles, the appearance of a second nucleus in the cells of the liver should give us something to think about. In this case there was obviously nothing to gain with a restriction of the programme, and the organic environment actually enforced a new cell form which has only remotely to do with the original plan of the germ cell.

Thus there isn't any command for "liver cells" on the DNA but organs, which grow stringed to each other, suddenly create conditions which evoke a syntheses of the liver cells, and so the DNA is not alone in command but everything is involved in the game which contributes to the specific environment: the cell plasma, the organelles, and the cell function itself, i.e. the products which are created or consumed.

If an error of any kind occurs - disturbing chemical substances and viruses can wreak a lot of havoc here - the cell does not only lose its specialisation but does not gain a new function either, least of all will it become an original germ cell because all essential steps of the programme have been eradicated long since. If the complete blueprint still existed, however, cases of this kind would have to occur from time to time. That it does never happen proves our opinion - because the disturbed cell becomes at best a helpless object which begins to proliferate rampantly like a primeval cell. This is nothing else but cancer, the feared scourge of mankind, a direct consequence of our variable DNA. It can hardly be assumed that a rigid DNA which remains completely operative over millions of years suddenly suffers such drastic pathological errors during cell division because of its reduplication process - therefore no one has ever heard of cancer in insects.

It is our misfortune that carcinogenic substances can intervene during the disassembly and reassembly of the DNA - i.e. in the stage of dissolution of the chromosomes during which the amount of DNA is reduced to a quarter. For the weak spot lies in the interphase of cell division: just as the DNA causes design and function of the cell, i.e. creates the environment, this environment has to react upon the DNA in return in order to reassemble it identically. When this environment changes, the correct plan is lost...

Finally, one has to become aware of the fact that nature obviously found several ways of dealing with and using the DNA. A safe one but it restricted the development and required metamorphoses and is keen on development which can unfortunately also lead to such distressing results like cancer in a toxic and unsuitable environment. Therefore this terrible disease is also a tribute for our higher development.

In any case we hopefully undermined a general difficulty that should have weighed heavily on the evolutionists: the unreliability of chance to which the creation of life and its high development could not be attributed alone for mathematical reasons. Chance was in fact already restricted by the development of systems and purely spatial regulations but this was no particular consolation for the sceptics.

Well, we found another restriction of chance: the polarisation of space, i.e. the effects of a finestructure that leads to electrical controls which complement or even exceed those of the spatial structures by far. Here is an example for that: the possibilities of two dice to meet one another with two particular sides are much too great as long as all sides of the two dice are absolutely equal. But when we discover opposite polarisations in addition, these dice (or atoms and molecules) already carry a programme - and only those sides will combine which fit to another. Apart from the stereometric (spatial) conditions there are also electrostatic and magnetic effects in the molecular activity, which don't leave a very great repertoire to chance. With that it can finally be demonstrated that life is a natural process, which does not require any higher cause.

One should probably relativise it in that way: if we didn't know anything about the growing conditions of a crystal, even the rocks of our Earth would evade every explanation...

Is our universe perfect? Why does it seem to have exactly does properties which make life possible? Of course, life as we know it is not likely without the existence of planets, stars, and galaxies. Many researchers believe that the creation of stars depends on a precisely coordinated relation between the three "constants of nature", on gravitation, on the weak nuclear force, and on the electromagnetic force. If only one of these constants was a little higher or lower, no stars and consequently no life either could have been created in our universe. From that one could derive that the universe was made to measure for us. But this perspective is the wrong one.

One could also see the eternal transformation of this universe as a succession of a variety of universes. Quantum cosmologists like Andrei Linde advocate for example the theory of the "eternal universe reproducing itself ", in which new universes are created continuously. In each of these universes, the constants of nature have other values set by chance. That our universe, which possesses exactly the values required for the creation of life, is among them at one time is almost inevitable.

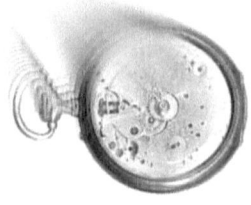

38 Eternity

The successes of natural scientific discoveries were often unintentionally supported by the statements of some religions. Interestingly enough, because of the behaviour of some churches which – as in particular the Christian catholic one - felt obliged to insist on keeping God's living room clear, it happened as a rule that exactly those hypotheses were the wrong ones with great certainty which had been hesitantly and reluctantly acknowledged by the churches.

Probably this has to be understood as follows: in defence of their ready-made answers the churches feel compelled again and again to modify their dogmas and to express an opinion on natural scientific insights. Especially the catholic church has always, and more than ever since Galileo, disapproved of all "laws of nature" just to acknowledge them finally after tenacious struggles in order not to jeopardise its own survival.

But this acknowledgement has always been, as is to be expected of a church, nothing else but a new form of devoutness or a new content of faith. After all, supply depends on demand in this field, too. Thus the church took on a new viewpoint now and again to adapt to the times, to be "modern", and to remain attractive. And whenever it did so, whenever it deviated from the old answers, it seemed to err. Because the old answers were better! They had come from people who had not yet divided or catalogued nature, who had still lived in naive, impartial concord with the universe.

The Genesis of the Bible astonishes us: there aren't any "missing links" in this creation; God created all living things according to their kind. Considering that the Bible itself goes back to even older traditions - at least where the Genesis up to the Flood is concerned - God was not a personality in the time of first thoughts. He was the epitome of Adoration, namely the one which remained inexplicable because it could not be defined and was not defined at all, either. At the times of Jesus, the Aramaic word for "God" meant "that which consists of itself ". It was the epitome of the very source of the cosmos - and it is exactly such a lack of origination which we assumed in this book as well. What is more, the ancient peoples did not in the least doubt that the source of power of the visible and invisible was eternal and not subject to any temporal concept - and therefore the world itself had to be infinite and not subject to any spatial measure, either. This world carried its own origin. Only when the philosophising man was looking for someone to blame for anything and everything, this self-evident naturalness was lost.

While the Eastern religions did not know any doubt in the fact that matter and mind were the same, it was Plato who divided this world in all clarity and since then it has remained divided and incompatible. All of a sudden the world was the effect of a metaphysical cause. This handed a play area on a plate to all mystics, who built their own self-justifiability on this constructed realisation and gained from proclaiming a transcendence which has never existed. In that way they invented, for example, the sin toward a higher authority and pictured a Heaven for us, which they often enough sold at a high price.

For thousands of years our world remained a machine given by God until Einstein found another apparent cause for it: the four-dimensional space-time to which, however, no less mysticism has been attached and which has remained no less unexplainable than the mystical work of the gods. The scientists had tended to see the world as a focal point of simple natural laws - which corresponds at least to our hypothetic reality – before it became a mathematical model with Einstein which also manages and works without the world...

In the year 1951, the catholic church under Pope Pius XII. officially professed the Big Bang theory. With regard to the biblical answers this is a surprising decision, and it seems reasonable to suspect that this new merchandise in the catalogue of professional sellers of the truth has to be just as forged as the concept of hell, which does not occur at all in the Old Testament since there is only mention of the grave in that part of the Bible.

God can neither be a mathematician nor a pyrotechnist! If there was an origin of the world from a preceding nothing because of a divine will, it would also be necessary to clarify the origin of God. Otherwise God is just as little of an answer as the Big Bang. If God Himself is the origin, it would imply an endless chain of questions for the origin of the origin...

On the other hand, it doesn't make any difference in principle whether a physical spectacle is replaced by the adorable Divine,. Does not the inability of the physicists to explain what there was before this spectacle immediately demonstrate the artificiality of their theory?

Putting it mildly, the hypothesis of the Big Bang is one of the most ridiculous and useless theories which have ever been cooked up by the brains of scholars. It is nearly only surpassed by the black holes. At the latest with the discovery that the speed of expansion does not only increase with distance but even exhibits an acceleration, the only argument in favour of the Big Bang was lost. The spacious structures in the universe, stars which are older than the calculated age of the cosmos, unexplainably high amounts of iron and deuterium, cosmic radiation or high-energy protons from far-away galaxies which should not exist at all ... yes, even the latest measurements of background radiation ... they all banish the Big Bang theses into the land of fairies tales. We don't have to go at all into the auxiliary hypotheses postulated to rescue the Saga of the Big Bang, like Dark Matter or Dark Energy. Apart from the fact that it goes without saying that not all the energy of the cosmos is glowing and that therefore a big portion remains invisible, the Dark Energy is to explain exactly those phenomena which have been impossible to explain by means of the gravitation hypotheses – the repulsive forces in the universe which one could no longer ignore in spite of the greatest blindness.

We, on the other hand, found only the illusion of gravitation, evoked by one single self-evident force, and we didn't see any beginning of the cosmos either. We discovered an expansion which isn't any at all because real movement^2 does not exist anywhere. Everything without exception consists of images which are drawn by oscillating impulses in the T.A.O. matrix! As definitions, energy, space, and time have only come into this world with the thinking human being. This world is without size as long as nobody measures it; it is without time because it is eternally present. Neither future nor past exist anywhere.

But as a world of changes, the universe did not always look as it does today. Only the impulses in T.A.O. gave us the possibility to comprehend time, space, and structures. These impulses don't have any real beginning either because their opposite, absolute rest, was just impossible. Where should this world rest? Would the assumption of rest not force us to the assumption of a reference point which would be contrary to this rest - and would this not raise the question for the reference point of this reference point?

Questions asked wrongly result in wrong answers. T.A.O. is eternal existence - but not in the material sense. As the only non-material something, T.A.O. requires only a word to name it which we are free to chose. Whoever absolutely wants to can also call it God - but he has to be aware of the fact that nothing can be expected of this God apart from the continued existence of this world, which is left to its own devices as for the rest.

Exactly for this reason the world is fair after all because it contains both the evil and the good, depending on how we see and experience it. Because we have the freedom to fashion our world just the way we like it.

Still, however, there is something like a beginning and an end of the world for us. It is our very own beginning, the moment in which we begin to perceive the world. Our own birth is also the birth of the universe in us. Our awareness gradually crystallised into something completely new, born by an organic order which sprang from old material orders.

No doubt the term beginning has to be understood correctly. Are the colours on the palette of the artist the beginning of a picture? Are the iron atoms as such the beginning of an automobile? From the unpredictable development of our consciousness the world itself was created along with its centre, our ego, which has never existed before. And since it came from nowhere, it will not go anywhere when the awareness-creating function of our body has stopped. But the end of "our world" will occur inevitably ... Although life as a principle is eternal, the individual passes away ... this is the price we pay for everything we receive, for our existence...

Our development has a gradual beginning: slowly, step by step we were immersing into this world, which only gained its significance and meaning through our perception. And just as unknowing and unconscious we will cross over into the sphere of non-perception, into an existence without form, without colour, without pain, and without misery. All problems are solved - and with them all questions as well.

This invincible end is defined as such only by the human consciousness, and only for those left behind this insight is painful at all.

Our ego - used to dealing with hypothetic realities - promptly creates new hypotheses to find consolation. It would not be in accordance with the ambivalence of our mind if it did not invent even the opposite or something disadvantageous: the Divine Judgement, Heaven, and Hell...

But one of the wise men of this world already said Heaven was like the sourdough in the bread; the world was pervaded by it. Heaven and Hell in the sense of experiencing the good and the evil already exist here and now, in the change of everything in us and around us - and nowhere else. Only this one universe exists, of which we learn and experience a fraction during the short flash of our life. There is no division into the earthly existence and the hereafter; the universe - as its name already implies - comprises everything as a great and elemental unit, in fact for eternity but not unchangeably. From chaos - it was nothing else but a particular free order of the energy quanta - new orders have been created incessantly. This is a succession of "worlds", a blossoming and fading of worlds... like the Buddhists have put it.

The image of this world is just as co-incidental as the pictures of the kaleidoscope which suddenly makes sense provided there is somebody there who wants to see them. The individual little glass stones of the kaleidoscope, however, don't know about it, they laid down next to each other in causal succession and will continue to do so in order to transform the temporarily meaningful picture into new pictures, which may be meaningful again but which may also be inevitably meaningless.

Since the meaning is not immanent in the picture, it always depends whether a subjective meaning is recognised as well in the neutral reality surrounding us. The cause of this reality, the world of impulses, of energy quanta, of shapes and proportions is free of meaning like the play of waves on a lake. Probably the means in our life only consists subjectively in making this world into one which is acceptable and suitable for us. And for that reason, those organs which manage to do so are called sense organs.

Our Earth came to an end at least three times. Two of these catastrophes are well known to us. One of them is the last Flood which took place at a time when mankind had already established high cultures. Thus this apocalypse - maybe a cosmic cataclysm because of the orbital jump of the Earth after a preceded cooling of the sun and its re-inflammation – was handed down in many legends around the globe.

One of these three catastrophes happened presumably 66.7 million years ago - if one is to believe the clocks of radioactivity. At that time, dinosaurs dominated on Earth but there were already mammals as well, and one of them was certainly already on its way to become human. And of course almost all insects already existed in the form in which we still find them today. The cosmos in which the Earth was travelling had become an ecosphere. A lush vegetation provided the gigantic dinosaurs with enormous amounts of food. But one day the sun was suddenly aglow in a burning giant ball, whose corona brushed over the Earth with a breath of fire. The hour of birth had come for Mercury. The sun was hurling mighty masses into space; a dense flow of particles settled between Earth and sun, and a rain of hot solar matter fell down all over the globe.

Since the sun became a little smaller because of the ejected masses, all the planets went on their journey across the equipotential spaces; the planet between Mars and Jupiter broke apart; the Earth captured a big fragment as moon, and many other fragments impacted on the Earth as colossal meteors, hurling vast amounts of earth and dust into the atmosphere.

The sky, which had only just been aglow with the renewed sun one moment, darkened ("...a night came over Earth..."). Probably it remained less radiolucent for years. The axis of the Earth got dislocated; where once there was life abounding, soon an armour of ice formed. South Africa, South America, and Australia were covered under extensive glaciers...

The solar matter which descended on Earth can still be found today as a wafer-thin layer which contains a high content of iridium, an element that is otherwise rare on Earth. This layer was discovered by researchers only in 1981, and there can be no doubt about the cosmic origin of the iridium. The impact of a meteor alone, however, would not have been able to produce this amount of iridium. For that reason, it must have come from the sun, which had already produced a high degree of heavy elements.

The dinosaurs, as reptiles on no account prepared for such strong variations in temperature, did not survive. In addition, most of the vegetation died. Mighty movements of the Earth and continental drifts turned everything upside down; crude oil and coal still bear eloquent witness to this apocalyptic change. At that time, only those could survive which were small and nimble and could get by on small amounts of food. The hour of the mammals had come. And the only ones which were not distressed by all this were the insects with their enormous resistance.

The regular pole reversals of the Earth's magnetic field, however, also had devastating effects because they were always accompanied by a collapse of the protective Van-Allen belt.

However we look at the history of the world, be it the history of nature or the succession of human civilisations, it was always written in blood. With justification, the first Earth-based religions knew only evil demons, and whatever came over the Earth, it was always a punishment of God.

It is rather immaterial for the course of this "evil" world whether we see a meaning behind it which is more than the biological usefulness that shows neither intention nor aim itself. But exactly because the function of the world has to appear barbaric to us, because it really is, to the individual it may be of help from time to time to create sense and higher meaning for himself and to chose what his "happiness" depends on.

How hard it is to define "happiness" at all may have been noticed by many a reader. We already mentioned that, for instance, euphoria as a kind of feeling of happiness consists mainly of "not to feel oneself" - i.e. to be liberated from the straightjacket of life. This is not to be confused with death, though. "Not to feel oneself" is absolutely synonymous with "to feel oneself", both are a product of our consciousness. It is therefore hardly possible to sleep "euphorically", but we can of course dream of euphoria. Is sleep thus the same as death? Is it a "little death" as some often like to put it? Is limited activity of the senses the same as no activity of the senses? The question is answered according to logic: it cannot be the same!

Assuming that there is something like an absolute reality in the world of wavelengths and proportions which remains free of evaluation, we have to admit that our senses sift a constructed truth out of this absolute reality. Their activity is selective, they narrow the whole spectrum of the absolute down to certain spheres. We hear only certain sounds, recognise only certain structures and colours, feel only certain temperatures, and experience only certain flavours. We know the intensification of this selectivity, of this limitation as sleep. That means that our senses are not working poorer while we are sleeping but – considering their restricting function - even stronger. Thus our senses don't "show" us the world at all but they conceal a part of the world from us and just this act of concealing lends the characteristic picture to our world. It is just as if there was a kind of universal consciousness which comprises everything first. When we compare it to an empty sheet of paper (fig. 148) and when we draw symbolic limitations on this sheet as set by our sense organs we get a new picture of which we can now make sense.

On the sheet of paper a roughly star-shaped structure is created. It is to show the limited sphere of our hypothetic reality clearly. It has a certain size, and we can shift the boundaries by expanding our consciousness. The star is getting bigger through experience and knowledge, therefore that also means it defines the degree of our waking state. When the restriction of our perception is getting bigger, the star is getting smaller: we are sleeping!

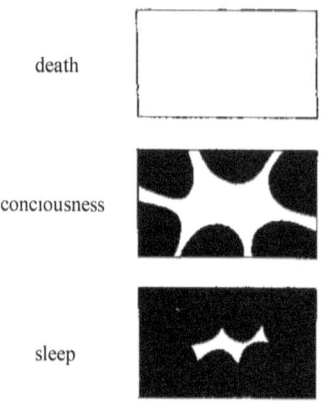
Fig.148

But what happens if this activity of the senses stops completely? Then there aren't any boundaries anymore! One picture is swallowed by the whole. From the whole of the universe our ego came, into this whole it will return in death. There is no better expression for this state than "Nirvana". It is the same as "Nothingness" that means: no perception, no reality, no suffering. This state is neutral, spaceless, and timeless. But this nothingness is not the darkness of sleep but the brightness of death because this nothingness means the same as T.A.O. itself, thus the same as the existence, which has no shape and does not accept any definition apart from one word. Can death therefore represent an end? Yes and no; an end to everything that determined our ego, for certain, and there is no consolation for that. No end, however, for the cosmic consciousness itself. Because the consciousness of all individuals forms a unit. Every one of us carries it in oneself. Although it is not the same "star", yet it is the same "sheet of paper", the same basis of reality for this star.

Is this esoteric hair-splitting? On no account because we saw in a quite comprehensive way that substantially, matter does not exist at all and that it is already a manifestation of a causal something, just like the energy is only born by this something and works in it. For this something we choose the term T.A.O. but we could just as well call it cosmic consciousness. There is only one T.A.O., thus only one material world, one power, one universe, one cosmic consciousness, yes, even one consciousness as such ... From this whole, the many images of the senses developed. The cause remains always the same but the images are changing...

What does this mean? Isn't that as if all living things were looking at one and the same sheet of paper so to speak? Yes, of course! One world takes place, and one consciousness takes place - isn't it mine, yours, ours, theirs? Well, does the consciousness not behave just like T.A.O. itself, then? Is its existence compelling regardless of its appearance? In that case, does an opposite of the consciousness not become just as impossible as an opposite of the world? Exactly!

The present picture is called "ego". It changes and is lost in death. But the "it" is eternal. It happens continuously. Again and again it forms a new ego which has no reference to any of the others because there isn't any before or afterwards. "It" is timeless - only the ego knows about clocks! If it happens continuously, it will never get dark. It shines the "Eternal Light" on us!

Isn't is strange how well this is described in some religions? Are these answers not really the wisest ones? They are because they contain a lot of truth. And as we have seen, they are quite consistent with the discoveries of our viewpoint. But what have the churches made of the religions! And the scholars of the sciences! We said it already: the history of the Earth is a chapter written by evil demons...

Now a bit of sober, plain speech. Just like the material event represents an uninterrupted succession of events, the spiritual of this world also takes place uninterruptedly. There is no death which comprises everything, just like there cannot be a nothingness which comprises everything. If we understand ourselves as consciousness event, it will be infinite and eternal. This is the same as if people took over from each other who didn't know and didn't learn anything about each other - but was each standing in the same centre of the world, and there each would find himself as an eternal but changeable ego. This circumstance has also been realised intuitively when the thought of reincarnation occurred to us - a misunderstood thought, however, since one believed the "ego" would be preserved personally and would adopt a new place after death, i.e. the soul as carrier of the self would wander.

Seen this way it is certainly wrong. Where should a soul go to if it already represents the sum of all souls? What light should shine up in the middle of eternal brightness? There is always an ego in the centre, and there is always somebody looking out of the centre, recognising the world. Today, our ego is in this place. After its extinction, there will immediately be another one - in exactly the same place, again located in the centre. How will this "other" one, who entered just as imperceptibly, call himself? "Me!" of course and he will believe to be just as unique and unrepeatable as we did.

We even sense this kind of eternity in ourselves. We wouldn't know about our arrival if there weren't any birth certificates and calendars. So gradually and smoothly did we develop our ego that we would have to say we had always been there. Because we would not remember any beginning if we didn't know about the date of our birth.

And since we can neither predetermine death nor perceive it as such and in the same manner just slipped into this world without sensing any "beginning", it might be the same as if we were here forever.

This is a very simple answer, worthy of this other answer which we found to the question of matter. One single principle created it. One single force exists, and it exists because it has to if there is a world. Therefore it is explained completely by itself. That is exactly the goal: to finally understand the world completely and not to interpret it only as a hotchpotch of laws of nature which are only applicable in the reality of our schoolbooks.

To see the world as a matter of course means to be allowed to love it without fear! The great game is eternal, only its characters and scenes are changing. Our Earth is only one of many countless scenes of life within the endless universe.

Unfortunately it also seems unavoidable and certain: the next apocalypse of this little blue planet belongs to the merciless rules of the game which we discovered. Even if we disregard the unpleasant ability of mankind to exterminate itself, for which it already has the means, there is no guarantee for the eternal existence of its civilisations.

The planetary series of catastrophes will continue furthermore. Of course, the next eruption of the sun is expected to happen but in several thousand years. It will not come as a surprise because the surface of the sun will darken in advance and a new ice age will take hold of our planet. Since 1980, the sun has gotten darker by a thousandth. If the loss of brightness is to continue for another 50 years, the temperature of the Earth will cool down by one to two degrees. That is already sufficient for a "small ice age". But probably life, mankind, will find the same way out which it has chosen once before...

Life is invincible, and the planet of the future lies in store for us: Venus. In several million years, it should be a really cosy place to live.

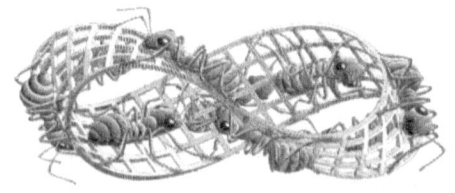

39 Future

The evolution continues ... The highly developed mammal man will be walking through the history of the Earth and the planets for a long time to come. Long since, evolution has shifted to the society, has become intellectual, the evolution of information and of knowledge and of sociology. And for the first time, a development conditional on nature has to set itself a goal consciously in order to survive: humanity. Only if we attain this goal will we have set us apart from the animal completely. But still, this goal appears to be very far away and it is uncertain whether we will achieve this ideal one day or if the so-called "evil" will win in the end. It is likely that the universe would not suffer a bad loss. After all, even the decline of mankind would only be the price for its existence over millions of years.

Whatever happens on and with the Earth - the universe will probably remain unaffected by it. The galaxies will continue to displace one another and to get smaller. Suns and planets will finally be pushed into the centres of the galaxies. An enormous hyper star will develop which hurls matter in gaseous state back into the universe.

In this way the disturbance of T.A.O. sustains itself. It is also very likely that the hyper star will carry out the same processes as the sun of its own accord and produce further suns and finally galaxies from colossal ejection rings and shells. Such young galaxies have really been proved in the framework of the IRAS Mission[101]. The spiral arms of many galaxies prove in addition graphically that they haven't been rotating for very long...

A final state of this universe would be T.A.O. at rest... This state as beginning and end is hypothetical, it has never been realised and will never be achieved. The universe expands; and when all galaxies have become hyper stars one day, they will in turn again create galaxies because once more new impulse centres, stars, and planets will develop... In this way, new matter is spontaneously created from the "vacuum", and that is only possible because energy can be transported back in the fields through which all matter is interwoven (cosmic radiation, background noise) and the expansion is compensated by that. Otherwise the density of matter would diminish constantly, more and more matter, stars, and galaxies would move away from the event horizon, and the cosmos would become dreary and desolate all around our milky way. It doesn't look as if this would happen one day. Although it could be that burnt out stars are not completely replaced by newly born ones. Then the lights will finally go out in the cosmos...

And so the event of a changing universe is repeated in eternity and infinity. There is no plausible reason to fear that the expansion of the universe could ever be finished one day. After all there is no gravitation. Matter only seems to attract each other because it is compressed by the surrounding matter. For that reason, it will always obstruct and repel itself, a process which - so simple and natural it may seem - means the Principle of Existence as such. Even the "pulsating" universe is a fairytale of the cosmologists. Figure 92 in this book demonstrates the structural arrangement of the galaxies although the figure actually shows "thermal spheres". But in the macrocosm, the same principle applies, on which the displacement patterns of dissipative structures are based. Naturally enough there is no necessity for the hypotheses of dark energy and dark matter in this cosmology and we don't need any "cosmological constant" or any other coefficient of corrections, either, in order to explain why gravitation did not contract the whole universe into one single clot long ago.

The universe is structured like giant soap foam because of the displacements, and therefore Geller and Huchra had to make their sensational discovery in 1986 - as we already mentioned briefly.[102] Future measuring results will confirm the repulsion principle. Only a short while ago, Ephraim Fischbach discovered deviations from Newton's law according to which the gravitational effects do not only depend on mass but also on the chemical composition of the bodies involved.

We believe that the universe works very simply in principle. Metaphysics, mysticism, and esotericism are in fact a lot of fun but they are not required in the complex event "world". The earthly existence and the next world, Heaven and Hell ... they are all fictions, bizarre excesses of our imagination – just like black holes or quarks or superstrings.[103] Not everything that man can think off exists without exception!

Well, that were quite optimistic considerations – but the truth is that we are unable to know anything about the future of the cosmos.

All that appears to be reasonably definite from a cosmological point of view so far is the endless expansion in all eternity and the fact that the universe is "flat"[104], whatever that should be. In any case it is not curved. Perhaps that may reassure many a person but for the majority a look into the near future will certainly be more interesting.

There is the pressing question for future forms of energy. Nuclear fission will not be able to solve the problem in the long run. An increase of operating accidents together with their serious consequences will call the technology into question. Moreover, the expenditure on security will become too expensive; for that reason, atomic energy will be of no economic interest anymore one day for sure. Nuclear fission may appear a little more promising if one really discovers the trick of "cold fusion" one day. In principle it is not impossible.

If we disregard the use of solar energy and the reactivation of methods close to nature, like tidal or wind driven power stations and the exploitation of geothermal energy, there remains another great glimmer of hope: the generation of energy by means of complete transformation of matter. This could only be achieved by means of antimatter, i.e. through the collisions of particles (protons) with opposite spin. Let's give free rein to our imagination: maybe one could make good use of the waste products from nuclear fission, which are very strong gamma radiators down the line.

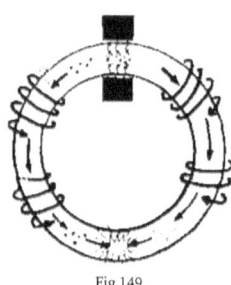

Fig.149

Analogous to the original beginning of matter as we described it two gamma rays directed at one another would have to created both matter and antimatter, i.e. both "right-hand" and "left-hand" protons or some other particles with different spin. They could be separated by magnetic fields and shot onto one another again. An energy synchrotron of the future could basically look as shown in figure 149. It would be necessary to provide energy for the creation of the magnetic fields which separate and unite the opposite protons again. Their mutual destruction could therefore bring a gain in energy because the gamma quanta themselves don't cost anything since the gamma radiators are yielding them willingly. Of course, this could not yet be done with today's technology but superconductors and Bose-Einstein condensate already offer some interesting perspectives in this respect...

It seems even more obvious to exploit the fact that matter practically consists of electricity. Direct conversions of energy, as for example of light and heat into electrical power, like it is already put into practise today, are quite possible to a larger extent. The completely dry battery is within the realms of possibility - one will certainly invent it one day. On the other hand one will make the application of energy more efficient, technical machines and communication devices will yield a better performance while consuming less energy.

But even the magnetic field of the Earth theoretically represents a still unused source of energy. At least it could induce currents into appropriately arranged conductors in a cheap way. One already tried this with big satellite antennas. But unfortunately the long wires got tangled up. Besides, the magnetic field is in the course of breaking down at present which will entail some unpleasant phenomena. But in 1000 years, a new one will surely have developed again...

In any case, whatever one does with matter, electric current will always get going. The energy drop existing in the elements can be utilised. The specific combination of certain elements produces energy already.

The main emphasis of a future generation of energy, however, is with biochemistry. The slogan is to learn from life how to deal with energy. The cold light of deep sea fish is produced without any loss in energy. It proves that it is possible to convert energy by almost 100 percent and without doubt mankind will make this method their own one day. Artificial photosynthesis lies within reach, the same applies to the artificial production of protein molecules.

It is pointless to speculate about the development of mankind itself. Nobody could have ever predicted the past development of nature, and in the face of aimless ways we don't know in any way where the signpost will point to. He who dares to make prognosis in this respect is a fraud.

Almost everything is possible within the function of this universe, and man can discover it if he overcomes the beast inside himself one day and if he has the time and leisure to develop a new spiritual understanding for matter which exceeds the fantastic theories of our age. Because these theories have become so independent by now that their objective accordance with reality is no longer expected - as is already the case in quantum physics. But quantum physics and quantum mechanics are still good and successful theories and will develop further. And it is to hope that one will understand one day that this cosmos is born on a basic structure which is not the ether; that matter does neither consist of ether nor of T.A.O. - but that everything without exception manifests, unfolds, and propagates in this T.A.O. through impulses and oscillations without T.A.O. moving itself or taking part in it in any way.

One can understand and comprehend this world in its entirety and finally know why and how it exists. The Tree of Knowledge is full of unpicked fruit, and the solutions to many questions are often simpler than they seem. Let's hope that we will still have the opportunity to ask these questions and to learn the answers...

The world is left to its own devices and we are in with it. Nobody protects us, and nobody takes revenge. We are responsible to nobody but ourselves. That is a valuable insight because it makes us free and makes us concentrate on life itself as the meaning of existence. Every ego is unrepeatable, individual, and worth to be lived. To be a fellow player in a game whose rules one knows and not to ask pointlessly who invented the game, that is the task. Because the game was not created at any time, in any place, it is the game of Eternity, of the essential T.A.O.: the unique Principle of Existence!

40 Footnotes

The Internet Community and the readers of this book's first edition contributed to most of these footnotes in form of comments, and links, letters, forum discussions, and emails. The author thanks everyone for their active participation in the development of this new edition.

---

[1] The philosopher and physicist Ernst Mach said in the general sense: "Why do we believe that a body ends where we do not feel it anymore? Why not where we cannot hear or see it anymore? In short: could it perhaps be that every body expands into eternity on its own even if we do not perceive this expansion with our limited senses? Is it possible that every body is connected with all other bodies of the universe in an immensely fast way by means of gravitation and the electric and magnetic forces which are presumably just as fast?"

[2] Most questions, which readers of the first edition asked, referred to their difficulty to understand the definition of movement within T.A.O. An atom is a pulsating field whose impulses are determined by the matrix, both concerning their velocity, their cohesion, and their propagation. Since the atom is not a compact, ponderable (solid) object for that reason but the product of a local impulse oscillation, it cannot move compactly or solidly through the matrix of T.A.O. but only relocate its propagation within this structure - which causes the "movement" of the atom. Several atoms are doing likewise while the information they carry through their intact constellation (molecule, body, object, item, organism, etc.) is preserved.

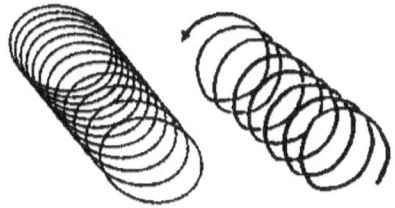

Fig. I

Figure I symbolises the difference: the circle (on the left) is moving compactly and closed. Actually it cannot do that in T.A.O. because it can only propagate by being temporally dispersed into impulses but it cannot "move" - that's why it develops into a spiral (on the right) in the matrix. The high velocity (c), however, will create the impression of a moving, closed circle.

All movements in the universe take place only by means of the propagation of impulses within T.A.O. The supporting structure to be assumed cannot be a running and flowing or all pervading ether (it could not achieve the cohesion of the impulses) but only an absolute structure that is motionless itself and carries the vibrational image of the universe in a kind of holography. This explains the cosmos administration of energy in quanta as well as the geometry of gravitation which results from the repulsion principle.

[3] Nature does not know any straight paths. Wherever something grows or moves a spiral is the final result. Since Galileo and Newton, the physicists have put in our heads: that the most natural form of movement is the uniform progressive motion in a straight line. But in truth everything in nature deviates from the straight line and moves in the form of spirals. Everything in nature expands or flows - from inorganic crystals to animated beings up to star clusters and galaxies. But almost nothing grows or flows uniformly. Let's imagine something is rising like a tree – the trunk of a plant, the calcium carbonate skeleton of a mussel, which grows vertically upwards, or the stream of gas exhausted by a star. As long as there are no disturbances, the cohesive mass – cells or gas molecules – fills the space uniformly forming a hose. But as soon as one side is growing faster (because more energy is flowing there) or slower (due to friction) than the other, the hose will bend to one side - in fact the stronger, the more it grows or the more it is retarded. A spiral will finally originate from the bend.

[4] The spin is a property of electrons and other particles which could not be described within the scope of Schrödinger's equation. Already in the first quarter of the previous century several experimental facts, like e.g. the double nature of atomic spectrums, the Stern-Gerlach experiment (1921), or the Einstein-de-Haas effect suggested the existence of the spin. In 1928, Dirac set up an equation replacing the inadequate Schrödinger equation with a combination of quantum theory and ToR and in that way he could solve the "one body problem" of the electron. This covered both spin and magnetic moment of the electron, the Sommerfeld formula of fine structure

could be derived from it and it helped to explain the Zeeman effect. (In quantum physics, the spin is not a true intrinsic angular impulse of a "particle" but a property which has only the same effects as an angular impulse.)

The spin was not "predicted" by the ToR but the Dirac theory is a completely relativistic quantum mechanical theory formulated in a Lorentz covariant form. Dirac has thus not "discovered" or invented the spin but developed a mathematical method, to be exact a relativistic derivation, from formulas which had previously been insufficient for the mathematical description of the spin. Dirac also set up the Fermi-Dirac statistic. The fact that especially particles with half-integral values of the spin follow the Fermi-Dirac statistic is called spin-statistics theorem. It can be derived from the quantum field theory in a makeshift manner, whereas the nuclear spin is covered by the Bose-Einstein statistics.

[5] The term "apparent mass" is on no account absurd. In old physics textbooks the term "apparent mass" was used for the apparent gain in mass due to kinetic energy. We are just extending this concept to every kind of mass action and with the fan wheel we are symbolising that *every* action of mass results from kinetic energy. (The connection of energy and apparent mass becomes quite obvious in toy cars with flywheel motor.)

[6] Prior to his death physics genius and Nobel laureate Richard P. Feynman left the following cryptic words to a puzzled posterity: "You cannot say A is made out of B - or vice versa. All mass (*here also in the sense of matter - the author*) is interaction".

[7] Heisenberg's indeterminacy relation, an apparent cornerstone of quantum physics, according to which it is impossible to discern simultaneously and with accuracy both the position and the momentum of a body, is pure illusion. The physicist James Paul Wesley demonstrated by means of some simple calculations that there is no indeterminacy with common light in cells, with transistor radios or with scanning tunnelling microscopes. The Physicist Wojciech Hubert Zurek of the Los Alamos National Laboratory in New Mexico proved that the indeterminacy of the double-slit experiment, in which a beam of light passes through two slits and forms interference patterns on a screen behind them, is not correct.

[8] There is practically no difference between protons and neutrons. It seems reasonable to suspect that the neutron was postulated only for reasons of theory (periodic system of chemical elements) in order to explain the different weight of atoms which are chemically identical on the outside (isotopes). The scientists of the Florida State University in Tallahassee and of the Michigan State University in East Lansing in the United States discovered unambiguously: proton and neutron appear to be different only in their respective electrical charge and are otherwise as like as two peas in a pod. (Physical Review Letters, volume 88, reference number 172502) One could also conclude from the fact that free neutrons can "decay" spontaneously into protons and electrons that one is dealing *with protons only*!

[9] In the proton, which physicists have considered for a long time to be an empty structure consisting of three elementary building blocks (quarks), surges a regular ocean of smallest "particles" in truth. This knowledge was gained thanks to HERA, one of the biggest charged particle accelerators of the world, which is located in the Hamburg research centre DESY and has been used for exploring the structure of matter for the last ten years. "HERA is some kind of big microscope for the proton", says research director Prof. Robert Klanner. The "Hadron Electron Ring Accelerator" makes it possible to notice structures which are 2000 times smaller than the proton itself. "Prior to HERA the idea prevailed that there were essentially three quarks in a proton ", Klanner explains. "With HERA we gained a completely new picture. Actually, the inside of a proton looks like a big soup in which numerous quarks, anti-quarks, and gluons float."

[10] How big something is always depends on who is looking at the object to determine its "mass". According to theory, atomic nuclei are minute. But to extremely slow "neutrons" the nucleus gives the impression to be at least as big as the whole atom. For the first time now, physicists confirmed this prediction by experiment.

[11] Every student of the natural sciences learns that the *indivisible* bond of the electric charge is that of the electron. Two years ago, however, scientists detected that under certain circumstances charge can be distributed to "quasi-particles" in such a way that they will bear a third of the elementary charge. Now physicists also found some with a fifth of the charge - a crucial discovery which suggests

to delete the indivisibility of the electron's charge from the physics textbooks for once and for all.

[12] The neutrino predicted by Wolfgang Pauli belongs to these elementary particles which are the most difficult to detect. It reacts only very rarely with ordinary matter, and for that reason, giant detecting instruments are required for rendering proof of it. In Europe, such a detector is operated in the Italian Gransasso Massif. If neutrinos have a mass or not is not answered by the standard model of elementary particle physics. Meant to be a "Saviour Particle" for inconsistencies in decay processes, the neutrino, however, proves to be a tough nut to crack for particle physics and jeopardises the standard model more and more. As it is, experiments concerning the interaction of neutrinos lead to results which cannot be explained with the concepts of the physicists. This makes some of them even think of a new fundamental force ("extra-weak force"). About one percent of the neutrinos unfortunately deviate from the predictions of the standard model (discovered by Sam Zeller, Northwestern University in Illinois and Fermilab near Chicago). According to the previous expert opinion, neutrinos interact with the quarks of the atomic nuclei by means of the so-called electroweak force which is, among other things, also responsible for the so-called beta decay of the atomic nuclei. The experiment of physicists of the Northwestern University now revealed that this thesis probably has to be revised, thinks Jens Erler, a theoretical physicist of the University of Pennsylvania. Experiments which were conducted at the Los Alamos National Laboratory in New Mexico from 1993 to 1998 even suggest the existence of a *fourth* type of neutrino which is not at variance with the standard model either. (David Caldwell in Physical Review D, volume 64, 112007). According to the standard model, there are three neutrinos at the moment. In the first place, it was assumed that the three neutrinos had no mass. This had to be revised *in order to explain* by means of the transformation of anti particles from muon neutrinos into anti-electron-neutrinos why so much less electron-neutrinos from the sun arrive on Earth than were calculated theoretically. The mass difference between each of the two neutrino types involved can be determined from each of the three neutrino measurements. The problem: from two mass differences the third can be calculated - and this calculation does not correspond with the experimental result. To crown it all, during the

neutrino-free double beta decay now observed by researchers two neutrons transformed into two protons and two electrons simultaneously without ejecting any anti-neutrinos. This decay obviously violates the conservation of the lepton numbers, and one would have to conclude that the neutrino is its own anti-particle. If one attributes a mass to the neutrinos, which are as fast as the light, one will collide with the SToR – a fact of which the physicists are obviously not quite aware yet...

[13] The flux behaviour of the fields of magnetised material was already discovered under the name "Barnett-Monstein effect". The measurements give grounds for the assumption that magnetism is neither a static magnetic field nor a static B-field but an active flux of smallest particles (or impulses) around the longitudinal axis of a magnet with a clearly detectable direction of the flux. For that reason, the physicist Alois Ludwig Siegrist has been speaking of a magnetic "flux coat" or a magnetic "space-quantum flux" since 1992. ("Central Oscillators and Space Quanta Medium" published by Universal Experten Verlag, CH-8640 Rapperswil/Schweiz. ISBN no. 3-9520261-0-7).

[14] Already at the beginning of the 1990ies atoms were observed which could adopt far more "photons" then admitted by the quantum-mechanical orbital model. In addition, these excited atoms, emitted photons again which had a higher energy than actually permitted. All attempts to explain this phenomenon with quantum-mechanics failed. Therefore physics cannot substantiate that the quantum-mechanical explanation of the origination of light or the absorption represents a precise theory.

[15] In a large-scale simulation a team of German and American scientists unearthed the submicroscopic details of the diffusion of protons in an aqueous solution. In a mysterious way, the protons proved to be faster than all other atoms and molecules. It was revealed that the protons used the old trick by means of which the hedgehog of the fairy tale defeated the faster hare in running. Instead of setting off on the long road themselves *they transmit the information*, and at the end of the racetrack an identical hedgehog or proton appears. The discovery of this structural diffusion should not only make the run of a process in chemistry and biology easier to comprehend but will also lend a new meaning to the word "motion".

[16] A group of researchers at the University of Rochester retarded a light impulse to a velocity of 57 metres per second at ambient temperature. For that purpose the scientists fired a short laser pulse onto a ruby crystal which became transparent for a narrow range of wavelengths. That way the velocity speed of the pulse could be reduced to less than the five-millionth part of the velocity of light in vacuum. A team of Japanese and American researchers (Yukiko Shimizu of the University of Tokyo and his American colleagues of the National Institute of Standards and Technology in Colorado) were even successful in retarding a beam of light by the interaction of only ten atoms. (Physical Review Letters, volume 90, reference number 113903). That the velocity of light can be broken in every school laboratory was proven by American researchers (Jeremy Munday and Bill Robertson) of the Middle Tennessee State University. They guided an electric signal over a distance of 120 metres at four times the velocity of light. For that purpose they used only customary coaxial cables as well as two electric A.C. power supplies as can be found in most well equipped school laboratories. (New Scientist). The fact that the velocity of light is not constant has long been confirmed by experiments (Georges de Sagnac, 1913; Michelson & Gale, 1925; Ives & Stivell, 1938 ; Macek & Davis, 1963; Brillet & Hall, 1979; Marinov, 1977, and Bilger, 1995.)

[17] Physicists (Jerzy Dudek and his colleagues) of the Louis Pasteur University in Strasbourg claimed that atomic nuclei could possibly also be found in pyramidal form in nature. The nuclear particles would combine to tiny triangular pyramids or tetrahedrons. The triangular pyramid is made of four triangles joined at the corners. The results of the calculations revealed that this form should be found with many elements straight through the periodic system of chemical elements. A good candidate is for example the element zirconium but on top of the list even better known elements like calcium and uranium could possess pyramidical nuclei. ("New Scientist" in its edition of June 8th, 2003)

[18] Proof of an oxygen atom with 4 atoms, already predicted in theory in 1920, was really established by Italian researchers in the meantime. It is a dumbbell-shaped bond of two atmospheric oxygen molecules (O_2).

[19] Why so many things in the universe are spherical is explained with

gravitation on the whole. This, however, leads to an illogical circular argument: the heavy mass is the cause of gravitation which acts upon the inert mass. The equivalence of these masses has applied since Einstein: with that the effect becomes its own cause. Why smaller celestial bodies, asteroids for instance, which are not solid bodies but accretions of dust, are not spherical cannot be explained with gravitation either. In the opinion of astronomers, these "cosmic heaps of debris" are held together by electrostatic forces.

[20] The conventional explanation of surface tension assumes that molecules in a liquid attract each other and that each is subject to the same force from all its neighbours. A molecule on the surface doesn't have any neighbours on one side and there are not any forces acting on it there so it is drawn into the liquid for that reason. Due to that the surface molecules have a higher energy than those inside. The surface tension of the liquid is defined by this difference in energy. It does not seem to make any difference at first glance if one assumes attraction or repulsion of the molecules as explanation for the surface tension - but it does. An attractive force would actually draw the molecules on the margin inside - therefore a counter energy had to be *postulated* which holds the molecules on the surface - otherwise there would be no tension. For that reason, the explanation is relating to the purpose (teleological).

[21] Electrophoresis (Tiselius 1930); the migration of electrically charged particles in liquid media in the – if possible homogenous – electric field. The velocity of migration v is always proportional to the field intensity E and to the ionic charge Q and inversely proportional to the radius of the particle r and the viscosity η of the suspension: $v = QE / 6\pi r\eta$.

[22] Teleological explanation: a teleological explanation explains the occurrence of an event by the fact that a telos (a goal) is immanent to it: event E occurs so that E' is the case.

[23] The design of a Kirlian device is for example as follows: a metal plate is connected to a high-frequency alternating voltage of usually more than 20 000 Volt. On this metal plate there is an insulating layer, e.g. a glass plate. Photographic paper or a film is put onto this insulating layer. On top of it all, the object to be "photographed" is placed, e.g. the leaf of a tree. This object is connected with the mass of the apparatus. The high voltage causes a brushing discharge or

corona discharge and exposes the film which is then developed as usual. The corona has a certain resemblance to how some people imagine the aura to be. However, it has nothing to do with an aura but it is just a high-voltage brushing discharge. Even "dead" objects, like for example coins, create very beautiful corona discharges whereas electrical non-conductors (insulators, e.g. plastic materials) do not produce any corona discharge. The high-voltage discharge demonstrates the impulse field around a body in a very direct manner. If there was no such field, the current could not jump over.

[24] Since basically everything we encounter in the world and in the cosmos is chaotic by nature, the idea of the unchangeable laws and constants in classical physics appears to be absolutely unrealistic. Alfred North Whitehead said in this connection: "If we drop the old idea that laws are *imposed* on nature and think instead that of laws being *immanent* in nature, it would necessarily follow that they evolve along with nature." This means the values of the constants change simultaneously with the evolution of the universe. According to the theories, however, they should be unchangeable. The contradiction between empiric reality and theory is usually dismissed with the remark that variations were mere experimental errors and that the most recent values were the best. ... But nature itself is not uniform. Constants are not constant, and in addition they are only measured in our small region of the universe - and most of them have been measured only for a couple of decades. Besides, the values alternate from year to year. The opinion that constants are the same all the time and in every place is not derived from data, though. Because they all have just been determined by definition. In case of the velocity of light, even the units in which it is expressed are defined by the light itself. Today, the *second* is based on the frequency of light which is emitted by excited caesium 133 atoms. One second corresponds to 9 192 631 770 vibrational periods of this light. And since 1983, the *meter* has been defined on the basis of the velocity of light which in turn was determined by definition. If the velocity of light changes we wouldn't even notice it! Because such changes remain practically undetected if the units are defined in such a way that they are changed when the velocity of light changes and the value of *kilometres per second* would therefore remain exactly the same!

[25] The standard model of the particle physicists is also jeopardised by an experiment in the particle accelerator Brookhaven in which a muon behaviour was found which significantly deviates from theory. (wissenschaft.de/wissen/news/155235)

[26] Our view of the capillary effect is not so naive at all as it may appear at first glance. Typical school book explanations of the effect are: "The water *wants* to increase the water-glass boundary surface in unfavour of the air-glass boundary surface. Therefore an upward suction is created in the capillaries opposed to the weight load of the water. In big tubes the force is too small to evoke a change of the water surface. In small capillaries the force makes the water rise in dependence on the diameter..." That liquids don't *want* anything but are influenced by the surrounding field pressure seems more likely since a force also acting against gravitation cannot be generated by the "wants" of the water – nor by the unrelated comparison of two concepts, though (boundary surface *water-glass : air-glass* or *cohesion : adhesion*).

[27] The shadowing of the universal pressure and the changes in gravitation related to that, which do *not* correspond to the *attraction* thesis, were proved in experiments during solar eclipses (the moon shields off the solar pressure), last time by the Institute of Geophysics, Chinese Academy of Sciences on March 9th, 1997. Many researchers have developed pressure theories of gravitation in the meantime. They all have the problem to explain the meanwhile undoubtedly existing gravitational eclipses by means of particle currents. Unequivocal results were obtained by examinations of the orbit of the LAGEOS satellites. In the Earth's shadow (the Earth shielding off the sun), significant gravitational changes were the result which indicated some *pressure*.

[28] In general, the astronomers have great problems with the formation of structure because the postulated absolute homogeneity and isotropy of the universe apply only approximately on the basis of newer observations and are inconsistent with the formation of structure which took place. This concerns the existence of very big structures in the same way as the *Clustering* and its spatial distribution, which could both not be reproduced in the framework of the cosmological *standard model*. The *voids* and the discovery of very old objects are hard to explain, either. According to the

formation of structure would have taken place extremely fast in view of the observed high isotropy. No mechanisms are conceivable within the framework of the cosmological standard model which could produce well-developed structures from an almost homogenous distribution of matter in such a fast way. The maximum density of matter determined on the basis of the relative frequency of chemical elements is plainly inconsistent with the values which are required as a minimum for a *gravitative* bond of galaxies and clusters of galaxies. In addition to that, so far one has been searching in vain for stars of the first generation with a correspondingly low metal content; at least the proportional shares of boron and beryllium are just as persistently excessive as those of iron (deuterium is also found too frequently).

[29] Strong magnetic fields are responsible for the creation of hot gas rings around some stars. This was discovered by Myron Smith of the Space Telescope Science Institute in Baltimore and Detlef Groote of the University of Hamburg by analysing the ultraviolet light of four stars with rings. As the researchers reported in the specialist journal Astronomy and Astrophysics, the rings around the stars are presumably at least twice as frequent as previously thought. Their study also revealed that stars of different composition produce rings according to the same principle.

[30] Astronomers of the NASA Jet Propulsion Laboratory (JPL) discovered young stars in the Orion Nebula and in the galaxy NGC 2264 which rotated slower than expected. This could be an indication that planets have formed in the dust disks of these stars. "A young, shrinking planet should behave like an ice skater who puts her arms against her body and therefore rotates faster", explains Luisa Rebull of the JPL. She and her colleagues think that planets were created in the dust disks of these slowly rotating stars which are stealing the angular impulse from their mother star. The scientists hope that the space telescope SIM (Space Interferometry Mission) whose launching is planned for 2009 will bring them final clarification. By making the most of optical interferometry SIM will be able to discover planets down to the size of the Earth. (March 2003!)

[31] An international team of astronomers discovered a planetary system which is just in the phase of creation. It is the first time that

scientists are able to watch the birth of new planets directly, NASA reports. The star "KH 15D" which is 2400 light-years away emits a light which fades every 48 days for a period of 18 days. The astronomers around William Herbst suspect that an accumulation of smaller objects like dust, rocks, or asteroids screen off the light from time to time. The Earth and the other planets also developed from such a so-called proto-planetary disk. The material gathers so quickly to form planets that researchers can directly follow the process over a period of months and years. Further observations of KH 15D will also show the origins of our solar system in a new light, the astronomers hope.

The geologist Brigitte Zanda-Hewins of the Museum of Natural History in Paris writes, that it took only about 20 million years until the Earth had developed from a dust disk around the original sun (Science, March 1st, 2003, vol. 295, p. 1705). By means of the most modern instruments, the geologists examined five billion year old meteorites. They stem from a time when the Earth was just developing and convey a picture of the epoch at that time. Up to now the researchers have started out from the fact that it had taken more than twice as long for the Earth to be created.

[32] Based on a computer model, a team of astronomers of the universities of Berkeley and Kingston as well as of the Southwest Research Institute in Boulder in the United States around Ed Thommes postulated that Uranus and probably Neptune had come into existence closer to the sun. If Uranus and Neptune had been created at the distance of their current orbits around the sun, they could only have a weight of about 10 times the Earth's mass according to the computer simulations. The two planets, however, have a weight of approximately 15 and 17 times the Earth's mass.

[33] In 1905, Albert Einstein postulated the photons for the interpretation of the photoelectric effect. David Blohm and other researchers, however, realised four decades later that the photoelectric effect can also be explained without the hypotheses of the photons. Light could be a variable electromagnetic field, that interacts with the individual atoms of a metallic surface which can only absorb certain amounts of energy. Strictly speaking, this means that Einstein received the Nobel prize undeservedly.

[34] A supercomputer at the Grainell University, by means of which an

extraordinary collapse of gravitation in the universe was simulated, surprised astrophysicists with results which should not occur according to Einstein's GToR. The scientists explained the simulation method had probably uncovered an error in at least one aspect of Einstein's theory about the behaviour of space, time, matter, and gravitation. Through this simulation it was revealed that a giant cloud of matter whose particles were kept together by gravitation in form of an egg-shaped (American) football dissolves into infinitely small matter particles and infinitely big gravitational forces upon its sudden internal collapse. Up to now scientists have calculated this process in the context of the GToR as so-called "naked singularities". "Naked singularities", so the previously valid assumption, exist in the familiar "black holes", i.e. in regions of the universe where the gravitational forces are supposed to be so strong that neither matter nor energy nor even light could escape from them. According to the results of the supercomputer simulation, however, nature is on no account capable of producing this occurrence at all. "Naked Singularities do not exist at all", says Dr. Stuart Shapiro, an astrophysicist at the Grainell University, who developed the simulation method. "So when the results of the simulation reveal", Shapiro continues, "that Einstein's theory leads to such indeterminable quantities, to the release of unbound forces, it is a sign that the theory itself has to be verified or that it is at least appropriate to have doubts concerning the applicability of the theory in this special context."

[35] In an experiment, scientists of the Massachusetts Institute of Technology (MIT) proved the dependency of the gravitational constant on the orientation in space. Michael Gerschtein, the senior scientist of the group, explained to United Press International that the modification of G could come to more than one half per thousand which would require a completely new theory of gravitation. Many other physical laws would have to be rewritten, too. That is to say the effect measured by Michael Gerschtein is even bigger by a multiple than Einstein's corrections of Newton's law of gravitation. (wissenschaft.de/ wissen/ news/ 148908)

[36] At the RHIC accelerator in Brookhaven, physicists came across unexpected problems when evaluating their data. The result of their experiment violated one of the most important symmetries of particle

physics, the Lorentz boost invariance. "Something seems to work fundamentally different as previously thought", Steven Manly of the university of Rochester noticed. (Physical Review Letters, vol. 89, no. 22, 222301)

[37] The physicist J. J. Shapiro already measured the alteration of the gravitational constant experimentally in the seventies. Published in Physical Revue Letters: G diminishes every year by about $2 * 10^{-10}$ of its value (hobby no. 18, 1-9-1971, page 128). A similar result was published by Stephen Merkowitz on May 1st, 2000 (Congress of American Physical Society).

[38] Cosmologists postulated a "dark matter" which is said to fill at least 90% of the universe - but so far nobody has discovered even a whiff of this ominous substance. We don't need it, though, astrophysicist Mordehai Milgrom says, who consolidated the MOND theory first proposed by Stacy S. McGaugh. MOND stands for „Modified Newtonian Dynamics", a simple modification of Newton's laws of gravitation. According to Newton, the heavy mass (responsible for the gravitational force) is always equal to the inert mass (responsible for the centrifugal force). If one of them is known, the other can be calculated. Now this identicalness is just doubted to be applicable for the giant masses at the outer fringe areas of the galaxies. There, inert and heavy mass are not equivalent anymore. The consequence is: the centrifugal force is getting lower (and the GTR is no longer valid!). Milgrom arbitrarily calculated a "reduction ratio" without substantiating it (an absolutely usual way of proceeding in physics!) and found his law "confirmed" with several galaxies. Moreover, one believes to be able to deduce the inertia of all bodies casually from the heavy masses of the whole universe by means of the MOND hypotheses (Mach principle).

[39] The idea of the accelerated expansion of the universe stems from Saul Perlmutter (University of California in Berkeley) and Brian Schmidt (Mount Stromlo Observatory, Australia). They realised that the light from supernovas is diminished by about 20%. From that they concluded that the world had expanded slowlier in former times - and will expand faster in future. But the astrophysicist Michael Rowan-Robinson of the Imperial College, London, claims to have proved blatant errors in the measurements, calculations, and interpretations of the authors. As is generally known, cosmic dust

dims the light of stars behind it. Mark Phillips of the Las Campanas Observatory in Chile determined a dimming factor of 25% for close supernovas - something which had been ignored by the supporters of the accelerated expansion. In addition, the supernovas were only observed when they had already reached their maximum luminosity. Thus their greatest brightness could not have been measured at all. When calculating the raw data again the phenomenon of too little brightness vanished immediately. The acceleration of the expansion could therefore be figments of the imagination.

[40] The question why it is dark at night although there are almost infinitely many stars is a problem which was already discussed in the 17th century and became popular through Olbers in 1823. Olbers' paradox asks why the night sky does not appear bright if the universe is infinitely big and there are everywhere as many stars as in our vicinity. Olbers thought that there had to be dark matter between the stars which, however, cannot be the solution at present. We know meanwhile that the light of far away stars is shifted to red by the expansion of the universe and - depending on the distance - into a non-visible range of the spectrum.

[41] When the physicists Wilson and Penzias discovered the cosmic background radiation, it had exactly the wavelength which it should have according to predictions of the theoreticians (especially of George Gamow). It corresponded to a "black body", a uniform emitter of radiation, of 2.7 Kelvin. And the cosmic background radiation was also as uniform as the cosmologist needed it. But one does not need a Big Bang for explaining the cosmic background radiation. As the physicist André K.T. Assis of the University of Campinas (Brazil) demonstrated there were other physicists before Penzias and Wilson who calculated the temperature of the empty universe and they did it from the radiation of the stars and galaxies alone by means of the fourth power law of radiation. And they made better predictions than Gamow! Here are some examples (K = degrees above absolute zero): C.E. Guillaume (1896): 5-6 K; Arthur Eddington (1926): 3.18 K; E. Regener (1933): 2.8 K; George Gamow (1952) 50 K (!). All authors who started out from the light of the stars alone achieved pretty good values. Only Gamow, who took the Big Bang as a starting point, calculated an absolutely wrong temperature. What's even more: When the insights about the

background radiation gained acceptance among experts, Gamow pointed out in a letter to the discoverers that he had predicted exactly the measured temperature (2.7 Kelvin) - yet his value was twenty times as high!

[42] According to current understanding, the radius of the universe is to be about 10^{23} km (100,000,000,000,000,000,000,000 km). But the determination of distances is a bit of a problem in astronomy. Many distances can at best be determined relative to others, some distances on the other hand only on certain assumptions. One of these assumptions is that supernovas of type Ia always have the same brightness distribution curve. But if they don't, *and there is cause to suppose so according to the latest insights*, the astronomical house of cards will collapse.

[43] The movement of our galaxy through the universe can also be proven by means of faraway radio galaxies. The astronomers Chris Blake and Jasper Wall used a radio telescope of the National Radio Astronomy Observatory's Very Large Array for studying the number of radio galaxies far away from our own galaxy. The density of these galaxies was found to be higher by one percent in the direction of movement of our galaxy than in the opposite direction. The study also matches observations of the Doppler shift of cosmic background radiation which is also caused by the movement of our galaxy. (Nature, volume 416, page 150)

[44] Andromeda Nebula M 31, object type: spiral galaxy, distance from Earth: ca. 2,500,000 light years (77,000 parsecs), diameter of the galaxy: 160,000 to 200,000 light years. The great galaxy in the constellation Andromeda is the biggest galaxy in the cluster of galaxies which also contains our milky way. The galaxy M 31 contains more than 300 billion suns. It is orbited by three times as many spherical star clusters as the milky way. M 31 is also the object farthest away which is visible with the naked eye. Two satellite galaxies NGC 205 and M 32 can be seen in the same region. By measurements of the background radiation one also knows today that our milky way is moving towards the Andromeda Nebula.

[45] An international team of the European Space Agency (ESA) under the direction of Max P. Bernstein (USA) and Guillermo M. Caro (Europe) simulated the conditions of the universe in the laboratory. They produced the dust grains responsible for the interstellar dark

nebulae in special pressure chambers where they created a temperature of -260° C and a nearly ideal vacuum. They also attached great significance to degermination. They equipped the chambers with the ingredients of interstellar nebulas: carbon monoxide, carbon dioxide, ammonia, and hydrogen cyanide. Now the researchers exposed the artificially created clouds of dust to ultra-violet radiation (in space, this is done by hot stars). In doing so amino acids like glycine, alanine, and serine developed by themselves - all in all 16 different components. Because such nebulae have an extension of thousands of light years and penetrate other nebulae and already finished solar systems the researchers assume that the amino acids produced in these clouds of dust are widespread - as it were the seeds for future life on worlds suitable for it.

[46] For comprehending the genetic development of life one began to examine the dynamics of the RNA molecules under various external conditions. For that purpose, Ralf Bundschuh of the Ohio State University and his colleagues of the University of California in San Diego analysed the temperature behaviour of RNA molecules by means of computer simulations. They found out that RNA, like water, adopts different phases in different temperature ranges. The molecules behave like glass at low temperatures and like molten material at high temperatures. The temperature-dependent mechanical properties of the RNA have in turn profound consequences for their three-dimensional spatial structure – they restrict the molecule's possibilities of folding. By means of his own computer simulations about the folding of RNA, Ranjan Mukhopadhyay, a scientist working with the NEC Laboratories, discovered that the possible spatial structures of an RNA molecule are exactly the most stable when it consists of a sequence of exactly four different bases. This explains why the RNA molecules with four bases were more successful in any step of the evolution than variants with more or less bases.

[47] The now clearly detectable blatant deviation from the conventional theories of biology and biochemistry is thoroughly intended. The functioning of the ribosome has remained completely unsolved up to today. We are proposing an absolutely new variant here. According to popular theory, the ribosome reads the genetic

code of the DNA strands, and on the basis of this sequence it composes the proteins required by the cell. In the meantime it turned out to be a big tangle of more than 50 proteins and various ribonucleic acids (RNA). The new "map" of the protein factory, developed by Harry Noller and his colleagues of the University of California at Santa Cruz, serves as a basis on which it will be possible to join other partial structures discovered earlier complete the picture. For example the structure of the two ribosome halves was already known – the new map, however, shows the position of the two halves together with a gap in-between where the production of protein takes place.

[48] The "data processing" of the DNA by means of the electron spin was discovered by researchers not until the end of 2002. US scientists proved by means of large-scale computer simulations that the strands of the genetic make-up can even influence the flux of electrons in dependence on their polarisation. With that DNA molecules could provide an interesting building block for future molecular switching circuits. In their models, Michael Zwolak and Massimiliano Di Ventra of the Virginia Polytechnic Institute discovered that DNA molecules did not conduct electrons with opposite spin equally well. This should be suitable for designing an electron valve or a spin switch on a molecular level. (from Applied Physics Letters).

[49] Of course, DNA strands do not swim around separately in the cytoplasm. Due to the negatively charged phosphate groups they bind to so-called histone proteins and form specific units (nucleosomes, chromatin fibrils etc.). In order to save the legibility of the text, all microbiological processes have been depicted in an extremely simplified way since we are only interested in the fundamental, schematic comprehension of processes whose complexity is unsurpassed in the universe.

[50] The currently applicable theory of the protein biosynthesis on ribosomes differs only slightly from our description and takes place in three steps: 1st Initiation: an m-RNA binds to the 40s-subunit of a ribosome. 2nd Elongation: beginning at the starter triplet or starter codon, transfer ribonucleic acids (t-RNAs) with specifically bound amino acids settle down on the ribosome one after the other according to the copied genetic code on the m-RNA. The amino

acids of which the protein consists are tied together by means of the enzyme peptidyl transferase. In doing so the t-RNAs dissociate from the ribosome again after they have released their amino acids. 3rd Termination = destruction of the chain. When the codon for termination of the m-RNA has been reached, the ribosome disintegrates into its subunits by consuming the GTP, and the finished protein detaches from the last t-RNA.

[51] Scientists now also established this fact with the bacterium mycoplasma genitalium: merely a few hundred genes would be required for its life. By means of the so-called mutagenesis of the transposons they detected that the micro organisms could manage without all their other genes.

[52] The eucariotic cells of our animal and plant kingdom contain much more DNA than required for the sequences of amino acids of the proteins. Living beings on low classification which have used up less genes in comparison with the human being therefore exhibit an enormous surplus – the newt, for example, has more DNA in one cell than humans. Since plants still represent a generally lower order of life it is to be expected that they possess a relatively unspent collection of information. Many plants, e.g. lilies, have considerably more DNA than any animal cell! As a rule, only 1% of the DNA is even used for the blueprint of the cell, thus the collection of the remaining 99% of the sequences is obviously unused programme. This unused DNA contains, however, transposable elements, and it has been revealed that parts of them spread like an infection and can influence a vaster and vaster portion of the genetic material.

[53] American researchers discovered that the differences in the DNA of man and chimpanzee are far greater than originally assumed. So far, it had been believed that the difference was about 1.5 percent. Actually, it is, however, five percent, Roy J. Britten and his colleagues write in the specialist journal "Proceedings" (Doi10.1073). The scientist (California Institute of Technology, Pasadena) explains the new results with the fact that until then only the differences of the base exchange of the DNA had been determined. Nobody ever dealt with the question if the results of deletion and insertion of the human and the chimpanzee's DNA matched or not. But by breaking out (deletion) or introducing (insertion) bases, a pattern characteristic for every species is created.

Compared to the exchange of a single base, deletion and insertion are in fact ten times rarer than the exchange of an individual base. In return these events concern, however, several hundred bases. When the differences of the base exchange are added to the events of insertion and deletion, the genetic make-up of the chimpanzee and the human genome differ from each other by five percent in the end – which separates mankind far more from the ape than assumed.

[54] Possibly the evolution of life proceeds much faster than previously thought. Scientists from New Zealand examined hereditary molecules from the bones of fossil penguins with an especially precise method. They discovered that the molecules had changed twice to seven times as quickly in the last seven thousand years than they should have done according to textbook opinion. The discovery was reported in the magazine "Science".

[55] By using the so-called transposon mutagenesis, a group of researches found out that micro-organisms like, for instance, the bacterium Mycoplasma genitalium would get by with a few hundred genes and could do without all their numerous other genes.

[56] Neuron = nerve cell; cell of the nerve tissue. Nerve cells are the only kind of cell which serve for creating and transmitting stimuli. Their cell body (perikaryon) possesses always only one cell nucleus with one or several nucleoles and, besides the usual cell organelles Nissl granules (also called Nissl substance, Nissl bodies or tigroid substance = basophilic ergastoplasm, consisting of granular or rough endoplasmic reticulum and polyribosomes) which only occur in neurons. In addition, Nissl granules (Nissl bodies) are only found in great amounts in the dendrites (cellular branchlets). The distinction of a neuron is discerned especially by the increase of Nissl substance. Decrease of the Nissl substance in case of fatigue, damage, or poisoning; reversible loss with ischaemia, irreversible reduction with Alzheimer's disease type II. Regeneration and creation of new substance is done mainly during sleep. Motoneurons or motor nerve cells (they trigger and control muscles) contain particularly many and big Nissl granules.

[57] We use the designation "Nissl bodies" intentionally although it is antiquated and the corresponding structure in the neuron is now called granular rough endoplasmic reticulum (rER) since we do not share the currently common opinion of the molecular biologists that

all RNA conglomerates in the cell are ribosomes. See also the previous footnote!

[58] In 1989, Swiss scientists could actually take the first picture of changes in the nerve cells of the brain through the electron microscope. The examined nerve cells were responsible for the constitution of the long-term memory. The scientists could prove photographically with the brain tissue of rats that the long-term memory is based on the formation of additional neuronal junctions (synapses) between the neurons (nerve cells).

[59] This restricted freedom of will is characteristic of all living things whose neurons work to the method of inhibition. Even with the human being, neuronal processes are crucial for the behaviour. "The free will is only a useful illusion", says neurobiologist Gerhard Roth (University of Bremen). Experiments by the American neurophysiologist Benjamin Libet suggest the conclusion: human beings don't do what they want but they want what they do... Libet asked test subjects to spontaneously make the decision to move one finger or the whole hand, and recorded the moment of decision with a clock. In the transcript, it was recorded: firstly this moment of time, secondly the moment when, in preparation of the movement, a so-called readiness potential built up in the brain for the first time, and thirdly the moment of the actual movement. The result was a surprising sequence: the conscious decision for action occurred 0.2 seconds before the movement set in but only more than 0.3 seconds after the readiness potential.

Thus can volition be the cause of the neuronal activity at all? For Gerhard Roth, the volitional act occurs really only after the brain has already decided which movement it is going to make. For Libet, the same result means that the power of volition is restricted. Volition is not an initiator but a censor. In the discussion it was also doubted if decisions are momentary acts. And not rather processes whose results one sometimes becomes aware of only after they have ended. Thus some researchers think it is quite possible that the momentary decision assumed by Libet is only the last step of a decision process which began earlier. The conclusion of the neurobiologists, that all processes in the brain are deterministic (exclude the freedom of will) and that the cause of every action is the immediately preceding overall states of the brain, seems just as appropriate.

Professor of philosophy Hans Goller (University of Innsbruck) stated that the brain research was far from having identified the neuronal foundation for experiencing the freedom of will. Goller: "There are first interesting indications. They prove the fact that certain areas and functions of the brain are a necessary condition for experiences of the will. But are they also a sufficient condition? The interdisciplinary discussion of the freedom of will shows that our knowledge about the brain and its performances are incomplete in a fundamental sense."

[60] This memory allegory with a metal cube is on no account a high-flown idea. Experiments with superconductors showed that metals really exhibit some kind of memory: rising temperatures or a strong magnetic field can turn a metallic superconductor back into a conventional conductor again. But experiments with the element aluminium yielded a surprise. To be exact with a certain alignment of the magnetic field the height of the transition temperature depends on the fact if the sample *already is or has yet to become superconductive* - the aluminium "knows" its *past*, so to speak. Even if no scientist knows how this information is stored.

[61] Researchers could prove with the brain tissue of rats that the long-term memory is based on the formation of additional junctions (synapses) between neurons (nerve cells). These works were conducted within the framework of the International Human Frontier Science Programme which was brought into being by the G7 states in 1989.

[62] "The radio waves evoke consciousness by joining the information stored in the brain to one overall picture which can be experienced," says Johnjoe McFadden, microbiologist at the University of Surrey. With that the human mind could be an electromagnetic field. "Many unsolved questions of consciousness research", McFadden thinks could be explained that way. For example the "combination problem": information belonging together can be combined in the consciousness nevertheless without any problems. For that purpose, the visual impression in the brain evokes electrical activities of the nerves which build up a radio field. The related memories are then activated by this electromagnetic field. The Britons also explains the free will with this theory: the electromagnetic field could select certain neurons, i.e. information processing units of the nervous

system, by blocking or supporting them. But: the neurons are connected with each other. With every activity of the nerves, this connection is growing, too. In this way, the influence of the field could be diminished in the course of time because many couplings are later done automatically.

[63] Einstein himself proposed in a speech – delivered on May 5th, 1920 in the University in Leiden – a structure similar to the T.A.O. matrix (motionless ether), when he said: "Recapitulating, we may say that according to the general theory of relativity space is endowed with physical qualities; in this sense, therefore, there exists an ether. According to the general theory of relativity, space without ether is unthinkable; for in such space there not only would be no propagation of light, but also no possibility of existence for standards of space and time (measuring-rods and clocks), nor therefore any space-time intervals in the physical sense. But this ether may not be thought of as endowed with the quality characteristic of ponderable media, as consisting of parts which may be tracked through time. *The idea of motion may not be applied to it.*"

[64] As everybody knows, in the SToR the fundamental magnitude v really reverses its sign in the counter transformation although the Lorentz transformations should be absolutely symmetrical between the primed and the unprimed frame of reference. An absolutely symmetrical inertial process therefore contains asymmetric transformations. This flaw has been ignored by relativists for one hundred years although it questions the whole theory. Students at every university of the world have complained about this incomprehensibility to the lecturers. "How is it possible that the inverse Lorentz transformation reverses the sign of the fundamental magnitude despite the absolute symmetry of the inertial process?"

[65] The frequency of a clock of any model is, ... as has been proved theoretically and practically, linearly depending on the gravitational potential. An atomic clock which has a certain frequency at sea level and which is transported to a place at a higher level, for example to the US Bureau of Standards in Boulder (Col.) at 1650 metres above sea, is going faster there by a factor of $+ 1.8 \cdot 10^{-13}$. This is not an illusion because when the clock is taken back to sea level, one can read on it how much time it has gained on the higher level. (Quotation from Brockhaus multimedial 2001). The question is

probably not rarely asked: what happens to the clock when it enters a different gravitational potential and changes its frequency accordingly. The clock does not go faster on a mountain simply because the time is going faster. It goes faster there because explicitly those structural components alter which determine the frequency. This observation describes actually only an identity: the modification of the frequency determining components is identical with the statement that the clock changes its frequency. Foucault pendulums and clock pendulums turn out to be the key for understanding the cosmological conclusions from Mach's principle.(Prof. Dr. Klaus Strobach, Stuttgart)

[66] This altitude of 4.90 m stems from calculations by John Archibald Wheeler (A Journey into Gravity and Space-time, p. 176). Other authors, like for instance Thomas Fischbacher, University of Munich (1.20 m) achieved completely different values which deviate from each other. This shows that the mathematics of the GTR is not a simple matter.

[67] See: "ABC of the Theory of Relativity" by Bertrand Russell, page 95 of German edition, published by Fischer Taschenbuch Verlag GmbH, Frankfurt a. M., 1989.

[68] William of Ockham (around 1285 to ca. 1349), English philosopher born in Ockham (Surrey), theological writer and Franciscan friar. The rule of economy of formal logic ascribed to William of Ockham according to which simple hypothesis are to be preferred to complicated ones, is called Ockham's razor.

[69] The concept of Black Holes is not new and did on no account arise but with Einstein's theory: already in 1799, Pierre Simon Laplace (1749–1827) discussed the question whether the gravitational force of a body could be so strong that it would prevent light from escaping. Since black holes cannot be proved directly of course, one is looking for indications for the existence of the black hole by means of the radiation emitted by bodies falling into the black hole. Thus it is meanwhile considered as "proven" that black holes occur in the centre of many galaxies.

[70] Mach's principle: in 1883, Ernst Mach (1838-1916) formulated the hypothesis that the forces of inertia were caused by the entirety of matter available in the universe. In a thought experiment to that effect, the inertia of a body was expected to disappear when all other

matter was removed. According to Newton's bucket experiment, the parabolic curvature of the surface of a water-filled rotating bucket marks a frame of reference rotating against the absolute space. But since there is no absolute space according to Mach, the centrifugal force as a cause of the curvature is generated on the basis of the rotation relative to the fixed stars. According to Mach, the reversed situation, namely the rotation of the fixed stars around the stationary bucket cannot be distinguished from Newton's bucket experiment neither by thought nor by experiment. Therefore the water surface has to be curved in this as well. Mach's principle was one of the starting points for developing the GTR.

[71] Curved beam of light (mirage): a cuvette is filled with 4 cm of water and placed on the optical bench. Then the table salt solution is filled in by means of the tube at the bottom of the cuvette so that two different layers are created in the cuvette, water on top and the table salt solution at the bottom. One has to make sure that the layers don't mix. The laser is mounted on the table in such a way that the beam enters the cuvette only just below the boundary of the layers, pointing slightly inclined upwards. Because of the continuously changing refraction index along this boundary the beam will run in a curved way.

[72] In GPS (Global Positioning System), a correction of the relativistic effects (the clocks are going faster because of the altitude of the satellite orbits) is actually made by slightly reducing the frequency of the atomic clocks in the satellites (from 10.23 Mhz to 10.229999995453 Mhz). It cannot be verified if this correction makes sense at least with regard to the GTR (the SToR errors would be too insignificant) since the errors from other causes are substantially more significant and conceal the relativistic ones. The errors can have following extent:

- Atmospheric effects ± 5 metres
- Variations of the satellite orbits ± 2.5 metres
- Errors of the satellite clocks ± 2 metres
- Disturbances due to reflection of signals ± 1 metre
- Disturbances due to the troposphere ± 0.5 metres
- Computational and rounding errors ± 1 metre
- Relativistic effects ± 0.13 metres

With a probability of 95 percent a position measured by means of GPS does not deviate more than 100 m in horizontal position and not more than 156 m in altitude from the actual value (Hofmann-Wellenhof & Lichtenegger 1994). The "natural" errors make the lion's share of inaccuracy in the balance of errors of the GPS; they are by far greater than those 13 centimetres from the Theories of Relativity so that they scarcely play a role in practice. The correction is an academical industrious piece of work. Franz Embacher (University of Vienna): "Because of this simple solution the GPS technicians don't have to grapple with the Theory of Relativity."

[73] Actually, this expectation is incomprehensible: Galileo's or Newton's principles of relativity imply that it does not depend on the motion or the rest of a body when we conduct a physical experiment. That means that we cannot distinguish at all between the Earth at rest or in motion. Thus when we shoot cannon balls into different directions we could not establish the motion of the Earth around the sun from their velocities. Why did one actually believe that Newton's principle of relativity could be broken if one took beams of light instead of cannon balls? Michelson proved that there is no ether - and what more? All right, forget the ether. Why should the light reveal the motional state of the Earth when it was already known that no experiment would permit it? Why did one expect that corpuscles of light behaved different to cannon balls? One only had to accept Newton's principle of relativity and did not require any SToR at all to explain the result of Michelson's experiment (and those of other people). We would get exactly the same result with cannon balls - but nobody would come up with the idea that they were moved along with the "ether". (Posted to the forum of "Bild der Wisssenschaft", a German scientific magazine).

[74] In the years 1976 to 1977, experimenters of the Lawrence Berkeley Laboratory in California flew in a U2 airplane high above in the Earth's atmosphere. They found that there were differences in the measured velocity compared to a cosmic frame of reference defined by the 3-K radio energy. There also were distinct results for the motion of our milky way through the universe. In his book "Einstein's Universe" Nigel Calder said to that: "What is false is nothing less than one of Einstein's fundamental assumptions: that it is impossible for an astronaut moving at a steady speed to tell

whether he who is moving or the outside world is moving. In fact it turns out that he can, and the democracy of Einstein's theory is compromised."

[75] Why should the presented swimmer analogy not be admissible for the behaviour of the light? In short it can be said that in case of the swimmers there is a modification to the speeds whereas in the MICHELSON interferometer a modification of the distances takes place, and we should therefore examine the experiment very thoroughly.

For easier comprehension we imagine an enormous interferometer with arm lengths of 300 000 kilometres:

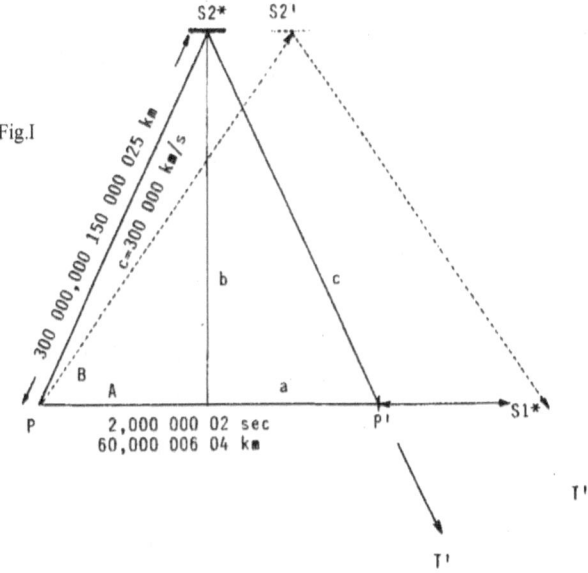

Fig.I

Figure I shows the situation of the vertical arm of the interferometer which is in motion for the period which the horizontal beam requires until it returns to P'. Michelson expected a difference in time according to:

$$\Delta t = \frac{L}{c} \frac{v^2}{c^2} \qquad (1)$$

Michelson calculated the time of the vertical arm with:

$$t = \frac{L}{(c^2 - v^2)^{\frac{1}{2}}} \qquad (2)$$

Translated to our giant imaginary instrument a time results of

$$\frac{600000}{299999.999} = 2.000000006 \quad s$$

The running time of the arm in direction of the motion is calculated with

$$t = \frac{1}{c-v} + \frac{1}{c+v} = \frac{300000}{299970} + \frac{300000}{300030} = 2.00000002 \quad s \qquad (3)$$

Therefore one expects an advance of the perpendicular beam of

2.000 000 02
-2.000 000 006
0.000 000 014 seconds

With approximation this value is also the result of formula (1):

$$\Delta t = \frac{L}{c}\frac{v^2}{c^2} = \frac{600000}{300000} * \frac{900}{9000000000\,0} = 0.00000001 \; s \qquad (1)$$

Now let's take a closer look a the distance of the perpendicular beam. On the condition of Galileo's addition procedure, a triangle P-P'-S2* is the result whose sides are 300 000.000 150 000 025 kilometres long and whose base line is 60.000 006 04 kilometres long. This is because the horizontal beam returns to P after 2.000 000 02 seconds whereas P has wandered off to P' in the meantime.

The perpendicular beam needs about 1.000 000 0005 seconds for one distance, hence it arrives at P' after 2.000 000 001 seconds, obviously really exactly with an advance of

2.000 000 02
- 2.000 000 001
0.000 000 019 seconds.

We see that this agrees with the previously calculated difference with regard to the dimension and that Michelson must have really proceeded on the assumption of such a situation. But we also realise at once that something is a bit fishy about this matter.

If the distance P-S2* was already more than 300 000 kilometres at the time when the beam was reflected but light cannot be faster than 300 000 km/s, how could it reach and hit mirror S2*?

In view of the swimmer example we have to discover to our surprise that it really seems to make a difference whether the river or the bank is moving.

Still, in the interferometer, the situation presents itself in an even stricter manner. The beam of light is bound to the laws of reflection; the angle of incidence determines the angle of reflection. When Michelson expected the beam at P', the reflection should take place at S2* but that could never happen. Because if the beam wanted to hit the mirror at all (when it really reaches the point S2*, the mirror has moved away in the meantime), an additional angle had to be given.

To repeat it: in the swimmer example only one of the points is imaginary - either start or finish. In the interferometer the distance is: from where P was to where S2* will be - *both* points are imaginary!

In any case, Michelson's experiment was not suitable to demonstrate a "being left behind" of the light. Because when aiming at the mirror S2, the angle is already given automatically because the image of the mirror needs time to reach P. When one now sets the Galilean angle to be on the safe side in order to hit the mirror, one has in truth used this angle - without knowing - twice. And only on this condition can the mirror really be hit. When the beam returns this angle results automatically twice because of the reflection. The beams can therefore impossibly come together at P'. But they do so promptly in the telescope, for Michelson overlooked in addition that an additional correction crept in: the horizontal beam was reflected into the perpendicular one in order to hit the telescope. Figure II illustrates the situation drastically (of course in an exaggerated way).

The interferometer is portrayed in three situations. The chosen interval in time is that time which the horizontal beam requires to hit P again. According to Michelson's expectations and calculations, the horizontal beam (A) should run as follows:

L-S1*-P'-T'.   The perpendicular beam (B): L-P-S2*-P'-T'.

The relation of the distances can be measured already in the rough sketch: the running distance B from P to T' is a little shorter compared to the distance A from P to T'. One sees: B should arrive sooner in the telescope (all distances are traversed at c!). This was Michelson's expectation: as the second sketch shows, this difference is translated exactly from one arm to the other when the instrument is turned by 90 degrees. The true path of the light, however, looks differently: beam A remains the same for the moment until it reaches P', but then it pulls towards T'' ! Beam B can hit the mirror only at S2' and from there it is directed to T''. Now path B (from P to T'') is of the same length as path A!

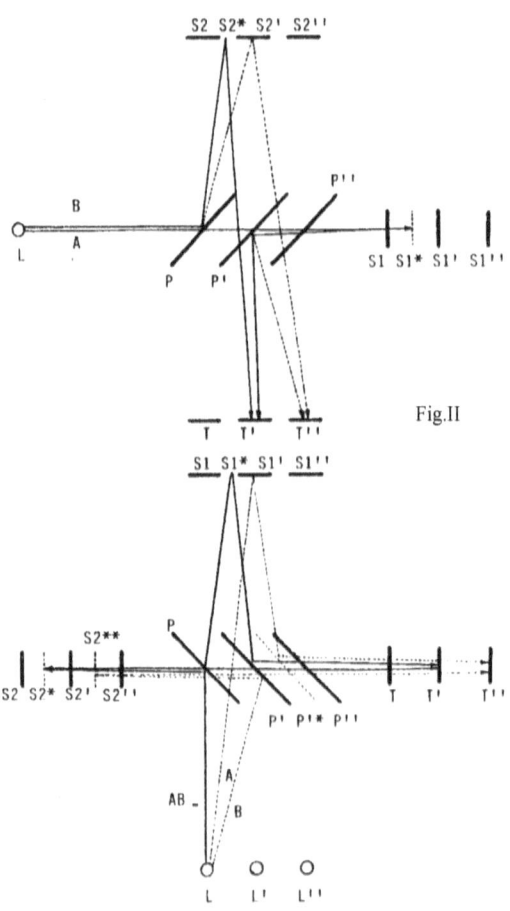

Fig.II

As there is yet a correction to A, a difference is to be expected which has to be essentially smaller than the one assumed by Michelson. After turning the instrument, Michelson expected the distances to be as follows (he considered P as start); for B: L-P-S2*-P'-T'. For A: L-P-S1*-P'-T' . In this case, B would now have the longer distance whereas distance A would become a little shorter. Michelson hoped to see this difference in the telescope.

This hope was wrong because in truth the distances are following the path L-P'-S2**-T" for B and L-S1'-P'*-T" for A! Again the two distances P-T'' are of the same length!

For that reason, there was not much that could change in the telescope. Of course the sketch exaggerates the changes at mirror P a lot. In truth, the angles are so minute that such a change (namely the correction of the train of waves to P) would be merely noticeable. It should also be mentioned that Michelson reflected the beam of light several times to and fro in order to get a greater arm length which did not change anything in the situation, of course.

Because of the "being-left-behind" of the light and its unfaltering path both events ensue: relative to the interferometer, the perpendicular beam has the velocity according to Galileo but the distance actually covered is (in our imaginary instrument) not 300000 km but the distance from P to S2', i.e.: $(l^2+v^2)^{1/2}$

The time of the perpendicular beam can therefore be calculated with good approximation with

$$t = \frac{2(l^2+v^2)^{\frac{1}{2}}}{(c^2-v^2)^{\frac{1}{2}}} = \frac{600000 \cdot .004}{299999.999} = 2.0000000200\ 0000006 \text{ sec} \quad (4)$$

The actual difference is therefore only about

        beam B: 2.00000002000000006 seconds
        <u>beam A: -2.00000002</u>
        0.00000000000000006 seconds

But even this difference is almost compensated by path A: p'-T'[1]. It is therefore no wonder when Michelson could not find the wrongly expected shifting of the interference fringe to the theoretically expected extent, no matter how he turned his instrument.

It should be noted that even after turning the instrument the beams arrive temporally at T'' so that the turning corresponds absolutely to the temporal displacement. Since the distances P-T'' adopt practically the same lengths for both beams in all cases, Michelson did not only fail in providing evidence for the ether but would have been unable to notice the absolute propagation of light relative to the Earth either - therefore the various contrasting speeds of light.

This experiment, which is often designated "best verified experiment in physics" in literature, proves to be unsuitable as a foundation of the ToR. Many critics of the Theory of Relativity examined the Michelson-Morley experiment with a fine-toothed comb. And there are several explanations for the failure of the experiment: Paul Wesley, for example, is said to have proved that standing waves develop in the interferometer which are taken along by the laboratory in any case.

In the Michelson interferometer it was thus not a possibly carrying ether which determined the path of the light but firstly the circumstance that the light remains absolutely fixed, and secondly that it observes the laws of reflection, a fact that should actually be expected.[110]

The situations at the half-transparent mirror P cannot be accounted for exactly in a drawing since the reflection times of A and B do not correspond, of course. It is important that the total distances don't change and that after turning the instrument mirror S1' can certainly only reflect that train of waves which reaches it. He who is a little confused with the events at mirror P because he knows that the beam is split up here, should consider that it is still a wave front despite the focussing of the beam. Because of the inclination of the mirror the wave front remains sufficiently broad to impart so much scattering to the light that the selection of the corresponding paths becomes possible by means of mirrors S1 and S2. The occurring Doppler effects are compensated by the mirrors, which are each working in opposite directions, as well as by the moved telescope itself. In this respect there is nothing to gain here, either.

[76] In 1864, James Clerk Maxwell (1831–1879) submitted his dissertation "A Dynamical Theory of the Electromagnetic Field" to the Royal Society in London. With his equations he provided the

theory by means of which all electromagnetic effects have been explained until today. The theory, however, had a crucial disadvantage: it was no longer Galileo invariant. Its equations resulted, for instance, in the velocity of light being of the same value in all frames of reference. This was a contradiction to Galileo's opinion according to which the light, which is emitted, for example, at c by a source of light moving away from the observer at 0.3c, should arrive at the observer at only 0.7c. But this seemed to be contradictory to the experimental results. Maxwell's theory was no longer Galileo invariant but Lorentz invariant. That means that it is invariant at a peculiar transformation, the so-called Lorentz transformation. The peculiarity of this transformation is that moving bodies appear to be shortened and that moving clocks go slower.

[77] The conventional expert opinion that, for instance, the electric charge of the proton is always distributed in a spherical structure was refuted by the result of a study concerning interactions of a high-energy electron ray with hydrogen atoms. The examination carried out under the direction of Charles Perdrisat of the Jefferson Laboratory in the US County Virginia provoked intensive disputes in the expert world. Together with about eighty research colleagues Perdrisat conducted his examinations on an electron accelerator of the Jefferson Laboratory. In their experiment the scientists fired an electron ray into a vessel which was filled with extremely cold hydrogen. When the electrons hit the hydrogen atoms and accelerated them, they were deflected into an unexpected direction through the interaction with their protons. The group of researchers interpreted the results of their experiment in that way that the positive electric charge of the proton did not adopt a spherical form but rather that of an egg. As was to be expected, other researchers are not convinced of this interpretation, though. They rather suspect that the results of the experiment could be explained with the relativistic interactions between the high-energy electrons with the protons.

[78] According to the SToR, a couple of paradoxes and inconsistencies in argumentation result, like for example: the faster a car drives, the slower its motor would have to run because of the time dilatation, or tanks could cross a crack in the earth for one observer but not for the other observer, balls would fit through the gaps of a fence passing by

or they wouldn't..., just think of the twin paradox or the Ehrenfest dog-flea paradox etc... Here is another one: a submarine travelling at near-light speed appears shorter to an observer on land. For that reason, it looses its buoyancy and should sink to the ground. But from the view of the submarine crew, the situation is just reversed, and the submarine should rise to the surface. With astonishment we can read in the specialist magazine Physical Review D (volume 68, article 027701): "This paradox of the SToR has now been resolved by a Brazilian researcher... When an object is moving past a stationary observer at close to the speed of light, it appears to get shorter to him. This so-called Lorentz contraction should therefore make a submarine, which is of the same density as water in a system at rest and is therefore swimming at a constant altitude, sink since its density increases because of the contraction. According to the frame of reference of the submarine crew, however, the sub is stationary, and the water is rushing past. It therefore appears to be denser than the sub and as a consequence the sub should float. In his study, George Matsas of the State University of Sao Paulo in Brazil used the equations of the General Theory of Relativity in order to calculate a generalised buoyancy for objects which are moving almost at the velocity of light in a liquid. Since the General Theory of Relativity accounts for gravitational forces, the submarine paradox could be solved in this way - the submarine sinks even from the viewpoint of the submarine crew. Reason for this is the gravitational field of the water rushing past which also reduces the buoyancy in this frame of reference. Matsas has shown in an elegant way that this contradiction dissolves when considering the energy of acceleration of the gravity field. His solutions should also be applicable to the theory of the Hawking radiation emitted by black holes which can exert a sort of " buoyant force " on nearby matter according to some researchers."

Comment: so the contradictions of the SToR can be solved by means of the GTR. Well done, really! And what does this have to do with the SToR at all?

[79] All so-called "tests of the SToR" concern predominantly only "tests of light propagation" and can therefore not confirm the SToR at all (because even the theory according to Lorentz would be confirmed by that). A verification of the constancy of the velocity of

light cannot at the same time be a verification of the SToR for the simple reason that it is not a prediction of the theory but a basic assumption! (Vicious circle: MM experiment measures constancy of c, Einstein bases his theory on it, establishing the constancy of c "confirms" theory...)

[80] Actually particles are not "discovered"! We should not forget that all those "particles", mesons, kaons, muons, etc. materialise as spherical fields, spherical waves, impulse fields, etc... because of the conditions of encounter in T.A.O. and are for the most part produced in the charged particle accelerators.

[81] Georg Galeczki/Peter Marquardt: "Requiem für die Spezielle Relativität" (= *Requiem for Special Relativity*), Haag + Herchen 1997.

[82] The different operation of the clocks is easy to understand. One circumnavigation was flown towards the East and one towards the West. Both journeys lasted for three days. The result of the experiment:

The clock travelling eastwards lost on average 59 nanoseconds compared to the clock in Washington whereas the clock travelling westwards gained on average 273 nanoseconds. Since one of the planes was flying with the rotation of the Earth, the other against it, and the clock in Washington was going along with the rotation of the Earth, all three clocks were moving at a different speed through the matrix of T.A.O. The clocks reacted with changes in their operation because of their inertia compared to the higher absolute system of the matrix. One difference results from the flight level of the two travelling clocks compared to the clock in Washington (faster operation) and from the retardation of running due to this motion. The fastest clock which gained the rotation of the Earth when flying eastwards therefore lost again most of the seconds gained by the flight level because of its high speed and therefore it was 59 nanoseconds slow, whereas the slower one lost little of its increase in frequency through the flight level and therefore was 273 seconds fast.

The values can only be reconciled with the predictions of the SToR and the GTR if they are relativised to an imaginary stationary clock (i.e. if they are not compared with the clock in Washington). That time itself had nothing to do with these incorrectly operating clocks is proved by the fact *that the rotation of the Earth did not change during these three days and that the course of the world was not disturbed at all...*

[83] Aberration of the stars: since light inside a telescope needs time for traversing, it receives a diagonal path in the moving telescope behind whose elongation we falsely locate the star. The angle of aberration results simply from v/c; during one revolution of the Earth there is thus an East-West drift of the observed star of *2 v/c* = $2*10^{-4}$ degrees, that's about 41 angular seconds. The aberration, which was first determined by James Bradley, corresponds very well with this value. Since the velocity of the Earth was quite well known at this time, Bradley could measure the value of *c* essentially exacter because of the angles of aberration.

Already in 1871, Sir George Airy had the idea to determine the velocity of the Earth immediately by means of the aberration (fig. I):

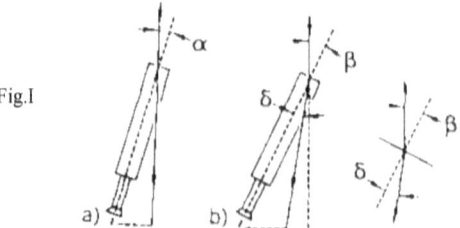

Fig.I

The physicist assumed a telescope set to a star whose true direction includes an angle of 90 degrees with the direction of the ecliptic plane of the Earth. The unknown angle of aberration would be α and the also unknown velocity of the Earth (relative to the "ether" as Airy assumed) would be *v*. Now Airy completely filled the telescope with water. Since the velocity of light is lower in water than in air, the time which the light requires to travel through the tube of the telescopes was increased by the factor *n*. For that reason, Airy expected that in order to keep the image of the star in the centre of the visual field he would have to tilt the telescope by the new aberration angle β, and that he could use the value of this correction to the adjustment for calculating the velocity *v*.

Well, the angle β is not simply given by *nv/c* because there was air on one side of the objective lens and water on the other side and the incident beams of light were therefore refracted to the axis of the instrument (fig. 153 on the right). Inside the telescope, the beams of light would include an angle δ with the axis so that

$$n = \frac{\sin \beta}{\sin \delta} \approx \frac{\beta}{\delta} \qquad (1)$$

Since the light traverses the telescope at a velocity c/n and the telescope is moving horizontally at the velocity v, the conditions for centring the constellation in the telescope is

$$\delta \approx \frac{\frac{v}{c}}{n} = \frac{nv}{c} \qquad (2)$$

Well, Airy did not know the true values of α, β, and δ but he hoped to be able to measure the change in the direction of the telescope in order to receive

$$\beta \approx n\delta \approx \frac{n^2 v}{c}; \alpha \approx \frac{v}{c} \qquad (3)$$

Hence

$$\beta - \alpha \approx (n^2 - 1)\frac{v}{c} \qquad (4)$$

Since all quantities with the exception of v can be measured directly, it should be possible to determine v through them. For that reason, Sir George Airy conducted this experiment. To his surprise there was not the slightest change in the apparent position of the star.

If one tends to the hypothesis that the light is at least partially dragged by the medium water, the negative expression of the experiment could be explained as follows for the time being: we assume the water - which certainly moves perpendicular to the light – drags the light at a fraction f of its own velocity. The experiment revealed that the angle β equals the original angle of aberration α (α=v/c) and that therefore the angle δ equals α /n. The length of the telescope would be l; the time for traversing the water filled telescope $t=nl/c$. In time t, however, the telescope covers the distance vt. When the light is to leave the telescope again through the centre of the eyepiece, the lateral displacement of the light has to correspond exactly to this value. The displacement of the beam of light would be equal to the sum of $l\delta$, the component caused by refraction, and of fvt, the one implied by the water dragging the light. Hence

But

$$vt \approx l\delta + fvt \quad (5)$$

$$l = \frac{ct}{n} \text{ and } \ldots \delta = \frac{\alpha}{n} = \frac{v}{nc} \quad (6,7)$$

Hence

$$vt = \frac{ct}{n}\frac{v}{nc} + fvt \quad (8)$$

which results in

$$f = 1 - \frac{1}{n^2} \quad (9)$$

This quantity is known as Fresnel's drag coefficient.

At first glance it seems strange that exactly this drag coefficient really exists in nature by means of which Airy's experiment - and many other similar ones as well - led to the same results which one would get if the Earth was in rest relative to the "ether". Just like the result of the Michelson-Morley experiment one also interpreted Airy's experiment subsequently as evidence for the correctness of Einstein's assumptions.

But when Airy's experiment is analysed from our point of view, the quantity f does on no account seem strange, for it has to result of necessity. What Sir George Airy did not consider (nor did many other physicists) is the possibility that the refraction on the moving water-filled telescope does not have to be the same as on the stationary one. When the law of refraction is interpreted by means of the Huygenian principle, we realise that the motion of the refracting medium at the moment of incidence slightly changes the wave front and with that the direction of refraction.

The easiest way to explain this is by means of our simple beer mat model in which the Huygens-Fresnel principle is fundamentally hidden (fig. II, centre).

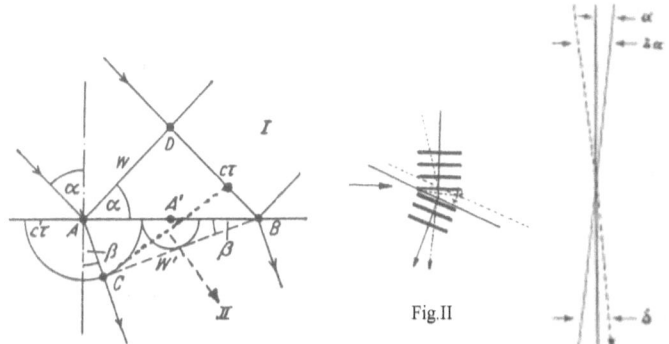

Fig.II

We clearly see that the refraction is caused and determined by the difference in velocities inside and outside of the medium. The decisive factor lies in the time in which the wave front (beer mat) still remains partially "in the open" after its fringe immersed in the retarding medium. When the medium is in motion, it comes to meet the wave front (or runs away from it) and abbreviates (or prolongs) this time...

The motion changes the refraction in such a way as if the beam was more inclined by the angle of v/c. That means an additional inclination of the beam by v/c=0.0001 degrees would cause the same refraction in the motionless medium. In the specific case of the Airy experiment the actual inclination of the instrument of 0.0001 degrees and the correction of the motion to the same extent results in a refraction as if the incident beam of light had an inclination of 0.0002 degrees. This results in an angle δ with $2\alpha/n$=0.00015 degrees. Since the instrument itself is and remains inclined by 0.0001 degrees, the beam is preset to 0.00005 degrees by the refraction of motion; that is exactly the angle which it has to include in order to exit in the centre of the ocular despite the velocity reduced by the factor n!

For that reason, Airy expected in vain an apparent modification in the position of the star. The drag hypothesis didn't play any significant role, either. There isn't any drag in the actual sense but the motion changes the refraction and that in turn annihilates the measurability of the motion. Therefore Arago had to notice already in 1818 that the refraction of the star light occurred obviously in such a way as if the Earth was resting in the "ether".

What applies to refraction applies of course in an analogous manner to absorption as well. Therefore Fizeau's measurements of the drag coefficient had to provide the same result as the aberration. The physicist sent opposite beams of light through flowing water and measured the modification in the optical path lengths with an interferometer. Apart from the fact that the conditions were similar to those in the Michelson instrument, the coming-towards-the-light and the running-away-from-the-light of the medium water caused differences in the optical path lengths. In flow direction of the water the wavelengths are getting longer, against the flow the are getting shorter. The extent depends on the velocity of the medium in the same way and in the same relation as in case of the change in refraction. Hence the result in this case is also an apparent drag. We must not fail to notice that the moving medium represents in a certain way the same as an "observer" who has to experience for sure what is caused by his motion: the Doppler effect!

[84] The SToR also predicts, for instance, that with the same particle one observer will measure a mass *smaller* than Planck mass, another observer, however, will measure a mass *bigger* than Planck mass. This is of course nonsense.

[85] Experiments in the manner of Michelson's have been repeated many times, even in a variety of variations, with laser beams for the first time in 1964, even with different arm lengths and cooled equipment (Kennedy-Thorndike experiment), with microwaves in echo boxes, etc... Most of the time the frequencies of two laser beams directed perpendicular to each other were compared and the resulted difference between the frequencies (the beat frequency) was recorded. These cases also revealed (although not without exception) that no change in the frequency followed the turning of the experimental set-up which was always celebrated as new, modern evidence for the SToR.

Well, the absolute propagation of the light in T.A.O. also applies to many other electromagnetic processes. Since in case of the laser there is a fixed relation between the causing and the emitted light-waves, which are arranged perpendicular to each other in addition, a differential compensation has to be expected from that alone. When the causing wave is subject to shortening, the emitted one is extended. The working frequency of a laser, however, is determined also by the distance of the two mirrors at the ends of the laser. The perpendicular laser beam corresponds thus absolutely with the vertical arm of the Michelson interferometer.

Since the distance in the perpendicular laser will be of the same length as the one of the horizontal laser for the same reasons of reflection as in the original Michelson instrument, no result is to be expected in this case, either. In the theory of this experiment, factors are also paying a role which include, among other things, the exact consideration of atomic behaviour. But we must not forget at all that eventually all matter is created of electric fields and that their absolute fixation in the T.A.O. is given, from which firstly comes the peculiar phenomenon of the inert mass and of which secondly a Lorentz contraction has to be expected.

[86] The Doppler effect could offer a good possibility to directly locate the time dilatation postulated by Einstein. In fact by means of the spectrums of far away milky way systems, which, as is commonly known, move away from us at very high speeds. Their light is distinctly altered in its colour by that.

But what cannot transform is that message which *is not transmitted*: the absorbed light whose lines of absorption we recognise in every spectrum (Frauenhofer lines). Without thinking about it the concepts red or blue shift are usually combined with the ideas that the lines of absorption shift in the spectrum - and this assumption is wrong. These lines are in fact exactly that which does *not* change. What shifts is the spectrum! Therefore we can assign these lines to particular elements for certain and identify them in every spectrum (like the lines H or K of calcium) and at the same time establish the shifting of the light spectrum relative to them.

That should make many any disciple of the Theory of Relativity suspicious, though, for the reason that if something like an expansion of time happened in one of the fast moving galaxies, these dark lines would have to shift as well - because in an altered time, calcium would on no account absorb the same wavelength as in "our" time!

This altered absorption would have to present itself clearly to our eyes because it doesn't cause *any signal*, so to speak it is a "hole" in the spectrum and thus it is not subject to any relativistic effects. But a shift of this kind, namely of spectrum *and lines at the same time* (as is to be expected to a different extent), has never been observed up to now. That means that calcium atoms behave in the same way in far away galaxies as here on our Earth. Obviously all calcium atoms remain faithful to their characteristic absorption frequency all over the universe - and that proves that they all exist in one and the same "time". In this connection it should be noted that Einstein's time dilatation would have to result from the relative velocity of the galaxy whereas the clock retardation which we discovered always results from the absolute motion which is of course essentially lower with the galaxies.

[87] The paradox can only be solved by one concept which has actually no right to be in the Theory of Relativity: bias. Because both the travelling brother and the brother who remained at home should testify that the travelling one ages less than the one left at home. Even for the fanatic relativist this is not immediately plausible because it is exactly the impossibility to differentiate between "station" and "train" from which one should be able to conclude that every brother would claim the same of the other. One searched for distinctive features of the systems moving away from each other in order to achieve an asymmetry in aging. One of these reasons is based on the fact that the traveller is subject to accelerations and the stationary one is not. Apart from the fact that the fields of acceleration and of gravitation are equivalent to each other (GTR), one can forget this argument right from the start: accelerations are not considered in the SToR so to speak. Those authors who want to see the GTR applied to an analysis of the twin paradox are piquantly right – because the SToR can be refuted by means of the GTR. Because, as it is, one has to acknowledge that the "stationary state" of the one at home does not apply since the spaceship which leaves its system does of course transmit an impulse to it according to the principle of action and reaction. As for the rest, this impulse is only equalised by the return of the spaceship. *Both* brothers are therefore subject to accelerations. It has to be noted here that the traveller is only able to achieve such accelerations which correspond to the fuel taken along - a mass that has to be taken from a stationary system. The take-off mass therefore determines both the impulse of one system and of the other system. The event is still symmetrical!

In addition, the exact calculation of the problem would have to include the field quantities (acceleration and gravitation). It is impossible to consider the event biased because due to the laws of conservation the calculation must always be symmetrical - otherwise one would have to mistrust the laws of conservation but we certainly don't want to go that far.

Another method argues with the Doppler effect: each of the twins has to send impulses separated by the same intervals according to his own time. Since A is moving away from B each will receive the signals of the other at a reduced frequency... But how long will this be the case? And here one senses asymmetry: namely as soon as A returns, he immediately receives signals from B at a higher frequency. For B, however, the case is completely different, one would think: the last signal which A sends out prior to returning will reach B only after a certain time. Thus B receives the signals with the low frequency from A far longer than half the total travelling time; each of the two observers, however, receives exactly as many signals as the other sent out... How should their respective measurements of the total time correspond nevertheless?

The error of this arguments arises from the fact that a symmetry is assigned to the Doppler effect of the light which it cannot have in truth. Basically two causes are possible: either the light comes towards us or we are coming closer to the light. In the first case, the impulse of the light has the velocity c relative to us; in the second case it has it relative to the source. Of course, this slightly changes the corresponding moment in which the impulse is received - as one can also notice with the sound whose Doppler effect admits a differentiability between moving and stationary source (provided the carrying medium is at rest). That this is the case with the acoustic Doppler effect will not surprise any physicist; but what may astonish many of them is the fact that the asymmetry of the Doppler effect with light was practically proved in experiments by H.E. Ives and G.R. Stilwell already in the year 1938 (J.Opt.Sci.Am., 28,215-226 ; 1938). Their measurements dealt with the light emitted to the front or to the rear (relative to the direction of motion of the source). A hydrogen discharge tube was the source of H_2 and H_3 ions. The emitted light quanta corresponded to the characteristic lines of the atomic hydrogen. The apparent wavelength of the $H\beta$ line was determined with greatest care, the lines shifted by the Doppler effect were measured exactly for three different voltages. In doing so it was distinctly revealed that the lines of the ions moving forward did not shift to the same extent as the lines moving backwards. This experiment has already been interpreted in a variety of manners - both by opponents and by supporters of the Theory of Relativity. The ones think it only proves the actual slower operation of moved clocks, the others saw it as a proof for time dilatation.

But what the experiment really showed (analogous to Fizeau's flow experiment) was nothing but the independence of the velocity of light from its source - but not from the observer. In the "stationary" medium, even the speed of sound is independent of the source; in this case, the medium takes part in any velocities of the system, like for example the atmosphere of the Earth. On the other hand, a dragged "ether" of the light does not exist - and with that the absoluteness of the velocity of light of all systems is proved so to speak, it is thus independent either from the observer or from the source conditional on the situation of movement. Only a system in which the light propagates really to all sides at the same speed is absolutely at rest!

For that reason, there is no twin paradox because the symmetry of the event is not violated by the Doppler effect. It is always ignored with the often quoted examples that the traveller is unable to return immediately but has to come to a standstill first in any case before he returns! With that the familiar claim, B would receive the low frequency far longer than A, is of no importance because A will receive the higher frequency longer during his return.

[88] H. W. Thim, "Absence of the transverse Doppler shift at microwave frequencies", *Digest of the IEEE Instrumentation and Measurement Technology Conference 2002*, pp. 1345-1348, ISBN 0-7803-7218-2, ISN 1091-5281, IEEE Number 00CH 37276.

[89] For Poincare, $E_s = m_S c^2$ was nothing mysterious. Other scientists as well, like Joseph Larmor, Joseph John Thomson, Oliver Heaviside, and Friedrich Hasenöhrl were familiar with this relation. $E=4mc^2/3$ had already occurred to Hasenöhrl (1874 - 1915) in 1904. But the roots of $E = mc^2$ go back even farther. Peter and Neal Graneau write in *Newton versus Einstein, How Matter Interacts with Matter*, 1993, p. 122: "Writers of electromagnetics have been poor historians. They usually give Maxwell the credit for having discovered the velocity of light in electromagnetic theory. This honor

belongs to Weber. Weber deserves credit for another theoretical discovery which is normally attributed to Einstein. This concerns the increase of mass with velocity and $E = mc^2$. Many textbook writers consider this to be one of the most important revelations of the special theory of relativity. Weber had stumbled on this fact 50 years before Einstein discussed it in detail." Already in 1846, Wilhelm Eduard Weber calculated the potential voltage bound in 1 mm^3 water according to the formula $E = mc^2$. The first indication of the formula goes even back to Lagrange. Einstein's main credit was only that this relation later became a worldwide sensation because of clever publicity.

[90] Physicists calculated the temperature of empty space starting out from star light and achieved values which corresponded quite well with the predictions of the theoreticians (blackbody of 2.7 degrees Kelvin). Only Gamow, who proceeded on the assumption of the Big Bang, calculated a completely wrong temperature. When the discovery of the background radiation became known, Gamow claimed that he had exactly predicted the measured temperature of 2.7 degrees Kelvin - yet his value was twenty times higher.

[91] The number of satellites of the big planets should in fact be constant but in recent years more and more of them have been discovered. Most of them are, however, tiny boulders so that these are more likely captured asteroids. At the moment, the statistics of the "moon gatherers" looks like this: Jupiter 60, Saturn 31, Uranus 21, and Neptune 11 moons. (ds/May 8th, 2003)

[92] A similar deviation from Kepler's principles or Newton's law of gravitation can also be found with the rotational velocity of stars at the edge of galaxies.

[93] At the time of the dinosaurs, Saturn did probably not have any rings yet, planetologist Jeff Cuzzi of the NASA Ames Research Center in Moffett Field (USA) claims. At former times, researchers thought that the rings were created together with Saturn itself barely five billion years ago. But soon it became apparent that they have to be much younger: in the telescope they appear in bright colours as if they were new. In older rings, more interstellar dust would have accumulated and darkened the colours. Moreover the moons of Saturn take away kinetic energy from the rings which means that the rings are gradually dissipating and will fall down onto the planet.

Perhaps an asteroid scattered one of Saturn's satellites which then formed a disc of particles around its old home planet. All the matter of the only a few metres thick disc taken together would make a celestial body of the size of the satellite Mima which still orbits around Saturn.

[94] As a result of the evaluation of Jupiter's data collected by the spacecraft Galileo the theories of the astronomers concerning the creation of the planets have to be rephrased. As it is, they still don't know about Jupiter neither how nor where nor when it came into existence. So far they have always assumed the big planets, like Jupiter, Saturn, Uranus, and Neptune had been created at the same time through condensation of gases around a core of rocks 4.6 billion years ago. But according to the composition of Jupiter, it rather looks as if the creation took place in a completely different way, as if Jupiter did not belong to our solar system at all. It is feared that similar surprises await them with the other planets. The internal heat of Jupiter which is greater than one would expect because of its distance to the sun could also be produced by violent ionic winds which even attain supersonic speed from time to time and heat up the atmosphere.

[95] The surface structure of the much too hot Venus proves that it must be a younger planet. Storms with a speed of 350 km/h (near the poles 700 km/h) would have covered up all irregularities with sand on the surface of Venus. Fumes of sulphuric acid in the almost 500 °C hot atmosphere would have corroded every stone long ago. The flanks of the highest mountain (10.8 km) slope with 30°. This indicates that the mountains are growing faster because of tectonic deformation than they could crumble due to the enormous erosion by strong winds and sulphuric acid rain.

[96] The comparison of the genome of Thermotoga maritima - an eubacterium - with the DNA sequences of other organisms brought a big surprise: almost a quarter of the genes originally stems from bacteria called archaea which are less related to the eubacteria than we human beings are to the daisies. Apparently life was carrying out the *exchange of genes* to an up to then unknown extent.

[97] The theory of capturing the moon is not undisputed. The orbit of the moon with its stabilising effect on the Earth contradicts a capturing manoeuvre. Captured asteroids or meteorites mostly have a

considerably elliptic orbit and a high velocity. The moon, however, has a slow circular orbit with slight eccentricity (0.05). An indication to the capturing theory is, on the other hand, that the rocks of the moon contain traces of a magnetic field which the moon could only have had as a constituent of a bigger planet. According to another theory, the creation of the moon was thanks to an enormous catastrophe. About 4.5 billion years ago, the primeval Earth is said to have collided with a planet the size of Mars. The force of the impact smashed and evaporated the surfaces of *both* bodies and hurled them into space. Part of it accumulated in an orbit around the Earth and rather quickly reaccreted to a new body, the Earth's moon. This theory is even more improbable. Fragments in a rotating circular system crush one another through impacts and their particles are getting smaller and smaller (see the dust rings of the planets). It cannot be observed anywhere that a planet, a moon, or an asteroid has composed itself from *cold* matter.

[98] Evaluations of the measurements from the probe *Mars Global Surveyor* brought astonishing things to the light. In its earlier history, Mars was probably much more similar to Earth than has been assumed so far. According to an article in the American scientific magazine „Science", researchers found indications that there could even have been plate tectonics. The traces which the scientists discovered by means of the magnetometer of the probe "Mars Global Surveyor" have an astonishing similarity to formations which are found on Earth at the bottom of the ocean where the continental plates are drifting apart and new matter is flowing upwards from the interior of the Earth. Dr. Jack Connerney of the NASA Goddard Space Flight Center: "The discovery of these traces on Mars could revolutionise our opinion with regard to the evolutionary history of the Red Planet...."

[99] The terrestrial globe is surrounded by a magnetic field whose magnetic flux density is between about 30 μT and 60 μT (1 μT = 10^{-6} Tesla). The field exhibits a higher flux density in the vicinity of the magnetic poles than in the area of the equator; moreover, the field varies locally. For example, the field around Moscow is very weak. According to the theory applicable at present, the field is divided into a main field (share 95 %) which is said to have its origin in the electric current systems in the interior of the Earth below the

core mantle boundary located at a depth of 2,900 km and in addition comprises the magnetic fields of the electric currents induced by external influences in the interior of the Earth, and into a residual field which for a great part comes from variable electric currents in the higher atmosphere, particularly in the ionosphere, as well as in the magnetosphere and a generally very small, but occasionally significant portion is produced by rocks of the Earth's crust (crust field).

[100] The apparent force of gravitation is still higher above the Himalayas than for example above the areas around the equator. The lowest gravitation reigns above the Indian Ocean or the Lesser Antilles, for instance, which is explained by the "centrifugal force" but is connected with the bigger diameter of the Earth in these places. If all factors are considered, the "attractive force" above the Himalayas is relatively lower than expected.

[101] The Infrared Astronomy Satellite (IRAS) was a mutual project of Great Britain, the USA, and the Netherlands. IRAS was launched in January, 1983 and finished its mission ten months later. IRAS possessed a special instrument for sampling the sky and was the first satellite which discovered a comet (IRAS-Araki-Alcock). IRAS observed 20 000 galaxies, 130 000 stars, and 90 000 other celestial objects and stellar groups. It discovered a disc of dust around the star Vega of which maybe a new solar system will develop. The most famous discovery by IRAS was a new type of galaxies, the Starburst Galaxies. In Starburst Galaxies, new stars are created faster than in other types of galaxies.

[102] Some teams of astronomers raised a question again that had actually been settled long ago: Was the distribution of matter in the young universe really accidental? Their observations give grounds for the assumption that little variations, which we see today as stars or galaxies in the otherwise fairly homogenous space are not distributed completely statistically. That would, however, contradict all conventional theories and would therefore set back research by astronomic lengths

[103] An experiment conducted by John Price at the University of Colorado in Boulder revealed that the additional spatial dimensions postulated by the string theory don't exist because in case of very short distances gravitation would diminish much faster with distance

than is claimed in Newton's law of gravitation. Consequently, Price and his colleagues were looking for deviations from Newton's law of gravitation with very short distances. Result: Down to a distance of one tenth of a millimetre there is no deviation from Newton's law of gravitation. (Nature, volume 421, p. 922)

[104] According to an international team of researchers, the universe will continue to expand eternally as a result of latest analyses (Nature, volume 404, p. 955). They interpreted their measurements as proof for a cosmos which has exactly the critical density at which the drifting apart can never come to a stop. In this case cosmologist speak about a "flat" geometry of the universe.

[105] In this connection we would also like to mention the theory of the "jumping genes" by Nobel price laureate Barbara McClintock (1902-1992) who discovered that certain genes can obviously jump between the individual chromosomes. For decades, McClintocks jumping genes had been ignored by scientists, who declared the researcher to be insane. Oswald Avery (1877-1955) made a similar experience when he identified the DNA as carrier of genetic information and met with a complete lack of understanding. Nobel price laureate James Watson, who discovered the double helix, described the behaviour of the scientists in his book (1968) as follows: "Many of them were self-opinionated fools who always backed the wrong horse with unerring certainty. One could not be a successful scientist without realising that – in contrast to popular conception (...) – a good number of scientists are not only narrow-minded and dull but also just stupid."

[106] In the opinion of Nobel price laureate Hannes Alfvén, galaxies are formed in the intergalactic plasma by electric and magnetic forces, not by gravitation.

[107] After the Earth had been only populated by unicellular organisms for almost three billion years, life suddenly unfolded in unexpected abundance about 540 million years ago. The reason for this "cambric explosion" of life is still unclear. Kathleen Grey of the Geological Survey of Western Australia and her colleagues report in the specialist journal Geology (volume 31, p. 459) that a tremendous meteorite impact could have been the cause.

[108] Ludwig Boltzmann: "The general struggle for survival of the living things is not a struggle for basic materials,... nor for energy

which ... exists in plenty in every body but a struggle for entropy."

[109] The addition of solar and lunar gravitation would make one expect the opposite. Pendulum experiments carried out by Erwin J. Saxl and Mildred Allen during the solar eclipse on March 7th, 1970 indicated an increase in the period of oscillation, consequently a surprising and inexplicable amplification of the Earth's gravitational field ("Physical Review", 1971). Not "gravitation" but the pressure (shove!) from sun and moon had added up!

[110] We have already described that a sphere of light is the sum of several individual spheres which set out and spread like rings of waves from the place of origin (absolutely anchored in space). This propagation takes place at a constant velocity ($"c"$). Each sphere consists of a vibration or tremor (of *one* per triggered process!). The image and the properties of the wave can be put down to the sequence of spheres triggered in succession. That means this constant new creation of the sphere follows the possible movement of the source of light (fig.I).

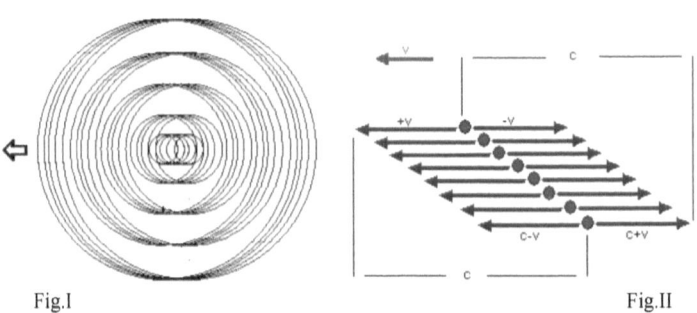

Fig.I   Fig.II

Every singly sphere is anchored in space. Spheres move together with the source of light at v. Result: the light pulses spread isotropically with c and are only apparently depending on the movement of the source.

Therefore the peculiar propagation of the light simply goes back to the fact that the "speed of light" is composed of two velocity factors.

This looks as if the propagation of a sphere of light is in fact independent of its source – once it has been produced - but actually the points of origination move along with the source! That means the spheres created one after the other shift together with the place of their creation. Among other things, this is the reason for the Doppler effect, and among other things, it demonstrates that the velocity of light is always a velocity relative to both the receiver and the creator. At the same time, every mirror, every lense, and every measuring instrument becomes a new source of light once a beam has been captured to make it visible. A beam of light arriving with c-v or c+v would therefore not be reflected with this velocity but again only with c. But the motion of the source reveals itself to the receiver through the corresponding shifting of the impulse fields! There would not be any Doppler effect if this was not the case.

In figure II the tips of the arrow ("photons", "light pulses", "quanta") symbolises the "light". They are added to a sequence which contains both the periods of their creation (frequency) and the movement of the source (Doppler). The tips themselves always move away from the source at c, their sphere of propagation, however, is left in the space ("absolute ether", T.A.O. matrix). When the source is moving at v, the sphere which is created next is also shifted by this amount. Hence

$$(c-v)+v=c.$$

All unsuccessful drift experiments, which are designed similar to the experiment by Michelson-Morley, can already be explained on the basis of this definition without requiring the Special Theory of Relativity.

T.A.O.: It is the way and the waygoer. It is the eternal road along which walk all beings, but no being made it, for itself is being. It is everything and nothing. From it all things spring, all things conform to it, and to it at last all things return. It is a square without angles, a sound which ears cannot hear, and an image without form. It is a vast net and though its meshes are as wide as the sea it lets nothing through. It is the sanctuary where all things find refuge. It is nowhere, but without looking out of the window you may see it. Desire not to desire, it teaches, and leave all things to take their course. He that humbles himself shall be preserved entire. He that bends shall be made straight. Failure is the foundation of success and success is the lurking-place of failure; but who can tell when the turning point will come? He who strives after tenderness can become even as a little child. Gentleness brings victory to him who attacks and safety to him who defends. Mighty is he who conquers himself..."

W. Somerset Maugham

(The painted veil, 1953)

The book

The first notes of "The Principle of Existence" were already written down in 1975. For more than 10 years, the author verified his ideas and studied the experimental data of the scientists for inconsistencies and proofs. Actually, however, the latest discoveries of the researchers seemed to confirm his "Principle" more and more. When some of the predictions already noted down in 1975 (volcanoes on Venus, planetary rings, irregular expansion of the universe, dependency of gravitation on the composition of matter, repulsive forces in particle physics and in astronomy, superclusters and foam structure of the universe, surplus of information on the DNA etc.) really became true in the course of time, the book was published in 1987. Almost 16 years later, in March, 2003, the author discovered that readers had scanned and posted the book on the internet. After making some cursory corrections, he did the same - with surprising success. From hundreds of emails and contributions to the forum, where readers discussed topics of his book, he received valuable indications to uncertain points, errors, and mistakes in the text. He didn't have any other choice than to revise and reprint the book with updated data and facts and some completely new chapters and additional figures.

The author

Harald Maurer, born in 1944, trained electrical engineer, caused a sensation as Europe's youngest author in 1963; he wrote several books for young readers, novels and screenplays, published articles of scientific content, and presented his first work of non-fiction with the "Principle of Existence". He lives as freelance writer and painter in Graz, Austria.

Contact

Please send corrections, criticism, and suggestions to EDITION MAHAG, Lindweg 9, A-8010 GRAZ, AUSTRIA

Discussion forum and guest book on **www.mahag.com** !